Conservation and Development in Cambodia

Written by leading authorities from Australasia, Europe and North America, this book examines the dynamic conflicts and synergies between nature conservation and human development in contemporary Cambodia.

After suffering conflict and stagnation in the late twentieth century, Cambodia has experienced an economic transformation in the last decade, with growth averaging almost 10 per cent per year, partly through investment from China. However, this rush for development has been coupled with tremendous social and environmental change which, although positive in some aspects, has led to rising inequality and profound shifts in the condition, ownership and management of natural resources. High deforestation rates, declining fish stocks, biodiversity loss and alienation of indigenous and rural people from their land and traditional livelihoods are now matters of increasing local and international concern.

The book explores the social and political dimensions of these environmental changes in Cambodia, and of efforts to intervene in and 'improve' current trajectories for conservation and development. It provides a compelling analysis of the connections between nature, state and society, pointing to the key role of grassroots and non-state actors in shaping Cambodia's frontiers of change. These insights will be of great interest to scholars of Southeast Asia and environment-development issues in general.

Sarah Milne is a Postdoctoral Fellow in the Resources Environment and Development group, Crawford School of Public Policy, College of Asia and the Pacific, Australian National University.

Sango Mahanty is an ARC Future Fellow in the Resources Environment and Development group, Crawford School of Public Policy, College of Asia and the Pacific, Australian National University.

Earthscan Conservation and Development series
Series Editor: W.M. Adams
Moran Professor of Conservation and Development,
Department of Geography, University of Cambridge, UK

Conservation and Sustainable Development
Linking Practice and Policy in Eastern Africa
Edited by Jon Davies

Conservation and Environmental Management in Madagascar
Edited by Ivan R. Scales

Conservation and Development in Cambodia
Exploring frontiers of change in nature, state and society
Edited by Sarah Milne and Sango Mahanty

For further information please visit the series page on the Routledge website: www.routledge.com/books/series/ECCAD

Conservation and Development in Cambodia

Exploring frontiers of change in nature, state and society

Edited by Sarah Milne and Sango Mahanty

LONDON AND NEW YORK

First published 2015
by Routledge
2 Park Square, Milton Park, Abingdon, Oxon OX14 4RN

and by Routledge
711 Third Avenue, New York, NY 10017

Routledge is an imprint of the Taylor & Francis Group, an informa business

© 2015 Sarah Milne and Sango Mahanty, selection and editorial material; individual chapters, the contributors.

The right of the editors to be identified as the authors of the editorial material, and of the authors for their individual chapters, has been asserted in accordance with sections 77 and 78 of the Copyright, Designs and Patents Act 1988.

All rights reserved. No part of this book may be reprinted or reproduced or utilised in any form or by any electronic, mechanical, or other means, now known or hereafter invented, including photocopying and recording, or in any information storage or retrieval system, without permission in writing from the publishers.

Trademark notice: Product or corporate names may be trademarks or registered trademarks, and are used only for identification and explanation without intent to infringe.

British Library Cataloguing in Publication Data
A catalogue record for this book is available from the British Library

Library of Congress Cataloguing in Publication Data
A catalogue record for this book has been requested

ISBN: 978-0-415-70680-3 (hbk)
ISBN: 978-1-315-88730-2 (ebk)

Typeset in Baskerville
by Swales & Willis Ltd, Exeter, Devon, UK

Printed and bound in Great Britain by
TJ International Ltd, Padstow, Cornwall

In memory of Chut Wutty

Contents

List of figures	ix
List of tables	x
Notes on contributors	xi
Preface	xv
Acronyms and abbreviations	xvii

1 The political ecology of Cambodia's transformation   1
   SARAH MILNE AND SANGO MAHANTY

2 Shackled to nature? The post-conflict state and its
   symbiotic relationship with natural resources   28
   SARAH MILNE, PAK KIMCHOEUN AND MICHAEL SULLIVAN

PART 1
Transformation, complexity and contestation in
nature-society relations   51

3 Lost in transition: Landscape, ecological gradients
   and legibility on the Tonle Sap floodplain   53
   ANDREW S. ROBERTS

4 Can market integration improve livelihoods and
   safeguard the environment? The case of hybrid rice
   varieties in Cambodia's agricultural heartland   75
   MAYLEE THAVAT

5 Land is life: An analysis of the role 'grand corruption'
   plays in enabling elite grabbing of land in Cambodia   95
   MEGAN MACINNES

viii Contents

6 Contested development and environment: Chinese-backed hydropower and infrastructure projects in Cambodia   120
MICHAEL SULLIVAN

PART 2
Interventions in natural resource management   139

7 Managing protected areas in Cambodia: The challenge for conservation bureaucracies in a hostile governance environment   141
RICHARD PALEY

8 In whose name and in whose interests? An actor-oriented analysis of community forestry in Bey, a Khmer village in Northeast Cambodia   160
ROBIN BIDDULPH

9 The forest carbon commodity chain in Cambodia's voluntary carbon market   177
SANGO MAHANTY, AMANDA BRADLEY AND SARAH MILNE

PART 3
Social movements and radical responses to transformation   201

10 What about the 'unprotected' areas? Building on traditional forms of ownership and land use for dealing with new contexts   203
JEREMY IRONSIDE

11 Cultures and histories of resistance in Cambodia   225
MARGARET SLOCOMB

12 A 'people's' irrigation reservoir on the Tonle Sap floodplain   238
JOHN MARSTON AND CHHUON HOEUR

13 Story-telling and social change: A case study of the Prey Lang Community Network   258
TERRY PARNELL

Index   280

Figures

1.1	Map of forest loss in Cambodia 2000–2012	19
1.2	Map of concessions and protected areas in Cambodia, May 2014	20
1.3	Study sites discussed in this volume	21
2.1	Truck of illegally harvested rosewood leaving the Cardamom Mountains, 2011	28
3.1	Regional map indicating Tonle Sap Lake dry season margin	55
3.2	Regional map indicating Tonle Sap Lake wet season margin	56
3.3	Map indicating the location of the study area	61
4.1	Different perspectives on globalization and the role of small-scale farmers	79
7.1	Rangers demarcating the Community Zone inside a protected area	141
9.1	The forest carbon commodity chain for Oddar Meanchey and Seima Protection Forest	185
9.2	Village representatives and the Mondulkiri provincial governor sign the REDD+ Free Prior and Informed consent agreement at a public ceremony, January 2013	188
10.1	Intensive swidden farming near the present-day site of Ratanakiri's provincial capital, Ban Lung	211
10.2	The decentralized arrangement of village sites on the central basalt plateau in the centre of Ratanakiri Province in 1953	212
10.3	Beine Village land use, also showing the overlapping claim by a rubber company	214
12.1	Cambodian and CPP flags erected around the People's Reservoir, as the community appeals for it not to be destroyed	238
13.1	Kuy woman dressed as an avatar. Pregnant, she completes a long protest walk through the forest. When the child is born, she names it Prey Lang	258
13.2	Activists from the Prey Lang Community Network and elsewhere attend a solidarity event in memory of Chut Wutty, after his assassination in 2012. The sign says: "We are all Chut Wutty".	272

Tables

4.1	Resource security and seed uptake	85
8.1	Time-line of community forestry in Bey 2002–2009	162
9.1	Key actors in the Oddar Meanchey (OM) and Seima carbon schemes	183
9.2	Key steps in forest carbon production and exchange	189

Notes on contributors

Robin Biddulph is a researcher at the University of Gothenburg's Human Geography Unit. Robin has worked extensively on property relations in Cambodia and the attempts of the development industry to intervene in and influence poor people's rights. His 2010 doctorate examined tenure interventions in rural Cambodia and led to the proposition of an 'evasion hypothesis', which suggests that conflicts between official public policy agendas and unofficial elite agendas may be 'resolved' by implementing reform programs away from the problem they are explicitly intended to address. His more recent research focuses on the effects of mass tourism booms in impoverished settings.

Amanda Bradley has over 15 years' experience in the environment sector in Asia, specializing in community-based natural resource management, stakeholder engagement, consultation processes and gender. She is currently a REDD+ tenure specialist with the UN Food and Agriculture Organisation in Rome, but her contribution to this book was written while working for TerraCarbon as Senior Manager – Social and Community Benefits. Prior to that, Amanda was the Forestry and Climate Program Director for Pact Cambodia where she initiated and managed Cambodia's first REDD+ project. She holds a Masters from the Fletcher School of Law and Diplomacy and a Bachelor in French Literature from Amherst College.

Chhuon Hoeur is an independent researcher and teacher based in Phnom Penh, Cambodia. He has completed Bachelor and Masters degrees in Law at the Build Bright University. Hoeur has worked as a research assistant for several foreign-based scholars working in Cambodia. He is a native of Stoung district, the area he writes about in this volume. In addition to his research and teaching on law and rural communities, he has worked extensively on Cambodian Buddhism.

Jeremy Ironside has lived on and off in Cambodia since 1994, advising and consulting on community livelihoods, sustainable agriculture, resource management and indigenous land tenure issues, especially in Ratanakiri province and the Cardamom Mountains. He has written extensively on the traditional resource governance systems of indigenous peoples in Cambodia. Jeremy's PhD (2013) from Otago University explored communal land ownership in Ratanakiri. He presently works as a consultant for the McKnight Foundation, supporting indigenous and local communities in Cambodia, Laos and Vietnam to secure their land and natural resources. He also carries out independent and collaborative research.

Pak Kimchoeun completed his PhD at the Australian National University in 2011, in the field of Policy and Governance. His doctorate is entitled 'A dominant party in a weak state: How the ruling party in Cambodia manages to become and stay dominant in power'. Kimchoeun is currently working as a researcher and consultant in Cambodia where he specializes in decentralization, public budgeting and the political economy of state reforms. He has been affiliated with the Cambodian Development Research Institute since 2003.

Megan MacInnes has more than 10 years' experience working on land and natural resource governance in Southeast Asia, and has been with Global Witness since July 2009. She currently manages Global Witness' land campaign and was the lead author of high-profile reports 'Dealing with Disclosure' and 'Rubber Barons'. Megan lived in Cambodia from 2002 to 2009 while working on a range of grassroots, NGO and advocacy projects that focused on policy and dispute resolution processes around land and resources. Megan received her undergraduate degree from the School of Oriental and African Studies (SOAS) (2000) and her MSc in Environment and Development from the University of East Anglia (2007).

Sango Mahanty is based at the Australian National University and researches the social and political dimensions of commodity networks, forests and agrarian change. Through funding from the Australian Research Council she is currently working on two projects in Cambodia. The first examines the political ecology of REDD+ in Cambodia, Laos and Vietnam. The second explores the role of cross-border commodity networks in environmental, social and political change on the Cambodia-Vietnam borderland. Sango has held teaching, research and professional advisory roles in a range of organizations. For the last 9 years, she has worked in mainland Southeast Asia, but her PhD research focused on India.

John A. Marston is a Professor and Researcher at the Center for Asian and African Studies of El Colegio de México in Mexico City. He completed a doctorate in Anthropology at the University of Washington in 1997. John has published three edited volumes about Cambodia and Southeast Asia, including *History, Buddhism and New Religious Movements in Cambodia* (University of Hawaii Press, 2004), *Anthropology and*

Notes on contributors xiii

Community in Cambodia (Monash University Press, 2011) and *Ethnicity, Borders, and the Grassroots Interface with the State* (Silkworm Books). He has also produced numerous articles in books and scholarly journals.

Sarah Milne is a postdoctoral research fellow at the Australian National University. Her work investigates the political ecology of environmental intervention in Cambodia, with a focus on the complex effects of projects that advance community-based conservation, indigenous resource rights and market mechanisms like Payments for Environmental Services (PES). Sarah has lived on and off in Cambodia since 2002, working on various projects as a conservationist, ethnographer and advocate. Her PhD, completed in Human Geography at the University of Cambridge in 2009, explored the multi-faceted and cross-scalar politics of global conservation in the Cardamom Mountains, Southwest Cambodia.

Richard Paley has been involved in conservation and natural resource management in Asia and Africa for the past two decades. Much of Richard's recent work has focused on protected area management, especially in Cambodia where he worked for 7 years from 2001 onwards. His PhD thesis, completed in 2011 in Human Geography at the University of Cambridge, focused on the political and organizational challenges of biodiversity conservation in Cambodia. Richard is currently the Director of the Wildlife Conservation Society's program in Afghanistan.

Terry Parnell worked in Cambodia with East West Management Institute's Program on Rights and Justice from 2004 to 2014. Terry has almost 30 years' experience in development and humanitarian relief programs, including more than 20 years in Southeast Asia. For the past decade, much of her work has been devoted to assisting grassroots and indigenous groups in advocating for their land and natural resource rights in Cambodia, especially in Prey Lang. Terry has a Masters in Education and a Masters in Agriculture Education and Extension, with a focus on sustainable development.

Andrew Roberts' research focuses on the intersection of agrodiversity, landscape history and vegetative ecology on the Tonle Sap floodplain in Cambodia. He received his PhD in Biology from the Graduate Centre of the City University of New York and the New York Botanical Garden in 2011. Andrew now manages a diversified farm with his wife and three children in the Seacoast Region of New Hampshire in the United States.

Margaret Slocomb has a PhD in History from the University of Queensland. An education specialist, she worked with international aid organizations and local civil society groups in Cambodia for almost two decades after 1988. Margaret has authored numerous scholarly articles and books on Cambodia. Her latest work is *An Economic History of Cambodia in the Twentieth Century*, published by the National University of Singapore Press.

Michael Sullivan is a researcher living and working in Phnom Penh. He is the author of 'China's Aid to Cambodia' a chapter in the 2011 edited volume by Caroline Hughes and Kheang Un on Cambodia's economic transformation. Michael's doctoral research at the University of London's School of Oriental and African Studies (SOAS) critically examined international support for Cambodian elections from 1993 to 2003. He is currently writing a book on this subject.

Maylee Thavat completed her PhD in Resource Management and the Environment at the Australian National University in 2010, focusing on agricultural value chain development in Cambodia. Maylee is now an international consultant and independent researcher. She has taught in the ANU's Masters of Applied Anthropology and Participatory Development, at Deakin University, and at the University of Melbourne. She has also completed a number of major consultancies in climate change, environment, disaster risk reduction and rural development, especially in the context of the Australian government aid program. She is currently conducting new research on inclusive energy systems in agri-food value chains.

Preface

The idea of producing an edited volume on conservation and development in Cambodia first emerged in late 2011, at the suggestion of Bill Adams. Immediately, the potential of such a project was clear. Cambodia was emerging from its first decade of 'global conservation', in which efforts to implement ideas such as protected areas, community-based natural resource management and sustainable livelihoods had produced mixed and ambiguous results. Meanwhile, the dramatic transformation of Cambodia's natural environment and socio-political life was rapidly gathering momentum, seemingly unaffected by the well-intended and well-financed interventions of international donors and non-government organizations. It was time to take stock.

For the first time since the civil war, there was a fresh batch of empirical research emerging from rural and remote areas of the country, along with a rich set of recent practitioner experiences to reflect upon. Our project in developing this book was therefore to gather and synthesize this new knowledge, gleaning essential insights into Cambodia's environment-development nexus. The research and experience that are shared here by contributing authors come from their many years of deep immersion in Cambodian life, work and scholarship, often for the causes of social justice and the environment. Their contributions offer an authoritative and diverse range of perspectives on Cambodia, as well as wider insights on the relationships between nature, the state and society. Thus, this volume should be of use to scholars and practitioners working in Cambodia and elsewhere.

Although the thinking behind this book commenced in 2011, our eventual direction was shaped and inspired by certain key events in 2012 and 2013. First was the tragic assassination of one of Cambodia's most high profile environmental activists, Chut Wutty, in April 2012. Wutty was shot by Military Police in the Cardamom Mountains of Southwest Cambodia, while gathering evidence on illegal logging. He was a collaborator and friend to several people involved in the production of this book. The second key event was the Cambodian national election in July 2013, which saw an unprecedented popular groundswell against the ruling party and took many by surprise. As Cambodia's political life transformed, we reflected upon the environmental dimensions of this change; especially the role of social movements and resistance in response to land alienation and deforestation. Thus, the contributions in this volume are not an end point, but they mark out an exciting agenda for future research on conservation and development in Cambodia.

The development of this volume has benefited from generous financial support provided by Forest Trends (with DFID and NORAD funding), the Centre for International Forestry Research (CIFOR), and two groups within the Australian National University's (ANU) College of Asia and the Pacific: the Resources Environment and Development Group and the Asia-Pacific Environmental Governance Network, both housed within the Crawford School of Public Policy. Aside from supporting production costs, these sponsors allowed chapter authors and other interested scholars to gather for a workshop on 'Conservation and Development in Cambodia', hosted at the ANU in October 2013. Each book chapter was presented and discussed at this event, leading to a very productive dialogue that eventually shaped the volume's overall framing and narrative. Significant contributions were made at the workshop and in subsequent thinking about the book by Mr Keo Piseth, Mr Marcus Hardtke, Dr Meas Nee, Ms Hanneke Nooren and Dr Keith Barney. Although they are not contributing authors, their voices are heard.

In early 2014, the development and fine-tuning of the manuscript benefited greatly from our two reviewers, Jonathan Rigg and Margaret Slocomb. Both contributed their valuable time and provided constructive suggestions for improvement – we thank them sincerely. But above all, we extend our thanks to the contributing authors in this volume, who shared inspiring ideas, ongoing smiles and maintained a tremendous level of effort over the course of our frenetically paced 9-month writing period.

Finally, we thank Sandra Davenport for her copy-editing; and, for the preparation of maps, CartoGIS at the ANU's College of Asia and the Pacific and Mathieu Pellerin at the Cambodian League for the Promotion and Defence of Human Rights (LICADHO). All demonstrated admirable patience and attention to detail.

Disclaimer

The views expressed in this publication are not necessarily those of the publisher or funders.

Acronyms and abbreviations

AFD	Agence Française pour le Développement
AQIP	Agricultural Quality Improvement Project
BOT	Build Operate Transfer
CBNRM	Community-based Natural Resource Management
CBD	Convention on Biological Diversity
CCB	Climate Community and Biodiversity Standard
CCPF	Central Cardamoms Protected Forest
CDA	Children's Development Association
CDC	Council for the Development of Cambodia
CEPF	Critical Ecosystem Partnership Fund
CETIC	China Electric Power Technology Import and Export Corporation
CF	Community Forestry
CFI	Community Forestry International
CFN	CF Network
CI	Conservation International
CIAP	Cambodia-IRRI-Australia Project
CLV-DTA	Cambodia, Laos and Vietnam Development Triangle
CNRP	Cambodian National Rescue Party
CoM	Council of Ministers
CPN	Community Peacebuilding Network
CPP	Cambodian People's Party
CSO	Civil Society Organization
CSPG	China Southern Power Grid
DoE	Department of Environment
EIA	Environmental Impact Assessment
ELC	Economic Land Concession
EWMI	East West Management Institute
FA	Forestry Administration
FFI	Flora and Fauna International
FPIC	Free Prior and Informed Consent
Funcinpec	National United Front for an Independent, Neutral, Peaceful and Cooperative Cambodia

FWUC	Farmer Water User Group
GDANCP	General Directorate for the Administration of Nature Conservation and Protection
GEF	Global Environment Facility
GMS	Greater Mekong Sub-Region
ICDP	Integrated Conservation and Development Project
IIED	International Institute for Environment and Development
JICA	Japan International Cooperation Agency
MAFF	Ministry of Agriculture, Forestry and Fisheries
MEF	Ministry of Economy and Finance
MIME	Ministry of Industry Mines and Energy
MoE	Ministry of Environment
MoI	Ministry of Interior
MOWRAM	Ministry of Water Resources and Meteorology
NRPG	Natural Resource Protection Group
PA	Protected Area
PES	Payments for Environmental Services
PD	Project Design Document
PLCN	Prey Lang Community Network
PRK	People's Republic of Kampuchea
PWG	Party Working Group for Helping the Local Level
RCAF	Royal Cambodian Armed Forces
RECOFTC	Regional Community Forestry Training Centre
REDD	Reducing Emissions from Deforestation and Forest Degradation
RGC	Royal Government of Cambodia
SADP	South-East Asia Development Programme
SCS	Scientific Certification Systems
SIA	Social Impact Assessment
SNA	Sub-National Administrator
SoC	State of Cambodia
SOE	State-owned Enterprise
SPF	Seima Protection Forest
SRP	Sam Rainsy Party
TGC	Terra Global Capital
UNCED	United Nations Conference on Environment and Development
UNTAC	United Nations Transitional Authority
VCS	Verified Carbon Standard
VVB	Validation and Verification Body
WA	Wildlife Alliance
WB	World Bank
WCD	World Commission on Dams
WCS	The Wildlife Conservation Society

1 The political ecology of Cambodia's transformation

Sarah Milne and Sango Mahanty

The *Churning of the Sea of Milk* is an epic Hindu creation myth. Spectacularly carved into the walls of Angkor Wat, it is also etched into the psyche of Cambodian people. The story involves a great tug-of-war in which gods and demons struggle to find the elixir of life, upheaving nature in the process. Pushing and pulling their 'rope', which is the giant serpent *Vasuki*, their efforts steadily turn the 'churning stick' of Mount Mandara, deep in the cosmic sea. The massive creative friction that they generated is said to have moved mountains, turned the sea into foam and given rise to the essence of life and immortality, as well as a deadly poison.[1] Representing tension and change, destruction and creation, this iconic myth from Cambodia's past bears down upon the present with piercing archetypal relevance. Such are the dramatic struggles and transformative changes unfolding within the realm of people and nature in the Royal Kingdom today. In this dynamic and productive domain, human endeavours are embedded recursively within nature, through interconnected processes of conflict, convergence, social turmoil and environmental change.

Although these 'frontiers of change' bear the imprint of Cambodia's unique and troubled history, they also resonate with wider transformations in the environment-development nexus of Southeast Asia. This book considers how relationships between nature and society in contemporary Cambodia are changing and why. By engaging with and developing the concept of *transformation*, especially its inter-linked social, environmental and political frictions, we ask how nature-society relations are being re-worked in this relatively small Southeast Asian nation: What new configurations, dynamics and forms are emerging in the realm of nature-society? What are the implications of these changes for people and nature? What can Cambodia's experience tell us about the frontiers of change that are unfolding more broadly in Southeast Asia?

In light of these questions, this introductory chapter aims to describe, problematize and re-theorize Cambodia's transformation. We propose, drawing from some of the basic tenets of political ecology (e.g. Blaikie and Brookfield, 1987), that the social and environmental dimensions of change are dynamic, inter-linked, multi-scalar and power laden. The major actors in this drama – government officials, conservation organizations, villagers, local NGOs, armed forces, elites and private interests – are caught in an interplay which, at a fundamental level, involves struggles over resources such as land, forests, fisheries and floodplains. Examining this interplay is a central focus of this volume: together, the book's empirical chapters provide a vivid illustration of how social interactions, political dynamics and market processes are shaping environmental change in Cambodia, and vice versa.

Building on recent work about Cambodia's post-conflict economic transformation (Hughes and Un, 2011), we also argue that the socio-political, economic and environmental dimensions of this transformation are inseparable, and must be examined together. Drawing on diverse areas of scholarship, we achieve this by expanding the notion of *frontiers*, seeing them as windows into change processes that expose 'productive' encounters between nature and society. In broad terms, this chapter considers how these ideas apply to and illuminate the transformative processes that are now underway in Cambodia.

Mirroring the structure of this volume, we first outline the major dimensions and dynamics of nature-society relations in contemporary Cambodia. Here we develop the notion of environmental transformation and conceptualize the key frontiers of change that are now shaping Cambodia's environment-development nexus. Second, we critically examine attempts to intervene in nature-society relations in Cambodia, as seen through the wide range of conservation and development projects implemented across the country over the last decade, including the creation of protected areas, community forests and 'market-oriented' conservation schemes, alongside various efforts to reform policy and build government capacity. Third, we explore political mobilizations that have a strong environmental dimension; these are occurring beyond and in spite of conventional interventions in conservation and development. Engaging with these more radical and endogenous processes enables us to speculate about how Cambodia's deep struggles over land and natural resources also have the potential to become a source of hope and social change, both for Cambodians and others in the region.

Cambodia's environmental transformation

Much has been made of the *economic* dimensions of Cambodia's recent transformation, which are of undeniable importance. Cambodia has experienced one of the highest economic growth rates in Southeast Asia in the last decade, almost 10 per cent per year between 1998 and 2008 (World Bank, 2012). This growth, and its associated processes of marketization and wealth generation, have been characterized as 'Cambodia's economic transformation' – the subject of an insightful volume edited by Caroline Hughes and Kheang Un (2011). Their volume draws from the work of Karl Polanyi, a Hungarian economist who described the social and political upheavals wrought by capitalism, as it advanced through pre-modern Europe during the industrial revolution, in his book *The Great Transformation* (1944). Studying the processes and side effects of capitalism, as it moves into new spaces and configurations, is fundamental to our task here; especially in considering the notion of frontiers, which we elaborate on below. Primarily, we contend that economic transformation cannot be understood in isolation from the environment, which is a key source of goods, services and capital; but also a source of disruption, since nature's encounter with capitalism is necessarily awkward, as Polanyi observed (Prudham, 2013).

Not surprisingly, therefore, Cambodia's environmental transformation has been just as dramatic as its economic transformation, and the two processes are intimately linked. If we consider Cambodia's economic growth alone, then what appears to emerge is an outstanding success story in human development: higher average incomes, improvements in infrastructure, increased exports and rising life expectancy (World Bank, 2012; Hughes and Un, 2011). Key contributors to this development process have been Cambodia's regional integration through infrastructure corridors, special economic zones and the facilitation of trade, promoted over the last two decades through the Greater Mekong Subregion initiative (Strange, 2013) and through growing Chinese aid and investment (Sullivan, 2011). However, macro-economic indicators provide only one crude measure of a country's development, as Cambodia's ongoing labour unrest indicates,[2] and as Polanyi suggested in his analysis of the 'social dislocation' wrought by intense market integration. Yet it is in the environmental domain that some of the most profound changes and challenges of economic development are seen, particularly through shifts in the condition, ownership and management of natural resources such as forests, fisheries, customary lands and biodiversity conservation areas. Furthermore, as the natural world transforms, so too do the institutions and political economy that govern human interactions with it.

An unprecedented recent study of global deforestation rates showed that Cambodia had the third highest national deforestation rate in the world, with forest cover loss of over 7 per cent in the decade 2002 to 2012 (Hansen *et al.*, 2013, see Figure 1.1).[3] Most of this deforestation is attributed to the conversion of forests for agriculture through Economic Land Concessions (ELCs): long-term leases for the development of state land, issued by the Cambodian government to private companies, normally for around 70 years. These concessions now cover over two million hectares of Cambodian land, with over 24 per cent of the country's land area now under some form of leasing arrangement (see Figure 1.2). Given the scale of this resource appropriation, often implemented as forced dispossession or land grabbing, it has inevitably been accompanied by rising landlessness and thousands of land conflicts, which now pose a significant political problem (Subedi, 2012; Neef *et al.*, 2013). But the government continues to downplay these issues, providing official estimates that overstate forest cover, and which highlight the political nature of environmental knowledge in Cambodia (Frewer and Chan, 2014).

In addition to the conversion of forests for ELCs, there has also been widespread and systematic degradation of forests (ODC, 2014). This degradation has especially occurred within dense or evergreen forests, which are often designated for conservation, and is associated with illegal logging activities (ibid).[4] Since the suspension of formal logging concessions in 2001, and subsequent new laws and bans on commercial logging across the country, timber extraction has been almost entirely permit-based illicit.[5] While mainstream narratives blame forest loss on impoverished contemporary villagers, and/or Cambodian logging operations are often operated by powerful individuals or companies, with direct connections to the government, and are frequently associated with ELCs and infrastructure projects (e.g. Global Witness, 2013; Boyle and May, 2012; Le Billon and Springer, 2007; Frewer and Chan, 2014). Drawing on the cheap labour of local villagers and migrant workers, these operations have ensured a steady supply of luxury tropical hardwoods, such as rosewood, to Vietnam and China. Often this logging takes place inside or adjacent to conservation areas, where the most valuable forest reserves lie (see Figure 1.2). Hundreds of millions of dollars in timber sales have now enriched a new elite class of Cambodians, many of whom have become identified as *okhnya* or tycoons, with special links to the ruling Cambodian People's Party (CPP).[6]

Beyond the forests, there has also been heavy exploitation of Cambodia's fisheries, particularly on Tonle Sap Lake. The lake, which expands annually into the vast surrounding floodplain, has been hailed as the world's most productive freshwater fishery (Baran *et al.*, 2007). The hundreds of thousands of tonnes of fish harvested annually from this system have supplied Cambodians with vital income and nourishment for generations (ibid). However, as in the forests, the last two decades have witnessed heavy exploitation of the fishery – often through sub-legal or illicit fishing activities, as well-connected commercial operators, with monopoly licences to private fishing lots, have systematically ignored regulations and dispossessed local fishers (Sneddon, 2007). Apart from over-fishing, a range of other environmental changes and effects are being felt in Cambodia's aquatic areas more generally: large-scale sand dredging is changing entire coastal and riverine eco-systems (Marschke, 2012); fish populations on Tonle Sap are being affected by increased siltation, loss of flooded forests and construction of reservoirs for dry-season agriculture (Baran *et al.*, 2007); and serious productivity declines are likely as hydropower dams in Cambodia, Laos and Vietnam disrupt the Mekong and Tonle Sap 'flood pulse' and associated fish migrations (Kummu and Sarkkula, 2008; Ziv *et al.*, 2012). Together, these environmental changes have the potential to halve Cambodia's per capita fish catch by 2030, with significant food security implications (Fisheries Administration, 2013).

Finally, apart from the steady physical degradation of natural resources and ecosystems, there are other hidden but pervasive issues also driving Cambodia's environmental transformation. First is pollution, deriving from increased use of agricultural chemicals, and the expansion of factories, livestock production and mining activities, among other things (e.g. Minh *et al.*, 2006; Dasgupta *et al.*, 2005; Azimi *et al.*, 2000). Monitoring and regulation of these polluting activities is almost entirely absent. The accumulation of heavy metals is also beginning to affect human health and ecosystems. For example, mercury from artisanal gold mining in Cambodia's northeast has entered the Sesan and Mekong rivers, exposing thousands of villagers and water users to mercury levels well beyond World Health Organization standards (Murphy *et al.*, 2013). The other looming environmental issue is, of course, climate change. The potential effects of extreme weather and variable rainfall on Cambodia's predominantly rural population, who have limited adaptation options, mean that the country's 'climate change vulnerability' index is the highest in Southeast Asia, alongside the Philippines (Yusuf and Francisco, 2009, p. 11).

The list of environmental threats and changes goes on, but our aim is not to catalogue these. Rather, we are interested in the socio-political dimensions and effects of these environmental transformations. For instance, we ask about conflicts and social upheaval, as tens of thousands of villagers respond to forced dispossession from the land and natural resources upon which they depend (Neef *et al.*, 2013; STAR Kampuchea Organization, 2007). Other dynamics are appearing too: rural families gradually adjust their livelihoods to accommodate emerging constraints and vulnerabilities, while also taking up new opportunities (Marschke, 2012); advocacy groups gain skills and connections to fight for villagers' rights and leverage international support (Henke, 2011; Parnell, this volume); protestors are subject to threats and violence, leaving imprints of fear and anger in their hearts.[7] Yet the state must also appease and respond to local demands, as seen in the lead-up to the 2013 elections, when dramatic policy reforms restored community access to fisheries through the abolition of private fishing lots on Tonle Sap Lake (Kong, 2012); and awarded thousands of land titles to farmers and informal settlers at the forest frontier (Milne, 2013). Cambodia's contemporary rural dynamics are therefore distinct from classic peasant resistance of the past, as they now involve the deep penetration of the state,[8] along with international reform agendas and their associated 'frictions' (Hughes, 2013). Like the churning of the sea of milk, this socio-environmental realm is full of tension and struggle, which together have the potential to galvanize into sources of hope and change.

Frontiers of change in Southeast Asia: Theorizing transformation in nature-society

The notion of *frontiers* enables us to observe the processes and effects of transformation and its interconnected social, political and environmental dimensions. We view frontiers as 'sites' as well as 'interfaces' where change processes are particularly intense and visible, manifesting in ways that exemplify or illuminate broader underlying transformations. Frontiers may therefore be multi-scalar, ephemeral, material, socially constructed, human and non-human. The point is that they are *situated expressions of transformation*; windows through which the workings of change may be viewed and framed.

The frontiers of change that we deal with in this volume are those within the realm of nature and society, or nature-society. This is a realm of mutual production and interdependence, in which nature and society cannot be separated. Nature is not pristine or free from human impact; nor can it be controlled or made external to human existence (Smith, 1998). As Donna Haraway (1997) told us, we exist in 'a cyborg world that dissolves sharp boundaries between human and non-human nature'. Thus we must take socio-natures as a given and as a starting point in our analysis.

Often scholars of Southeast Asia have cast frontiers as places at the edge of modernity, or at the interface between spaces of modernity, or subject to capitalist expansion and those that have previously escaped such expansion. For example, forest frontiers are conceived as spaces where the advance of timber extraction, land commodification and industrial agriculture 'eats into' a non-capitalized and non-commodified forested world, often inhabited by indigenous people (Tsing, 1993; McCarthy, 2006). As Anna Tsing wrote, these are places at the 'edge of space and time: a zone of not yet – not yet mapped, "not yet" regulated' (2003, p. 5100). Thus frontiers are often spatial, existing at the physical boundary between more and less exploited landscapes; as well as social, given their intense processes of commodification, dispossession and class formation (Nevins and Peluso, 2008).

In this vein, and echoing world-system studies, frontiers are also sites of incorporation into the world capitalist economy (Wallerstein, 1989). That is, they are spaces subject to the forward movement of capitalism, beyond which further capitalist expansion can occur so long as uncommodified land and labour are available (Moore, 2000). Recent Southeast Asian scholarship distinguishes three features of these capitalist or commodity frontiers. First, a key mechanism for capitalist expansion is the opening up of new commodity markets, whether for land or land-based commodities such as rubber and timber, or for newly commodified forms of nature and its ecosystem services such as carbon sequestration (Nevins and Peluso, 2008; Mahanty *et al.*, 2013). Second, Southeast Asia's typically undemocratic states play a crucial role in facilitating this capitalist expansion (Wolford *et al.*, 2013), which has enabled elites and state actors to benefit from the processes of accumulation by dispossession and primitive accumulation (Hall, 2013). Third, capitalist frontiers are complex in their cross-scalar and transnational dynamics, often setting in train new processes of state-making and government. These include the introduction of much larger 'projects' of citizenship (Tsing, 2005), the extension of state territorialization

(Vandergeest and Peluso, 1995), and the emergence of hybrid forms of neoliberalism (Springer, 2010).

A key aspect of these frontier dynamics, whether they emerge from the advance of markets or simply the transmission of ideas, is that they give rise to intense sites of cultural production (Appadurai, 1996) or social 'friction' (Tsing, 2005). Friction occurs at sites of 'global connection' and may precipitate new identities and social movements, or enable 'universal' aspirations of freedom and development to take root locally (ibid). The capacity for friction of this kind to generate hybrid social and political forms has been observed in Cambodia, especially in the context of international aid and post-conflict reconstruction (Öjendal and Ou, 2013; Hughes, 2013). But hotter and more dynamic frictions are also emerging through Cambodia's recent political turmoil, fuelled in part by popular resistance to elite accumulation, and in response to the effects of exclusion, social marginalization and environmental depletion (e.g. Neef et al., 2013; Ngoun, 2013). As Tsing's (2005) concept of friction highlights, with 'agrarian angst' (Turner and Caouette, 2009) comes new space for agency and creative transformation, a point that is explored further in Part 3 of this volume.

Finally, studies of agrarian change remind us that frontiers are not necessarily exceptional spaces (Walker, 2009). Rather, they are a culmination and intense expression of ongoing processes of change in rural society more widely, such as migration (de Koninck, 2000; Rigg, 2005) and agricultural intensification (Cramb et al., 2009). These transformations are in turn connected to the opportunities and risks of national and global political-economic processes. While some local actors can strategically take up new livelihood opportunities that emerge from this, others may experience heightened social vulnerability (Rigg, 2005), as well as altered resource access and exclusion (Hall et al., 2011). Like a mysterious fungus that occasionally manifests above ground, frontiers provide us with special insights into transformative processes that are everywhere, yet may be hard to see.

Key frontiers in Cambodia's changing nature-society relations

The early chapters in this volume examine how and why nature-society relationships are changing in contemporary Cambodia. This endeavour begins with an account of the fundamental role played by the post-conflict state, in creating the mechanisms and conditions for Cambodia's transformation (Chapter 2). The pronounced influence of powerful state actors and the ruling party in Cambodia's development trajectory has been observed (Hughes and Un, 2011); but this analysis is extended to the environmental realm, providing a vital state-society framing for the volume as a whole. The subsequent four chapters then showcase major dynamics and processes in Cambodia's environment-development nexus, highlighting: the presence of intricate socio-ecological systems in which rural villagers are intimately connected to their environment (Chapter 3); the strained modernization of lowland rice farming, in which new technologies and markets do not necessarily integrate smoothly with existing practices (Chapter 4); the role of forced dispossession and land grabbing in rupturing nature-society connections (Chapter 5); and the multi-scaled implications of Cambodia's authoritarian-developmentalist drive to transform landscapes and 'harness nature' through hydropower (Chapter 6). Together, these chapters illustrate how change processes in nature-society relations in Cambodia can be thought of in two broad categories: (i) continuous change or gradual transitions in the micro-dynamics of rural livelihoods and production systems and (ii) discontinuous change or violent ruptures in nature-society caused by spectacular transformations and physical conversion of environments. These diverse change processes entail different kinds of frontiers and frictions, but a key mediating force across all of them is power, especially that of the state.

The role of the state

An overarching frontier or interface, present in all of Cambodia's nature-society dynamics, relates to the shifting presence and power of the state. The state and its 'rulers' have played, and continue to play, a key role in determining how natural resources are owned, used and managed. This phenomenon is not unique to Cambodia – Polanyi (1944) also emphasized the fundamental role of the state in facilitating Europe's economic transformation – but the Cambodian case is exemplary because of the state's powerful and reflexive relationship with nature-society. It is in this domain that the state derives and consolidates its power: extracting vital revenue from natural resources, and dealing with the inevitable agrarian push-back and potential grassroots movements that arise as a result. This is the subject of Chapter 2, by Sarah Milne, Pak Kimchoeun and Michael Sullivan, who provide us with an account of Cambodia's post-conflict state formation and how the current regime 'came into being' through the enclosure, commodification and exploitation of natural resources. They explain how the ruling CPP was able to co-opt the state apparatus and dismantle political opposition over time; in particular through the use of techniques such as elite accommodation and mass patronage, which hinged upon and were financed by natural resource rents.

Understanding the formation and functioning of the CPP-backed regime is therefore vital for any analysis of Cambodia's conservation and development outcomes. For example, the party's eager facilitation of market integration, property reform, agricultural investment and ambitious infrastructure projects over the last decade and a half, through the 'Rectangular Strategy' for national development, has profoundly shaped nature-society dynamics.[9] Indeed, this policy context alone has created a formidable force for conservationists and resource-dependent villagers to contend with. But it is the regime's treatment of land, forests and fisheries reforms that reveal most about its real or unofficial character, which is widely identified as predatory and neopatrimonial (Cock, 2010; Un and So, 2011; Milne, 2013). This is because state authority and legal mechanisms have been used to territorialize forested land and fisheries, at the expense of local claims to resources, leading to enclosure and dispossession (Neef *et al.*, 2013; Sneddon, 2007; Springer, 2013). In turn, this has paved the way for appropriation of public resources by ruling elites, including party leaders and those tied to the regime through familial, patrimonial or business relationships (Global Witness, 2009). The result of this state-backed privatization process has been a trajectory of conjoined resource exploitation and regime strengthening.

However, with the enclosure and appropriation of land and resources, rural livelihoods are inevitably squeezed. Responding to this dispossession, farmers, fishers and forest-dependent villagers have become increasingly vocal and determined in Cambodia; and they now represent a major force for social change that the ruling party cannot ignore. This dynamic was first visible among Cambodian fishers who, facing a bleak future due to declining stocks on Tonle Sap in the early 2000s, organized themselves into a grassroots coalition and stood up to the government. This took the CPP by surprise and led to the unprecedented move by Hun Sen of the cancellation of some private fishing lots, to allow villagers to gain access to fish – an action he repeated in similar circumstances in 2012. Some identify this early movement on Tonle Sap as 'the spark' that awakened Cambodia's people, and which has now developed into a national-level struggle around resource rights in general, especially land.[10] This resistance has changed the country's political landscape; as seen in the populist reforms to land ownership and fisheries prior to the 2013 election, and in the ongoing pressure for change post-election (see Chapter 2). Arguably, these dynamics resemble a Polanyian 'double-movement', which we explain below and adopt as the focus of Part 3 in this volume.

Gradual transitions and constant dynamism in rural production systems

Another frontier of change in Cambodia's nature-society relations is to be found in the gradual transitions or 'micro-dynamics' of rural production systems. In Chapter 3, Andrew Roberts combines insights from ecology, geography and anthropology to illustrate the intimate and contingent interactions between rural people and their environment on the Tonle Sap floodplain, Cambodia's most productive fishery and rice-producing area (see Figure 1.3, which shows the location of this and subsequent study sites). In Kompong Thom, Roberts finds that villagers 'make a living' in a place that is constantly changing, in part through their exploitation of the interstices between landscape types and seasons. Problematically, these cracks or grey-areas are rendered invisible by conventional classifications of land-use and resources used by NGOs and government actors. Thus Roberts demonstrates the practical and inherently political challenges faced by conservation and development practitioners in their attempts to intervene in natural resource management on Tonle Sap, but elsewhere too. For these actors, complex nature-society interactions must be simplified for the purposes of intervention (Li, 2007) and made 'legible' through the production of maps and plans for natural resource management (Scott, 1998). Roberts conveys what is obscured in this process; an ephemeral and fragile world of complex inter-dependence between people and nature.

Chapter 4 by Maylee Thavat shifts our focus to the myriad and often unintended effects of development interventions in such finely-tuned rural environments. Examining Cambodia's rice-growing heartland of Prey Veng province, Thavat explores donor-backed efforts to 'improve' farm productivity and encourage market integration for the purposes of poverty alleviation. At first glance, this lowland agricultural landscape conforms to Cambodia's quintessential rural idyll: boundless rice paddies, interspersed with sugar palm, farmed for generations by local families. But this chapter reveals a more socially differentiated and environmentally precarious situation. In particular, the contrasting assets and farming practices of poor, middle-income and wealthy farmers shape their different engagements with donor-introduced environmental technologies and schemes, in this case improved rice seed distributed through new market mechanisms. While delivering increased yields for some, the adoption of improved seed also highlights the challenges and risks of commodifying rice production, which until recently was subject to more traditional management practices that ensured risk-aversion, local subsistence and agro-biodiversity, in farmers' interests. Now, it seems that such 'yet-to-be-commodified' approaches to farming are a privilege retained by the middle class only, with poor and rich farmers locked into more marketized modes of production.

Dramatic ruptures and spectacular transformations in nature-society

Beyond the incremental transformations taking place in some rural production systems, another set of more dramatic and violent changes to nature-society relations have been highly visible in Cambodia. Chapter 5 by Megan MacInnes is illustrative, as she takes us to the highly dynamic 'forest frontier', where new spaces of capitalist production and accumulation have been created over the last decade through land grabbing and forced dispossession of various kinds, but mainly due to state-backed ELCs (see Figure 1.2). Across the country, these processes have ruptured the underlying relationships between people and land, in which local residents, often ethnic minority or indigenous people, have been separated from their homelands: landscapes that they have shaped, inhabited and 'belonged to' over hundreds of years.[11] Through two high-profile cases, MacInnes examines the conditions and processes that have facilitated land grabbing in Cambodia. Her analysis reveals the central role played by the CPP-controlled state apparatus in enabling land accumulation and resource access for elites. The government's manipulation of legal mechanisms and the judicial system, alongside the use of state authority and violence, emerge as key ingredients in Cambodia's land and resource grabbing phenomena.

The final chapter in this section on contemporary nature-society relations in Cambodia (Chapter 6) addresses the profound and discontinuous changes wrought by major infrastructure projects. In this chapter, Michael Sullivan describes the proliferation of Chinese-backed hydropower investments, which in turn are connected to wider geo-political and transnational agendas. Often established in remote forests and protected areas, these projects bring massive transformative potential for society and the environment. Indeed, Prime Minister Hun Sen has hailed a new set of hydropower dams in the Cardamom Mountains as the future 'battery of Cambodia', given their ability to generate energy from plentiful un-tapped water resources. While some international agencies and donors see these developments as the key to sustainability and a new 'green economy' for Cambodia (e.g. Killeen, 2012), Sullivan's analysis reveals a more nuanced view of the transformative effects of hydropower. In particular, he explores the role of Chinese state-owned companies in planning and financing these developments, especially their opaque interactions with the Cambodian government. The chapter therefore asks whether Cambodia's environment and development trajectory will converge with that of China's, or whether Cambodia can find an alternative 'sovereign' pathway that secures environmental values alongside development.

Attempts to intervene: Practices of 'conservation and development' in Cambodia

Although the Cambodian government has made strong commitments to nature conservation in the last decade,[12] especially given pressure and interest from donors and non-government organizations, the practical outcomes have often been socially and environmentally problematic. This cannot be understood without critical analysis of the practices, institutions and power relations that mediate all interventions seeking to achieve environmental and development goals. Often the limitations of international conservation projects in settings like Cambodia emerge from their underlying assumptions and logics, which tend to derive from Western-centric ideas or values around nature, and paradigmatic thinking about how it should be saved (Adams, 2009). However, another compromising factor is the sheer complexity of project implementation, inherent in the myriad transnational and cross-cultural collaborations that must be forged between NGOs, government officials, local villagers and others in the course of pursuing 'improvement' in nature-society relations (Mosse, 2005; Long, 2001). In the Cambodian context, a distinguishing feature of these collaborations is the influence of the state; especially its ability to resist donor-led reform (e.g. Un and So, 2011; Cock, 2010; Hughes, 2013) and manipulate the practices and outcomes of environmental projects on the ground (Milne and Adams, 2012; Biddulph, 2011). In the following paragraphs we develop these critical insights, providing a conceptual framing for Part 2 of this volume, which examines the outcomes of a range of conservation and development interventions in Cambodia over the last decade (Chapters 7, 8, 9). These chapters problematize the major modes of conservation that have been attempted across the country, highlighting how their inherent paradigmatic, social and political complexities complicate the realization of intervention goals.

Problematizing interventions in conservation and development

In order to study the practice of conservation, and to gain an appreciation of its political nature, we analyse it as a form of intervention. That is, conservation is a set of externally driven activities that are guided by an overall rationale to ameliorate or 'govern' the relationships between people and nature (Li, 2007). Typically, this entails the propagation and implementation of powerful ideas about the value of biodiversity and how it should be protected, for example, through the creation of protected areas or new markets for environmental services (Adams and Hutton, 2007; Igoe and Brockington, 2007). However, by implication, this also entails the implementation of ideas about how people should relate to or co-exist with nature. For example, early Western and colonial conservation efforts tried hard to remove people from natural areas, by fencing-off 'wilderness' and national parks (Adams, 2004). But as the conservation movement evolved into its contemporary global form in the 1970s, this model attracted sharp criticism, due to the negative effects of protected areas on local and indigenous peoples who were already facing issues of poverty and marginalization (Brockington, 2002; Adams *et al.*, 2004). Thus, from the 1990s onwards, international conservation efforts have been coupled with human development, both practically and intellectually, as seen in the proliferation of schemes such as integrated conservation and development projects (ICDPs), community-based natural resource management (CBNRM) and later market-based schemes such as payments for environmental services (PES) and carbon trade. These interventions try to harmonize conservation and development, thus alleviating perceived tensions and trade-offs between the two goals (e.g. Brandon and Wells, 1992; Western *et al.*, 1994; Ferraro and Kiss, 2002).

The problem is that the pursuit of these good intentions – saving wildlife, helping indigenous people, building strong communities – entails the formulation and implementation of complex projects that are rarely apolitical, and can have perverse side-effects in practice. Scholars of international development have long studied this problem, offering important insights. For example, Tania Li (2007) examined how development interventions are driven by a 'will to improve' that is assumed to be universal and good, but in practice can be colonial and political. Analysis of how such interventions work in practice highlights their profoundly problematic nature. For example, project proponents must first construct and frame the problems that they wish to solve. This involves processes of simplification and representation that make the site of intervention 'legible' for the roll-out of new projects and ideas (Scott, 1998), in turn reducing complex political problems into mere technical matters (Li, 2007). Second, having socially constructed the field or the realm of intervention, a project's interpretation of reality must be perpetuated through its practices and logics. This can lead to 'systems of representation' within projects and programs that make it difficult for practitioners to acknowledge complicated local realities or unintended consequences (West, 2006; Mosse, 2005). Thus, interventions in conservation and development typically entail a particular 'anti-politics' that filters out messy details or problems on the ground (Ferguson, 1990; Milne and Adams, 2012). With these politics in train, contemporary conservation and development projects often proceed with insufficient attention to the complexity of local situations in which they are embedded, and nowhere is this more evident than in Cambodia.

Cambodia's engagement and experiences with the conservation movement

International NGOs and donors have been attempting to intervene in the governance of Cambodia's natural resources since the late 1990s. At that time, emerging from 30 years of civil war, Cambodia retained forests and wildlife that had disappeared from much of the rest of mainland Southeast Asia. This, combined with an apparently imminent post-conflict rush to exploit natural resources for development purposes, made Cambodia a priority area or 'hotspot' for conservation intervention.[13] The country became a poster child for donors and international NGOs: by 2001–2002, most of the major players[14] in global conservation had acquired a 'Cambodia program', with an office in Phnom Penh and at least one field site or critically endangered species to protect. There was a lot of hope and promise at this time, as Hun Sen had just suspended all commercial logging concessions in response to international pressure, leaving vast tracts of apparently 'untouched' and 'unmanaged' forested land in government hands. This was fertile ground for conservationists, and their interests were galvanized by the World Bank in 2002, when it committed millions of dollars in funding for biodiversity conservation and protected area management through the Global Environment Facility (GEF).[15]

Subsequent interventions saw about one-third of Cambodia's surface area committed to some kind of conservation management, including protected areas under the Ministry of Environment (MoE); protected forests and community forests under the Forestry Administration (FA); community fisheries under the Fisheries Administration and other areas under complex transnational governance arrangements, guided by the United Nations, such as the Tonle Sap Biosphere Reserve and the Angkor Wat World Heritage Site. Taken together, these territorial designations for 'conservation and development' have all involved the strengthening of government claims to resources, albeit often in contested ways, for example, as different government departments compete against each other for control over particular areas.[16] In this complex political environment, international conservation organizations and donors tried hard to push for reforms and management practices that would sustain natural resources and biodiversity.

The chapters in Part 2 of this book focus on how these international conservation efforts have played out. Together, the chapters illustrate the inner workings and political dynamics of three key modalities of conservation practice in Cambodia, which are seen across Southeast Asia and other global biodiversity 'hotspots', particularly: the creation of protected areas and national parks (Chapter 7); attempts to foster CBNRM through 'community forestry' (Chapter 8) and efforts to conserve forests through international carbon markets, under global climate change mitigation protocols (Chapter 9). These chapters showcase how conservation gives rise to contested and transnational 'spaces' or frontiers, in which global policy ideas and project implementation must be negotiated across scales and through a maze of hidden institutions and pressures that influence local decision-making, such as patronage networks and the accommodation of elite interests.

Thus, the most profound challenge for Cambodia's conservation movement emerges: that there is frequently a dissonance or disconnect between what government counterparts say they will do, and what they actually do. Richard Paley analyses government resistance to reform in the MoE, a 'conservation bureaucracy' charged with running Cambodia's enormous protected area system (Chapter 7; see also Chapter 2 for broader analysis). He demonstrates how formal conservation goals, typically those sponsored by international actors, are almost impossible to achieve given the informal regime of patronage and CPP-dominance in which the ministry is embedded. In this light, the way in which most international conservation NGOs and donors continue to position themselves as *government partners* or counterparts to the MoE and FA in Cambodia is increasingly problematic; attracting warranted criticism and debate (e.g. Milne, 2012; Global Witness, 2007).

The final two chapters on conservation practice are intended to illustrate approaches that are less government-heavy, focusing instead on solutions inspired by neoliberal thinking, which claim to rely on communities and the market (Igoe and Brockington, 2007). Chapter 8 by Robin Biddulph examines Community Forestry – an idealistic mode of intervention that seeks to 'empower' villagers, while helping them to sustain and manage 'their' forest resources. Through detailed ethnographic analysis of one project in Kratie, Biddulph reveals just how challenging it is to achieve the stated ideals of community forestry in Cambodia, given the dynamics of under-resourced NGOs, government territoriality and a local political economy that is tied to CPP-backed elites. Similarly, the latest innovation in global conservation thinking – which promises conservation through the creation of new markets for environmental services – also appears to be constrained by Cambodia's governance context. Chapter 9, by Sango Mahanty, Amanda Bradley and Sarah Milne, reveals how this problem manifests in the context of voluntary forest carbon markets, where pilot schemes are currently being established, ultimately to become part of Cambodia's national REDD[17] framework for generation of carbon credits. Through a commodity chain analysis of the two most advanced REDD projects in Cambodia, this chapter shows how substantial donor resources have been spent on the highly technical 'production phase' of generating forest carbon credits, with benefits so far accruing mainly to international experts and government and civil society service providers. Meanwhile, the carbon commodity chain fails to incorporate many of the actors that drive forest loss, and the much anticipated resources and actions for 'avoided deforestation' on the ground are yet to materialize in the face of market hurdles and state reticence.

Given the frustrations of mainstream conservation practice in Cambodia, and the mounting critique of NGOs and donors who continue to engage with a government that shows little commitment to sustaining its natural resources, new questions and alternative responses are emerging. As the final section of this book suggests, it is now time to re-think the models, approaches and assumptions of conventional 'conservation and development' practice; thus creating space for nature-society to rebound and reform.

Social change and radical possibilities in response to transformation

The final section in this book considers how the frictions and struggles involved in transformation are contributing to grassroots social movements and government opposition in Cambodia, with implications for elsewhere. These emerging social dynamics and forms must contend with their own internal divisions and contradictions, as well as the coercive pressures of authoritarian and predatory actors aligned with the ruling party. Government attempts to manipulate or undermine community organizing and supress people's mobilization have been fierce and effective in recent years.[18] But the state-society dynamic continues to shift and evolve, as new modes of resistance emerge, and as government actors respond with a combination of violence and accommodative reforms (e.g. Öjendal and Ou, 2013; Springer, 2010).

These responses to transformation can be examined through the lens of Polanyi's double-movement, as suggested in the edited volume by Hughes and Un (2011), and by other scholars examining similar contemporary contexts (e.g. Cotula, 2013; Li, 2010). Polanyi's thesis was that processes of commodification and marketization would be countered by efforts for social protection; for 'the conservation of man and nature ... relying on the varying support of those most immediately affected by the deleterious action of the market' (Polanyi, 1944, p. 179). We argue that this dynamic has become increasingly evident in Cambodia since 2010: first, as disenfranchised people challenge their loss of land and resources through anti-government protest; and second, as state and NGO actors attempt to implement social protection measures, whether genuinely motivated or politically expedient. Polanyi's emphasis on how the double-movement attempts to reunify society-nature, or in Marxian terms, attempts to reconstitute labourers with the 'means of labour' (Chatterjee, 2008),[19] has particular importance for this volume. Much remains to be understood about the specific mechanisms and spaces through which this double-movement might evolve in Cambodia, including the challenges faced by actors involved and the implications for state-society relations more broadly. All of these themes are explored in the final section of this volume.[20]

Part 3 (Chapters 10, 11, 12, and 13) examines emerging and more radical modalities for conservation and development in Cambodia. Case studies explore grassroots social movements and transnational advocacy networks that have begun to challenge state authority and elite appropriation of natural resources, while calling for environmental justice and strengthened resource rights. On the one hand, these developments demand the extension of conventional thinking in conservation and development – signifying a move *beyond* the interventions of mainstream NGOs and the state, to encompass more horizontal and dynamic organizational forms, and more innovative spaces for nature-society such as anthropogenic landscapes and community-owned resources. On the other hand, they signal the central importance of environment and development linkages in what appears to be Cambodia's double-movement.

Thus, the final section of this book begins with an exploration of relationships between people and nature that are not governed by the dichotomous post-enlightenment thinking that dominates conventional conservation (Adams, 2004). Asking 'what about the unprotected areas?', Chapter 10 by Jeremy Ironside, explores the potential for more holistic thinking about people–nature relationships, through an exploration of indigenous land use in Ratanakiri. Ironside reviews indigenous land management practices in three villages, showing how traditional landscapes are anthropogenic and often perceived as 'boundless' by local residents. He demonstrates the merits of communal management of land, which can accommodate gaps and gradations between farm and forest, arguing that privatized or 'fenced in' land can lead to social and ecological damage. In this light, he explores nascent efforts to implement indigenous communal land title as a defence against the encroachment and alienation that inevitably emerge with capitalism. The results are mixed, but the chapter highlights how communally held land can play an important role in contemporary landscapes, as it re-situates people in nature and can foster new kinds of belonging.

Probing further into Cambodia's capacities and possibilities for radical change, we look to the past. Chapter 11 by Margaret Slocomb explores the history and culture of peasant resistance in Cambodia, particularly to colonial enclosures and state predation. This chapter is important because some observers question whether sustained social movements are even possible in Cambodia, given the war-weary and dominated populace, who have until recently chosen not to pursue collective action against their rulers (e.g. Bit, 1991; Henke, 2011; Brinkley, 2011). But, Chapter 11 debunks this narrative by exploring the country's historical precedents of resistance, particularly against French colonizers. Indeed, Slocomb shows that both Khmer and upland indigenous populations have a track record of resisting domination, often violently. The historical roots of people's movements in Cambodia are therefore exposed, providing context and shedding light on current grassroots mobilizations around the environment that are explored in the final two chapters.

Building upon Slocomb's historical discussion, Chapter 12 by John Marsten and Chhuon Hoeur examines a contemporary story of resistance, in one village of Kompong Thom Province near Tonle Sap Lake. By following a local movement to demand a 'people's irrigation reservoir', in response to elite-backed reservoir developments in the area, the authors reveal a grassroots resistance story that is complicated and contradictory. In particular, they show how local CPP leaders and elite business interests interacted with the villagers' movement, causing it to become entangled in party politics. Thus they offer a cautionary tale, showing us the potential for community leaders to be co-opted or corrupted by the dominant regime, with ambiguous ends. This raises important questions about the internal workings of resistance and the double-movement, highlighting the almost inevitable need for grassroots movements to negotiate both internal dysfunctions and external pressures.

A critical component of this analysis is the final chapter by Terry Parnell, which details the emergence and continuing strength of Cambodia's most prominent social movement around forest conservation, the Prey Lang Community Network. Parnell explores why this movement formed and consolidated, and the challenges and opportunities it now faces. Vital lessons for nurturing, but not controlling, grassroots actions are provided. The story of Prey Lang therefore offers us an alternative vision to the interventionist conservation efforts of the last decade, led by NGOs and state officials, which is grounded in an enduring concern for social justice. Parnell also reveals the importance of a social movement's narrative, which in this case suggests that there is not a final end-point or particular goal in the movement; rather it functions as a 'never ending story', evolving organically from the frictions at play. This offers another perspective on the inner workings of Polanyi's double-movement, as a source of social change that flows continuously.

Conclusion

The frontiers of change discussed in this volume yield important insights into pervasive processes of transformation that are affecting not only Cambodia, but Southeast Asia more broadly. Cambodia's nature-society transformations range from incremental and insidious to dramatic and cathartic. They also entail multi-scalar and highly power-laden processes of resource appropriation, market extension, environmental degradation and intervention; all of which resonate throughout Southeast Asia, given its 'frontier nature' and rapid pace of development and economic integration (Fold and Hirsch, 2009).

As the chapters in this volume reveal, a key frontier that cuts across all of these processes in Cambodia is the role of the state – including its power, its limitations and its dynamic and fluid relationship with society (Migdal, 2001). At first glance, we see the post-conflict state at the apex of a striking recursive relationship between the country's political economy and its environmental trajectory. In particular, the ruling party's efforts to drive a transformation process that is uniquely neoliberal and authoritarian (Springer, 2010) have produced dramatic environmental change and social marginalization. But diverse responses to this trajectory have emerged, exposing the limits of state power. This volume demonstrates that 'non-state agency' is evident in the rise of resistance and social movements, especially around natural resources. However, this state-society dynamic is also subject to nature's agency (Grundy-Warr *et al.*, 2014) and the influence of non-human or spirit entities (Beban and Work, 2014), all of which can ultimately disrupt order. These factors, viewed alongside recent political history, suggest that state power in Cambodia is becoming more contingent and negotiated.

Yet, as state power and legitimacy are challenged, so must the state respond. In a post-colonial world where violent crackdowns against peasant resistance are no longer normalized, governments must find other ways to accommodate the demands of those who bear the brunt of capitalist transformation (Cotula, 2013; Chatterjee, 2008). Or, as Chatterjee explains, echoing Polanyi, governments must find ways to 'reverse the effects' of primitive accumulation so that such accumulation may continue. Typically this occurs with reforms that attempt to reduce the extremes of poverty, restore some local resource rights and conserve the natural environment; all of which have been prominent in Cambodia since the early 2000s, with the support of donors and NGOs. But, as this volume illustrates, such interventions in nature-society are often blunt or ineffective, having consequences that are hard to control or predict. Either they are undermined by their crude 'simplifications' of the complex domains that they seek to manipulate; or they suffer from deep contradictions, as they must be implemented by or in partnership with an authoritarian regime that until now has systematically facilitated peasant dispossession and elite accumulation. Profound questions therefore remain about how Cambodia will respond to the upheavals of transformation.

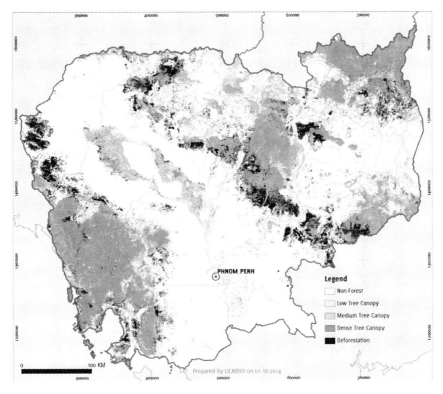

Figure 1.1 Map of forest loss in Cambodia 2000–2012.
Source: Global Forest Change interactive tool, developed by Hansen *et al.* (2013), available at http://earthenginepartners.appspot.com/science-2013-global-forest. The original data from the website are in colour. They were converted to greyscale using QGIS by Mathieu Pellerin.[21]

For now, the chapters in this volume expose the frictions, negotiations and 'productive' encounters that are taking place as Cambodia's transformation unfolds. Like the churning of the sea of milk, which produced upheaval and a potent poison, our contributing authors document the myriad social, political and environmental challenges being generated at Cambodia's frontiers of change. They show that efforts to manipulate and intervene in these complex and multi-scalar trajectories are inherently limited. However, they offer a degree of hope too. The frictions at Cambodia's frontiers, like the creative essence of the cosmic sea, also have the potential to generate a new 'elixir of life' – through emerging social movements, akin to Polanyi's double-movement. These forces, while unpredictable and not without their own internal challenges, will inevitably breathe vitality and fresh dynamics into Cambodia's strained and inequitable political economy. Thus, the sites of struggle that we see around 'conservation and development also have the potential to become sources of hope.

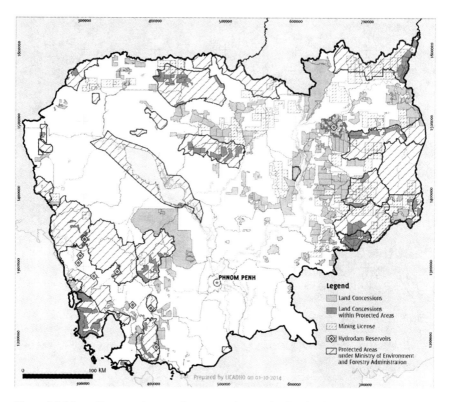

Figure 1.2 Map of concessions and protected areas in Cambodia, May 2014. Land concessions cover 2,289,490 hectares and mining concessions cover 2,027,979 hectares. (Land concessions include ELCs, divested rubber plantations, the Union Development Group Lease, and Special Economic Zones of Try Pheap and by Yong Phat.)

Source: Licadho, Phnom Penh

Notes

1. The original Hindu text that describes this myth is: *Mahabharatha*, Volume 1, The Book of the Beginning, Verse 16.1 (sourced from van Buitanen, 1973). This translation refers to the 'ocean of milk', but the term 'sea of milk' is often used with reference to Angkorean representations of the myth, hence our use of it here.
2. For example, see Smallteacher (2014).
3. For interpretation of Hansen *et al.* (2013) see Morgan (2013).
4. For interpretation, see Worrell (2013).
5. Legal logging now occurs only with special permits from the Forestry Administration, for example, in association with forest clearing for ELCs and hydropower dams.
6. For example, see Global Witness (2007) and countless recent articles on illegal logging by tycoons, such as May and Pye (2014).
7. For example, as seen in the 2012 murder of Chut Wutty, who was trying to expose illegal logging (Milne, 2012); and in widespread violent crackdowns on protesters resisting forced evictions (HRW, 2014).

The political ecology of Cambodia's transformation 21

Figure 1.3 Study sites discussed in this volume.
Source: Cartography, The Australian National University

8 This observation of state interaction with peasant resistance in the 21st century is owed to Partha Chatterjee, in his discussion of economic transformation in India (2008). The same dynamic arguably applies to Cambodia, in light of recent work (e.g. Hughes, 2013).
9 The rectangular strategy has had multiple phases. The latest is phase III (2013), see http://cnv.org.kh/en/wp-content/uploads/2013/10/26sep13_rectangular-strategy_phaseIII.pdf, accessed 26 September 2013.
10 Terry Parnell, personal communication, 2014. Also see Henke (2011).
11 See 2013 special issue of *Asia Pacific Viewpoint* 54(3) on indigeneity and natural resources in Cambodia.
12 For example Cambodia signed the UN Convention on Biological Diversity (CBD) and government agencies have created numerous protected forests, biosphere reserves and protected areas; over 20 per cent of the country's surface area is under some form of legal protection (ICEM, 2003).
13 The term 'hotspot' was popularized by Conservation International (CI), for setting global conservation priorities (Brooks *et al.*, 2006). Cambodia is in the Indo-Burma hotspot, defined by CI.

14 For example, international conservation NGOs included CI, World Wildlife Fund, Wildlife Conservation Society, Birdlife International and others. They received funds from the Danish Embassy, the Department for International Development UK, the US Agency for International Development, the GEF, the Critical Ecosystem Partnership Fund (CEPF), the French Agence Française pour le Développement (AFD), the MacArthur Foundation etc.
15 Multiple tranches of GEF funding have been awarded to Cambodia over the last decade and a half, amounting to over $179 million. Source: 'Cambodia and the GEF', February 2013 factsheet. Available at http://www.thegef.org/gef/sites/thegef.org/files/publication/Cambodia%20-%20Fact%20Sheet%20-%20Feb2013_EN.pdf, accessed 30 February 2014.
16 This is most evident on Tonle Sap, with at least four ministries and one authority involved in management. See Chapter 2 this volume for discussion of this problem of 'overlapping mandates'.
17 REDD stands for Reducing Emissions from Deforestation and Forest Degradation.
18 For example, activists contesting land grabbing and illegal logging have been murdered, threatened and imprisoned. See the cases of Chut Wutty, Mom Sonando and those involved in the struggles around Boeung Kak Lake, Borei Keila and Kratie (e.g. HRW, 2014).
19 Marx's analysis in *Capital* focused on peasants and artisans' loss of the 'means of production', with the transition to capitalist production. Chatterjee sees this as equivalent to labourers being dissociated from the 'means of labour' (2008, p. 54).
20 Note that one chapter in Hughes and Un's edited volume (Hughes *et al.*, 2011) speculates about whether a Polanyian double-movement is actually possible in Cambodia, given the lack of conclusive evidence of social movements around natural resources at the time of their research (*c.* 2009). Cambodia's political landscape has clearly changed dramatically since then.
21 The conversion to greyscale was achieved by merging two sets of colour categories in the Hansen *et al.* map. First, red (forest loss 2000–2012) and pink (forest loss and gain) were merged into a single category that is called 'deforestation' in Figure 1.1. This relies on the premise that 'forest loss and gain' is equivalent to deforestation; easily justified because 'forest gain' in Hansen *et al*'s work represents either new agricultural plantation or forest regrowth, signifying a loss of the original forest cover since 2000. Second, the original blue 'forest gain 2000–2012' and green 'forest extent' were merged to create the category of current 'forest cover' in Figure 1.1, shown in varying degrees of density in grey. The premise here is that forest regrowth and new plantations, which appeared from non-forest since 2000, do not constitute deforestation in the time period of interest. Furthermore, the area of land that falls under 'forest gain' in Cambodia is extremely small when compared to the area of land under original or natural 'forest extent'. Thus, the merging of forest gain and forest extent in Figure 1.1 makes sense for analytical and representational purposes.

References

Adams, W. (2004) *Against Extinction: The Past and Future of Conservation*, Earthscan, London.
Adams, W. (2009) 'The politics of preservation', in *Green Development: Environment and Sustainability in a Developing World*, Routledge, Oxon, pp. 275–298.
Adams, W., Avcling, R., Brockington, D., Dickson, B., Elliott, J., Hutton, J., Roe, D., Vira, B. and Wolmer, W. (2004) 'Biodiversity conservation and the eradication of poverty', *Science* 306, pp. 1146–1148.

Adams, W. and Hutton, J. (2007) 'People, parks and poverty: Political ecology and biodiversity conservation', *Conservation and Society* 5(2), pp. 147–183.

Appadurai, A. (1996) *Modernity at Large: Cultural Dimensions of Globalisation*, University of Minnesota Press, Minneapolis.

Azimi, A., Knowland, W., Carew Reid, J., Ruzicka, I. and Zola, A. (2000) 'Environments in Transition: Cambodia, Lao PDR, Thailand, Viet Nam', Asia Development Bank, Manila, http://tnmckc.org/upload/document/bdp/2/2.7/External/Envir_in_transition.pdf, accessed 14 April 2014.

Baran, E., Starr, P. and Kura, Y. (2007) *Influence of Built Structures on Tonle Sap Fisheries*, Cambodian National Mekong Committee and the WorldFish Centre, Phnom Penh.

Beban, A. and Work, C. (2014) 'The spirits are crying: Dispossessing land and possessing bodies in rural Cambodia', *Antipode* 46(3), pp. 593–610.

Biddulph, R. (2011) 'Tenure security interventions in Cambodia: Testing Bebbington's approach to development geography', *Geografiska Annaler: Series B, Human Geography* 93(3), pp. 223–236.

Bit, S. (1991) *The Warrior Heritage: A Psychological Perspective of Cambodian Trauma*, S. Bit, El Cerrito, CA.

Blaikie, P. and Brookfield, H. (1987) *Land Degradation and Society*, Methuen, New York and London.

Boyle, D. and May, T. (2012) 'Blind eye to forest's plight', *Phnom Penh Post*, 26 March, p. 1.

Brandon, K. and Wells, M. (1992) 'Planning for people and parks: Design dilemmas', *World Development* 20(4), pp. 557–570.

Brinkley, J. (2011) *Cambodia's Curse: The Modern History of a Troubled Land*, PublicAffairs Books, New York.

Brockington, D. (2002) *Fortress Conservation: The Preservation of the Mkomazi Game Reserve, Tanzania*, James Currey, Oxford.

Brooks, T., Mittermeier, R., da Fonseca, G., Gerlach, J., Hoffman, M., Lamoreux, J., Mittermeier, C., Pilgrim, J. and Rodrigues, A. (2006) 'Global biodiversity conservation priorities', *Science* 313(5783), pp. 58–61.

Chatterjee, P. (2008) 'Democracy and economic transformation in India', *Economic and Political Weekly* 43(16), pp. 53–62.

Cock, A. (2010) 'External actors and the relative autonomy of the ruling elite in post-UNTAC Cambodia', *Journal of Southeast Asian Studies* 41(2), pp. 241–265.

Cotula, L. (2013) 'The new enclosures? Polanyi, international investment law and the global land rush', *Third World Quarterly* 34(9), pp. 1605–1629.

Cramb, R. A., Colfer, C. J., Dressler, W., Laungaramsri, P., Quang, T. L., Mulyoutami, E., Peluso, N. L. and Wadley, R. L. (2009) 'Swidden transformations and rural livelihoods in Southeast Asia', *Human Ecology* 37(2009), pp. 323–346.

Dasgupta, S., Deichmann, U., Meisner, C. and Wheeler, D. (2005) 'Where is the poverty-environment nexus? Evidence from Cambodia, Lao PDR, and Vietnam', *World Development* 33(4), pp. 617–638.

de Koninck, R. (2000) 'The theory and practice of frontier development: Vietnam's contribution', *Asia Pacific Viewpoint* 41(1), pp. 7–21.

Ferguson, J. (1990) *The Anti-Politics Machine: 'Development', Depoliticization, and Bureaucratic Power in Lesotho*, Cambridge University Press, Cambridge.

Ferraro, P. and Kiss, A. (2002) 'Direct payments to conserve biodiversity', *Science* 298, pp. 1718–1719.

Fisheries Administration. (2013) 'Key considerations: Food and nutrition security vulnerability to mainstream hydropower dam development in Cambodia', Policy brief from project by Inland Fisheries Research and Development Institute, Fisheries Administration, with support from DANIDA, Oxfam and WWF, https://www.oxfam.org.au/wp-content/uploads/2014/02/key-considerations-dams-and-nutrition_english-2.pdf, accessed 15 February 2014.

Fold, N. and Hirsch, P. (2009) 'Rethinking frontiers in Southeast Asia: Editorial', *The Geographical Journal* 175(2), pp. 95–97.

Frewer, T. and Chan, S. (2014) 'GIS and the "usual suspects" – [Mis]understanding land use change in Cambodia', *Human Ecology* 42(2), pp. 267–281.

Global Witness. (2007) 'Cambodia's family trees: Illegal logging and the stripping of public assets by Cambodia's elite', http://www.globalwitness.org/sites/default/files/pdfs/cambodias_family_trees_low_res.pdf, accessed 28 November 2013.

Global Witness. (2009) 'Country for sale: How Cambodia's elite has captured the country's extractive industries', http://www.globalwitness.org/sites/default/files/library/final_english.pdf, accessed 28 January 2014.

Global Witness. (2013) 'Rubber barons: How Vietnamese companies and international financiers are driving a land grabbing crisis in Cambodia and Laos', http://www.globalwitness.org/rubberbarons/, accessed 14 February 2014.

Grundy-Warr, C., Sithirith, M. and Li, Y. M. (2014) 'Volumes, fluidity and flows: Rethinking the "nature" of political geography', *Political Geography*, http://dx.doi.org/10.1016/j.polgeo.2014.03.002, accessed 24 May 2014.

Hall, D. (2013) 'Primitive accumulation, accumulation by dispossession and the global land grab', *Third World Quarterly* 34(9), pp. 1582–1604.

Hall, D., Hirsch, P. and Li, T. (2011) *Powers of Exclusion: Land Dilemmas in Southeast Asia*, NUS Press, Singapore.

Hansen, M. C., Potapov, P. V., Moore, R., Hancher, M., Turubanova, S. A., Tyukavina, A., Thau, D., Stehman, S. V., Goetz, S. J., Loveland, T. R., Kommareddy, A., Egorov, A., Chini, L., Justice, C. O. and Townshend, J. R. G. (2013) 'High-resolution global maps of 21st-century forest cover change', *Science* 342(6160), pp. 850–853.

Haraway, D. (1997) *Modest_Witness@Second_Millennium.Female©_Meets_OncoMouse™*, Routledge, New York.

Henke, R. (2011) 'NGOs, people's movements and natural resource management', in C. Hughes and K. Un (eds) *Cambodia's Economic Transformation*, NIAS Press, Copenhagen, pp. 288–309.

HRW (Human Rights Watch). (2014) 'Cambodia universal periodic review submission 2013', 07 January, New York, http://www.hrw.org/news/2014/01/07/cambodia-universal-periodic-review-submission-2013, accessed 30 January 2014.

Hughes, C. (2013) 'Friction, good governance and the poor: Cases from Cambodia', *International Peacekeeping* 20(2), pp. 144–158.

Hughes, C., Netra, E., Vimealea, T., Sivhouch, O. and Tem, L. (2011) 'Local leaders and big business in three communes', in C. Hughes and K. Un (eds) *Cambodia's Economic Transformation*, NIAS Press, Copenhagen, pp. 245–265.

Hughes, C. and Un, K. (2011) *Cambodia's Economic Transformation*, NIAS Press, Copenhagen.

ICEM (International Centre for Environmental Management). (2003) 'Cambodia national report on protected areas and development: Review of protected areas and development in the lower Mekong River Region, International Centre for Environmental Management (ICEM) for Royal Cambodian Government', http://www.mekong-protected-areas.org/cambodia/docs/Cambodia_nr.pdf, accessed 15 December 2014.

Igoe, J. and Brockington, D. (2007) 'Neoliberal conservation: A brief introduction', *Conservation and Society* 5(4), pp. 432–449.

Killeen, T. (2012) *The Cardamom Conundrum: Reconciling Development and Conservation in the Kingdom of Cambodia*, NUS Press, Singapore.

Kong, K. (2012) 'Cancelling fishing lots in Tonle Sap', http://www.iucn.org/about/union/secretariat/offices/asia/asia_where_work/cambodia/?9491/Canceling-Fishing-Lots-in-the-Tonle-Sap-Benefits-and-Risks, accessed 15 April 2014.

Kummu, M. and Sarkkula, J. (2008) 'Impact of the Mekong River flow alteration on the Tonle Sap flood pulse', *AMBIO: A Journal of the Human Environment* 37(3), pp. 185–192.

Le Billon, P. and Springer, S. (2007) 'Between war and peace: Violence and accommodation in the Cambodian logging sector', in W. De Jong, D. Donovan and K. Abe (eds) *Extreme Conflict and Tropical Forests*, Springer Netherlands, Dordrecht, pp. 17–36.

Li, T. (2007) *The Will to Improve: Governmentality, Development and the Practice of Politics*, Duke University Press, Durham and London.

Li, T. (2010) 'Indigeneity, capitalism, and the management of dispossesion', *Current Anthropology* 51(3), pp. 385–414.

Long, N. (2001) *Development Sociology: Actor Perspectives*, Routledge, London and New York.

Mahanty, S., Dressler, W., Milne, S. and Filer, C. (2013) 'Unravelling property relations around forest carbon', *Singapore Journal of Tropical Geography* 34(2), pp. 188–205.

Marschke, M. (2012) *Life, Fish and Mangroves: Resource Governance in Coastal Cambodia*, University of Ottowa Press, Ottowa.

May, T. and Pye, D. (2014) 'Big logging cartel alleged' *Phnom Penh Post*, 1 April, http://www.phnompenhpost.com/national/big-logging-cartel-alleged, accessed 1 April 2014.

McCarthy, J. (2006) *The Fourth Circle: A Political Ecology of Sumatra's Rainforest Frontier*, Stanford University Press, Stanford, CA.

Migdal, J. (2001) *State in Society: Studying How States and Societies Transform and Constitute One Another*, Cambridge University Press, Cambridge.

Milne, S. (2012) 'Chut Wutty: Tragic casualty of Cambodia's dirty war to save forests,' http://asiapacific.anu.edu.au/newmandala/2012/04/30/chut-wutty-tragic-casualty-of-cambodia%E2%80%99s-dirty-war-to-save-forests/, accessed 30 April 2012.

Milne, S. (2013) 'Under the leopard's skin: Land commodification and the dilemmas of Indigenous communal title in upland Cambodia', *Asia Pacific Viewpoint* 54(3), pp. 323–339.

Milne, S. and Adams, W. (2012) 'Market masquerades: Uncovering the politics of community-level payments for environmental services in Cambodia', *Development and Change* 43(1), pp. 133–158.

Minh, N., Minh, T., Kajiwara, N., Kunisue, T., Subramanian, A. , Iwata, H., Tana, T., Baburajendran, R., Karuppiah, S., Viet, P., Tuyen, B. and Tanabe, S. (2006) 'Contamination by persistent organic pollutants in dumping sites of Asian developing countries: Implication of emerging pollution sources', *Archives of Environmental Contamination and Toxicology* 50(4), pp. 474–481.

Moore, J. (2000) 'Sugar and the expansion of early modern world-economy: Commodity frontiers, ecological transformation, and industrialization', *Review (Fernand Braudel Center)* 23(3), pp. 409–433.

Morgan, J. (2013) 'Forest change mapped by Google Earth', *BBC News (Science and Environment)*, 14 November, http://www.bbc.com/news/science-environment-24934790, accessed 15 November 2013.
Mosse, D. (2005) *Cultivating Development: An Ethnography of Aid Policy and Practice*, Pluto Press, London.
Murphy, T., Guo, J., Irvine, K., Slotton, D., Wilson, K., Lean, D. and Lim, S. (2013) 'Emerging problems with mercury in Cambodia', *Global Health Perspectives* 1(2), pp. 113–134.
Neef, A., Touch, S. and Chiengthong, J. (2013) 'The politics and ethics of land concessions in rural Cambodia', *Journal of Agricultural and Environmental Ethics* 26(6), pp. 1085–1103.
Nevins, J. and Peluso, N. (2008) *Taking Southeast Asia to Market: Commodities, Nature and People in the Neoliberal Age*, Cornell University Press, Ithaca and London.
Ngoun, K. (2013) 'Rethinking Cambodia's political transformation' *New Mandala*, 5 August, http://asiapacific.anu.edu.au/newmandala/2013/08/05/rethinking-cambodias-political-transformation/, accessed 6 August 2014.
ODC (Open Development Cambodia). (2014) *Forest Cover: Briefing*, March, Phnom Penh.
Öjendal, J. and Ou, S. (2013) 'From friction to hybridity in Cambodia: 20 years of unfinished peacebuilding', *Peacebuilding* 1, pp. 365–380.
Polanyi, K. (1944) *The Great Transformation: The Political and Economic Origins of Our Time*, Beacon Press, Boston.
Prudham, S. (2013) 'Men and things: Karl Polanyi, primitive accumulation, and their relevance to a radical green political economy', *Environment and Planning A* 45, pp. 1569–1587.
Rigg, J. (2005) *Living with Transition in Laos: Market Integration in Southeast Asia*, Routledge, London.
Scott, J. (1998) *Seeing Like a State: How Certain Schemes to Improve the Human Condition Have Failed*, Yale University Press, New Haven.
Smallteacher, R. (2014) 'Cambodian police open fire at garment workers protest, killing four', *Global Research*, 6 January, http://www.globalresearch.ca/cambodian-police-open-fire-at-garment-workers-protest-killing-four/5363982, accessed 13 April 2014.
Smith, N. (1998) 'Nature at the millennium: Production and re-enchantment', in B. Braun and N. Castree (eds) *Remaking Reality: Nature at the Millennium*, Routledge, London, pp. 271–285.
Sneddon, C. (2007) 'Nature's materiality and the circuitous paths of accumulation: Dispossession of freshwater fisheries in Cambodia', *Antipode* 39(1), pp. 167–193.
Springer, S. (2010) *Cambodia's Neoliberal Order: Violence, Authoritarianism, and the Contestation of Public Space*, Routledge, Oxford.
Springer, S. (2013) 'Illegal evictions? Overwriting possession and orality with law's violence in Cambodia', *Journal of Agrarian Change* 13(4), pp. 520–546.
STAR Kampuchea Organization. (2007) 'Landlessness and land conflicts in Cambodia', http://www.landcoalition.org/sites/default/files/legacy/legacypdf/07_r%5Bt_land_cambodia.pdf?q=pdf/07_r[t_land_cambodia.pdf, accessed 30 November 2014.
Strange, L. (2013) 'Cambodia, its development, and integration into the GMS: A work in progress', in O. Shrestha and A. Chongvilaivan (eds) *Greater Mekong Subregion: From Geographical to Socio-Economic Integration*, Institute of Southeast Asian Studies, Singapore, pp. 18–30.

Subedi, S. (2012) *A Human Rights Analysis of Economic and Other Land Concessions in Cambodia*, Report of the Special Rapporteur on the Situation of Human Rights in Cambodia, A/HRC/21/63/Add.1/Rev.1 United Nations, Human Rights Council.

Sullivan, M. (2011) 'China's aid to Cambodia', in C. Hughes and K. Un (eds) *Cambodia's Economic Transformation*, NIAS Press, Copenhagen, pp. 50–69.

Tsing, A. (1993) *In the Realm of the Diamond Queen: Marginality in an Out-of-the-Way Place*, Princeton University Press, Princeton, NJ.

Tsing, A. (2003) 'Natural resources and capitalist frontiers', *Economic and Political Weekly* 38(48), pp. 5100–5106.

Tsing, A. (2005) *Friction: An Ethnography of Global Connection*, Princeton University Press, Princeton, NJ.

Turner, S. and Caouette, D. 2009. 'Agrarian angst: rural resistance in Southeast Asia', *Geography Compass* 3(3), pp. 950–975.

Un, K. and So, S. (2011) 'Land rights in Cambodia: How neopatrimonial politics restricts land policy reform', *Pacific Affairs* 84(2), pp. 289–308.

van Buitanen, J. A. B. (translator) (1973) *The Mahabharata*, University of Chicago Press, Chicago.

Vandergeest, P. and Peluso, N. (1995) 'Territorialization and state power in Thailand', *Theory and Society* 24, pp. 385–426.

Walker, A. (2009) 'Conclusion: Are the Mekong frontiers sites of exception?' in M. Gainsborough (ed.) *On the Borders of State Power: Frontiers in the Greater Mekong Sub-Region*, Routledge, Oxon, pp. 101–111.

Wallerstein, I. (1989) *The Modern World-System, III: The Second Great Expansion of the Capitalist World-Economy, 1730–1840s*, Academic Press, New York.

West, P. (2006) *Conservation Is Our Government Now: The Politics of Ecology in Papua New Guinea*, Duke University Press, Durham and London.

Western, D., Wright, M. and Strum, S. (1994) *Natural Connections: Perspectives in Community-Based Conservation*, Island Press, Washington, DC.

Wolford, W., Borras, S., Hall, R., Scoones, I. and White, B. (2013) 'Governing global land deals: The role of the state in the rush for land', *Development and Change* 44(2), pp. 189–210.

World Bank. (2012) 'Cambodia – Country overview', Phnom Penh, http://www.worldbank.org/en/country/cambodia/overview, accessed 12 December 2013.

Worrell, S. (2013) 'Can't see the forest...', *Phnom Penh Post*, 12 December, http://www.phnompenhpost.com/national/can%E2%80%99t-see-forest-%E2%80%A6, accessed 13 December 2013.

Yusuf, A. and Francisco, H. (2009) 'Climate change vulnerability mapping for Southeast Asia, Singapore, economy and environment program for Southeast Asia', supported by International Development Research Centre (IDRC), http://www.ccfsc.gov.vn/resources/users/6D696775656C/Climate%20Change%20Vulnerability%20Mapping%20S-E%20Asia%20%28IDRC%29.pdf, accessed 31 March 2014.

Ziv, G., Baran, E., Nam, S., Rodríguez-Iturbe, I. and Levin, S. (2012) 'Trading-off fish biodiversity, food security, and hydropower in the Mekong River Basin', *PNAS* 109(15), pp. 5609–5614.

2 Shackled to nature? The post-conflict state and its symbiotic relationship with natural resources

Sarah Milne, Pak Kimchoeun and Michael Sullivan

Figure 2.1 Truck of illegally harvested rosewood leaving the Cardamom Mountains, 2011.
Photo supplied anonymously by owner

In July 2013, the Cambodian People's Party (CPP) suffered a surprising challenge in the national elections. For the first time in over a decade, an apparently viable and re-constituted opposition movement formed and faced the CPP at the polls. This movement, operating under the banner of a new party, the Cambodian National Rescue Party (CNRP), mustered popular support and voter sentiment that have now called into question the dominance of the CPP regime and its self-professed legitimacy. This is not the first time that Hun Sen and the CPP have been challenged, but the nature of the challenge this time is qualitatively different; particularly since this is the first decline in electoral performance for the CPP since 'democracy' was initiated in 1993.[1] New forces are now at play, deriving from an unpredictable combination of influences such as young urban voters, who are plugged-in to social media; a vibrant civil society and protest movement that has galvanized around land conflicts and natural resource depletion; and the struggles of garment factory workers, who have come to embody and articulate ordinary people's demands for viable livelihoods across the country. Thus Cambodia stands at a crossroads, facing a political moment that is unprecedented in its peace-time trajectory.

But why should a nation's political life matter to the observers and practitioners of conservation and development? And what, if any, are the environmental dimensions and implications of Cambodia's current political dynamics? The purpose of this chapter is to engage with these questions and to create a 'political ecological' foundation for the chapters that follow. We start from the premise that all nature-society interactions and outcomes are shaped by power dynamics (Neumann, 2005); arguing that, in the case of Cambodia, these power dynamics are particularly influenced by the demands and behaviour of the post-conflict state. Thus, we begin this chapter with an explanation of the origins of the contemporary Cambodian state in the 1980s. This analysis of state formation in turn enables us to characterize the recent peace-time era of CPP dominance, leading up to the 2013 election. We then show how the CPP's 'state-making' processes have interacted with the environmental realm, based on analysis of the forest and land sectors. This provides critical insights into the symbiotic inter-relationship between the state, the ruling party and natural resources in Cambodia, which together have underpinned conservation and development outcomes over the last decade, as subsequent chapters reveal.

On a theoretical note, we take a broad view of the state, seeing it not just as the formal and visible apparatus of government, with bureaucratic, territorial and militaristic features (Levi, 2002); but also as an idea or 'force field' that is embedded in society, and is often contested or contradictory in nature (Migdal, 2001). Our analysis therefore engages with the direct and indirect effects of the state, as seen through its practices and discourses, which interact constantly with both social and environmental realms. Seeing beyond the formal exterior of the state also enables a focus on its rulers: those individuals who control and enact the mechanisms of state power and authority, often to serve their own private interests through 'predatory' rule (Levi, 1988). This is necessary in the case of Cambodia, where the patrimonial practices of its ruling elite have been well documented and likened to a 'regime' (e.g. Cock, 2010b; Un and So, 2011). Our approach also follows Vu's (2010) example of studying states through their *processes of formation*. This chapter therefore places a strong emphasis on explaining how the Cambodian state evolved from the mid-1980s onwards. We proceed by focusing on the origins and evolution of the dominant CPP, which survived the transition to multi-party democracy in a uniquely authoritarian way.

State formation: The socialist-authoritarian origins of the current regime

The origins of the contemporary Cambodian state lie in the early 1980s, in the period that followed the disastrous Khmer Rouge experiment of 1975–1979. The Vietnamese military intervention that removed the Khmer Rouge from power led to the establishment of the People's Republic of Kampuchea (PRK), led by former Khmer Rouge cadres who had earlier escaped to Vietnam to avoid Pol Pot's internal purges. This new regime, with Vietnamese and Soviet backing, attempted to introduce a more benign socialist state system, based on the Vietnamese communist bureaucratic model. However, by the mid-1980s, these efforts had largely failed and Cambodia's civil war persisted, with armed conflict being sustained by insurgents from previous Cambodian regimes, including the Khmer Rouge, and supported variously by China, the United States and its allies. As fighting to remove the PRK regime dragged on, and regional geo-political relations shifted with the easing of the cold war, conditions emerged for an international political solution to end the Cambodian conflict. The potential for a peace agreement at this time was also facilitated by lucrative deals over logging rents, shared between insurgents and competing factions within the post-conflict state (Le Billon, 2002). This helped build alliances and patronage networks that formed the basis for peace, and which persist to this day (Global Witness, 2007).

After a lengthy period of tough negotiations, a solution to the conflict was finally agreed by all sides. This was formalized by the Paris Peace Accords in October 1991. The centrepiece of these agreements was a commitment to multi-party competitive democratic elections, to be organized and managed by the United Nations Transitional Authority (UNTAC). For the PRK leadership, already led by Prime Minister Hun Sen, the prospect of competing politically with previous Cambodian state power holders and their international supporters was a major challenge. In order to survive politically, Hun Sen and the PRK had little choice but to accept the new international political-economic realities and to prepare for the transformation of the state from one governed by a single party system to one under some form of democratic pluralism.

Since becoming Prime Minister in 1985, Hun Sen was fully aware of the threat posed to his party by competitive elections. He knew that political survival unavoidably involved reform of the state and diplomatic engagement with insurgents. Furthermore, after the devastation caused by the Khmer Rouge's radical policies, many state officials outside the higher echelons of the party, along with the majority of ordinary Cambodians, were uninterested in the PRK's socialism and opposed the continued presence of the Vietnamese under Hun Sen's leadership. In an effort to counter this unpopularity, and to ensure political loyalty from state officials, Hun Sen adopted a pragmatic strategy of economic liberalization. This was formalized in 1989, when liberalizing reforms were enacted and the government changed its name from the PRK to the State of Cambodia (SoC), officially discarding any pretence of socialist ideology. At the same time, to demonstrate its apparent commitment to political transition, the ruling party changed its name to the CPP. In parallel, Hun Sen also pursued 'national reconciliation' through diplomacy with Cambodia's former King Sihanouk (Gottesman, 2003).

In practical terms, these reforms meant that state power holders were formally acknowledging their inability to control centrally the informal economy and black markets that had emerged out of the post-Khmer Rouge chaos. Re-building the Cambodian state post-1979 had been a task of monumental proportions, hampered by (i) the fact that Cambodia was denied vital aid for reconstruction and development by Western nations and their allies due to Cold-War rivalries and (ii) that Vietnamese and Soviet-bloc aid alone were not enough to re-build an effective socialist state system and fight insurgency. To cope with these huge challenges, the PRK had therefore developed a 'culture of tolerance', allowing the resurgence of petty commerce and the emergence of black markets. This also meant that state employees, local authorities and party members were permitted to engage in uncontrolled or informal economic activities to supplement their meagre salaries (Gottesman, 2003; Roberts, 2002). But as Soviet aid began to dry up in the mid-1980s, and as the Vietnamese prepared to withdraw from Cambodia, the situation worsened. This left the PRK leadership at the mercy of market forces, a restless populace, a difficult-to-finance public service and ongoing geo-political pressures. With all of these dynamics at play, conditions were set for the emergence of a patrimonial system of rule, operating in parallel to the formal state, which could secure the CPP's grip on power.

To maintain control of the state and protect party interests, key leaders like Hun Sen and Chea Sim actively built upon their personal patronage networks and bases of power. Extending from the centre in Phnom Penh to the provinces and districts and beyond, these networks engaged in profiteering from various entrepreneurial activities including cross-border trade and the exploitation and smuggling of natural resources like timber and fish. Following the liberalization of the economy in 1989, even more opportunities emerged for state officials to enrich themselves, such as from the privatization of land and the sale or leasing of state property. As a result, local authorities and military personnel in the countryside gained more independence, leveraging their ability to control revenues from resource exploitation and entrepreneurial activity. The party therefore gave them generous concessions, in exchange for political loyalty and a share of the profits. In this way, systems of informal extraction and patronage became entrenched throughout the state apparatus, relying particularly on the predation of forests and land (Le Billon and Springer, 2007; Roberts, 2002; Gottesman, 2003).

By the time of the UNTAC elections in 1993, the SoC/CPP leadership was presiding over a congenitally weak and increasingly corrupt state system, dominated by powerful mutually dependent networks of personal patronage with military backing. The shoring up of the party's power through its unique mode of 'self-interested state capitalism', however, was not enough to secure an outright victory in elections managed by the United Nations. The disenfranchised population of war-weary Cambodians, many of whom were excluded from the CPP's lucrative patronage networks, posed a significant threat to the unpopular and ideologically moribund party that had ridden to power on the back of the Vietnamese army. Therefore, in spite of CPP efforts to control the election outcome through the mobilization of state resources and the use of violence and intimidation, it failed to win a majority share of the vote. Instead, the popular Royalist party, Funcinpec,[2] led by former King Sihanouk's son Norodom Ranariddh emerged victorious.

Not prepared to accept defeat, the CPP capitalized on its control over the state apparatus and issued threats of a return to armed conflict. This brought enough pressure to bear to force Funcinpec and the United Nations to accept a power sharing arrangement in which Hun Sen and Ranariddh would serve as co-Prime Ministers. Although it did not reflect the election results, this coalition government was finally formed and a new constitution promulgated in September 1993. Officially Cambodia was now a constitutional monarchy following a pluralist system based upon liberal democratic principles. Sihanouk was reinstated as King and head of state. Under the new political arrangements, aid for reconstruction and development previously denied to Cambodia by Western powers and their allies began to flood into the country.

Irrespective of the circumstances in which it was formed, there was hope that the new coalition government could make the most of this international support to tackle Cambodia's myriad and complex socio-economic problems. But initial hopes were short-lived as relations between the co-prime ministers deteriorated, and the development of state institutions suffered as a consequence. At the heart of the matter was the struggle for control over state institutions and their associated revenues, particularly given impending commune elections in 1997 and parliamentary elections in 1998, from which only one Prime Minister was expected to emerge.[3] Again, the key to consolidating political power in this new multi-party system was the ability to control access to resources, whether rents from forested land and fisheries (e.g. Sneddon, 2007; Van Acker, 2003; Le Billon, 2002), or new financial flows from international aid (Hughes, 2003). Amidst this jostling over resources, the new government also sought to maintain international legitimacy by committing to reforms, including democratic elections and a range of covenants covering human rights and environmental safeguards.

But these commitments were for the most part ignored as political infighting between the two prime ministers intensified, culminating in the violent removal of Ranariddh by military forces loyal to Hun Sen in July 1997. The reasons for Hun Sen's military action were deeply rooted in the previous two decades of Cambodian politics, involving dissident Khmer Rouge elements that needed to be satisfied, but they were also guided by the prime minister's desire to avoid another electoral defeat in 1998. Hun Sen's forces therefore moved to destroy any organized political opposition to the CPP, killing up to a hundred senior Funcinpec military officials in the process (HRW, 2012). This fundamentally altered Cambodia's political landscape, but international donors were reluctant to interfere, insisting only that elections be contested with all parties able to participate 'freely'. For Hun Sen, this acquiescence was enough: he then skilfully employed authoritarian controls to ensure the CPP won the largest share of votes in 1998, in what was a deeply flawed election process (Heder, 2005).

In the 15 years since these 1998 elections, Hun Sen has consolidated power and maintained international legitimacy. He and the CPP have successfully managed to manipulate electoral administration, control the media and resist democratic reform. In addition, they have used violence, coercion and intimidation against a large number of the electorate and circumscribed the capacity of opposition parties to compete on a level playing field. This has led to CPP 'victories' in the three commune council elections of 2002, 2007 and 2012; and in the three national parliamentary elections of 2003, 2008 and 2013. Thus, the post-1998 era of stability and CPP dominance was secured through a combination of Hun Sen's authoritarianism and the proven political strategy of alliance-building through informal sharing of resources. Importantly, this could not have been achieved without the networks of patronage and power that were developed by the CPP leadership in the 1980s, which were financed and fuelled by the easy availability of natural resources. These networks and their modes of extraction have consolidated over time, becoming so intertwined with the political economy of the Cambodian state that extricating the two is likely to involve major upheavals.

The contemporary state: Architecture of a neopatrimonial regime

Hun Sen's regime has benefited enormously from the stability brought about by the post-1998 government and the prolonged period of impressive macro-economic growth that followed. But these benefits have not been channelled into the creation of strong government institutions or state capacity in the conventional sense (Larsson, 2013). In spite of substantial international support and resources directed towards essential reforms to the judiciary, civil service and property rights, little progress has been made. Instead, there is demonstrable resistance to reform, or where necessary, careful manipulation of reforms to serve the interests of the regime, as seen in the forest and land sectors (Cock, 2010b; Un and So, 2011). A major part of the problem is that substantive reforms threaten the very edifice and resource base upon which CPP power rests. For this reason, Cambodia's system of rule may be characterized as a neopatrimonial regime: one that is adept at maintaining appearances in the formal domain of the state, with rhetorical overtures to reform, while also nurturing informal patronage-based alliances and resource flows (Erdmann and Engel, 2007). In the next section we illustrate how this works in the contemporary Cambodian context, enabling ongoing CPP dominance, through (i) the manipulation of government decentralization processes and (ii) the creation of off-budget mechanisms for mass patronage (Craig and Pak, 2011).[4] Understanding this 'system of rule' is essential because, as we reveal in the final section of this chapter, it drives and relies upon the depletion and commodification of natural resources.

Consolidating and centralizing power

After losing the first national election in 1993, the CPP fought doggedly to ensure that it did not lose control over the state apparatus and its associated resources. To secure its power base, the party, together with the Prime Minister, worked hard to nourish and expand its/his patronage networks, which relied upon rents from the state (Hughes, 2003). This practice has since evolved, becoming stronger and more centralized around the Prime Minister and elite factions backed by party members in key ministerial positions. Power has therefore become concentrated around particular national government bodies, including: the Council of Ministers (CoM), the Ministry of Economy and Finance, the Ministry of Interior and other regulatory and income generation agencies such as Customs and Excise, the Ministry of Agriculture, Forestry and Fisheries (MAFF), the Ministry of Land Management Urban Planning and Construction and the Ministry of Mines and Energy. Provincial governors who used to be powerful in the late 1980s and early 1990s became less so as a consequence of this consolidation of power in Phnom Penh, even though decentralization reforms had been initiated under international guidance in 2002 (Pak, 2011).

The trajectory of Cambodia's decentralization process and the concomitant politicization of government administrative systems provide key insights into the regime's functioning, particularly the continual need for informal or off-budget funds that are often derived from natural resources. The state is now formally divided into national and sub-national levels, the latter consisting of the capital and 23 provinces; 194 districts and municipalities; and 1633 communes and *sangkat* (urban communes).[5] Since decentralization, each commune has a commune council, elected directly by local residents for a 5-year term. Commune councillors in turn elect district and provincial councils, and they are also responsible for selecting village authorities under their control.

After more than a decade with decentralized systems in place, however, Cambodia remains a centralized state, both administratively and fiscally. For instance, sub-national administrators (SNAs) such as the commune councils have never been given clear functions, other than for basic infrastructure development. Although they are officially in charge of 'promoting people's welfare and environmental protection', the SNAs have never received explicit authority over these key areas, most conspicuously in forestry and land management.[6] Furthermore, communes and districts are not permitted to collect their own revenue on a formal basis and must rely on higher levels of government for their budget. Provinces too are dependent on national fiscal transfers, but they have some discretion to collect minor taxes and other revenue items. The result is that, with power and resource hungry rulers at the centre, Cambodia's sub-national institutions have remained financially starved, with the total SNA budget amounting to less than 6 per cent of the national budget.[7] These peripheral arms of the state are therefore forced to seek revenue elsewhere, typically from the surrounding resource base.

In addition to fiscal dysfunction, Cambodia's decentralization program was also manipulated by the ruling party to create 'centralizing effects'. In essence, the CPP used the rhetoric of decentralization to legitimize its local ruling, while maintaining and increasing strict central government control over valuable resources. Thus, ministries and line agencies responsible for land, forestry, mining and fisheries have in practice become *more* centralized in the last 15 years. This is particularly evident in the forestry sector, where donor-driven efforts to ensure stronger rule of law and local decision-making resulted in a more top-down and centrally controlled Forestry Administration, able to accommodate elite interests (Cock, 2010b). This corresponds with the 'recentralizing while decentralizing' observed in other countries undergoing similar environmental reforms (Ribot *et al.*, 2006).

Meanwhile, lines of authority in Cambodia's natural resource management have also been fragmented. Many actors are now involved, with unclear, overlapping or even conflicting roles. Nowhere is this more pronounced than in the contested governance of Tonle Sap, in which officials from the Fisheries Administration, the Ministry of Environment (MoE), the Tonle Sap Authority and the Ministry of Water Resources and Meteorology jostle with local authorities over 'management' of the lake (Milne, 2013a). Similarly, forests are controlled not only by the Forestry Administration, but also by MoE, MAFF, the CoM, local authorities such as police and commune councils and even the Ministry of Rural Development. These piecemeal arrangements make overall coordination particularly challenging, ultimately undermining prospects for sound natural resource management. Indeed, the main function of this confusion may well be that it enables informal resource extraction by powerful elites and allows arbitrary controls 'from the top'. In turn, both of these mechanisms often serve the purpose of generating off-budget revenue; the significance of which we now explain.

Off-budget financing for political projects and mass patronage

Off-budget patronage systems are of fundamental importance to the CPP regime and Cambodia's state-dominated politics of natural resource management. These systems emerged after the CPP's electoral defeat in 1993, which taught the party leadership that in a democracy power cannot be retained through force alone, but requires legitimacy in the eyes of the populace as well. This realization led to the establishment of a key political mechanism – the Party Working Group for Helping the Local Level (or PWG) – which over time has become central to the CPP's quests for dominance in electoral politics. The PWG's main purpose is to institutionalize popular gift-giving or 'mass patronage' as a strategy for winning voters' favour, especially before elections, but also as a general *modus operandi* of the party (Hughes, 2006; Craig and Pak, 2011; Pak, 2011). The mechanism is significant for the apparent political success it has achieved over the last decade, meaning that its 'conceptual model' has been replicated through other CPP-backed organizations like the Cambodian Red Cross and Party Youth Groups. Even more significant, however, is the amount of financial investment attracted by these party mechanisms. In many instances, PWG funding exceeds formal government budgets and is consistently derived from off-budget sources associated with illicit extraction of natural resources and/or informal resource rents derived by state officials.

Established in 1995, the PWG is a decentralized and semi-formal mechanism, headed by key party officials whose responsibility is to mobilize resources for building local infrastructure, purchasing 'hand-outs' for voters and covering election-related expenses. There is a PWG for each province, under which there is a PWG for each district and commune. Funding for these PWGs comes from many sources, mostly informal, including the personal wealth of PWG heads and donations collected from their 'networks' that encompass businessmen, tycoons (*okhnya*) and even NGOs. Indeed, the system requires that all state and party officials contribute to the PWG. Even ordinary government staff, who generally have less chance to seek rents than their more resourceful or powerful counterparts, are asked to make regular contributions to the PWG. For instance, an official with a salary of $120 per month has to make a contribution of $5 every month to the PWG, or other party initiatives.[8]

Through the PWG, the CPP has spent millions of dollars in constructing school buildings and countless kilometres of rural roads since the late 1990s. In his 2008 cabinet report, the Prime Minister outlined that the PWG mechanism had been used in his name to build 3,030 schools, equivalent to 15,267 classrooms or about 35 per cent of the total number of classrooms in Cambodia. Not surprisingly, therefore, evidence suggests that off-budget

PWG support given to some commune councils is around three times greater than what they receive through the formal government budget, which is delivered through the Commune Sangkat Fund as an unconditional grant of around $25,000 per year per commune (Pak, 2011). Thus, semi-formal PWG projects appear to compete with, or even out-compete, formal government systems for public service delivery.

Similar mechanisms to the PWG are the Cambodian Red Cross and Party Youth Groups. Headed by the Prime Minister's wife, the Cambodian Red Cross is seen as 'the charity' of the CPP, given its work on social issues ranging from emergency relief to awareness-raising about traffic accidents. Apart from unconfirmed international support, the organization relies on a state budget from the Ministry of Social Affairs of roughly $1.5 million annually,[9] but more importantly it also receives donations from 'resourceful' government officials, tycoons and businessmen. For example, in a fund-raising event in May 2013, the Red Cross mobilized roughly $15 million from wealthy benefactors, in the presence of the Prime Minister and his wife. Out of this, $3 million came from a South Korean company, and $300,000 came from the former Phnom Penh governor.[10] As with the PWGs, 'normal' government officials and villagers are also expected to make contributions to the Red Cross. For example, one mid-level ministry official interviewed on this subject said that he and his colleagues each contributed $15 annually to the Red Cross. At the village level, village chiefs are asked to collect roughly $60 per village annually: poor households are not asked to contribute, but the better off ones need to contribute around $1 to $2 per year. Apparently, these local fundraising activities have created some resentment among villagers towards their leaders, especially relating to how village chiefs collect donations, and the lack of transparency with which they are managed or passed up the chain.[11]

Furthermore, in an effort to secure the support of younger generations and junior state officials, the CPP has established Party Youth Groups, currently headed by a son of the Prime Minister. These groups have been established inside all ministries and administrative offices in provinces, districts and communes, using a structure that mirrors that of the PWG. Within ministries, Youth Groups are usually led by the Ministers' sons or daughters, showing the close connections between elite families, the state and the party. A key role of the Youth Groups is to participate in election campaigning. For example, leading up to the July 2013 election, the party youth were mobilized to join in rallies and events. On the election day, one of their key jobs was apparently to transport older people to polling stations.[12] But little is known about how these groups are now interacting with the politics of other young and politicized Cambodians, which would be a fruitful area for further research.

The wider implication of the PWG system, with its opaque and politically motivated mode of 'public giving', is that it severely weakens formal state institutions. Not only do the PWGs rely on the informal extraction of public resources, but they also create excuses for government officials to seek rents from their public duties and/or not come to work regularly.

Despite these insidious impacts, the CPP shows no sign of reducing its reliance on the PWGs, which, if there were political will, would entail reforming and strengthening the formal state system. On the contrary, the party has become increasingly reliant on the PWG to ensure its electoral dominance and to 'keep tabs' on sub-national government bodies and their income streams. This strategy has proven so successful that it is now a habit of the CPP leadership to avoid any strengthening of the formal state system, instead creating parallel structures to address specific social needs as they arise. This means that tasks and services conventionally performed by the state – such as the financing of schools, temples, roads and health centres – now fall into the domain of politically motivated off-budget finance. Even the government's massive recent push to issue tens of thousands of land titles to rural Cambodians was pitched and financed through this 'party logic'. This initiative, known as Order 01, was launched by Hun Sen, who used his 'personal funds' to finance thousands of student volunteers to map land use across the country (Milne, 2013b). Overall, the effect of such prominent off-budget financing is that direct taxes still play an almost negligible role in state revenue generation in Cambodia, and consequently public services are not adequately financed through central or conventional government budgets. In this regard, Cambodia is the 'stand out' case in Southeast Asia (Larsson, 2013).

The last notable feature of the PWG system is its inclusion of Cambodian tycoons, and some foreign investors, as key financiers. Their contributions cultivate political ties that in turn facilitate their commercial undertakings, both nationally and locally. Political contributions of this kind have therefore become a vital component in the 'license to operate' of any tycoon or company.[13] This is important for natural resource management because most tycoons in Cambodia are involved in land transactions, logging, dam construction and concessions for mining and plantations (Global Witness, 2009). The PWG system and its related mechanisms therefore represent a formidable nexus in which elite interests, regime maintenance and the exploitation of natural resources are tied together. Until the 2013 election, this strategy worked remarkably well for its beneficiaries. It helped to secure party dominance, concentrate political power around a few individuals or rulers holding key government positions, and ensure that elite groups accumulated stunning wealth (Evans, 2014). But the consequences of this 'boom' have eroded state capacity, increased authoritarianism, and contributed to environmental degradation: problems that voters are becoming increasingly aware of, and now call into question the viability of the PWG system as a political strategy.

The role of natural resources in Cambodia's regime

The magnitude of the CPP's off-budget financing of public goods and services, and the importance of this for sustaining the regime, raises significant questions about the political economy, and indeed the political ecology, of these arrangements. For example, how is it possible that hundreds of millions of dollars in donations are used to finance party-backed mechanisms that operate in parallel to and belittle formal state budgets? What do elites, businessmen and ordinary government officials have to gain from this system? And where does the money come from to sustain this system? As hinted earlier, the answers to many of these questions lie in the environmental domain, particularly the recent dramatic privatization and appropriation of state-owned commons like fisheries and forested land (Van Acker, 2003; Neef *et al.*, 2013). State predation of this kind has led to the transfer of billions of dollars of public wealth into the hands of party-connected elites, from the 1980s onwards (Le Billon, 2000; Global Witness, 2007; Evans, 2014); meaning that natural resource rents have played a fundamental role in the formation and evolution of the contemporary regime in Cambodia. In the following paragraphs we examine the practices and trajectory of this symbiotic relationship more precisely, particularly analysing the forest and land sectors, but recognizing that similar patterns exist around other natural resources too (Cock, 2010a). We examine first the role of logging revenues in early state formation, and second the role of state predation of forests and land in subsequent regime consolidation.

State formation and resource rents: The role of logging from 1989–2001

As noted, Cambodia's political culture entails an expectation that government officials use their role to extract revenue: some of the proceeds are for personal benefit, while a 'due portion' must be allocated in patronage payments up the chain to one's superiors and to the party itself (Un and So, 2011; Cock, 2010b). These dynamics and rules form an extractive regime that, although ostensibly illegal, is well known and quite openly practiced. For low-level state officials, practices of resource extraction are often simply a matter of survival, given that their government salaries are insufficient to cover living costs. For example, in interviews with park rangers across the country,[14] most convey their expectation of deriving income from bribes or informal taxation with the Khmer adage: 'If the chicken sits on the rice, then why shouldn't it eat the rice?' In other words, as guardians of the nation's resources, they imply that it is somehow *natural* for them to feed off these resources, as though it were an implicit entitlement of state employment (see Chapter 7).

This practice of informal extraction has only been encouraged by Cambodia's rulers, who know that they must keep peripheral state officials, especially the military, satisfied in order to secure their loyalty to the party. The informal allocation of resources in this way is a well-known technique of regime maintenance or state-making in resource-rich postcolonial states like Indonesia (Ascher, 1998), and in Africa too, where centralized control in nascent or transitional states is typically achieved through informal deals with powerful and potentially regime-threatening individuals (Bayart, 1993; Reno, 1999). Bayart referred to this process as 'elite accommodation', which Reno translated into his concept of the shadow state, defined as:

> a very real, but not formally recognized, patronage system that is rigidly organized and centred on rulers' *control over resources*. This control binds rulers' potential rivals to them in exchange for largesse without the need to create strong bureaucracies [that could] ... heighten independent tendencies among elites.
>
> (Reno, 1999, p. 2)[15]

Thus, the formal state is emasculated and maintained only as a façade to service rulers' interests. Cambodia's regime has been likened to a shadow state, especially in light of the foundational role played by forest resources in the post-conflict period (Le Billon and Springer, 2007; Heder, 2007), but also in relation to elite capture of other resources such as land and petroleum (Global Witness, 2009; Cock, 2010a; Neef *et al.*, 2013).

As we have suggested, the practices that now constitute Cambodia's shadow state, and dictate its reliance on natural resources, emerged from the processes of post-conflict state formation. With the easing of fighting in 1989, it was possible for commercial logging to commence. This ushered in an era of struggle and accommodation, in which logging revenues played a critical but paradoxical role: on the one hand financing the ongoing civil war by providing revenue to the Khmer Rouge and competing military factions; but on the other hand enabling the brokering of political alliances and deals (Le Billon, 2000, 2002). Potentially disloyal figures within the armed forces were placated and enticed into alliance with the new CPP regime, through offers of unhindered access to valuable resources such as timber, land and gems (ibid). Thus, over the decade 1989–1999 'strongmen' in the country's periphery such as provincial governors and generals operated like warlords, controlling logging in order to finance their personal wealth and maintain their troops (Le Billon and Springer, 2007). Consequently, only 5 per cent of the value of the timber exported from Cambodia during the 1990s, which was estimated to exceed $2.5 billion, was captured by the central government for public spending.[16] This period is often referred to by officials as 'the era of anarchic logging', a notion that reflects the CPP's relatively limited control over the country's peripheral forested regions and their associated revenues at the time.

However, the logging-fuelled warlordism that helped to shape Cambodian politics of the 1990s was not antithetical to state formation. As John Sidel described in the case of the Philippines, this type of 'petty sultanistic' rule can flourish alongside formal national-level state building, and even 'buttress' local state power (1989, p. 19). In other words, local strongmen agree to provide stability for state leaders in exchange for a degree of autonomy and personalistic power, which allows them to extract revenue unhindered. Cambodia's transition to peace exhibited these dynamics precisely, as the state coalesced around alliances that hinged upon logging revenues (Neak, 2007; Le Billon, 2002).

A conspicuous tactic used by the Phnom Penh-based CPP at this time, to gain access to forest revenues, was the use of law-making. For example, over five successive logging bans were issued by Hun Sen in the 1990s, all of which were swiftly lifted as new revenue-sharing deals were brokered with opposition factions in the provinces (Neak, 2007). The government's claim over forest resources was also advanced through the introduction of a national concessions system that eventually spanned nearly seven million hectares, and was designed to counteract locally controlled illegal or 'anarchic' logging (ibid).[17] But eventually this too succumbed to the personal and political ambitions of individual government staff, who taxed rather than enforced the law. The transition period therefore did not produce a neatly articulated or centralized shadow state, but a dynamic conglomerate of dispersed and competing power nodes, all sustained by logging revenues.

As the CPP consolidated its grip on power after 1998, and as international pressure over illegal logging mounted, the government made new efforts to 'improve' its management of forests. Timber extraction at the time was generating 43 per cent of Cambodia's export earnings, the highest rate of logging dependency in the world, but still only a fraction of the revenues were reaching public coffers (Le Billon and Springer, 2007).[18] Hun Sen therefore declared dramatically that he would 'resign' if he could not stop the anarchic logging (Neak, 2007). He then initiated an aggressive military crackdown on illegal timber extraction, which effectively removed the small players or 'oxcart cutters', leaving behind only powerful loggers who had special permits and authorizations from central government (Global Witness, 2002). This crackdown was therefore more about ensuring the regime's control over logging revenues, than it was about stopping logging per se. But the strategy backfired somewhat, as concessionaires and logging syndicates accelerated logging and scrambled to 'get what they could' while conditions allowed. Eventually, amid mounting donor pressure over the government's failure to manage the concession system, Hun Sen suspended all commerical logging in late 2001. This opened the way for reform, in which donors and international conservation organizations engaged vigorously.

Regime strengthening through territorialization and predation of forested land

Following the 2001 logging ban, a government-declared monopoly over the Forest Estate and Protected Areas was established. This allowed for new and distinct modes of revenue generation, especially from land transactions, forest clearing and illegal logging (Global Witness, 2007; Neef *et al.*, 2013).[19] In this post-logging era, the state asserted its control over forested lands by working hand-in-hand with international donors and conservation organizations, advancing and strengthening the processes of territorialization and recentralization (Ribot *et al.*, 2006; Vandergeest and Peluso, 1995; Baird, 2009). This initially occurred with the promulgation of new laws, including: the Forestry Law of 2002, which made it illegal to cut trees on state land without a permit; and the Protected Areas Law of 2008, which provided a framework for natural resource management and the 'prevention of illegal activities' throughout Cambodia's national parks and wildlife sanctuaries. These laws reinforced the designation of State Land across vast areas. For example, the protected area system covers 21 per cent of the country's surface area,[20] while official forest cover under control of the Forestry Administration is said to be 'close to 60 per cent' of Cambodian territory.[21] This process of territorialization, while annulling competing claims to resources by local villagers and indigenous people, has also formed the basis of the contemporary regime's extractive practices.

The post-2000 era of CPP dominance has therefore been sustained through state predation of natural resources, particularly forested land. Government officials, local strongmen and tycoons, while making significant contributions to the CPP, have also secured windfall personal profits from this. For example, the post-2009 boom in luxury timber, fuelled mainly by demand for rosewood (genus *Dalbergia*), generated illicit profits that appear to match or exceed those from the logging of the 1990s. Indicative figures are available from the Cardamom Mountains, where rosewood extraction is estimated to have generated at least half a billion dollars of revenue in the period 2009–2012, shared between one tycoon and relatives of the Prime Minister (Figure 2.1).[22] More significant, however, is the outright clearing of forest for the establishment of Economic Land Concessions (ELCs), an illegal but widespread practice. This is estimated to generate $100,000/ha of timber revenue where primary evergreen forests are cleared.[23] Considering that these concessions now cover over two million hectares of the country, and many exhibit an uncanny overlap with forested areas and proximity to protected areas (see Figure 1.1), the likely resource flows from timber exploitation in and around ELCs are staggering. It is no wonder, then, that hundreds of millions of dollars in 'fees' are said to circulate through the upper echelons of government, in association with ELC approvals.[24]

The lack of transparency around land concessions, and the voracity with which the state has embraced them as a 'mode of development' in its official strategies since 2005,[25] exhibit many parallels with the country's commercial logging experiences of the 1990s. First, having territorialized vast areas of state land, the ruling party has effectively 'capitalized' this public asset for the purposes of private appropriation and patronage (Neef *et al.*, 2013; Loehr, 2012). For example, it is estimated that 20 per cent of the total land area allocated to concessions is held by just five senior CPP senators.[26] Second, although regulations exist to minimize the social and environmental harm of ELCs, these are rarely adhered to in practice (e.g. Global Witness, 2013). Law-breaking and circumvention of rules appear to be systematic, with ELCs regularly exceeding the legal size limit of 10,000 ha and/or overlapping with evergreen forest, which is also technically illegal.[27] This lack of regulatory enforcement hampers most prospects for formal taxation of ELCs, instead undermining state capacity and encouraging speculative and predatory 'investments' in land (Loehr, 2012). Recent reports from MAFF confirm this tendency: 'less than one-quarter of the land leased to foreign companies for plantations, including rubber, has been used for its intended purpose'.[28] Thus, ELCs have delivered few of their promised public benefits and development opportunities. Rather, instead they have produced spectacular profits for ruling elites.

Inevitably, the rapid proliferation of ELCs since 2005 has caused landlessness, social conflict and resource degradation; attracting high-profile international criticism and push-back from civil society (Subedi, 2012). Facing this looming political crisis, and seeking regime stability, Hun Sen's response in May 2012 was to declare Order 01.[29] This placed a moratorium on all new ELCs, and initiated the massive rural land-titling program that was financed using off-budget sources, as discussed above. Remarkably, Order 01 brings the regime's circular reliance on land dealings into focus: off-budget funds, generated from illicit practices such as land speculation and illegal logging, must be spent on massive state-backed projects to cope with the deleterious social effects of elite accumulation. Yet the regime's ameliorative actions should not be misconstrued as benevolent; rather, they provide the means for land and resource capitalization to continue, unhindered by political unrest. But, like the logging bans of the past, the ELC moratorium has also been manipulated and ignored. Over 30 new ELCs have been granted since the mid-2012 ban, covering over 200,000 hectares.[30]

Finally, it is notable that as personal and illicit profits from forests and land increase, so too do the obligations of this system's beneficiaries. This applies mainly to government officials and businessmen who must provide donations for mass patronage and election campaigning. Some tycoons are now said to be 'struggling to pay their bills', given their promises to finance infrastructure through the PWG or meet party dues.[31] Similarly, CPP members with prominent roles in the 2013 election campaign were said to be under considerable financial strain, due to their need to finance 'gifts' and voter hand-outs. This need for revenue apparently contributed to an acceleration of illegal logging in the lead-up to the election.[32] Ultimately, these political-environmental dynamics have caused Cambodia to demonstrate one of the world's highest deforestation rates since 2000 (Hansen *et al.*, 2013). Correspondingly it is said that 20 of Hun Sen's closest associates are now billionaires (Evans, 2014). However, this overt liquidation of resources to service elite accumulation and regime maintenance has now contributed to a looming political discontent, described below.

Cambodia's changing political context

Until the 2013 election, the CPP's dominance was overwhelming. It not only controlled more than two-thirds of parliamentary seats and the courts, but also the whole executive branch of government at central and sub-national levels. But the 2013 election left it with only a slim majority,[33] the CPP having lost in the major provinces and Phnom Penh. This took many in the party by complete surprise; and it signalled a groundswell within the body-politic that few imagined possible before 2018.[34] Nearly one year on from the election, at the time of writing, the results remain contested by the opposition. Post-election protests were maintained for months, with calls for a vote re-count and even the resignation of the Prime Minister himself. But after violent clashes in early 2014, all protesting has been banned, with the future uncertain. Protests of this kind are not new for Cambodia; but the key difference this time is that Hun Sen seems unable to divide the opposition through manipulation, or pressure it into acquiescence.

The current crisis, if nothing else, tells us that the CPP's domination strategy of pre-2013 has lost its effectiveness. In particular, it appears that the PWG mechanisms are no longer performing as intended, and may now have become counter-productive. This trend was already emerging in the 2008 election, when only a weak correlation between PWG support and CPP votes was observed (Pak, 2011). But widespread anecdotes after the 2013 election suggest that the correlation between the two might now be negative, with higher PWG support paradoxically leading to fewer votes for the CPP.[35] A possible explanation for this is that ordinary people are tired of the conspicuous consumption of rich PWG and CPP members, especially Phnom Penh elites, who manifest all too clearly the increasing inequality between high-ranking officials and the populace.

The 2013 election result also conveyed that the CPP risks further declines in popularity and legitimacy if it continues to hamper state reforms, like the provision of adequate civil servant salaries for basic service delivery. Here, the CPP's old 'loyalty problem' appears to be resurfacing, with post-election analysis suggesting that roughly 70 per cent of medium and low level civil servants might have voted against the party.[36] A key reason for this is low pay, combined with resentment over continued obligations to contribute to patronage mechanisms like the PWG. Low salaries have also led to poor service delivery in schools, health centres, natural resource management and among traffic police, angering the general public. These circumstances suggest that the popularity of the CPP will continue to slide if deep reforms are not implemented.

Overall, it appears that the CPP regime now faces a crisis of legitimacy, similar to what it encountered at the outset of multi-party democracy in

1993. But the problem this time is compounded by the effects of social change, a strengthening civil society, and the 'seeds of discontent' sown by increasing inequality and the conspicuous wealth of elites, fuelled especially by the liquidation of state-held assets such as land and forests. In response, a 'new consciousness' about justice and the potential for change appears to be taking hold among urban youth and some rural villagers (see Chapter 13). Stories, pictures and anecdotes now abound on Facebook and other media outlets about land grabbing, illegal logging and the role of the ruling party in this. Combined with ongoing village-level resistance to dispossession, transition of some kind seems inevitable.

Conclusion

This chapter has explored the formation of the contemporary Cambodian state, the nature of the CPP-dominated regime that formed post-1998, and the role of natural resources in this. A portrait has emerged of a regime that was created from and is sustained by natural resources in a symbiotic way. Wealth from the exploitation of resources, particularly forests and land, enabled Cambodia's transition to peace. Subsequently, it has provided vital off-budget revenue to finance the maintenance of the CPP regime and to satisfy the demands of powerful elites. Thus, even as Cambodia emerges from over a decade of stability and economic growth, the CPP-led dynamics of neopatrimonialism and predation have only become more pronounced. In particular, as demonstrated in this chapter, the regime found expression through increasingly formalized and generously financed party patronage mechanisms from the 2000s onwards. Perceived as necessary for securing votes and loyalty, these mechanisms also became a standard outlet for tycoons and elites to cultivate their ties to the regime, while securing their own access to resources. But the costs and demands of this party-mediated system of exploitation have risen over time, as though caught in a ratchet effect, with beneficiaries having to donate more, the more they receive. Correspondingly, the state's off-budget or shadow economy rivals formal budgets and undermines state capacity.

Taking stock of these patterns and cycles, it is now possible to discern how the CPP regime has indelibly shaped the dynamics and practices of Cambodia's environment-development nexus, particularly its natural resource management interventions (see Chapters 7–9). However, the regime's evolution has now reached a turning point, in which it must contend with the side-effects of depleted natural resources and increasing push-back from a populace that has generally missed out on the 'boom' of timber and land exploitation. Although the incredible wealth of natural resources effectively created and sustained the regime until now, the consequences of this destruction may now be its downfall.

Notes

1 Interview by Milne with political analyst in April 2014. Beyond vote-counting in 2013, the nature of the challenge to the CPP remains unclear. Certainly, the level of public support for CNRP seen on the streets during the post-election protests of late 2013 is unprecedented since 1993; but this may not be anything more than a 'wake-up call' for the CPP. Our sources suggest that, whether power changes hands or not, the political moment created by the July 2013 election is one that signals transition.
2 Funcinpec is an acronym of the party name, translated from the French as: National United Front for an Independent, Neutral, Peaceful and Cooperative Cambodia.
3 Because of the tense political situation in Phnom Penh the 1997 commune elections were postponed until 2002.
4 Off-budget financing refers to state financing that is derived from and spent through unofficial or informal channels. It works in parallel to formal government budgets, which are financed through taxation and other 'normal' means of state revenue generation. See Ascher (1998) for a description of off-budget development financing in Suharto's Indonesia.
5 The capital has a population of roughly 1.6 million people, while the average size of a province is roughly 550,000 people, over 75,000 for a district and 9,000 for a commune. Source: The Cambodia Inter-Censual Population Survey, 2013, National Institute of Statistics, Phnom Penh.
6 Royal Government of Cambodia (2008) 'Law on Administrative Management of the Capital, Provinces, Municipalities, districts and Khans.' Phnom Penh.
7 Or about 25 per cent of the national budget, if the centrally controlled budgets of de-concentrated line departments are factored in. Source: Royal Government of Cambodia (2013) National Budget Law.
8 Interview by Pak in Prey Veng, June 2013. Currency amounts are in US dollars.
9 National Budget Law for 2013, Royal Government of Cambodia, Phnom Penh (2012).
10 Neou, V. (2013) 'CPP's elite showers Red Cross with cash' *The Cambodia Daily*, 9 May 2013, http://www.cambodiadaily.com/archives/cpps-elite-showers-red-cross-with-millions-23079/.
11 Interviews in Prey Veng by Pak, June 2013.
12 Source: field interviews on election day by Pak, 2013.
13 Sometimes this link plays out very directly. For example, in villages around the controversial Areng Dam construction site in the Cardamom Mountains, the Red Cross has been active. The Cambodian tycoons involved in this project are the influential married couple Lao Meng Kin and Yeay Phu (see Chapter 5). Yeay Phu, along with Hun Sen's wife, is a key figure in the Cambodian Red Cross.
14 Field research by Milne in Tonle Sap (2013), Mondulkiri (2012) and the Cardamom Mountains (2007).
15 Emphasis added by authors; also, 'binds' was originally in past-tense as 'bound'.
16 See Le Billon and Springer (2007). Their period of analysis spans the signing of the Paris Peace Agreement in 1991, to the end of the first term of the newly formed government in 1998. By then, fighting with the Khmer Rouge had ended and Hun Sen's power was firmly consolidated over Funcinpec rivals.
17 The logic of the concession system was introduced by the World Bank, which promoted forest privatization and commercialization as a key management instrument for Cambodia (see Neak, 2007). The first concession was granted in 1994, and eventually 33 concessions were issued.
18 Data on export earnings are from the Food and Agriculture Organization's (FAO) 1997 report 'State of the World's Forests', Rome (cited in Le Billon and

Springer, 2007). Notably this report shows that, from 1991 to 1998, the government received only 12 per cent of what it should have received from logging revenues had a proper taxation system been in place.
19 Land sales and kick-backs from the issuance of ELCs probably represent the most prominent new revenue source for the ruling elite. But timber revenues are still relevant, as they are an inherent part of many land deals (e.g. Global Witness, 2013) and development projects such as hydro-power (see Chapter 6).
20 See ICEM. (2003) 'Cambodia national report on protected areas and development: Review of protected areas and development in the Lower Mekong River region', Queensland: International Centre for Environmental Management (ICEM) for Royal Cambodian Government. http://www.mekong-protected-areas.org/cambodia/docs/Cambodia_nr.pdf.
21 This figure from the National Forest Programme (FA, 2010) is contested, but the government has an interest in maintaining a high percentage of forest cover for territorial purposes.
22 See Milne S. (forthcoming) 'Cambodia's unofficial extractive regime: Logging in the shadow of transnational governance and investment.' *Critical Asian Studies*.
23 Source: NGO-led forest inventory and timber valuation for evergreen forest in Mondulkiri.
24 Key informant interview done by Pak, 22 August 2013; and interview with conservation NGO staff member by Milne, January 2014.
25 See Royal Government of Cambodia. (2005) 'Sub-decree No. 146 on Economic Land Concessions'; and (2013) 'National strategic development plan update 2009–2013'. http://www.opendevelopmentcambodia.net/briefing/economic-land-concessions-elcs/, accessed June 2014.
26 Cambodian Centre for Human Rights. (2013) *Policy Brief: Land Issues after the 2013 National Assembly Election and Recommendations*, Phnom Penh http://cchrcambodia.org/admin/media/analysis/analysis/english/CCHR_CLEC_EC_Policy_Brief_on_Land_Issues_after_the_2013_National_Assembly_Elections_en.pdf, accessed May 2014.
27 Legal provisions are outlined in: Royal Government of Cambodia (2005) 'Sub-decree No. 146 on Economic Land Concessions'. Another technique for exceeding the size limit is for large companies to create multiple smaller subsidiary companies that can each hold up to 10,000 ha (Global Witness, 2013).
28 See: Pye, D. (2014) 'New owners, old story' *Phnom Penh Post*, 6 March, http://www.phnompenhpost.com/national/new-owners-old-story, accessed March 2014.
29 See Royal Government of Cambodia. (2012) 'Prime Minister's Directive on Measures to Strengthen and Enhance the Effectiveness of the Economic Land Concession Management, Order No 01. 17 May 2012'. Unofficial legal interpretation states that: 'The order aims to settle land disputes between the concessionaire/concessionaire companies and land occupants and to strengthen the management of ELCs through the implementation of new policies', in DFDL (2012) 'New governmental policies in relation to ELCs in Cambodia', http://www.dfdl.com/easyblog/entry/new-governmental-policies-in-relation-to-economic-land-concessions-in-cambodia, accessed June 2014.
30 Zsombor, P. and Aun, P. (2012) '32 land concessions approved since moratorium', *The Cambodia Daily*, 18 November, http://www.cambodiadaily.com/archives/32-land-concessions-approved-since-moratorium-5725/, accessed December 2013.
31 Interview by Milne with high-level official in Phnom Penh, October 2013.
32 Source: Facebook commentary and interviews with park rangers and NGO staff.
33 The CPP won only 68 seats, down from 90. Meanwhile, the opposition won 55 seats. This is the first time the CPP's share of seats has declined since democracy began in 1993 (Ngoun, 2013).

34 Interview by Sullivan with high-level political figure in 2010. For these actors, the question of regime change is considered not a matter of 'if' but 'when'. Predictions then were that change may emerge in 2018, whether through elections and/or popular mass protest.
35 This negative correlation was apparently observed as early as 1998, when Hun Sen pumped 'development' money into Kraing Ov commune as an experiment to gauge voter responses, which he tested with a mock election. Here too the CPP lost (see Hughes, 2003). For this reason, the party must also rely upon other techniques such as electoral manipulation and intimidation.
36 Key informant interviews by Pak with high ranking CPP officials, late 2013.

References

Ascher, W. (1998) 'From oil to timber: The political economy of off-budget development financing in Indonesia', *Indonesia* 65, pp. 37–62.

Baird, I. (2009) 'Controlling the margins: Nature conservation and state power in northeast Cambodia', in F. Bourdier (ed.) *Development and Dominion: Indigenous Peoples of Cambodia, Vietnam and Laos*, White Lotus, Bangkok, pp. 215–248.

Bayart, J. (1993) *The State in Africa: The Politics of the Belly*, Longman Press, London.

Cock, A. (2010a) 'Anticipating an oil boom: The "Resource Curse" thesis in the play of Cambodian politics', *Pacific Affairs* 83(10), pp. 525–546.

Cock, A. (2010b) 'External actors and the relative autonomy of the ruling elite in post-UNTAC Cambodia', *Journal of Southeast Asian Studies* 41(2), pp. 241–265.

Craig, D. and Pak, K. (2011) 'Party financing of local investment projects: Elite and mass patronage', in C. Hughes and K. Un (eds) *Cambodia's Economic Transformation*, NIAS, Copenhagen, pp. 219–244.

Erdmann, G. and Engel, U. (2007) 'Neopatrimonialism reconsidered: Critical review and elaboration of an elusive concept', *Commonwealth and Comparative Politics* 45(1), pp. 95–119.

Evans, G. (2014) 'Cambodia's violent peace', *Poject Syndicate*, 26 February, http://www.project-syndicate.org/commentary/gareth-evans-examines-the-causes-of-ongoing-political-violence-since-the-1991-paris-peace-agreements, accessed May 2014.

FA. (2010) *Strategic Framework: National Forest Programme*, Forestry Administration (FA), Royal Government of Cambodia, February 2010.

Global Witness. (2002) 'Deforestation Without Limits', http://www.globalwitness.org/sites/default/files/library/Deforestation_Without_Limit.pdf, accessed 15 February 2014.

Global Witness. (2007) 'Cambodia's family trees: Illegal logging and the stripping of public assets by Cambodia's elite', http://www.globalwitness.org/sites/degault/files/pdfs/cambodias_family_trees_low_res.pdf, accessed 28 November 2013.

Global Witness. (2009) 'Country for Sale: How Cambodia's Elite has Captured the Country's Extractive Industries', http://www.globalwitness.org/sites/default/files/library/final_english.pdf, accessed 28 January 2014.

Global Witness. (2013) 'Rubber Barons: How Vietnamese Companies and International Financiers are Driving a Land Grabbing Crisis in Cambodia and Laos', http://www.globalwitness.org/rubberbarons/, accessed 14 February 2014.

Gottesman, E. (2003). *Cambodia after the Khmer Rouge: Inside the Politics of Nation Building*, Yale University Press, New Haven and London.

Hansen, M. C., Potapov, P. V., Moore, R., Hancher, M., Turubanova, S. A., Tyukavina, A., Thau, D., Stehman, S. V., Goetz, S. J., Loveland, T. R., Kommareddy, A.,

Egorov, A., Chini, L., Justice, C. O. and Townshend, J. R. G. (2013) 'High-resolution global maps of 21st-century forest cover change', *Science* 342(6160), pp. 850–853.

Heder, S. (2005) 'Hun Sen's consolidation: Death or beginning of reform?' *Southeast Asian Affairs* 2005, pp. 113–130.

Heder, S. (2007) 'Political theatre in the 2003 Cambodian elections: State democracy and conciliation in historical perspective', in J. Strauss and D. C. O'Brien (eds) *Staging Politics: Power and Performance in Asia and Africa*, I.B. Taurus & Co. Ltd, London, pp. 151–172.

HRW. (2012) 'Tell them I want to kill them: Two decades of impunity in Hun Sen's Cambodia', *Human Rights Watch (HRW)*, 13 November 2012, http://www.hrw.org/reports/2012/11/13/tell-them-i-want-kill-them-0, accessed June 2014.

Hughes, C. (2003) *The Political Economy of Cambodia's Transition 1991–2001*, RoutledgeCurzon, London and New York.

Hughes, C. (2006) 'The politics of gifts: Tradition and regimentation in contemporary Cambodia', *Journal of Southeast Asian Studies* 37(3), pp. 469–489.

Larsson, T. (2013) 'The strong and the weak: Ups and downs of state capacity in Southeast Asia', *Asian Politics and Policy* 5(3), pp. 337–358.

Le Billon, P. (2000) 'The political ecology of transition in Cambodia 1989–1999: War, peace and forest exploitation', *Development and Change* 31(4), pp. 785–805.

Le Billon, P. (2002) 'Logging in muddy waters: The politics of forest exploitation in Cambodia', *Critical Asian Studies* 34(4), pp. 563–586.

Le Billon, P. and Springer, S. (2007) 'Between war and peace: Violence and accommodation in the Cambodian logging sector', in W. De Jong, D. Donovan and K. Abe (eds) *Extreme Conflict and Tropical Forests*, Springer, Dordrecht, pp. 17–36.

Levi, M. (1988) *Of Rule and Revenue*, University of California Press, Berkeley and Los Angeles.

Levi, M. (2002) 'The state of the study of the state', in I. Katznelson and H. Milner (eds) *Political Science: The State of the Discipline*, W.W. Norton and the American Political Science Association, New York, pp. 33–55.

Loehr, D. (2012) 'Capitalization by formalization? – Challenging the current paradigm of land reforms', *Land Use Policy* 29, pp. 837–845.

Migdal, J. (2001) *State in Society: Studying How States and Societies Transform and Constitute One Another*, Cambridge University Press, Cambridge.

Milne, S. (2013a) *Situation Analysis at Three Project Sites on the Tonle Sap Lake, Cambodia: An Exploration of the Socio-economic, Institutional, and Political Context for Community-based Fisheries Management*, International Union for the Conservation of Nature (IUCN), Phnom Penh.

Milne, S. (2013b) 'Under the leopard's skin: Land commodification and the dilemmas of Indigenous communal title in upland Cambodia', *Asia Pacific Viewpoint* 54(3), pp. 323–339.

Neak, C. (2007) *Cambodia State in Society: Making the Forest Sector (1993–2004), A Case Study of Logging in Kompong Thom*, For conference 'Critical Transitions in the Mekong Region', Chiang Mai, January 2007.

Neef, A., Touch, S. and Chiengthong, J. (2013) 'The politics and ethics of land concessions in rural Cambodia', *Journal of Agricultural and Environmental Ethics* 26(6), pp. 1085–1103.

Neumann, R. (2005) *Making Political Ecology*, Hodder Education, London.

Ngoun, K. (2013) *Rethinking Cambodia's Political Transformation*, New Mandala, 5 August 2013, http://asiapacific.anu.edu.au/newmandala/2013/08/05/rethinking-cambodias-political-transformation/, accessed November 2013.

Pak, K. (2011) 'A dominant party in a weak state: How the ruling party in Cambodia has managed to stay dominant', PhD Thesis, Australian National University, Canberra.

Reno, W. (1999). *Warlord Politics and African States*, Lynne Rienner Publishers, Boulder, Colorado.

Ribot, J., Agrawal, A. and Larson, A. (2006) 'Recentralising while decentralizing: How national governments reappropriate forest resources', *World Development* 34(11), pp. 1864–1886.

Roberts, D. (2002) 'Democratization, elite transition, and violence in Cambodia 1991–1999', *Critical Asian Studies* 34(4), pp. 520–538.

Sidel, J. (1989) 'Beyond patron-client relations: Warlordism and local politics in the Philippines', *Kasarinlan: Philippine Journal of Third World Studies* 4(3), pp. 19–30.

Sneddon, C. (2007) 'Nature's materiality and the circuitous paths of accumulation: Dispossession of freshwater fisheries in Cambodia', *Antipode* 39(1), pp. 167–193.

Subedi, S. (2012) *A Human Rights Analysis of Economic and Other Land Concessions in Cambodia*, Report of the Special Rapporteur on the situation of human rights in Cambodia. A/HRC/21/63/Add.1/Rev.1 United Nations, Human Rights Council.

Un, K. and So, S. (2011) 'Land rights in Cambodia: How neopatrimonial politics restricts land policy reform', *Pacific Affairs* 84(2), pp. 289–308.

Van Acker, F. (2003) 'Cambodia's commons: Changing governance, shifting entitlements?' *Antwerp: Discussion paper No 42*, Centre for ASEAN Studies.

Vandergeest, P. and Peluso, N. (1995) 'Territorialization and state power in Thailand', *Theory and Society* 24, pp. 385–426.

Vu, T. (2010) 'Studying the state through state formation', *World Politics* 62(1), pp. 148–175.

Part 1
Transformation, complexity and contestation in nature-society relations

3 Lost in transition

Landscape, ecological gradients and legibility on the Tonle Sap floodplain

Andrew S. Roberts

Introduction

> ... The country, for nearly 100 miles around [Battambang], is flooded with water soon after the commencement of the rains; travelling becomes impossible, except in boats, and wild animals are driven off to the mountains ...
>
> (David Olyphant King's 1860 report to the Royal Geographic Society of London)

A unique socio-ecological system

The Tonle Sap floodplain is a landscape in motion, perpetually shifting from the terrestrial to the aquatic and back again. Rich in natural resources, it is subject to many, often competing, interests: a source of subsistence, crucial both locally and region-wide; a source of economic development and income generation for the Royal Cambodian Government; an ecosystem of global importance. It defies an uncomplicated characterization. It is the largest wetland and seasonally flooded grassland in peninsular Southeast Asia. It is the site of one of the most productive freshwater fisheries in the world, with annual catch estimates as high as 235,000 tons per year (van Zalinge, 2002).[1] It is also likely the site of the most productive snake harvest in the world, with an estimated 3.8 million snakes harvested per year (Brooks *et al.*, 2010). An estimated 1.5 million people depend upon the Tonle Sap for their subsistence, predominantly through rice production and fishing (Johnstone *et al.*, 2013). Despite the area's richness in natural resources, the Tonle Sap floodplain is home to many of the poorest people in Cambodia (Ministry of Planning and UNDP-Cambodia, 2007).

In the near future, the biological and economic productivity of the region may be subsumed by the dynamism which is a hallmark of this landscape. The grasslands of the floodplain are disappearing rapidly as land is converted to large-scale dry season rice production (Packman *et al.*, 2013; Evans *et al.*, 2005; Sokha *et al.*, 2004). Livelihoods, vegetation, fisheries and wildlife are all threatened by the potential change in flood regimens associated with both climate change and hydroelectric dam construction along the Mekong River and its tributaries (Arias et al., 2014; Ziv et al., 2012). Floodplain landscapes and vegetation are growing more homogeneous, and the livelihoods of floodplain residents who depend upon them may follow suit (Roberts, 2011). Meanwhile, as elsewhere in the region, rural and urban livelihoods continue to become further intertwined, channelling flows of people, money and ideas back and forth between the urban centres and the countryside (Rigg, 2006). The population in Phom Penh in particular has more than doubled in recent years, driven largely by the exodus of young people from rural areas seeking employment in the city (Ministry of Planning, 2012).

As a production landscape, the floodplain and its communities reflect the myriad multi-scalar social and ecological processes at play today, just as the landscape bears the marks of the recent and distant past. It is this dynamism, and the transitions it generates, which muddy the waters for governmental and non-governmental institutions involved in managing the Tonle Sap floodplain. The complexity of relationships between floodplain residents and the landscape thus remains obscured. Also lost is the importance of local natural resource management systems, as well as resource access rights and claims to land ownership. Lacking institutional validation of their ties to the land (ecological, economic and legal), local households are less resilient. Largely poor already, these households are left even more vulnerable to livelihood disruption, economic hardship and even outright dispossession.

What follows is an exploration of floodplain dynamism, with emphasis on the ecological gradients and transitions this produces. These physical manifestations of socio-ecological processes in motion are important in the livelihoods of floodplain residents, who recognize, produce, manage and utilize them as resources. Though recognized locally, these ecological gradients and transitions remain illegible to institutions attempting to manage and control the floodplain. They slip between the categories used by bureaucrats, technical specialists and development practitioners to understand the landscape. In exploring this problem, I present examples of ecological gradients and transitions I documented in a village on the floodplain, and detail why they are important to village residents and the implications of their illegibility to institutions. While the geographic focus of this study is very narrow, I contend that the critique presented here is broadly applicable throughout the Tonle Sap floodplain and beyond. Of course, local specifics will certainly vary, as the interactions of people, processes and the landscape assume many different configurations.

The flood pulse and the landscape

The great ecological and economic productivity of this region is driven by the flood pulse, with the annual water rise coming with the onset of the rainy season (Holtgrieve *et al.*, 2013; Arias *et al.*, 2013). This flush of productive waters, originating largely from the Mekong River and the inflow from tributaries around the lake (Kummu *et al.*, 2006), causes the lake to swell from a dry season area of about 2,500 square kilometres to a wet season peak of about 13,000 square kilometres, varying from year to year (Figures 3.1 and 3.2).

Likewise average depth of the lake jumps from 1–2 m during the dry season, to 8–10 m at the height of the flood (Hak and Piseth, 1999). This influx of water brings with it sediments which are deposited largely in the flooding forest at the lake's margin and on the adjacent floodplain (Kummu *et al.*, 2008). It also brings the fish, so important in the livelihoods of floodplain residents, which spawn in the flooding forest and migrate out onto the floodplain to feed and mature, before returning to the Mekong as the floodwaters recede. The aquatic and terrestrial phases of the landscape are connected by other channels as well, including flows of carbon and nutrients from the terrestrial to the aquatic through the breakdown of terrestrial organic matter

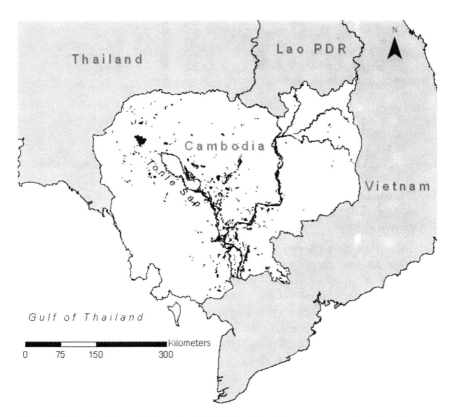

Figure 3.1 Regional map indicating Tonle Sap Lake dry season margin. Data date from March 1999.
Source: Tonle Sap Environmental Management Program/Fisheries Administration.

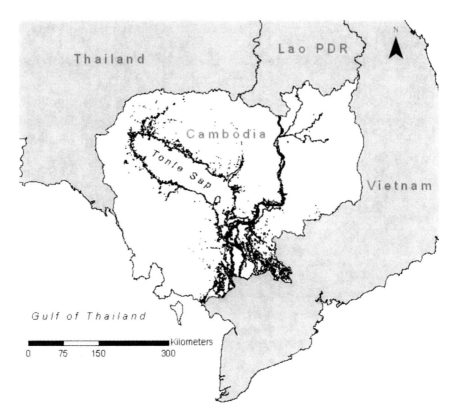

Figure 3.2 Regional map indicating Tonle Sap Lake wet season margin. Data date from October 2000.

Source: Tonle Sap Environmental Management Program/Fisheries Administration.

with the arrival of the floods, and also the stranding and subsequent decay of algae and aquatic plants as the floods recede. The density of these connections between the terrestrial and aquatic likely accounts for the high productivity of this system (Wantzen *et al.*, 2008; Junk and Wantzen, 2004).

Home to the majority of floodplain residents, the grass-dominated plant communities comprising the upper floodplains are typically glossed by geographers and biologists as 'flooding savanna' or even simply 'grasslands' (McDonald *et al.*, 1997; Delvert, 1994). While the use of this category is not inaccurate – the floodplains between the deeply flooding forested areas fringing the Tonle Sap and the uplands further from the lake are indeed covered by open grasslands and wooded savannas – the use of this category masks the diversity of plant communities and landscape features on the floodplain. It gives an impression of a homogeneous environment while concealing the diversity that makes this area so productive. It likewise obscures the hand prints and footprints of populations of fishers, farmers and herders who have made their lives on the floodplain for more than 1,000 years (Stark, 2006; Fox and Ledgerwood, 1999).

Gradients and transitions

Lacking clear physical, ecological and/or social order, ecological transitions and gradients are a challenge to be rendered into 'units that are visible' (Scott, 1998, p. 183), to be condensed into information which is legible to the sundry institutions attempting to control their management. Such a simplification and categorization is the first step in translating complex situations on the ground into legible schemata which may be used as the basis for institutional decision-making. Illegible, the information which might have been gleaned from ecological gradients and transitions is easily misinterpreted or overlooked. Unbeknownst to their authors, the models, plans and forecasts generated for institutional decision-making thereby remain faulty, lacking potentially important detail. In a more sinister light, simplification of complex floodplain livelihoods and environments may be used strategically to further the political, often predatory, agendas of individual elites, privately held businesses, as well as government institutions.[2]

Though difficult to resolve, the complexity lost between categories, between the 'units that are visible', is important. Here lies a network of linkages between livelihoods, landscapes and socio-ecological systems. This leaves institutions blind not only to these linkages but also to their significance to the goals and central questions posed by the institutions themselves. Additionally, this information left behind is important to local communities. For example, one important criterion for communities to retain access to the resources of the floodplain is to prove that they are managing them (Fox, 1998). Land considered vacant or unmanaged in the eyes of governing institutions is more readily converted to another use, and importantly not necessarily a use that is in the best interests of local communities.

Institutional setting

The bio-physical flux which characterizes the Tonle Sap floodplain is mirrored among the tangle of institutions involved in floodplain governance, influencing development, access to and use of natural resources and law enforcement (Sokhem and Sunada, 2006). They are organized at scales from the local to national, regional and global. As might be expected in such a complicated governance system, institutional perspectives are variously coincident or in conflict, resulting in a patchwork of jurisdictions and territories. Far from a level playing field, personal relationships, political connections and patronal networks are a particularly important factor in determining how institutions fit into in an unstable network of hierarchies of power (Sneddon, 2007).

The Royal Cambodian Government is represented by a number of ministries and other official bodies, each with their own goals and directives, implemented through local offices. These include, in part, the Ministry of Agriculture, Forestry and Fisheries; Ministry of the Environment (responsible for biodiversity conservation and ecotourism); Ministry of Foreign Affairs and International Cooperation (responsible for negotiating treaties and international agreements); Ministry of Water Resources and Meteorology; Cambodian National Petroleum Authority and Tonle Sap Basin Authority. Additionally, a great many international NGOs, foreign aid programs, international research institutions, as well as local NGOs are active in the region.

Operating in an inherently multi-disciplinary field, institutional vision is narrowed by sectoral focus in their mandates and by extension, their personnel (Sokhem and Sunada, 2006). Many specialize in a particular discipline such as agronomy, fisheries or economics, at the expense of a broader understanding of the complexity of the socio-ecological systems in their geographic areas of interest. These can lead to jurisdictional blind spots, which may not formally exist in the laws governing the landscape but take shape in practice in the field. For example, in Kampong Thom the harvest of wood from the flooding forest and shrublands reaching up from the margin of the Tonle Sap Lake is prohibited. These woodlands do not produce high value timber, and so fall outside the jurisdiction of the Forestry Administration, as it is understood by field personnel. The flooding forests are crucial as a spawning site for many economically important fish species. But, they are not themselves a fishery and so fall outside of the interests of the Fisheries Administration. Moreover, gaps in these shrublands are often opened for the expansion of agriculture and grazing. However, they seldom draw the interest of Department of Agriculture officials. As a result, there was little active planning on the government's part for the management of these resources and their use by floodplain communities. Likewise, there was little enforcement of the existing laws regarding wood harvest on the floodplain.

Complicating relationships among institutions, communication and feedback between them are lacking, as are collaborations between decision-makers, practitioners and academia (Nang *et al.*, 2011). Furthermore, these governmental and non-governmental institutions themselves are in flux (Keskinen and Varis, 2012). The waxing and waning of the political power of particular individuals and their patronal networks have a direct impact on the institutional tools used to manipulate the floodplain, including attempts to control resources, allocation of financial support and enforcement of laws (Kim, 2013). The same may be said of NGOs, which are subject to changes in leadership, staffing, funding and program emphasis.

Livelihoods and legibility

Despite such environmental and political dynamism, indeed possibly because of it, the people who make their livings on the floodplain cultivate a diverse portfolio of livelihoods which take advantage of the variety of productive and extractive opportunities offered in such a diverse environment (Roberts, 2011; Brooks *et al.*, 2008; Diepart, 2010; Keskinen, 2006; Balzer, 2003; Delvert, 1994). Livelihood diversity offers the most flexibility, nimbleness or adaptability with respect to change, and as such, the most household stability (Marschke and Berkes, 2006; Mortimore and Adams, 2001). Though, even the most flexible households may be unable to adapt when the pendulum swings beyond the normal range (Sopha *et al.*, 2007).

Dominant activities for most families include rice production, fishing and herding cattle or water buffalo, depending upon the season and household access to capital and natural resources. Relatively few (as little as 5 per cent) support themselves exclusively through commerce and trade (Keskinen, 2006). However, the floodplain is the site of many other productive activities, including both plant extraction (e.g. cutting firewood or gathering grasses for roof thatching) and animal extraction (e.g. collecting snakes and small birds for sale or consumption). As with elsewhere in the region, many families also take advantage of off-farm and non-farm income generating activities through wage labour, small commerce and sales of surplus production.

These many productive and extractive opportunities on the floodplain thus allow households to develop a flexible and diverse *productive bricolage*, fluidly engaging in different activities depending upon the availability of labour, skills and resources (Croll and Parkin, 1992, p. 12; Batterbury, 2001). Such diverse natural resource use portfolios, and the flexibility they engender, are vital for household survival in dynamic environments such as the floodplain (Bouzarovski, 2009; Ellis, 1998).

However, some activities important to floodplain families, as well as their relationships to the changing landscape, remain illegible to outsiders, particularly governmental and non-governmental institutions. This is due in part to the fact that many of these activities leave a light footprint on the landscape (e.g. edible insect collection, fodder collection). They thus range from being very subtle to outright invisible in remotely sensed imagery, commonly used as the foundation for institutional understanding of the landscape and thus broader planning schemes. Moreover, these activities taken individually typically make up small fractions of family incomes and caloric intake (though this is not always the case, see Brooks *et al.*, 2008, for an example). In the eyes of institutions and others focused on rural livelihoods, they are easily overshadowed by activities in the agriculture and fisheries sectors which typically comprise a larger fraction of household income and caloric intake. If these activities are detected at all, they may still slip between legible categories. Without extensive research at the household level, they are difficult to quantify in both material terms (e.g. aggregate amounts harvested) and economic terms. Harvest and effort vary among households and with the seasons, as does the fraction of products which are sold versus consumed in the home. Inability to value all of the products produced on and extracted from the landscape results in an incomplete accounting of the density, diversity and variability of the economic connections between people and the landscape.

Methodology

In order to explore land use and human ecology on the floodplain, I collected data over the course of three periods of research, focusing on a single village: May 2007–December 2007, March–June 2008 and January–May 2009. I used a range of methodologies; integrating methods from the fields of geography, ecology and anthropology (Brookfield *et al.*, 2002; Cunningham, 2001; Alexiades, 1996; Scoones *et al.*, 1994). These methods included semi-structured interviews and participant-observation alongside key informants (village elders and other local experts, but also including ministerial officers, local extension officers and employees of international development NGOs); field walks with key informants; unstructured interviews with village residents; written surveys focusing on land use (administered to 238 families, nearly 50 per cent of the households in village); as well as participant-observation of village life and resource management practices, joining village residents in their farming, fishing and livestock-keeping activities. I also performed a descriptive ecological inventory of floodplain vegetation, collecting data on both woody and herbaceous plants over 60 transects of 1,000 square metres each.

Research site description

The focal point for this research was Roka Village (in Sangkat Srayov, Steung Sen Municipality, Kampong Thom Province, at 12° 37' N 104° 55' E), a village of approximately 500 families on an old alluvial terrace jutting out from the edge of the Tonle Sap floodplain (White *et al.*, 1997). The village lies between 10 m and 15 m above sea level, and gradually slopes down on three sides to meet the surrounding annually flooding rice fields and grasslands at approximately 10 m above sea level. It is connected to National Road 6, the paved road running between Phnom Penh and Siem Reap, by four kilometres of improved dirt road (Figure 3.3).

The boundaries of the study area were selected based on preliminary interviews with Roka residents in order to incorporate as much of the floodplain utilized by village residents as possible. As a result, study boundaries do not exactly follow administrative boundaries. Rather they more closely

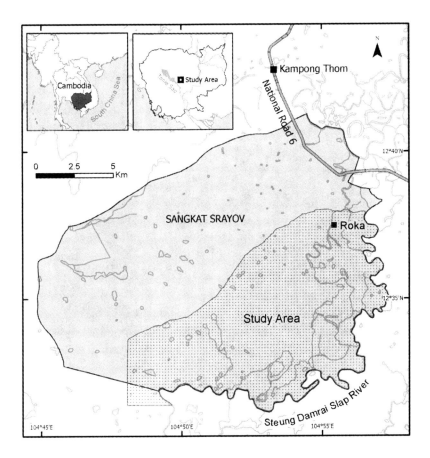

Figure 3.3 Map indicating the location of the study area.

Total area 122 km² south of Roka Village (Sangkat Srayov, Steung Sen Municipality, Kampong Thom Province). Sangkat Srayov is shaded grey, while the area of the study site itself is stippled. Mapping credit: Hannah Stevens, New York Botanical Garden GIS Lab.

follow natural features. The northern boundary of the study area is the administrative border between Roka and Kamraeng Villages. To the east and south, the area is bounded by the Steung Slap (referred to on some maps as Steung Damrai Slap), a river flowing from north to south, eventually turning to the west. West of the village, the boundary follows the dirt road which runs from the village southwest. The boundary ultimately turns due south, straying briefly into Kampong Chhnang Province at Toul Kok Preah. The area forms a rough right triangle of approximately 188 km².

A minority of village residents travel beyond the borders delineated for this study in order to fish, tend livestock or collect fodder and firewood.

However, such trips are not common. The daily activities of most village residents fall within the study boundaries.

Discussion

It is in this context that I now turn to the physical landscape itself, briefly characterizing it and subsequently presenting a typology of ecological transitions and gradients accompanied by specific examples from the village of Roka.

Landscapes (Il)legible to whom?

Topographically, the floodplain may be characterized by a gradual downward slope towards the Tonle Sap lake. But, fine-scale topographic features abound. In many areas the floodplain is punctuated by hillocks, ridges, depressions, ponds, streams and more. However, this microtopography is not legible at broader scales, either geographic or institutional. The 1:50,000 topographic maps prepared by the US Army Topographic Command in 1971 allude to a diverse landscape by noting 'numerous small and intermittent ponds' in some areas. However, many of these landscape features rise or fall as little as a metre or two from the surrounding landscape, and are so subtle as to be invisible on currently available topographic maps or even digital elevation models. Despite their invisibility to outside observers, local residents have detailed understandings of these landscapes, managing them through many different productive and extractive activities. Slight elevational difference from the surrounding plains forms ecological gradients of soil conditions, solar exposure, flood submergence time and more. Plant species vary in their environmental requirements, and therefore distribute themselves according to these requirements (Beatty, 1984; Schoener, 1974). These gradients therefore increase vegetative diversity. Seasonality and vegetative change throughout the year further contributes to landscape heterogeneity and temporal variation in biological diversity.

This landscape is actively managed and utilized by people. As relationships between vegetation and the landscape are locally recognized and managed, and as new ones are produced, an increase in agrodiversity at multiple scales follows.[3]

A simple typology

Different kinds of gradients and transitions pose different challenges in their discernment. To aid in this, a typology may be used, based on the characteristics which make them difficult to simplify and render legible to outsiders. *Interstitial environments* are places in the landscape characterized by a transition between vegetative communities and/or between production or land management systems. *Ephemeral environments* are highly seasonal and appear relatively briefly, most commonly associated with the rising or falling of the floods. Though there is overlap between these categories, this dichotomy is a convenient lens with which to examine transitions and gradients as they relate to livelihood portfolios, ecological processes and institutional readings of the landscape.

The many products which may be obtained from these spaces and the practices associated with them typically remain hidden, classed outside of landscape-based analyses of land use or livelihoods. Populated, knowingly or unknowingly, with incomplete information, institutional planning efforts undervalue the importance of the landscape in local livelihoods. The omission of information about interstitial and ephemeral environments might be easily dismissed as unimportant in the context of most land use and land cover studies, particularly those encompassing a large land area. Indeed, in areal terms they comprise a small fraction of the landscape. However, the socio-ecological mechanics of their production yield insights into the diversity of products derived from the landscape, how the landscape is managed to these ends and the social relationships involved in gaining access to these products (Ribot and Peluso, 2003). These are vital threads in the understanding of how changes in landscape composition or access might affect the resilience of floodplain households.

Interstitial environments

Interstitial environments are gradients between vegetative communities, production systems or other natural resource management schemes which may be produced purposefully, or may emerge as an artifact of land management performed with other goals in mind. Or, as is the case with vegetative communities associated with floodplain microtopography, they may be the result of plant communities self-organizing through successional processes and in relation to varying site conditions, such as elevation, slope and aspect.

Interstices between more dominant or persistent forms of land cover are readily lost in even a detailed reading of the landscape. On the ground, these environments may appear chaotic; their disorder attributed to mismanagement and neglect (Doolittle, 2001; Padoch *et al.*, 1998). Others, such as vegetation along bunds between rice fields, hide in plain sight and are overshadowed by adjacent land cover. Though in both cases, detailed local knowledge may shed light into these spaces.

For projects using remotely sensed data, detailed local knowledge is invaluable (Shepard *et al.*, 2004). But it is a data source seldom tapped in analyses of landscape and livelihoods. In addition, the use of remotely sensed data imposes its own suite of technical limitations. Some vegetative formations may not be visible at all due to limitations imposed by the image classification method, scale and resolution of an image or the minimum mapping unit chosen by the analyst (Sohl *et al.*, 2004). Even at appropriate scales of analysis, some may be impossible to discern from adjacent, differing vegetative formations either visually or through spectral analysis.

Moreover, application of remotely sensed imagery also privileges particular visions of the landscape. The perceived scientific objectivity of the technology equates that which is legible with scientific fact. The weight of modernist perceptions of science behind them, inequities in power relations between institutions and those that work the landscape day-to-day are reinforced (Pickles, 1995).

EXAMPLES FROM THE FIELD

Approximately 3 km down an unimproved dirt road running south from Roka Village is the largest permanent body of water within the study area, Boeng Trawsaing. Covering approximately 1 km^2, the lake along with the surrounding shrublands and rice fields supports approximately 20 families year-round, though the exact number likely varies from year to year. However, the area grows more crowded with the recession of the annual floods, around December. More families, by local estimates 60 or more, move into the area at this time to harvest the many fish stranded in the lake and surrounding seasonal ponds by receding floodwaters. Others cultivate small-scale flood recession rice along the margin of the lake, while many both fish and farm. Access to this land for rice cultivation is relatively controlled, with the same families returning year-after-year to the same sites. Many maintain a year-round residence in a village nearby, often Roka. Others travel from as far away as Phnom Penh. The number of fishing families not cultivating dry season rice is less predictable and likely more fluid from year to year as fish in that area, at that time of year, are an open access resource.

The vegetation stretching beyond the flood recession rice fields and the dry season margin of the lake is dominated by *Gmelina asiatica* L. In some areas, the thorny, small-statured tree grows relatively densely, forming thickets. In others, the trees are scattered across open areas dominated by grasses and sedges. While important much of the year for grazing livestock, as well as for the seasonal collection of grasses for thatching roofs, much of this area floods too deeply for the cultivation of all but the longest-growing varieties of deep water rice.[4] This description was confirmed in a land use/land cover classification of aerial photographs, that included 'shrublands', 'savanna' and 'rice field'. However, a closer examination on the ground reveals examples of interstitial environments between these categories. The two presented here share characteristics of all three land use/land cover categories, but are the products of very different social and ecological processes.

Near the lake, nestled among the *Gmelina* thickets may be found what appear to be old, abandoned flood-recession rice fields. Though grass-covered, their irregular gridwork of fields and bunds is still clear. These traits render these fields particularly difficult to identify in an aerial photograph, appearing as shrubland, savanna or rice field depending upon the resolution and timing of the image and the minimum mapping unit used for the classification. However, discussion with local informants revealed a more complex story. These fields are contingent rice fields. Not cultivated annually, they are brought into cultivation as needed such as when yield on other fields is threatened or when families face other hardships necessitating extra rice for consumption or sale. Unlike the majority of the rice fields in the study area, these fields are not privately owned. They are on commonly held land, but usufruct rights are allocated by the chairman of the community fisheries committee, who could also transfer these rights if the fields went uncultivated for too long. These fields shed light into different social and ecological processes: a fluidity in land tenure not seen elsewhere in the village, which provides a mechanism contributing to household resilience; and a process that maintains gaps in the *Gmelina* thicket, in an area which might otherwise have been a more homogeneous shrubland.

Further from the lake, the *Gmelina* grows more sparsely. Until relatively recently, much of this area had been owned by village residents under customary, locally recognized tenural arrangements. Prior to the civil war, these fields were typically planted with deep water rice varieties, fished when the floods were up and grazed when neither fished nor cultivated. However with the onset of the civil war, security decayed to a point where it was no longer safe to cultivate those areas. As a result, villagers withdrew from these areas and the distant fields lay abandoned up until the late 1990s, meanwhile successing back into the *Gmelina* shrubland which dominates the landscape. By the end of the 1990s, this part of the floodplain was calm enough to be returned to cultivation, fishing and grazing. However, due to a shortage of deep water rice seed, and government support for production of modern, high-yielding rice varieties, many Roka village residents left these fields idle. In the coming years, land values began to rise and attract the attention of investors and speculators. Responding to this new interest in what was then uncultivated land, many village residents sold their holdings.

This pattern of abandonment and sales, as well as government interest in the development of large-scale rice production on the floodplain, led to rampant speculation, soaring land prices and triggered further land sales by village residents (Sokha *et al.*, 2004). As a result, much of the land suitable for deep water rice production in the vicinity of the lake and beyond has been concentrated in the hands of a few wealthy investors, many of whom are numbered among Kampong Thom's urban elite (Diepart, 2010). Some of this land remains idle. However, some is being converted from *Gmelina* shrubland and savanna back into deep water rice fields.

These fields are cultivated by tractor, and are much larger in scale than those typical of village residents. Land preparation occurs in at least two steps. Initially, large trees are cleared and the land is ploughed. Typically in the following year, the land will be ploughed again and the remaining smaller trees and new, woody seedlings removed. However, it is not uncommon to find fields in-between these two stages, as for one reason or another their owners did not yet complete the land preparation necessary for deep water rice production. Some have been caught in-between these two stages for several years, giving the appearance of a young *Gmelina* dominated savanna or a gradient between savanna or shrubland. Even field borders are not always apparent, as they are often less obvious on the lower floodplain than in areas under other forms of rice cultivation. Appearing out of place on the ground, in aerial photographs they appear simply as grasslands or savannas, without any indication that they were a stage in an incremental process of land use change (Doolittle, 1984). Without the help of local informants who provided social and historical context, it would not have been clear what the origin of that vegetative formation was. These fields shed light into incremental processes of landscape change, notably that it is not necessarily teleological as stages in the process do not always follow a set sequence (Padoch et al., 2008, 1998).

The illegibility of these fields complicates land titling. According to an official in the Kampong Thom Provincial Office of the Ministry of Land Management, Urban Planning and Construction, field borders in areas typically planted to traditional tall and floating rice varieties due to the depth of annual flooding, are so difficult to consistently discern in aerial photography that as of 2009, they had been completely omitted from government land titling efforts. Supported at the time by Deutsche Gesellschaft für Technische Zusammenarbeit, titling efforts focused solely on fields closer to the village. These well-defined, shallowly flooding fields typically are used for the production of shorter, more rapidly maturing, modern rice varieties. Thus, ownership of deeply flooding fields further from the village, illegible to the government's formal titling process, assumes less formal arrangements, at best sketch-maps signed by the village chief. This lack of firm, legal documentation results in the increased vulnerability of village residents to land-grabbing or encroachment in these areas. Furthermore, it brings into question the legality of land sales agreements entered into voluntarily by village residents to transfer these areas to large landowners from beyond the village.

The landscape in these areas is beginning to show the effects of this concentration of land ownership. Roberts (2011) analysed changes in the spatial patterns of vegetation types over 47 years in these areas, finding that the landscape is becoming increasingly homogeneous. It also shows signs of more intensive management, as the formerly irregular patchwork of vegetation types near the frontiers of agricultural expansion into the shrublands, gave way to a more ordered, grid-like pattern in the landscape. This simplification of pattern points to increasingly large-scale and mechanized agricultural development. Such farms are privately owned, and typically their establishment leads to the loss of local access to the resources previously available at that location. The emergence of these farms signals decreasing natural resource-based livelihood flexibility for village residents due to diminishing landscape diversity and changes in access to the landscape.

In other situations, interstitial environments may be found nested within more legible categories. One example common throughout the study area is the rice field bund. Demarcating property and serving as both water-level controls and footpaths, bunds also serve a number of less obvious productive functions. Some farmers plant them to *sbauv*, a common grass on the lower floodplain used for thatching roofs. Aside from producing a useful product, this also adds to the durability of the bund, reducing the demands of annual maintenance. Others allow spontaneous grasses to grow along them, harvesting this as fodder for livestock. In a few areas where bunds are built up higher, or at the intersections of bunds, sugar palm ('*daum tnaot*', *Borassus flabellifer* L.) and pandanus ('*romchek*', *Pandanus* sp.) are planted along them. These palms yield a range of useful products from sap and fruit to construction materials. Production techniques associated with bunds are not confined simply to plants. For example, a hole punched in a bund for draining a field may be set with a fish trap to capture any fish trying to follow the water's flow. Simplified by both observers on the ground and those interpreting remotely sensed data as *just* rice fields, these areas nonetheless serve a variety of productive functions which can be important for household resilience.

Ephemeral environments

Environments associated with gradients may also be ephemeral. Particularly important on the floodplain are moisture gradients, their appearance and disappearance tied closely to rising or falling floodwaters, or the initiation or cessation of rainfall. Moisture gradients follow microtopography. Lower lying areas are wetter than higher sites, with many shallow ponds remaining behind in the lowest sites after the annual floodwaters recede. As with interstitial environments, these spaces present their own suites of plant communities and associated land uses. They may form in interstitial spaces as well, but are more strongly defined by their temporal aspect. Their discernment, both in the field or using remotely sensed data, presents many of the same pitfalls as interstitial environments. However, timing of data collection is particularly important. Data gleaned from either an aerial photograph or a field walk will vary depending upon what time of year the data are collected.

EXAMPLES FROM THE FIELD

Roka village residents are involved in a broad range of productive and extractive activities on the floodplain. Most are seasonal to some degree or another. However, some come and go quite rapidly, associated with highly seasonal ephemeral environments. Many appear only once in the annual flood cycle, such as harvesting rats from rice fields with the rising flood waters or harvesting snakes with gill nets strung in woodlands during the falling of the floods. A few are bimodal, as with firewood harvest in the woodlands on the lower floodplain. This peaks twice in the year: once when the floods are highest and harvest sites may be reached by boat and once when the landscape is driest and harvest sites may be reached by ox cart. In between these two periods, substantial woodland far from the village is difficult to access, particularly when heavily laden.

A NARRATIVE SEQUENCE OF LANDSCAPE CHANGE

Rather than focusing on isolated examples, a spatially situated narrative description of the sequence and flow from one vegetative community and productive activity to the next is illustrative (Lambin *et al.*, 2003; Reenberg, 1999). The following generalized sequence of environments is very common on the flooding grasslands and sparsely wooded savannas 3 km or more to the south of the village of Roka. Land use in areas around hillocks, *Gmelina* thickets, streams and woodlands associated with permanently wet sites will differ somewhat from this sequence. Areas closer to the village share some of the steps in the sequence. However, being higher in elevation and therefore flooded for a shorter period than more distant sites, rice cultivation plays a more dominant role in the annual cycle.

With the recession of the annual floods in December, the grasslands bustle with activity. Cattle are brought from wet season refuges in the uplands beyond the village to graze on the spontaneous grassy pasture which emerges on the newly revealed soil. Water buffalo also graze these pastures, though many spend the wet season out on the floodplain itself, at scattered herding camps on some of the larger hillocks. Many people also move into these areas to harvest the fish trapped in seasonal ponds remaining after the recession of the floods. At this time of year, these areas are treated as essentially open access resources. Access to sites closer to the village may be informally limited to village residents only; but at sites further from Roka, people from neighbouring villages, districts and even provinces also fish, and less commonly tend livestock.

As the dry season wears on, the grasses mature while the ponds are cleared of fish and begin to dry up. With this transition, many fisherfolk and livestock keepers move on to other areas. At the height of the dry season, through February and April, mature grasses are harvested for thatching roofs. This is an activity usually performed in small groups, often by women. Bundles of grass are collected to sell and to pay off debts, often under informal contractual agreements. They are also used in construction and repair projects by the collectors themselves. The season for thatch collection is relatively brief, curtailed as the grasslands are set afire to bring another flush of new growth for livestock. Burning is not in a single, organized event. Rather, fires are set here and there, by individuals engaging in other activities. Geographically, the fires are extensive but not complete in their coverage. The result is a mosaic of burned and unburned savanna, which changes annually. In addition to producing better pasture, annual burning maintains the patchwork of grasslands and sparse woody vegetation associated with this sequence of land uses (Laris, 2011).

The burning brings with it another flush of grassy regrowth, to the benefit of cattle and water buffalo graziers. With the onset of the annual rains in April and May, grazing tapers off in some areas as the cultivation of deep water rice begins. This portion of the grassland is not uniformly cultivated. Much of the grasslands are uncultivated, remaining open access pasture. Cultivated fields shift in ownership from open access to privately held, and are no longer grazed.

Throughout the rainy season, uncultivated areas of the grasslands are grazed. Once the flood waters from the Tonle Sap rise, fishing begins again throughout the floodplain, on cultivated land and uncultivated land alike. As with much of the rest of the year, access to this resource is not limited to landowners or village residents. Fish are an open access resource. The deep water rice crop is unaffected by this activity, as the shallow-draft boats typically employed in this fishery do not disturb the plants.

The flood tolerance and the elongating, floating stem of the deep water rice are also shared with the weedy relative of domesticated rice, *Oryza rufipogon* L., which forms floating meadows in these areas. It is very important as a source of fodder for livestock at this point in the production calendar. Most pastures are too deeply flooded for cattle to graze, leading many farmers to drive them into the uplands or to keep them in the village. Water buffalo fare better grazing in higher water, giving farmers the flexibility to graze them in shallow areas of the floodplain, keep them in the village or to send them to the uplands with the cattle, depending upon the availability of labour.

Weedy, undomesticated rice is not only important for wet season livestock management. It may be a significant generator of rice germplasm diversity, which is managed and maintained by farmers as they select which seeds to plant from year to year (Niruntrayakul *et al.*, 2009). Growing in proximity to each other allows cross-pollination and gene flow between domesticated rice and its wild relative. This genetic diversity gives farmers a broader palette with which to develop and fine-tune locally adapted rice varieties best suited to thrive in the variable floodplain environment.

Cessation of the rain and the recession of the floods reveal the terrestrial landscape again. Once fields are drained, rice is harvested. The crop is often threshed in the field for a fee by itinerant owners of mechanical threshing machines. Spontaneous pastures appear anew. Again, cattle and water buffalo are brought in to graze on the rice stubble and new grass growth. And, the busiest fishing season of the year begins.

This generalized schema illustrates the range of vegetation types and land uses associated with a single point in space. The sequence is not evident in a single field walk or in the analysis of a single image. Indeed, it is uncommon to have fine enough temporal resolution in a series of high resolution remotely sensed images to capture this sequence.

A challenge to render into visible units for institutional planning purposes, this sequence reveals nonetheless important information. It yields insight into mechanisms for building and maintaining landscape heterogeneity through burning, grazing and cultivation (Laris, 2011; Cingolani et al., 2005); management of livestock, fishing and other activities in village livelihood portfolios and maintenance and generation of seed varietal diversity. The fine-resolution and temporally continuous view also highlights the importance of grassland to people from beyond the village, especially during the fishing season following flood recession.

Conclusions

Products of dynamism, ecological transitions and gradients abound on the Tonle Sap floodplain. The resultant interstitial environments and ephemeral environments associated with them easily slip between legible categories and the units of measurement used by institutions beyond the village. Illegible, they are easily misinterpreted, overlooked or can be purposefully cast aside. They can also remain obscured from decision-makers and planners, as the dynamics are impossible to incorporate into models, maps and forecasts. Consequently, the local management systems in which they are situated remain unacknowledged. In the absence of detailed accounting of local management systems and their underlying socio-ecological processes, top-down impositions of new land management schemes therefore have few prospects for success. As illustrated by these examples from Roka Village, fine-grain analysis of information typically lost between categories sheds light upon the socio-ecological mechanics of land use and land cover change. To remedy this legibility gap, it is crucial that institutions involved in natural resource management expand methods of data collection and the types of data sought. Simply, they need to ask different questions.

The floodplain landscape is increasingly a contested landscape, as local residents, wealthy elites, governing institutions and development NGOs all struggle for control of the resource base. Rendering the illegible legible and bringing it to the fore may strengthen the case for increased local control and a validation of local management systems, slowing the progress of dispossession which has grown to characterize resource-rich rural areas in Cambodia.

Notes

1 Though widely cited, this figure is not unproblematic. See Lamberts (2006) for a discussion of how this figure was derived, as well as the challenges associated with harvest estimates in a fishery involving so many different fish species, fishing gear and social and legal arrangements for participants in the fishery.
2 While parsed out separately here for the sake of illustration, category lines between individual elite, privately held business and government institution

(more specifically, individuals and groups embedded within institutions) are more often than not, blurred.

3 Agrodiversity is a qualitative descriptor of production systems, and by extension livelihood portfolios, encompassing multiple aspects of diversity: agrobiodiversity (plants domesticated, semi-domesticated and managed); biophysical diversity (unmanaged biological diversity as well as physical aspects of the site, such as soils and topography); management diversity (farmers' technical knowledge and innovations as applied to production) and organizational diversity (farmers' allocation of labour). An agrodiverse system is more robust with respect to shocks and perturbations, while at the same time more flexible in allowing for innovation and capitalization on new opportunities (Brookfield, 2001, p. 41; Brookfield and Padoch, 1994).

4 Deep water rice varieties tolerate deep flooding. Their stems elongate to match the pace of the rising water, while the most distal portion of their stems floats atop the surface (Catling, 1992). These varieties are among the slowest maturing, least yielding and, when sold, the lowest value rice varieties planted in Cambodia. However, they fill a particular niche in production systems; thriving in deeply flooded areas far from the village, and requiring little attention from farmers during the growing season.

References

Alexiades, M. (1996) *Selected Guidelines for Ethnobotanical Research: A Field Manual,* New York Botanical Garden, New York.

Arias, M. E., Cochrane, T. A. and Elliott, V. (2014) 'Modeling future changes of habitat and fauna in the Tonle Sap wetland of the Mekong', *Environmental Conservation* 41(2), pp. 1–11.

Arias, M. E., Cochrane, T. A., Norton, D., Killeen, T. J. and Khon, P. (2013) 'The flood pulse as the underlying driver of vegetation in the largest wetland and fishery of the Mekong Basin', *Ambio* 42, pp. 1–13.

Balzer, P. (2003) 'Case study number 3: Traditional use and availability of aquatic biodiversity in rice-based ecosystems', in M. Halwart, D. Bartley and H. Guttman (eds) *Biodiversity and the Ecosystem Approach in Agriculture, Forestry and Fisheries,* UN FAO, Rome, pp. 50–71.

Batterbury, S. (2001) 'Landscapes of diversity: A local political ecology of livelihood diversification in South-Western Niger', *Ecumene* 8, pp. 437–464.

Beatty, S. W. (1984) 'Influence of microtopography and canopy species on spatial patterns of forest understory plants', *Ecology* 65, pp. 1406–1419.

Bouzarovski, S. (2009) 'Landscapes of flexibility: Negotiating the everyday, an introduction', *GeoJournal* 74, pp. 503–506.

Brookfield, H. C. (2001) *Exploring Agrodiversity,* Columbia University Press, New York.

Brookfield, H. C. and Padoch, C. (1994) 'Appreciating agrodiversity: A look at dynamism and diversity of indigenous farming practices', *Environment* 36, pp. 6–11, 37–45.

Brookfield, H. C., Padoch, C., Parsons, H. and Stocking, M. A. (2002) *Cultivating Biodiversity,* ITDG Publishing, London.

Brooks, S. E., Kebede, B., Allison, E. H. and Reynolds, J. D. (2010) 'The balance of power in rural marketing networks: A case study of snake trading in Cambodia', *Journal of Development Studies* 46, p. 1003.

Brooks, S. E., Reynolds, J. D. and Allison, E. H. (2008) 'Sustained by snakes? Seasonal livelihood strategies and resource conservation by Tonle Sap fishers in Cambodia', *Human Ecology* 36, pp. 835–851.

Catling, D. (1992) *Rice in Deep Water*, IRRI, Los Banos, Philippines.
Cingolani, A. M., Noy-Meir, I. and Díaz, S. (2005) 'Grazing effects on rangeland diversity: A synthesis of contemporary models', *Ecological Applications* 15, pp. 757–773.
Croll, E. J. and Parkin, D. J. (1992) *Bush Base, Forest Farm*, Routledge, London.
Cunningham, A. B. (2001) *Applied Ethnobotany*, Earthscan, London.
Delvert, J. (1994) *Le Paysan Cambodgien*, L'Harmattan, Paris.
Diepart, J.-C. (2010) 'Cambodian peasant's contribution to rural development: A perspective from Kampong Thom Province', *Biotechnologie, Agronomie, Société et Environnement* 14, pp. 321–340.
Doolittle, W. E. (1984) 'Agricultural change as an incremental process', *Annals of the Association of American Geographers* 74, pp. 124–137.
Doolittle, W. E. (2001) 'Learning to see the impacts of individuals', *Geographical Review* 91, pp. 423–429.
Ellis, F. (1998) 'Household strategies and rural livelihood diversification', *Journal of Development Studies* 35, pp. 1–38.
Evans, T., Gray, T., Chamnan, H., Mouyheang, S. and Vanny, L. (2005) *Farming and Its Impact on Flooded Grasslands around the Tonle Sap Lake*, WCS Cambodia Program, Phnom Penh, Cambodia.
Fox, J. (1998) 'Mapping the commons: The social context of spatial information technologies', *The Common Property Resource Digest* 45, pp. 1–4.
Fox, J. and Ledgerwood, J. (1999) 'Dry-season flood recession rice in the Mekong Delta: Two thousand years of sustainable agriculture?' *Asian Perspectives: The Journal of Archaeology for Asia and the Pacific* 38, pp. 37–50.
Hak, M. and Piseth, N. (1999) *Review of Flooding and Flood Management in Cambodia: Cambodia Country Statement. Flood Management and Mitigation in the Mekong River Basin*, UN FAO, Bangkok, Thailand.
Holtgrieve, G. W., Arias, M. E., Irvine, K. N., Lamberts, D., Ward, E. J., Kummu, M., Koponen, J., Sarkkula, J. and Richey, J. E. (2013) 'Patterns of ecosystem metabolism in the Tonle Sap Lake, Cambodia with links to capture fisheries', *PLoS ONE* 8, e71395, http://www.plosone.org/article/info%3Adoi%2F10.1371%2Fjournal.pone.0071395, accessed 17 May 2014.
Johnstone, G., Ranjitha, P., Declerck, F., Kosal, M., Oeur, I., Sithirith, M., Bunna, P., Sophat, S., Chan, S., Sochanny, H., Samnang, L., Sokheng, S., Proum Kimhor, P. and Sameth, R. (2013) 'Tonle Sap scoping report', *Project Report: AAS-2013-2*, CGIAR Research Program on Aquatic Agricultural Systems, Penang.
Junk, W. J. and Wantzen, K. M. (2004) 'The flood pulse concept: New aspects, approaches, and applications – an update', *Proceedings of the Second International Symposium on the Management of Large Rivers for Fisheries*, Vol. 2, FAO, Phnom Penh, pp. 117–140.
Keskinen, M. (2006) 'The lake with floating villages: Socio-economic analysis of the Tonle Sap Lake', *International Journal of Water Resources Development* 22, pp. 463–480.
Keskinen, M. and Varis O. (2012) 'Institutional cooperation at a basin level: For what, by whom? Lessons learned from Cambodia's Tonle Sap Lake', *Natural Resources Forum* 36, pp. 50–60.
Kim, S. S. (2013) 'Territoriality and state power in Cambodia: The case of demarcation in Tonle Sap', PhD thesis, University of Sydney, Australia, http://ses.library.usyd.edu.au/handle/2123/9522, accessed 9 February 2014.
King, D. O. (1860) 'Travels in Siam and Cambodia', *Journal of the Royal Geographical Society of London* 30, pp. 177–182.

Kummu, M., Penny, D., Sarkkula, J. and Koponen, J. (2008) 'Sediment: Curse or blessing for Tonle Sap Lake?' *Ambio* 37, pp. 158–163.

Kummu, M., Yin, S., Sarkkula, J. and Koponen, J. (2006) 'Tonle Sap Lake water balance calculations', Technical Paper, MRCS/WUP-FIN, Vientiane, Lao PDR.

Lamberts, D. (2006) 'The Tonle Sap Lake as a productive ecosystem', *International Journal of Water Resources Development* 22, pp. 481–495.

Lambin, E. F., Geist, H. J. and Lepers, E. (2003) 'Dynamics of land-use and land-cover change in tropical regions', *Annual Review of Environment and Resources* 28, pp. 205–241.

Laris, P. (2011) 'Humanizing savanna biogeography: Linking human practices with ecological patterns in a frequently burned savanna of southern Mali', *Annals of the Association of American Geographers* 101, pp. 1067–1088.

Marschke, M. J. and Berkes, F. (2006) 'Exploring strategies that build livelihood resilience: A case from Cambodia', *Ecology and Society* 11, p. 42.

McDonald, A., Pech, B., Phauk, V. and Leeu, B. (1997) *Plant Communities of the Tonle Sap Floodplain: Final Report in Contribution to the Nomination of Tonle Sap as a Biosphere Reserve for UNESCO's Man in the Biosphere Program*, UNESCO, Phnom Penh.

Ministry of Planning. (2012) 'Migration in Cambodia', *Report of the Cambodia Rural Urban Migration Project*, Phnom Penh, http://www.mop.gov.kh/Projects/CRUMP/tabid/213/Default.aspx, accessed 9 February 2014.

Ministry of Planning and UNDP-Cambodia. (2007) *Expanding Choices for Rural People: Cambodia Human Development Report*, Phnom Penh, http://www.mop.gov.kh/Others/CHDR/tabid/193/Default.aspx, accessed 9 February 2014.

Mortimore, M. J. and Adams, W. M. (2001) 'Farmer adaptation, change and 'crisis' in the Sahel', *Global Environmental Change* 11, pp. 49–57.

Nang, P., Khiev, D., Hirsch, P. and Whitehead, I. (2011) *Improving the Governance of Water Resources in Cambodia: A Stakeholder Analysis*, Phnom Penh, http://www.cdri.org.kh/webdata/download/wp/wp54e.pdf, accessed 30 September 2013.

Niruntrayakul, S., Rerkasem, B. and Jamjod, S. (2009) 'Crossability between cultivated rice (*Oryza sativa*) and common wild rice (*O. rufipogon*) and characterization of F1 and F2 populations', *ScienceAsia* 35, pp. 161–169.

Packman, C. E., Gray, T. N. E., Collar, N. J., Evans, T. D., van Zalinge, R. N., Virak, S., Lovett, A. A. and Dolman, P. M. (2013) 'Rapid loss of Cambodia's grasslands', *Conservation Biology* 27, pp. 245–247.

Padoch, C., Harwell, E. and Susanto, A. (1998) 'Swidden, sawah, and in-between: Agricultural transformation in Borneo', *Human Ecology* 26, pp. 3–20.

Padoch, C., Pinedo-Vasquez, M. and Roberts, A. S. (2008) 'Process in an Eventful Environment', in B. B. Walters, B. J. McCay, P. West and S. Lees (eds) *Against the Grain: The Vayda Tradition in Human Ecology and Ecological Anthropology*, Rowman, Altamira, New York, pp. 135–143.

Pickles, J. (1995) *Ground Truth: The Social Implications of Geographic Information Systems*, Guilford Press, New York.

Reenberg, A. (1999) 'Agricultural systems in space and time – the dynamic mosaic of land use', *Geografisk Tidsskrift, Danish Journal of Geography*, 99(1), pp. 181–190.

Ribot, J. C. and Peluso, N. L. (2003) 'A theory of access', *Rural Sociology* 68, pp. 153–181.

Rigg, J. (2006) 'Land, farming, livelihoods, and poverty: Rethinking the links in the rural South', *World Development* 34, pp. 180–202.

Roberts, A. S. (2011) 'Phytosociology, history and diversity in farmer-managed landscapes on the Tonle Sap floodplain, Cambodia', PhD thesis, Graduate Centre of the City University of New York.

Schoener, T. W. (1974) 'Resource partitioning in ecological communities', *Science* 185, pp. 27–39.

Scoones, I., Thompson, J. and Group, I. T. D. (1994) *Beyond Farmer First*, Intermediate Technology, London.

Scott, J. C. (1998) *Seeing Like a State*, Yale University Press, New Haven.

Shepard, G. H., Yu, D. W. and Nelson, B. W. (2004) 'Ethnobotanical ground-truthing and forest diversity in the Western Amazon', in T. J. Carlson and L. Maffi (eds) *Ethnobotany and Conservation of Biocultural Diversity*, New York Botanical Garden Press, New York, pp. 133–174.

Sneddon, C. (2007) 'Nature's materiality and the circuitous paths of accumulation: Dispossession of freshwater fisheries in Cambodia', *Antipode* 39, pp. 167–193.

Sohl, T. L., Gallant, A. L. and Loveland, T. R. (2004) 'The characteristics and interpretability of land surface change and implications for project design', *Photogrammetric Engineering and Remote Sensing* 70, pp. 439–450.

Sokha, P., Chhim, C., Vitou, S. and Ngak, O. (2004) 'Overview on dynamics of land tenure in Kamponh Thom Province and Sihanoukville Municipality', *Annual Research Report (No.1)*, Centre d'Etude et de Développement Agricole Cambodgien (CEDAC), Phnom Penh.

Sokhem, P. and Sunada, K. (2006) 'The governance of the Tonle Sap Lake, Cambodia: Integration of local, national and international levels', *International Journal of Water Resources Development* 22, pp. 399–416.

Sopha, A., Oeur, I. and McAndrew, J. (2007) 'Understanding social capital in response to floods and droughts', *Cambodia Development Review* 11, pp. 9–12.

Stark, M. T. (2006) 'Early mainland southeast Asian landscapes in the first millennium AD', *Annual Review of Anthropology* 35, pp. 1–26.

van Zalinge, N. P. (2002) 'Update on the status of the Cambodian inland capture fisheries sector with special reference to the Tonle Sap Great Lake', *Catch and Culture* 8, pp. 1–5.

Wantzen, K. M., Junk, W. J. and Rothhaupt, K. -O. (2008) 'An extension of the floodpulse concept (FPC) for lakes', *Hydrobiologia* 613, pp. 151–170.

White, P. F., Oberthur, T. and Sovuthy, P. (eds) (1997) *The Soils Used for Rice Production in Cambodia: A Manual for Their Identification and Management*, Cambodia-IRRI-Australia Project, Phnom Penh.

Ziv, G., Baran, E., Nam, S., Rodríguez-Iturbe, I. and Levin, S. A. (2012) 'Trading-off fish biodiversity, food security, and hydropower in the Mekong River Basin', *Proceedings of the National Academy of Sciences* 109, pp. 5609–5614.

4 Can market integration improve livelihoods and safeguard the environment?

The case of hybrid rice varieties in Cambodia's agricultural heartland

Maylee Thavat

Introduction

A key concern for developing countries experiencing rapid agrarian transformation is the loss of different agro-ecologies and on-farm biodiversity. As forest cover diminishes, discussions around environment and conservation often turn to debates over agro-biodiversity and land management by farmers. *Prey Veng* meaning 'Long' or 'Grand Forest' in Khmer, was densely forested prior to French rule; but it is now firmly planted as a central province of Cambodia's agricultural heartland, with the largest area of any province devoted to rice production, contributing around 10 per cent of the country's total annual rice harvest (USAID, 2008). Rice ecologies of the lower Mekong delta can present a seemingly endless landscape of monoculture. To the contrary, however, Cambodia's lowland rice ecologies are highly diverse and productive environments that yield not just rice but a range of flora and fauna important to food security for farmers and potentially the resilience of agricultural systems overall (Shams, 2007). Diversity among rice varieties is also recognized as important in the face of environmental uncertainty and climate variability (IPCC, 2002). Simply put, growing a diversity of rice varieties helps spread the risks of crop failure due to changing growing conditions or extreme climatic events to which Cambodia is prone.[1]

This chapter examines the dynamics of hybrid rice seed uptake by the Prey Veng Rice Seed Company, Cambodia.[2] In particular, it describes how different classes of farmers accessed and used both modern hybrid and traditional rice seeds, through formal and informal markets and the implications of this for on-farm agro-biodiversity and livelihoods. Hirsch (2012) noted that much political *ecology* work on Southeast Asia focuses on upland areas: but what of the agricultural lowlands? Studies of lowland agriculture have traditionally been dominated by political *economy* studies aimed at understanding 'capitalist transformations of the country-side' (Rigg and Vandergeest, 2012). Yet the environmental aspects of such transformations are now increasingly at the fore (ibid). This is because, 'small-scale producers are seen not only as the key to reducing rural poverty, but also as a pillar of global food security, stewards of natural resources and biodiversity, and part of the solution to climate change' (Vorley et al., 2012, p. 2). In this new light, conventional agricultural modernization projects must be re-examined to take account of new environmental challenges.

Using hybrid rice as an example, this chapter shows how new agricultural technologies interact with farmer livelihoods differently depending on levels of market integration, and resource security including the ability to produce surplus paddy rice for sale and access to irrigation. Initially, access to hybrid rice varieties bestowed a precarious prosperity on fully commercialized farmers by improving their ability to produce large volumes of uniform quality rice. Furthermore, it helped stabilize and subsidize the subsistence production of farmers partially involved in cash cropping. For the poorest farmers, hybrid rice enabled greater food security through enabling continuous cropping. However, follow up research conducted 8 years later in 2013 among the same villages found that despite cropping up to three times per year, both richer commercialized farmers and poorer subsistence oriented farmers now struggled with high input costs, labour shortages, debt and low rice prices. In one village up to 200 ha of land had been abandoned by farmers too indebted to plant another crop. Middle-income farmers, however (who cultivated the most diverse range of rice varieties including hybrid seed in 2005), continued to farm the greatest number of rice varieties, retaining the majority of their harvests for consumption. It was these farmers who had the most sustainable livelihoods with respect to the ability to maintain themselves and the landscapes they managed. By contrast, both rich and poor farmers who were more heavily reliant on hybrid rice seed varieties in 2005, by 2013, were struggling to maintain production.

Achieving a balance then between food security, agro-biodiversity and market integration is likely to be key in meeting the challenges noted by Vorley et al. (2012). Arguments over the modernization of agricultural production, and especially the introduction of modern or hybrid seeds, have typically centred on unequal social outcomes and diminished ecological integrity (see Griffin, 1974; Pearse, 1980; Shiva, 1991; Glaeser, 1987). Yet arguments that centre on the introduction of modern hybrid seed and the changes in agricultural production that they precipitate distract from the point: the need for coherent strategies that address the needs of all classes of farmers and their increasingly diversified livelihoods. Diversified livelihoods are a key feature of countries experiencing agrarian change. The following section defines and discusses the term 'agrarian change', and broadly identifies the mixed outcomes associated with it such as growing social inequality, rising smallholder productivity and improved food security. Borrowing from Rigg's (1997) analysis of the Green Revolution (the quintessential example of agrarian change), I argue that far from producing socially and environmentally deleterious effects, the introduction of hybrid seed and modern agricultural methods may in some instances improve the viability of subsistence production systems among some farmers, depending on their overall production and income mix.

Agrarian change in Southeast Asia

The term agrarian transition or change is used to encapsulate the interrelated processes of agro-industrialization, market integration and globalization; with reference to the implications and impacts of these processes beyond the agricultural production sector, for rural populations and society as a whole (Caouette and Turner, 2009). In Southeast Asia, these processes have typically resulted in greater degrees of inequality and therefore class differentiation among rural populations; often leading to a rise in the importance of off-farm work and remittances, which in turn increase the linkages between rural and urban areas (Rigg, 1997, 1998, 2006; Parnwell, 2001; Thompson, 2007; Hirsch, 2012).

Rigg and Hirsch (2012) noted that rural class differentiation has long been a central concept of political economy analysis in these contexts. Used to challenge modernization theories that posit peasant societies as backward and unproductive, class analysis instead reveals how existing social relations of production are transformed through new technologies and interventions resulting in 'differential control over production resources', especially land (Rigg and Hirsch, 2012, p. 16). Lenin's class formation among the peasantry, who he identified as either poor, middle or rich, is particularly useful then for understanding the variegated impacts of agricultural modernization projects (Bernstein, 2003, p. 6). For the poorest members of agrarian societies, the inability to meet the demands of simple biological or capital reproduction leads towards wage labour or proletarianism. An estimated 21 per cent of Cambodia's rural households are landless and are dependent on wages from agricultural labour. In addition, land poor households (those with less than 1 ha) comprise nearly half of Cambodia's rural population at 45 per cent (CDRI, 2006). Middle peasants are identified as those with the ability to meet reproduction (owning more than 1 ha of land), while rich 'peasants' are defined as those who not only meet their reproductive demands but expand, be it through land acquisition or diversification, into other areas including trading, money-lending, retailing or providing other goods or services (Bernstein, 2003, p. 6).

Broadly speaking the impacts of agro-industrialization and agrarian change in Southeast Asia have given rise to complex and often contradictory outcomes for different classes of farmers. Although a number of scholars point to increasing state violence, military rule and appropriation of land, resources and people via enclosure as the primary outcome of greater market integration in Southeast Asia (Nevens and Peluso, 2008; Caouette and Turner, 2009; Hall *et al.*, 2011), dramatic increases in standards of living across the region, reduced poverty and improved food security cannot be denied (Renwick, 2011). For instance, UN agencies assess that the region is on track to achieve Millennium Development Goal One – to eradicate extreme poverty and hunger – as a result of economic growth and market integration (UNESCAP, 2008, p. 11).

It can be difficult to make sense of such contradictory development trends in countries such as Cambodia that are undergoing rapid transformation. For example, the United Nations Development Program notes that between 1980 and 2012 Cambodia's life expectancy at birth increased by 24.9 years; mean years of schooling increased by 0.8 years; and gross national income per capita increased by about 163 per cent between 1995 and 2012 (UNDP, 2013). Indeed, in the 5 years prior to the Global Financial Crisis, the country experienced growth rates of nearly 10 per cent per year (CIA, 2009). Nevertheless, Cambodia remains in the unfortunate category of a Least Developed Country. Although human development indicators have improved in recent years in line with economic growth, some believe that the indicators have not improved as much as they should have in rural areas, where high levels of absolute poverty prevail (CDRI, 2006). Furthermore, poverty persists despite heavy investment by donors and government in rural infrastructure (Hughes and Un, 2011), and high growth rates in the agricultural sector (driven in part by increased rice production) of 5.6 per cent per year between 2000 and 2008 (Yu and Diao, 2011, p. 1). Also indicative is Cambodia's GINI coefficient (a measure of inequality where 0 is perfect equality and 100 implies perfect inequality) of 36 (World Bank, 2014). By comparison, many Latin American countries place within the 50s, South Africa at 63.1 and in 2010 Thailand's index was 39.4, Indonesia's 35.6 and India's 33.9.

The relationship between rapid economic growth, poverty reduction and inequality is varied and complex (Dollar and Kraay, 2007; Berg and Ostry, 2011). It can be hard to reconcile personal research experiences that present a mixed picture of changing landscapes and livelihoods with the critique of political ecologists who speak of exclusion and enclosure, and the view of economists who present the story of agro-industrialization as one of rising incomes, food security and development. Figure 4.1 organizes these different perspectives in relation to the role of small-scale farmers.

Taken from a 2012 study conducted by Vorley *et al.* for the International Institute for Environment and Development, the figure maps three main perspectives in agricultural development debates. The upper right quadrant typifies rights-based approaches to development that argue that smallholders must be protected from dominant and destructive market forces. This perspective is broadly defined by the food sovereignty movement which advocates for the rights of people to define and control their own food systems including rights to land, seeds, traditional agricultural knowledge and price setting (Vorley *et al.*, 2012, p. 11). The lower right quadrant, on the other hand, represents perspectives that currently dominate international development approaches in rural areas, which promote value chain development and Making Markets Work for the Poor (M4P) approaches. This perspective sees small producers as business people who can and must

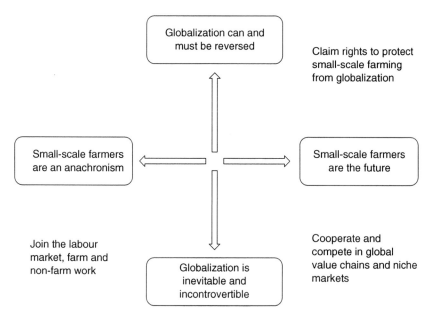

Figure 4.1 Different perspectives on globalization and the role of small-scale farmers.
Source: Vorley *et al.*, 2012, p. 11

compete if they are to stay viable in newly emerging global supply chains. Poverty in this view is thought to be the result of a lack of access to markets and globalization processes not a side effect of them (Marshall *et al.*, 2006, p. 4). The third perspective represents a plurality of views, all of which eventuate in farmers engaging in dynamic and diverse livelihood options. These options may include off-farm work and wage labour as economies diversify, or they may result in the emergence of entrepreneurial farms, or the persistence of subsistence farms depending on the types of agricultural policies at play (Vorley *et al.*, 2012). As Walker (2010, p. 1) put it:

> ... rural households are not making a simplistic transformation from agrarian to post-agrarian but are developing economically diversified and spatially dispersed livelihood strategies in which agricultural and non-agricultural pursuits are often intertwined.

This range of perspectives towards smallholders and agricultural development can be observed across the donor landscape in Cambodia, although few are addressing the full multiplicity of what sustainable rural livelihoods might entail.[3] The Cambodian government, meanwhile, has pursued 'high-input' agricultural production systems that Johnsen and Munford (2012, p. 9) argue are outmoded in the world and even in the region. The conditions under which staple agricultural crops such as rice are produced provide insight into agrarian changes processes overall.

Rice production in Cambodia

An estimated 60 per cent of Cambodians derive the majority of their income from agriculture, and mainly from the production of low-input, low-yielding rain-fed rice crops using traditional rice seed varieties retained from the previous harvest (WFP, 2014). A decade ago, average national yields were approximately 2.5 tonnes per hectare, which are the lowest in the region. This is changing rapidly, however, as growing numbers of farmers who, with access to a combination of irrigation, modern hybrid seed varieties and fertilizers, have expanded production into the dry season. Although the total area cultivated during the dry season tends to be smaller, yields are generally higher as production utilizes high-yielding hybrid varieties that are usually grown on more fertile soil, with better control over water, and during more beneficial climatic conditions (e.g. the dry season typically experiences higher total sunshine hours) (Nesbitt and Phaloeun, 1997, p. 19). In addition to favourable environmental conditions, external quality inputs are also key to the attainment of higher yields. That is, to maximize returns from the cultivation of modern rice varieties, the use of irrigation, chemical fertilizers, pesticides and fresh pure seed is important.

Traditional and modern rice varieties represent an important split in rice production and marketing in Cambodia. Cambodia contains an estimated 2,000 different landraces unique to the country. These indigenous rice varieties are well adapted to Cambodia's different agro-ecosystems and rain-fed production (Helmers, 1997, p. 2). Johnsen and Munford reported that modern hybrids are increasingly being substituted for local indigenous rice varieties (2012, p. 13). This, however, is debateable, as Fukai (2006) pointed out that modern rice seed varieties are typically used to supplement traditional wet season varieties rather than displace them. As we shall see in the proceeding sections, the degree to which hybrid seed may either complement or displace traditional varieties depends on different farmers' livelihood strategies and their class status.

The majority of traditional rice varieties are strongly photoperiod sensitive and begin reproductive growth at pre-determined day lengths (Nesbitt and Phaloeun, 1997, p. 32). Photoperiod sensitivity is an adaptive trait responsive to Cambodia's erratic rainfall patterns. For these varieties planting can be delayed up to 5 months until rainfall is adequate (Nesbitt and Phaloeun, 1997, p. 2). Thus planting can take place early or late in the season according to rainfall patterns and flowering will still take place once the required day length is reached. A crop is generally guaranteed. Overall, traditional photoperiod sensitive varieties are preferred for wet-season production due to their stress resistance and crop height which means that the rice towers above floodwaters (Javier, 1997, pp. 41–47). The drawback, however, is that yields for traditional varieties tend to be low. Indeed, Sokhen et al. (2004, p. 17) cited a study in Cambodia that correlated the lowest lying land with the tallest rice varieties and the poorest families. Nonetheless, Cambodian farmers prefer traditional varieties for consumption because they believe these taste better. Overall, there is little demand for traditional varieties outside of the domestic Cambodian market. Foreign Vietnamese or Thai buyers consider traditional varieties as low purity, low value and low grade. As a result of this lack of trade, Cambodian farmers tend to limit cash expenditure on this crop and produce their own seeds.

Modern, short-duration or hybrid varieties are not as tall, have shorter growing periods and are not photoperiod sensitive, meaning flowering is not dependent on day length so they can be grown throughout the year. These varieties tend to be grown in the dry season with irrigation, and they have higher yields than traditional varieties if used in conjunction with fertilizer. Modern varieties are generally not preferred for food. Farmers who grow these varieties tend to treat them as cash crops and sell the majority of their harvest. Modern, short-duration varieties are also considered to be low grade and low value and are often mixed with surplus traditional varieties when sold to foreign buyers.

Modern rice seed varieties were first introduced to Cambodia in the 1990s as part of the Cambodia-IRRI-Australia Project (CIAP), which was supported by Australian Aid.[4] A key output of CIAP was the testing and selective breeding of some of Cambodia's traditional rice varieties, leading to increased genetic purity of these landraces. Traditional Cambodian varieties were collected and pure genetic lines were singled out for multiplication. A total of nine 'improved' Cambodian rice varieties were released in Cambodia: three medium-duration (CAR 1 to CAR 3) and six late-duration (CAR 4 to CAR 9) (Javier, 1997, p. 53). In addition to the introduction of CAR varieties, CIAP also introduced foreign, modern photoperiod sensitive and non-photoperiod sensitive varieties. This included the medium-duration *santepheap* varieties and the high yielding short-duration variety IR66.

When I commenced this research in 2005, the most popular modern variety in Cambodia was IR66 (Mak, 2001). Like other modern varieties, IR66 seed does not possess the same in-built dormancy as traditional seed, which means it cannot be stored as long as traditional seed and must be renewed more frequently. Farmers therefore cannot retain this seed from season to season, and they must have access to fresh seed. Prior to the establishment of seed companies, there was no regular supply of modern seed in Cambodia. Instead, farmers exchanged seed with friends and family, or occasionally purchased it from a farmer rumoured to have extremely good quality, high-germinating seed. Since farmers expect to sell modern varieties for cash, they are less averse to purchasing inputs. The expansion of dry-season rice production using modern, short-duration varieties has dramatically increased some household's annual yields. This has occurred against a background of growing rice surpluses overall in Cambodia, resulting in increased and often informal trade.

The agricultural quality improvement project

In 2000, the Australian aid program (formerly AusAID) established the Agricultural Quality Improvement Project (AQIP). The primary purpose of AQIP was to 'improve food security and cash income for farm households to take them beyond the current levels of marginal subsistence in selected districts of selected provinces' (AusAID, 1999, p. 46). To this end the project spent a total of AU$17.2 million over 5 years (ACIL, 2006, p. 3). The major vehicle to achieve this objective was the establishment of four rice seed companies in four adjacent provinces of Cambodia. These companies were to 'improve the availability of varieties and quality of rice seed in target provinces' (AusAID, 1999, p. 57). The logic for this was that high-quality inputs – including seed – are required to produce high-quality, saleable outputs. This would thereby enable the market integration of Cambodia's largely subsistence-oriented rice crop and assist with poverty alleviation efforts. Australia had previously funded the Cambodia-IRRI-Australia Project (1987–1999) followed by the Cambodia Agricultural Research Development Institute (1999–present) – both of which aimed at selecting, testing and reproducing suitable rice varieties for Cambodia. The establishment of commercially successful rice seed companies was seen as key to maintaining the elusive 'institutional sustainability' of Australian aid efforts after the close of donor funding. Although the sustainability of farmer livelihoods and not of private seed companies would have seemed to be a more appropriate objective for an aid agency, securing the financial future of the seed companies was justified from the perspective that sustainable poverty alleviation would be achieved through greater market access for Cambodia's key agricultural products such as rice.

The target provinces were Takeo, Svay Reing, Prey Veng and Kandal, all located in the southern lowlands of Cambodia. These provinces were selected through participatory preference ranking with government, NGOs and international organizations. During project design, 20 preferences were identified and ranked accordingly. First among the preferences were provinces that displayed the highest capacity to take advantage of good quality rice seed especially in terms of irrigation, land tenure, market access and high levels of dry-season rice production, yet were nonetheless poor, densely populated and showed high levels of malnourishment, coupled with a disproportionate number of female headed households (AusAID, 1999, p. 40). In short, the provinces were identified as having commercial potential but were nevertheless poor.

Rice seed sales and distribution

The AQIP rice seed companies produced seed to internationally recognized standards and sold it to farmers and institutions. The two types of rice seed varieties they sold – modern and traditional – followed two distinct marketing channels. The first sales channel was of modern seed to farmers via seed dealer networks. Seed dealer networks were established by the seed company 'sales and marketing' officers. These networks usually enrolled men of stature within villages, such as village chiefs. Typically, village-level seed dealers received a day-long sales pitch on the benefits of high-quality seed and how to sell the seed to farmers. Those eager to sell company seed signed an agreement with a seed company to ensure that they followed company policy for storage, sale and promotion of the seed. Seed was then given to the dealers on credit at the price of 1300 *riel* per kilogram and sold for 1400 *riel* per kilogram, with dealers keeping the 100 *riel* or 2.5 US cents per kilogram commission (2005 prices). Around 85 per cent of sales via seed dealers to farmers were of modern, short-duration varieties, mostly IR66 which was preferred by farmers.[5]

The other sales channel was institutional sales to NGOs and government, consisting mainly of improved, traditional seed varieties. NGOs tended to give traditional seed on credit to farmers, as part of other development projects while government purchases were often used as part of relief to farmers who had lost their seed due to flood or drought. In the first years of the project, institutional sales far outweighed farmer sales. Although institutional sales supported the companies in the early years of establishment, institutional sales were generally seen by most involved in the project as undermining the market for seed, as farmers who were given seed were obviously far less likely to buy it. However, institutional sales were seen as useful in terms of the poverty alleviation aims of the project. By the end of the project, farmer sales increased significantly as market awareness was built and institutional sales declined. This was of some relief to project managers as sales to farmers were seen as crucial to the long-term commercial viability of the seed companies. By 2004, 76 per cent of total rice seed sales were to farmers, while sales to NGOs declined from 85 per cent in 2002 to 24 per cent in 2004. When I returned again in 2013, hybrid rice seed sales were being rapidly displaced by imported Vietnamese varieties.

Project impacts

In 2005, I conducted research with two project employees to establish the uptake of company seed among farmers and the impact of this along the rice value chain.[6] This was done through an Australian Research Council Industry Linkage Grant under which an agreement was made with the industry partner (AQIP) to host me as a PhD student. The primary aim was to understand who purchased the seed and who did not and why. Research was conducted in Prey Veng province, the province with the highest farmer company seed uptake. Within Prey Veng, 14 villages were rapidly surveyed to identify villages for further in-depth research.[7] Out of the 14 villages surveyed, four villages were chosen. The four villages each represented a varying level of AQIP company seed use. They were Prey Ankoing (non-AQIP seed use village), Prey T'bal (low AQIP seed use village), T'Lor (medium AQIP seed use village) and Chuen Tukor (high AQIP seed use village). Focus group meetings were conducted in each village with around 15 to 20 farmers. Since few farmers purchased improved traditional varieties, the study compared company IR66 with other non-company seed (unimproved IR66 and unimproved traditional varieties).[8] Information from focus group sessions was then supplemented by a survey of 35 farmers.[9] Finally, information on seed exchange, paddy trading and milling was gathered in informal interviews over a week-long period.[10]

Findings

Overall, the research found that farmers who purchased and grew company seed experienced yield improvements of between 20 and 40 per cent. This was supported by the AQIP 2005 Household Crop Production survey which found a 44 per cent yield increase with AQIP seed. The variation in yield benefits among farmers who used AQIP seed depended on factors such as differential soil quality, water supply, production techniques and timely and appropriate use of good quality fertilizer. These agronomic factors had the ability to render the benefits of high-quality seed negligible: one farmer complained that the poor quality fertilizer she purchased completely ruined her crop, a common problem in Cambodia's unregulated fertilizer market. Farmers were very aware of the impacts of environmental and other factors, and given the high price by Cambodian standards for the company seed, many farmers reported that they tried to provide the seed with the best growing conditions possible. They planted it on their best soils, close to irrigation sources and generally took greater care. Given this, it was difficult to make exact statements about the benefits of company seed alone as a number of other factors contributed to its higher yields. Importantly, however, 100 per cent of company seed users interviewed perceived the seed to have several positive attributes including higher germination rates (meaning they used less seed); higher yields; crop growth was considered stronger and more even; and the resulting paddy was perceived as higher quality and therefore easier to sell.

It is not surprising that the research also found that farmers with better and more secure resource endowments, such as good soil, access to irrigation and proximity to provincial markets, were better able to take advantage of company seed. From the focus group discussions and farmer surveys a graduated scale of farmers was identified.

In general, large-scale farmers who produced purely for commercial sale, tended to use high-quality, modern company seed purchased on a regular basis. They intensively produced IR66 and purchased traditional (often fragrant) varieties for household consumption. Some of these farmers had also moved into the production and marketing of second-generation company

Table 4.1 Resource security and seed uptake.

	Resource Security Secure → Insecure				
	2005 Higher-income	2005 Middle-Income		2005 Lower-Income	
Farm type	Commercial large scale farmers	Commercial medium scale farmers	Subsistence farmer with irrigation and large paddy surplus	Subsistence farmer with irrigation and small paddy surplus	Subsistence farmer with no irrigation and no surplus
Seed variety	Grows modern varieties ONLY	Grows modern and traditional varieties	Grows modern and traditional varieties	Grows modern and traditional varieties	Grows modern varieties ONLY
Seed source	From 1st generation AQIP seed	From 1st and 2nd generation AQIP seed	From 2nd generation AQIP seed	Retains and swaps seed	Retains and swaps seed
End use	Sells 2nd generation AQIP seed IR66, buys traditional rice for consumption	Sells IR66 surplus, buys traditional rice for consumption	Sells IR66 surplus. Retains traditional rice for consumption	Retains IR66 and traditional rice for consumption	Retains IR66 for consumption

Source: Long et al., 2005, p. 29.

seed for sale to other farmers at a price of 700 *riel* per kilogram – half the price of the company seed. These farmers were able to take advantage of the marketing efforts of the seed companies, which had built demand for high-quality seed; and without the overheads, they were able to undercut the seed companies by 50 per cent.

Second were the slightly less commercialized farmers who produced predominantly IR66 and used company seed or second-generation company seed for production. Generally, they sold at least 50 per cent of their yield. Third were farmers who were slightly less resource secure. They tended to have average sized land parcels (approximately 1 to 2 ha) with average soil quality and used a combination of ordinary or non-company IR66 and traditional varieties. They consumed and sold a combination of their production of both IR66 and traditional varieties. The wealthier among this group ate a greater proportion of traditional varieties. This made sense from a household perspective, because traditional varieties are differentiated in local markets and cost more to purchase. However, due to the dominance of Vietnamese traders' preferences, when traditional varieties are sold they are typically treated the same as IR66 and given a low price. Unless farmers had large parcels of land to achieve economies of scale, it made more sense for them to grow traditional rice for consumption, than to grow all IR66 and buy in traditional varieties. Some of these farmers purchased first- or second-generation company seed to enhance their surplus production of IR66. Some of these farmers had heard of, or were experimenting with, company seed.

Lastly were poorer farmers who, with limited land and larger families, tended to grow ordinary/non-company IR66 continuously from seed that they had obtained from seed swaps with other farmers.[11] Despite these households growing up to three crops a year, many only just managed to fulfil their consumption needs. Few of these farmers had even heard of the rice seed companies. Their poverty and inability to fulfil basic subsistence needs meant cultivating modern rice monocultures. That is, although the introduction of IR66 had undoubtedly helped such farmers achieve greater yields and therefore food security, without the backup of traditional varieties and the agro-ecological diversity they provide, they inhabited a precarious position, should hybrid crops fail (Ovesen *et al.*, 1996, p. 23). Few had options to access modern company seed which may have helped them move beyond subsistence and towards surplus production. Unless they received gifts of modern seed from institutions or second-generation company seed as part of an exchange with friends and family members, there was little scope for them to obtain this seed. None of these farmers reported receiving seed from government agencies, NGOs, friends or family.

Upon briefly returning to the four main case study villages in 2013, interviews with village chiefs revealed significant changes. All farmers involved in cash cropping had now swapped from growing hybrid variety IR66 to Vietnamese variety Nam Kong Bong. Village chiefs reported that the new Vietnamese variety grew faster than IR66 and had a ready commercial market among Vietnamese traders who dominate the paddy trade in this region. For the 'middle-income' farmers of Prey T'bal, this had not appeared to make a great deal of difference. These farmers continued to grow the largest variety of rice and maintained subsistence production of traditional varieties, using Nam Kong Bong to supplement their incomes.

Both rich and poor farmers also appeared to be in a similar situation as before: continually cropping Nam Kong Bong for commercial sale yet at decreased profitability. Village chiefs in the three other villages of Prey Angkoing, T'lov and Cheun Tukor all noted high levels of farmer debt associated with higher input costs for Nam Kong Bong production. High input prices for diesel water pumps, fertilizer and seed, as well as increased costs associated with mechanization for harvesting and tilling, contributed to this debt. Improved roads and better irrigation access had not alleviated these costs. Instead farmer livelihoods were now reliant on remittances sent by working-age family members employed in the garment and construction sectors. If remittances made up for the shortfall in farming costs, then rice production continued. When they did not, farmers had abandoned farming. This was especially the case in Cheun Tukor where recent floods combined with farmer debt had destroyed the prospect of planting for another year, leaving 200 ha fallow while farmers left the land in search of income.

Interpreting Cambodia's agrarian change and the impact of hybrid rice varieties

The above case study material resonates with concerns raised about Southeast Asia's earlier experience of the Green Revolution, which stands as the quintessential example of the complex and often contradictory outcomes of agrarian change propelled by agro-industrialization. The term, first coined in 1968 refers to a 'revolution' in agricultural production based on an agro-industrial package of hybrid seed, fertilizers, pesticides, irrigation systems, agricultural extension programs and mechanization. This package spread throughout the world, and in countries like India, Thailand and Indonesia it doubled rice yields. The Green Revolution, however, was strongly criticized for its impacts on the environment and biodiversity and rural social structures (see Bray, 1986; Griffin, 1974; Pearse, 1980; Shiva, 1991; Glaeser, 1987).

Chemical fertilizers and pesticides invariably accompany the use of hybrid varieties and their use tends to exacerbate soil degradation,[12] while reducing the availability of other flora and fauna important to farmer livelihoods and food security (Roberts, 2005). This is particularly problematic in Cambodia, where few farmers receive agricultural extension services or training regarding the appropriate use of agricultural chemicals. As the majority of agro-chemicals are illegally imported into Cambodia and have labels written in another language, the need for agricultural extension services is high (Chamroeun *et al.*, 2002; CEDAC, 2004). In a study conducted by Chamroeun *et al.* (2002) researchers found that Cambodian farmers involved in long-term chemical fertilizer use reported reduced soil quality, necessitating ongoing inputs. Compounding this problem, most soil types identified in Cambodia have low natural fertility (Johnsen and Munford, 2012) and many smallholding families do not produce sufficient compost or manure to improve soil fertility substantially.[13] Where labour is scarce, as it increasingly is in areas of Cambodia affected by high levels of urban migration, chemical fertilizers are an easy, labour saving method of improving soil performance.

Pesticide use is also more commonly associated with hybrid varieties grown by farmers during the dry season; a time when pest levels are the highest. But use of pesticides compromises agro-biodiversity and therefore food security. For example, Shams (2007) noted that Cambodian food systems are traditionally reliant on entire rice field eco-systems, not just the rice itself. Cambodian farmers often forage among rice fields for paddy rats, insects, frogs, fish and wild vegetables for sale and consumption. Shams argued that although rice production may be uncompetitive, taking into account the yield of non-cultivated products reveals Cambodian rice fields as highly productive. Indeed, Cambodia has emerged as a major regional supplier in the informal cross-border insect trade with Thailand and Vietnam (Macan-Makar, 2013). Agricultural modernization projects, however, are typically associated with increased agro-ecological simplification (monocultures) leading to reduced agro-diversity and therefore reduced eco-system services. This in turn compromises risk management and adaptation strategies in the face of natural disasters and ongoing climate change. The agro-ecological diversity of smallholders is therefore not just an issue for livelihoods; but as Thurpp (2000 in Lockie, 2009, p. 408) pointed out, it is an issue of global public goods, as it is commonly acknowledged that poor farmers in the developing world manage the largest stock of agricultural genetic resources in the most diverse agro-ecosystems.

The ability of smallholders to manage these stocks therefore depends on the stability and sustainability of their livelihoods. In Southeast Asia, sustainable agrarian livelihoods have their roots in urban linkages and off-farm work; in combining agricultural and non-agricultural pursuits. Indeed, Rigg (1997) argued that the persistence of smallholder subsistence farming in the region does not always imply the existence of autarchic rural communities impoverished by their lack of access to modern markets, trade and development. Rather, commercialization in the form of production for the market, monetary exchange, sale and rent of land, and migration for work all pre-date modern agriculture in the region. Rigg (ibid., p. 158) therefore argues that the quintessential perception of Southeast Asia as deeply agrarian, comprised of subsistence-oriented farming families toiling away in their paddy fields, is wrong. Instead, the persistence of smallholder agrarian landscapes is inextricably tied to the rural sector's interdependence on non-farm economies, trade and urban linkages. In other words, a symbiosis exists between the agricultural sector and the urban sector, with subsistence-oriented agricultural production subsidising the urban sector through keeping labour costs low, while off-farm wage sources remitted to the rural sector help drive productivity investments in mechanization, fertilizers, improved seeds and other labour-saving devices (ibid., p. 205). Thus, while agricultural livelihoods may subsidize industry, off-farm wages earned in the industrial or urban sectors bolster productivity and stabilize rural livelihoods (ibid., p. 247). Such symbiosis between rural and urban, market and subsistence systems, is often played out at the household level between different generations. The young leave the farm to seek their fortunes elsewhere, while the old maintain the village base (Rigg, 2006).

This situation has led some to champion the smallholder farm as not only a key foundation of social stability under conditions of rapid and uneven economic growth, but also as an often-overlooked buffer against the vagaries of economic growth. This is aided by the contention that small farms are often far more efficient and productive than large farms or plantations (Hazell *et al.*, 2007), shattering the widely perceived association between large-scale agriculture, economic development and modernity. Instead, numerous studies find that where smallholders exist, they often possess inherent productivity advantages relative to large farms (Lockie, 2009; Timmer, 2004; Agrifood Consulting International, 2005, p. 27). Furthermore, this inherent productivity does not automatically result in improved market integration for agricultural products. The low prices and high transaction costs associated with any subsistence crop such as rice typically negate widespread commercialization in all but the largest economies of scale. Thus, while agricultural subsidies protect and enable loss-making agricultural production in much of Europe and the United States, subsidies for agricultural production in Southeast Asia are largely facilitated by the private flows from remittance economies that may also stabilize rural livelihoods.

In the preceding cases, hybrid rice varieties combined with off-farm remittances enabled middle-income farmers to produce rice for both the market and their own consumption. This mix of modern and traditional production techniques, on and off-farm incomes also enabled the farmers of Prey T'bal to sustain themselves and their agro-ecological surroundings. For richer and poorer farmers in the study area, their ability to sustain themselves and the landscapes they managed through the production of hybrid rice varieties proved precarious, in the face of severe floods and low market prices. In some cases de-agrarianization has ensued (Rigg, 2001, 2006). Achieving sustainable smallholder livelihoods in these cases depended on a diversity of production methods and incomes.

Conclusion

Agrarian change in Cambodia is happening at a lightning pace. It can be difficult to keep up let alone interpret what these changes mean for rural livelihoods and ecologies. The contradictions inherent in rural landscapes undergoing rapid transformation are further exacerbated by the fragmented approaches of donors working in the rural space promoting a broad spectrum of agricultural development philosophies and perspectives. This chapter has examined the introduction of modern seed via private sector companies; and, while noting the drawbacks, showed that modern seed had the potential to benefit farmers and preserve agro-biodiversity in some instances. However, in other instances modernization of what has for centuries been Cambodia's subsistence crop has produced mixed results, leading to higher costs and risks for farmers, de-agrarianization, and loss of agro-biodiversity. These findings raise important questions about the nature of rural development debates in Cambodia that juggle: market-driven integration versus rights-based food sovereignty campaigns; and productivist agro-industrialization in the face of rising input costs versus agro-ecological approaches to farming that encourage the creation of post-productivist rural landscapes (Wilson and Rigg,

2003). While these debates rage among donor circles, Cambodian rural landscapes have rapidly transformed beyond simplistic models of rural development; with livelihoods becoming more economically and spatially diverse, highly differentiated and integrated into both rural and urban spheres. Donors promoting a plethora of ideologically driven agricultural development approaches would do well to consider instead the multiplicity of livelihood strategies required to maintain the integrity of Cambodia's agro-ecologies and rural communities.

Notes

1 Vulnerability mapping of Southeast Asia conducted by Yusuf and Francisco (2009) ranked Cambodia as being as vulnerable to the impacts of climate change as the Philippines.
2 Hybrid rice is produced by cross-breeding two different types of rice. It is typically more vigorous than non-hybrid varieties, producing up to 30 per cent more rice. As such, hybrid rice varieties are credited with helping countries achieve food security. The drawback of hybrid varieties, however, is that subsequent generations lose productivity quickly meaning that hybrid seed must be produced in laboratories, and farmers need to purchase new supplies each year. In addition, hybrid rice varieties also tend to be more vulnerable to disease and pests (Bray, 1986, p. 25).
3 Typically, NGOs have pursued rights-based approaches to smallholder livelihoods while bilateral donors such as AusAid and USAID have actively promoted value chain approaches. Official Development Assistance flows to Cambodia are highly fragmented. Thirty-nine multilateral and bilateral agencies provide the $529 million allocated by Development Assistance Committee members (Chanboreth and Hach, 2008, p. 3). Many donors also provide small amounts of less than $5 million. In 2008, 35 development agencies supported 1,300 separate projects of which 700 were ongoing (ibid., p. 23). More than 400 donor missions, reviews and studies are conducted each year in Cambodia. Consequently, government officials are estimated to spend at least 50 per cent of their time dealing with aid projects (Chanboreth and Hach, 2008, p. 2).
4 IRRI stands for International Rice Research Institute.
5 Mak (2001) stated that preference for IR66 by farmers is due to its suitable duration in relation to the field size and water availability, and other characteristics including plant height, straw and grain yield, eating quality and price (2001, p. 144).
6 This research was undertaken with a volunteer staff member and a paid staff member of AQIP and resulted in a small report entitled 'AQIP Seed Supply Chain Benefits, Pilot Study Report 2005'.
7 Village identification was conducted over a one-week period from 26 September 2005.
8 Focus groups research and farmer surveys were conducted over a 4-week period from 10 October 2005 to 4 November 2005.
9 These surveys were intended to verify the focus group data and collect further detailed information regarding seed use, inputs and production methods, outputs and harvest use, and perceptions of different seed varieties.
10 These interviews were conducted from 28 November 2005 to 5 December.
11 Data on landless farmers collected in 2005 were: Prey Angkoing 10 households; Prey T'bal 15 households; T'lov 70 households; Cheun T'ukor 120 households.

Follow up research in 2013 with village chiefs revealed that land was increasingly being abandoned by farmers; however, specific numbers were not available.
12 There is currently no reliable data on the extent of soil erosion in Cambodia (Johnsen and Munford, 2012).
13 Approximately 10 tonnes of manure and compost is needed per hectare (Thavat, 2011). Johnsen and Munford reported that average fertilizer use per household has now reached 115 kg per production season (2012, p. 4).

References

ACIL. (2006) *Final Activity Completion Report – Agriculture Quality Improvement Project*, Milestone 88, ACIL Australia, Hunter Consulting, CamConsult and AusAID, Melbourne.
Agrifood Consulting International. (2005) *Final Report for the Cambodian Agrarian Structure Study*, Prepared for the Ministry of Agriculture, Forestry and Fisheries, Royal Government of Cambodia, the World Bank, the Canadian International Development Agency (CIDA) and the Government of Germany/Gesellschaft für Technische Zusammenarbeit (GTZ), Bethesda, MD.
AusAID. (1999) *Draft Report Agricultural Quality Improvement Project: Project Design Document*, AusAID, Canberra.
Bernstein, H. (2003) 'Farewells to peasantry', *Transformations* 52, pp. 1–19.
Berg, A. G. and Ostry, J. D. (2011) *Inequality and Unsustainable Growth: Two Sides of the Same Coin?* IMF Staff Discussion Note, The International Monetary Fund, Washington, DC.
Bray, F. (1986) *The Rice Economies*, Basil Blackwell, Oxford.
Caouette, D. and Turner, S. (eds) (2009) *Agrarian Angst and Rural Resistance in Contemporary Southeast Asia*, Routledge, London and New York.
CDRI. (2006) *The World Bank's 2006 Cambodian Poverty Assessment: A CDRI Response*, Cambodian Development Resource Institute, Phnom Penh.
Cambodian Development Resource Institute (CDRI). (2014) *Impact of High Food Prices in Cambodia: Survey Report*, Cambodia Development Resource Institute, Phnom Penh.
Centre d'Etude de Développment Agricole Cambodgien (CEDAC). (2004) *Pesticide Use and Consequence in Cambodia*, Centre d'Etude de Développment Agricole Cambodgien, Phnom Penh.
Chamroeun, M., Kiet, V. and Votthy, S. (2002) 'Survey on environmental and health effects of agro-chemical use in rice production in Takeo province, Cambodia', in B. McKenny (ed.) *Economy and Environment: Case Studies in Cambodia*, Environment and Economy Program in Southeast Asia, Singapore, pp. 8–13.
Chanboreth, E. and Hach, S. (2008) *Aid Effectiveness in Cambodia*, Working Paper 7, Wolfenson Centre for Development, Brookings Institution, Washington, DC.
Central Intelligence Agency (CIA). (2009) 'Cambodia.' *The World Factbook*, https://www.cia.gov/library/publications/the-world-factbook/geos/cb.html, accessed 20 August 2009.
Dollar, D. and Kraay, A. (2007) 'Trade, growth and poverty', in J. Clift and E. Diehl (eds) *Financial Globalization: A compilation of Articles from Finance and Development*, International Monetary Fund, Washington, DC, pp. 70–75.
Fukai, S. (2006) *Rice Production in Southeast Asia for Sustainable Agriculture and Environment–International Collaboration for Rice Technology Development*, Paper

presented at the NIAES International Symposium, Evaluation and Effective Use of Environmental Resources for Sustainable Agriculture in Monsoon Asia–Toward International Research Collaboration, National Institute for Agro-Environmental Sciences, Tsukuba, Japan.

Glaeser, B. (ed.) (1987) *The Green Revolution Revisited: Critique and Alternatives*, Allen and Unwin, London.

Griffin, K. (1974) *The Political Economy of Agrarian Change: An Essay on the Green Revolution*, Harvard University Press, Cambridge MA.

Hall, D., Hirsch, P. and Li, T. M. (2011) *Powers of Exclusion: Land Dilemmas in Southeast Asia (Challenges of the Agrarian Transition in Southeast Asia)*, National University of Singapore Press, Singapore.

Hazell, P., Poulton, S., Wiggens, S. and Dorward, A. (2007) *The Future of Small Farms for Poverty Reduction and Growth*, 2020 Discussion Paper No. 42, International Food Policy Research Institute, Washington, DC.

Helmers, K. (1997) 'Rice in the Cambodian economy: Past and present', in H. J. Nesbitt (ed.) *Rice Production in Cambodia*, Cambodia-IRRI-Australia-Project, Phnom Penh, pp. 1–14.

Hirsch, P. (2012) 'Reviving agrarian studies in South-East Asia: Geography on the ascendancy', *Geographical Research* 50, pp. 393–403.

Hughes, C. and Un, K. (2011) 'Cambodia's economic transformation: Historical and theoretical frameworks', in C. Hughes and K. Un (eds) *Cambodia's Economic Transformation*, Nordic Institute of Asian Studies, Copenhagen, pp. 1–26.

Intergovernmental Panel on Climate Change (IPCC). (2002) *Climate Change and Biodiversity*, IPCC Technical Paper V, IPCC, Geneva.

Javier, E. L. (1997) 'Rice ecosystems and varieties' in H. J. Nesbitt (ed.) *Rice Production in Cambodia*, Cambodia-IRRI-Australia-Project, Phnom Penh, pp. 39–81.

Johnsen, S. and Munford, G. (2012) *Country Environment Profile*, Royal Kingdom of Cambodia, European Union, Euronet Consortium, Brussels.

Lockie, S. (2009) 'Agricultural biodiversity and neoliberal regimes of agri-environmental governance in Australia', *Current Sociology* 57, pp. 407–426.

Long, A., Sorn, V. and Thavat, M. (2005) *AQIP Seed Supply Chain Benefits*, Pilot Study Report 2005, Agricultural Quality Improvement Project, Phnom Penh.

Macan-Makar, M. (2013) 'Thailand's insect farms creating a buzz', *The Irrawaddy*, www.irrawaddy.org/asia/thailands-insect-farms-creating-buzz.html, accessed 28 October 2013.

Mak, S. (2001) 'Continued innovation in a Cambodian rice-based farming system: Farmer testing and recombination of new elements', *Agricultural Systems* 69, pp. 137–149.

Marshall, G. R., Patrick, I. W., Muktasam, A. and Ambarawati, I. G. A. A. (2006) *Alleviating Poverty by Linking Smallholders with Agribusiness: Roles of Social Capital and Common Property*, Paper presented at 11th Biennial Conference of the International Association for the Study of Common Property, Ubud, Bali, Indonesia.

Nesbitt, H. J. and Phaloeun, C. (1997) 'Rice-based farming systems', in H. J. Nesbitt (ed.) *Rice Production in Cambodia*, , International Rice Research Institute Manila, Phnom Penh, pp. 31–37.

Nevens, J. and Peluso, N. L. (eds) (2008) *Taking Southeast Asia to Market: Commodities, Nature and People in the Neoliberal Age*, Cornell University Press, Ithaca and London.

Ovesen, J., Trankell, I. and Ojendal, J. (1996) *When Every Household is an Island: Social Organization and Power Structures in Rural Cambodia*, Uppsala Research Reports in Cultural Anthropology, Department of Cultural Anthropology Uppsala University and Sida Stockholm Sweden.

Parnwell, M. (2001) 'Coping with crisis in Thailand: Migration reversal, survivalist strategies and development implications', in P. Masina (ed.) *Rethinking Development in East Asia: From the Miracle Mythology to the Economic Crisis*, Curzon, London, pp. 261–281.

Pearse, A. (1980) *Seeds of Plenty, Seeds of Want: Social and Economic Implications of the Green Revolution*, Clarendon Press, Oxford.

Renwick, N. (2011) 'Millennium Development Goal 1: Poverty, hunger and decent work in Southeast Asia', *Third World Quarterly* 32, pp. 65–89.

Rigg, J. (1997) *Southeast Asia: The Human Landscape of Modernisation and Development*, Routledge, London and New York.

Rigg, J. (1998) 'Rural–urban interactions, agriculture and wealth: A southeast Asian perspective', *Progress in Human Geography* 22, pp. 497–522.

Rigg, J. (2001) *More Than the Soil: Rural Change in South-east Asia*, Prentice Hall, Harlow.

Rigg, J. (2006) 'Land, farming, livelihoods and poverty: Rethinking the links in the rural south', *World Development* 34, pp. 180–202.

Rigg, J. and Vandergeest, P. (eds) (2012) *Revisiting Rural Places: Pathways to Poverty and Prosperity in Southeast Asia*, National University of Singapore, Singapore.

Roberts, A. (2005) *Fields in Transition, Livelihoods in Transition: Agro-Diversity and Incremental Change in Smallholder-Managed Landscapes in Cambodia*, Institute of Economic Botany, City University of New York.

Shams, N. (2007) 'Contribution of rice field ecosystems to food security strategies in Northwest Cambodia', *Journal of Sustainable Agriculture* 29, pp. 109–133.

Shiva, V. (1991) *The Violence of The Green Revolution*, Zed Books, London.

Sokhen, C., Kanika, D. and Moustier, P. (2004) *Vegetable Market Flows and Chains in Phnom Penh*, Sustainable Development of Peri-Urban Agriculture in Southeast Asia Project (Susper), CIRAD, AVRDC, French MOFA, Hanoi.

Thavat, M. (2011) 'The tyranny of taste: The case of organic rice in Cambodia', *Asia Pacific Viewpoint* 52, pp. 285–298.

Thompson, E. (2007) *Unsettling Absences: Urbanism in Rural Malaysia*, Singapore University Press, Singapore.

Timmer, P. (2004) *Food Security and Economic Growth: An Asian Perspective*, Center for Global Development, Washington, DC.

UNDP. (2013) *The Rise of the South: Human Progress in a Diverse World*, UNDP, New York.

UNESCAP. (2008) *A Future Within Reach*, United Nations Economic and Social Commission for Asia and the Pacific, Bangkok.

USAID. (2008) *Prey Veng: Cambodia's Untapped Business Locale*, Investment Profile, USAID, Washington, DC.

Vorley, B., Del Pozo-Vergnes, E. and Barnett, A. (2012) *Small Producer Agency in the Globalised Market: Making Choices in a Changing World*, International Institute for Environment and Development, London and Hivos, The Hague.

Walker, A. (2010) 'Royal sufficiency and elite misrepresentations of rural livelihoods', in S. Ivarsson and L. Isager. (ed.) *Saying the Unsayable: Monarchy and Democracy in Thailand*, NIAS Press, Copenhagen, pp. 241–266.

Wilson, G. A. and Rigg, J. (2003) ' "Post-productivist" agricultural regimes and the south: Discordant concepts?' *Progress in Human Geography* 27, pp. 681–707.

World Food Programme (WFP). (2014) *Livelihoods,* World Food Programme, http://www.foodsecurityatlas.org/khm/country/access/livelihoods, accessed 10 February 2014.

World Bank. (2014) 'GINI index', http://data.worldbank.org/indicator/SI.POV.GINI, accessed 8 April 2014.

Yu, B. and Diao, X. (2011) *Cambodia's Agricultural Strategy: Future Development Options for the Rice Sector,* A Policy Discussion Paper, International Food Policy Research Institute, Washington, DC.

Yusuf, A. and Francisco, H. (2009) *Climate Change Vulnerability Mapping for Southeast Asia,* Economy and Environment Program for Southeast Asia, SIDA, CIDA, IDRC, Singapore.

5 Land is life

An analysis of the role 'grand corruption' plays in enabling elite grabbing of land in Cambodia

Megan MacInnes

Introduction

On 22 November 2011, Mrs Chea Dara committed suicide by jumping off a bridge in the centre of Phnom Penh, Cambodia's capital (Licadho, 2011). Although she was leaving behind a husband and two children, her despair over the long-running dispute with a local development company who had illegally evicted her from her house and home in the centre of the city had become too much. Despite four years of advocacy, support from Cambodian civil society, international media and diplomatic and donor interventions – nothing was able to counter the power of the senator-tycoon who owned the company which had taken her land.

Cambodia is a 'country for sale'. As of late 2012, 2.6 million ha (hectares) of land had been leased to companies; equivalent to 73 per cent of the country's arable land and an increase of 16.7 per cent from 2011 (ADHOC, 2013, p. 7).[1] Of these investments, those which are large-scale land concessions ('economic land concessions', or ELCs) are intended to intensify agricultural production; be conducted in accordance with local land use plans; increase employment and contribute to living standards; protect the environment; and encourage investment while generating state revenues (Royal Government of Cambodia, 2005, Articles 3 and 5). However, they are failing on all counts. According to the government's own statistics, five tycoons hold 20 per cent of total land allocated through concessions, amounting to more than half a million ha.[2] This is despite the legal threshold of one company or individual's land holding being fixed at a maximum of 10,000 ha.[3] Moreover, it is estimated that land-grabbing resulting from weak control of ELCs has affected 400,000 Cambodians in 12 provinces since 2003 (Licadho, 2013). Protests against the concessions' advance are rising rapidly. In 2012, the government arrested more than twice as many people during housing and land disputes than the previous year and land disputes were at the top of the country's 2013 general election agenda (ADHOC, 2013, p. 32). As such, the phenomenon of land grabbing is having a transformative impact on Cambodia's people; from the forced dispossession of land, to the social deprivation, landlessness and landscape change which results, to the ultimate consequences for political and social action.

Corruption pervades Cambodia; global corruption perception indices rank it 160th out of 177 countries.[4] Cambodia's corruption is not just every day petty bribery, but 'grand corruption' wherein the problem is endemic and reaches the highest levels of the public sphere. The breadth and scope of this corruption means that decisions are made about land without a thought for their negative impact on local farmers and indigenous communities, or compliance with legal safeguards. Consequently, biased or corrupt decisions frequently result in the rich and powerful in Cambodia gaining all the benefits, while the poor and vulnerable, like Mrs Chea Dara, pay all the costs.

My objective in writing this chapter is to use two case studies of well-known land disputes in Cambodia to analyse the relationship between the phenomena of land grabbing and grand corruption. I examine first the role grand corruption plays by enabling such individuals to grab land, second how it prevents communities negatively affected by these land grabs from accessing justice and third how it consolidates elite capture of the state. In doing so, I provide a typology of the relationship between grand corruption and land grabbing. Both cases involve individuals of significant power within Cambodia's business and political elite, therefore in order to protect local activists involved in both disputes, I have anonymized the sources where necessary.

'Land grabbing' and 'grand corruption': Defining the terms and setting the scene

The rush for land playing out in Cambodia is not unique. Across the global south, the impact of increasing commercial pressure on land since 2008 has been well documented by policy makers, scholars and the media (Anseeuw *et al.*, 2012, Global Witness *et al.*, 2012; Deininger and Byerlee, 2011). However, the relationship between the phenomenon of 'land grabbing' and corruption is less well understood. Analysis by Transparency International (2011) took steps to understand the role of corruption in inequitable land distribution, however as this chapter identifies, the interplay between grand corruption and land grabbing is highly complex and needs additional empirical research. Furthermore, the secretive nature of how many large-scale land investments are undertaken hampers efforts to examine the extent, modalities and implications of corruption within this sector.

Although (following Hall *et al.*, 2011, p. 4) 'all land use and access requires exclusion of some kind', what has marked recent trends in land ownership in many developing countries is the pace and scale of exclusion, leading to dramatic negative social, environmental and governance transformations (Borras *et al.*, 2010; Borras *et al.* 2011). Such trends have received significant attention from international policy makers (e.g. Deininger and Byerlee, 2011) as well as researchers and scholars (e.g. Pollack *et al.*, 2014; Peluso and Lund, 2011; Borras *et al.*, 2011; and several special issues of the *Journal of Peasant Studies* Volume 37 Issue 4, 2010; Volume 38 Issue 4, 2011; Volume 39 Issue 1, 2012 and Volume 40 Issue 3, 2013). Hall *et al.* (2011) focused on these new forms of exclusion in Southeast Asia. In his *Journal of Peasant Studies* paper, Hall furthermore highlighted Southeast Asia's crop booms as providing insight into who is seeking to benefit from such acquisitions, how they are doing so (and to what extent such a resource capture directly involves the state; namely 'licensed exclusions') and in what way booms differentially effect areas under varying land tenure regimes (Hall, 2011 p. 844). Rising tension over land rights specific to Cambodia is also receiving increasing academic attention. For example, analysis of neopatrimonial restrictions on land reform (Un and So, 2011), how land titling interacts with the allocation of ELCs, as well as the drivers of current land grabbing trends (Dwyer, 2012; Neef and Touch, 2012) and the extent to which evictions are frequently under-written by law (Springer, 2013).

However, because of my position with Global Witness, I have chosen to embed this paper within the work of international organizations addressing such trends from an advocacy perspective. As such, I have used the definition of land grabbing adopted by a coalition of actors at the forefront of trying to reduce the phenomenon's negative impacts, during a conference in Tirana, Albania, in 2011.[5] This Tirana Declaration defines large-scale acquisitions or concessions as problematic if they do not: comply with human rights frameworks; take into consideration the social, environmental or economic impacts; provide transparency of contract terms and benefit sharing; or allow independent oversight and remedy. In terms of relevant, international normative frameworks, the Voluntary Guidelines on the Responsible Governance of Tenure of Land, Fisheries and Forests in the Context of National Food Security, endorsed in May 2012, are the first international standards explicitly focusing on the relationship between land rights, tenure governance and international human rights law, in response to increasing commercial pressure on land.[6]

Between 2000 and 2013, it is estimated that in low- and middle-income countries at least 49 million ha of land has been leased to companies, or is under negotiation.[7] Key drivers include increasing demand for food, fuel (biofuels), fibre and other raw materials. Speculation and international investors diversifying shareholdings away from stock markets since the 2008 economic crisis have also contributed, as described by McMichael (2012). As competition increases to control and exploit land, and the natural resources on and below it, the attractiveness of corrupting such processes for personal gain also increases. The way in which such a demand for land is manifesting in acquisitions or concessions which include one or more of the risks above, that is, fuelling 'land grabs', has been thoroughly analysed through the lens of rights violations, food security, land reform processes, environmental risks and transparency.[8] In the areas most recently targeted for investment in Africa, Asia and Latin America, neopatrimonial modes of governance have been instrumental in creating the conditions for land grabbing. Inequitable power dynamics, legal pluralism and state-licensed exclusion of people from their land is analysed by Hall *et al.* (2011); however, the role that corruption plays merits further investigation.

In terms of the second conceptual term which this chapter focuses on – corruption – policy makers, the World Bank and international organizations such as Transparency International, define it to be 'the abuse of entrusted power for private gain'.[9] According to Cockcroft, an economist and founder of Transparency International, corruption ranges from single acts of bribery to ultimately the decay of society: '[corruption] always involves the acquisition of money, assets or power in a way which escapes the public view; is usually illegal; and is at the expense of society as a whole either at a "grand" or everyday level' (2012, p. 2). Global institutions such as the World Bank embed their practical application of anti-corruption measures within the UN Convention against Corruption, adopted by the UN General Assembly in 2003.[10] Within academic literature meanwhile, Gupta (1995) examined the differentiated way in which corruption impacted on state functions, and people's interactions with them. Nuijten and Anders (2009) significantly evolved the conceptualization of corruption and its interaction with the state from an ethnographic perspective, recognizing the range of different responses from the actors involved, across moral and legal frameworks. However, it is Cockcroft's definition and manifestation of 'grand corruption' which I use in this analysis of the phenomenon's multi-faceted relationship with land grabbing.

Although I have more than a decade's worth of experience working on natural resource governance issues in Cambodia, my current position as a staff member of the international campaigning organization, Global Witness, has strongly influenced the framing of this chapter. First, I recognize that the context of escalating land disputes in Cambodia could have been analysed through a number of alternative frameworks; for example, the trade-offs between large-scale and small-scale investment modalities or the impact of decentralizing state-based decision-making on state-citizen accountability.

Second, (following Hall *et al.*, 2011), land exclusions in Cambodia can be both licensed by the state (as in case study one) and state-backed (as in case study two). Both examples highlight the way in which land grabs can violate a number of social and environmental protections in law, but none-the-less have the backing of the state. As such, and following Springer (2013), although the country's 2001 Land Law is considered relatively progressive in comparison to some neighbouring countries, the legal framework and its implementation in Cambodia as a whole is increasingly unjust and used with violence against its own people. In this paper, I therefore analyse how 'grand corruption' can help the facilitation of land grabbing by enabling individuals to ignore the law with impunity, to enable the promulgation of new laws which are themselves violent and unjust, and to misuse existing laws to underwrite land grabbing.

The tension between Cambodia's relatively strong social and environmental protection in law and its weak implementation can be regarded as a manifestation of structural violence. Galtung examined the latent and predictable nature of 'structural violence', particularly with regard to how power is used to maintain unequal distribution of (and control over) resources (1969). Mosse (2007) and others have further developed the concept of 'structural institutionalized violence' in relation to how the balance of poverty and inequality, and wealth and opportunity, can be institutionally maintained by the state and its rulers. This institutional misuse of power for personal gain closely aligns with the goal of grand corruption, according to Cockcroft ' . . . [p]ersonal enrichment is nearly always a key objective, although corruption may be engineered by a group with the intention of achieving or retaining political power, so that these motives can become closely entwined' (2012, p. 2).

It could be argued therefore that approaches to support victims of land grabbing in Cambodia which base advocacy positions on the legal framework and implementation of the rule of law could do better by targeting these underlying institutional structures. However, such a position presumes the Cambodian government to operate as a hegemonic entity. In my experience, there are in fact reformers and reform-minded institutions within government which are as equally convinced as the affected communities of the need for improved rule of law and are therefore responsive to such framings. Furthermore, Cambodia shows that the most effective advocacy activities, especially those involving international actors (e.g. via financial or supply-chain based relationships), are those which have articulated a clear and binding framework for analysis. The law, as it is written, being the most tangible currently. An additional rationale for focusing on legal frameworks is that international investment companies (who play an increasingly important role in Cambodia's land grabbing crisis) are duty bound to follow the national law, even if the state and its rulers chose not to. Further examples of what these responsibilities mean for ELC companies in practice are provided in the Global Witness report *Rubber Barons*, published in 2013.

In terms of addressing the challenge of land grabbing, policy and institutional responses have so far primarily targeted the state and state-based agencies. However, the presence of grand corruption (at every and all levels of government) can fundamentally undermine these basic state functions, as further outlined below. This potential contradiction has implications for the effectiveness of state-focused initiatives to tackle land grabbing, a question I attempt to address in this chapter.

An analysis of the theoretical relationship between land grabbing and grand corruption

Land grabbing, grand corruption and their subsequent deleterious impact on governance can be viewed as mutually reinforcing. Government officials and companies acting corruptly enable land grabbing when they ignore legal and regulatory safeguards, collude to capture the state and its natural resource wealth, or act with impunity. Following Levi (1988, p. 3) on state predation and Hall *et al.* (2011), in the most extreme cases the state itself becomes criminally and entrepreneurially involved in the capture of land. Once land is grabbed it provides revenues to business and political elites (this can be on-budget, but is frequently off-budget or illicit) which further strengthens their hold on influence and power. This subsequently increases the likelihood of future corruption. While the corrupt behaviours and actors themselves may be similar throughout these interactions, the dimensions, impacts and potential remedies differ, and therefore are analysed separately throughout the following section.

This institutionalization of perverted benefits and vested interests resulting from corrupt land grabbing are examples of how 'shadow states' are created.[11] According to Reno (2000) rulers in shadow states are able to 'manipulate external actors' access to both formal and clandestine markets, especially by relying on global recognition of sovereignty; and this in turn undermines formal government institutions (p. 434). However, reflecting on Galtung (1969), Levi (1988) and Mosse (2007), formal institutions can themselves operate in violent and unjust ways which may result in a shadow state operating symbiotically within a formal state structure.

Decision-making in the land sector that favours elite interests

Corruption facilitates land grabbing in a number of ways. Fundamentally, it is a manifestation of the vested interests and abuse of power involved when government officials at a national and/or local level, and companies interested in leasing or acquiring land (both public and private), act with disregard for the rule of law or negative consequences.

Corruption can occur in the land sector in various forms. First, government officials accept 'bribes' from a company in exchange for ignoring or perverting laws, facilitating swift transactions, giving preferential treatment or perverting justice. 'Bribes' include payments in cash and/or in kind, as well as other favours. These benefit flows give rise to ad hoc corruption where individual government officials act corruptly while their colleagues turn a blind eye, as well as the institutionalization of such behaviour across government and regulatory agencies. In some cases such corruption, especially at the local level, can be due to lack of capacity, budgetary resources and oversight from central levels of government, however in others it can be more organized.

Second, corruption can also occur when vested interests are endemic to the point that senior government officials, politicians and their family members directly own or are involved in companies which are being given land through leases and acquisitions, despite the fact that this violates some social and environmental protections in the law. In these cases, a physical bribe may not have actually been given or received, but the ownership or connections between the government official and the company mean that the official in question personally benefits from the deal, with the relationship kept deliberately secret. Again, this enables companies to receive special treatment, pervert regulations and justice, and ignore negative social, environmental and governance impacts.

Both forms of corruption can occur at all levels of government and are frequently organized, such that petty officials accept payments with the expectation that part of it will be passed up the chain of command, so as to share the revenues. Although local government officials receiving bribes from companies involved in large-scale land investments is a more common understanding of corruption, grand, or central-level, corruption which is institutionalized across government agencies is a more significant problem. When this occurs, policies and central functions of the state are distorted and leaders benefit at the expense of the public good. As a result, government decision-making about who gets to own and use what land, for which purpose, is not based on recognition of local rights, food security objectives, environmental sustainability or even economic growth. Rather, land and natural resources (which frequently already have a number of users dependent on them) are allocated to which ever company is best connected and willing to pay the highest price. When such corruption is present, and especially if it reaches the highest executive level, it undermines basic elements of accountability between the state and its citizens, detrimental even in fledgeling democracies such as Cambodia. Government officials, for example, ignore their public responsibilities in favour of allegiance to companies and patrons, giving rise to neo-patrimonial rule and structural violence. It also becomes almost impossible for any level of government department or international donor agency to implement reforms aimed at improving governance and mobilizing the country's own natural resource base towards developmental objectives.

Victims denied access to judicial and accountability mechanisms

In addition to corruption distorting legal procedure and due process when the decision-making around the acquisition and allocation of rights to large-scale land investments is being taken at the beginning of a project's life-cycle, corruption also occurs and has impacts throughout project implementation, and beyond. The most problematic way this occurs from the perspective of victims of land grabbing is when accountability, regulatory or judicial mechanisms responsible for ensuring that land investment projects are just, legally compliant and protecting human rights, are corrupted. This can occur, for example, when attempts by communities who have lost land to file complaints with the courts or non-judicial mechanisms are thwarted by officials paid not to cooperate. A separate impact during the implementation phase is when corruption prevents independent monitoring and evaluation of ongoing projects, enabling the company to ignore regulations and safeguards, operate outside of contractual terms and conditions and prevent regulatory authorities from enforcing sanctions or annulling contracts.

Another way in which this occurs is when companies or individuals acquiring the land are well-connected enough to employ police, military and the courts to silence or block community activism through threats and intimidation, wrongful arrest and detention, spurious charges and other tactics. Research by my colleagues at Global Witness revealed that land and forest activists around the world are facing increasingly deadly responses from governments, companies and the armed forces. At least 908 people were killed in 35 countries for attempting to protect their rights to land and the environment between 2002 and 2013, with the death rate rising in the last 4 years to an average of two activists a week (Global Witness, 2012, 2014).

How land grabs intensify and precipitate corruption?

The negative consequences of these interactions between land grabbing and corruption are multiple, transformative and reinforcing. They range from lost or perverted revenue streams, the consolidation of power and influence of the elites, the further disenfranchisement from state functions of the victims of such land grabs, all of which ultimately undermines state accountability.

According to the World Bank, large-scale transfers of land for commercial investment theoretically have a number of potential macro and micro economic benefits; including generating employment and revenue streams, improving food security and fostering technology transfer (Deininger and Byerlee, 2011). However, in reality (and apart from the direct negative impacts described above) there is significant leakage of actual and potential revenues from land deals. Corporate payments for acquiring concessions or property rights may, for example, be considered by state officials as bribes and as a result only a small percentage of such payments (if any) actually enter the national budget. Increased demand for land concessions (as natural resource exploitation has done in other sectors) can in fact fuel further corruption and subsequently erode state functions. Revenue generation can also be impacted when companies use their influence to negotiate favourable tax and royalty terms. In addition, corruption can prevent corporate taxes and royalties which are generated from these deals from trickling down to local levels of government or communities. If a government fails to generate taxes and other revenues from, for example, land leases, a deficit is created in the national budget which means it cannot afford to pay civil servants adequate salaries, fostering further demand for alternative incomes; namely bribes.

When land leases are speculative, if the company does not have the technical capacity, or if their financial backing is not secured, then local employment opportunities and other expected economic benefits do not occur. In some cases, even when the land is used productively, many local communities (often those who have lost significant areas of land to the company) are not offered employment opportunities as the company has brought in labour from other areas. In some cases, locally affected communities refuse to have anything to do with the company (such as accept work or salaries) because of their anger at losing their land. As a result, not only are such land grabs devastating to local livelihoods, food security, cultural well-being and the environment, they are also frequently not achieving their most fundamental theoretical economic objectives.

Communities impacted by land grabs are not only displaced by force from ancestral land, losing their livelihoods and blocked from accessing their share of the economic benefits; a deeper and more violent transformation is occurring. The impoverishment which comes from losing land and food security can disenfranchise households and create barriers against them participating in local level decision-making or accessing recourse or accountability mechanisms. Furthermore, certain rights as citizens, for example, the ability to register to vote in elections, can require residency at a permanent address. This means that once land is lost, so may be the ability to register as a citizen or be part of a community group, to vote or be recorded in censuses or other demographic data or have access to judicial and non-judicial forms of redress. In other situations, households who have lost land have no choice but to be employed as labourers for the plantation company which took their land; in doing so they are perceived by some as losing the last vestige of their right to denounce the company's operations.

Regimes characterized by such degrees of structural violence and 'shadow states' therefore enable the capture of power and resources by elites through two parallel processes. State rulers (formal and informal) undermine government institutions by manipulating bureaucratic structures and markets in order to 'enrich themselves and control others' (Reno, 2000, p. 437) and in such cases political power and private commercial operations become indistinguishable. Meanwhile, the poor and vulnerable households not only have their livelihoods directly affected, but impoverishment and disenfranchisement undermines their ability to hold such elites to account and the ability of basic state functions to respond.

Is the 'resource curse' extending to large-scale land investments?

For a number of years, Global Witness and other advocacy, policy and academic researchers have documented the way in which many countries rich in oil, gas and other minerals are, in spite of potential wealth, frequently mired in poverty due to the so-called 'resource curse' (also known as the paradox of plenty).[12] According to economist Jeffrey D. Sachs, this curse can be attributed to three phenomena: when resource-related capital inflows inflate currency values and crowd-out unrelated industries; the volatility of commodity prices and the negative impacts of resource abundance on fragile political institutions, providing opportunities for elite and illicit accumulation (Brown, 2008, p. 98). It is this third phenomenon and its implications for governance upon which Global Witness has traditionally focused.

Governance issues in countries such as Angola, Cambodia and Liberia show how natural resource abundance combined with poor governance, weak rule of law and tenure insecurity has enabled political and business elites to influence state processes and appropriate publicly held natural resources for personal profit.[13] It is this failure of governance which means that citizens of these countries have paid the costs of resource extraction but received very few of the benefits, and have no means to hold either the government or companies to account for decisions or actions which negatively affect them. In some of these countries, for example Cambodia, the gap between rich and poor, the powerful and the powerless has worsened as a result; inequality in these areas has increased in Cambodia since the 1900s.[14] Such trends cement interests within this elite to maintain the status quo and further disable ordinary citizens from demanding changes of policy and practice.

These problems have initially manifested in the extractive industries: oil and gas, minerals and timber. Since 2008, however, commercial pressure on the land itself has increased to the point that similar risks are now associated with large-scale land acquisitions and transfers. Again, this is particularly a problem in 'emerging markets' where political and regulatory institutions are fragile, where dubious investors rush in and where governments appear to be prioritizing investor interests over legislative safeguards and their duty to their citizenry. According to one global assessment of large-scale land acquisitions acquired by investors since 2000, 66 per cent of the land was in Africa and 21 per cent in Asia (Anseeuw et al., 2012). More than 20 per cent of all deals were given in forests, the study continued, frequently areas on which local livelihoods depend and which are under special protection for environmental purposes (on paper). Furthermore it concluded that globally, countries most affected by these deals are significantly poorer than average and struggle with significant agricultural yield gaps. Even more concerning is Deininger and Bylerlee's (2011) conclusions that lower recognition of land rights appears to increase a country's attractiveness for land acquisition by investors (pp. 96, 102).

The ultimate profitability of large-scale land investments is unlikely ever to equate to the revenue streams of the extractive industries sector. Nevertheless, the trends evident from increasing commercial interest in land indicate that fragile state institutions are already being undermined by such demand, thereby fitting one of Sachs' criteria for the resource curse. The question for countries such as Cambodia, who have already experienced the resource curse in other sectors, is whether they will learn from past experiences.

Case studies of the relationship between grand corruption and land grabbing

I selected these two case studies because they are exemplary and very well-known examples of licensed (in the case of Pheapimex) and state-backed (in the case of Kong Yu and Kong Thom) land grabs in Cambodia. The high level positions and personal connections of those involved in these cases provided detailed information about how power manifests in grand corruption and land grabbing. However, their notoriety also prevented a meaningful in-depth analysis without it becoming clear which individuals are involved, which is the basis for my decision to explicitly name the individuals involved. Nevertheless, the specific location and names of local people negatively impacted by both of these cases have been removed for their protection.

I undertook this research through a series of direct interviews with members of the affected communities and representatives from the civil society groups working with them, between November 2012 and February 2014. The fact that both cases are extremely well documented provided a wealth of direct and secondary source material through which the results of the interviews could be triangulated. Due to the highly sensitive nature of the allegations made against the named individuals, neither hearsay nor rumour was cited without additional evidence. Under the name of Global Witness, I wrote extensive letters to those involved outlining the allegations and asking for their perspective on the cases. Although these were sent by email, fax and hand-delivered, no responses were received by the date of publication.[15]

Case Study 1. Pheapimex: Overlapping state and private interests

The Director of Pheapimex, Mr Lau Meng Khin, is a Senator for the ruling Cambodian People's Party and his wife Choeung Sopheap (also known as 'Yeay Phu') regularly appears publicly alongside the prime minister's wife and used to be a leading member of the Cambodian Red Cross. Pheapimex, one of Cambodia's most powerful companies, currently holds a total of 335,142 ha in land concessions, equivalent to 13 per cent of the total area leased to companies.[16] Pheapimex first came to prominence as a logging concessionaire in the 1990s; every year between 2001 and 2004, Global Witness caught Pheapimex subcontractors and members of the Royal Cambodian Armed Forces illegally felling and processing significant volumes of timber in the company's Kompong Thom forest concession.[17]

In 2000 Pheapimex was given 315,028 ha of land in a 70-year lease located in Pursat and Kompong Chhnang provinces, for a eucalyptus plantation.[18] On 25 December 2000, at a ceremony attended by Prime Minister Hun Sen, the company signed a joint-venture with the Chinese Farm Cooperation Group to build a pulp and paper mill near the concession; a $70 million project financed by a loan from China's Import Export Bank (Lang, 2002; Cambodian Human Rights Committee, 2009).[19]

Between 2000 and 2004 Pheapimex began clearing and planting the area of their concession located in Pursat Province. This was done without any consultations with legitimate local land-owners, environmental impact assessments have never been done and details of the concession area (such as the maps) were not disclosed to locally affected households until 2010.[20] The social and environmental consequences of this concession have been devastating. It has affected access to farmland and forest resources of at least 100,000 local people. Villagers explained to me that the company had cleared significant areas of forest, including the resin trees on which many households rely on for an income source and which are given special protection in law, as well as clearing spirit forests, polluting the local environment with chemical fertilizers and destroying local water sources.[21] The promise of employment opportunities also never materialized. The company reportedly refused to employ local villagers on the concession, preferring to bring in labourers from other provinces, and employment conditions are poor with salaries low and paid late.[22]

Communities affected across both provinces have continually protested against this grabbing of their land and resources by Pheapimex. The company has employed members of Cambodia's armed forces (police and soldiers) to guard the concession area, who have responded with force. Protests escalated during 2004, with prominent activists being arrested on spurious charges. That year tragically culminated with a grenade attack on sleeping protestors on 13 November 2004, which left eight protestors severely injured. This has never been investigated by the government.[23]

In 2005 the Government introduced legislation governing all land leases, limiting company holdings to a maximum of 10,000 ha and requiring existing leases, larger than this, to be reduced (Royal Government of Cambodia, 2005, Article 38). However, according to the Government and the UN-OHCHR, Pheapimex has consistently refused to bring its concession within the law, has failed to pay its concession deposit and much of the land has remained unused since it was taken (UN-OHCHR, 2007, p. 11; Royal Government of Cambodia, 2008, p. 1).

Between 2004 and 2009, company operations on the concession ceased, but by 2010 land clearing began again, as did protests and subsequent violent responses and arrests by government authorities. Villagers filed complaints with the Pursat provincial court against the renewed clearing of their land and forest areas by the company, but by 2013 the courts had not yet responded.[24] In 2011 the Council of Ministers awarded communities in Pursat province rights to manage 6,000 ha of forest, under the Community Forestry model.[25] This included 500 ha located within Pheapimex's concession and should have been returned to the community, but up to the date of publication, the company has yet to give this land back.[26]

When I interviewed affected households from Kompong Chhnang in November 2013, they expressed concern that the company was about to start clearing the concession areas nearer to their villages. Although a new rapid land titling and dispute resolution process announced by Prime Minister Hun Sen in May 2012 and targeting land concessions had included Pheapimex's concession area, villagers were sceptical about whether this would result in their land being returned.[27]

Their scepticism reflected the company's other activities. Pheapimex has enjoyed a long relationship with the Cambodian armed forces, and has used members of the military to provide security and exert control over its forest concessions.[28] These relationships were cemented in February 2010, when the company was included in a list of 'official partnerships' announced by Prime Minister Hun Sen, between private businesses and Cambodian military units (Phalla and O'Toole, 2010; Brady, 2010). This policy officially sanctioned an arrangement wherein selected businesses were reported to get military protection in return for financial backing (Global Witness, 2010). Such partnerships are particularly concerning given the involvement of Cambodia's armed forced in exclusions, evictions and human rights violations by these same Cambodian companies (Brady, 2010).

Lau Meng Khin and his wife have previously accompanied Prime Minister Hun Sen on diplomatic trips to China.[29] The couple are formally involved in some of the most significant Chinese investments in Cambodia, indicative of their importance in maintaining Sino-Khmer commercial relations. These include the Chinese-owned Wuzhishan L.S. Group's concession; a 10,000 ha plantation which overlaps with indigenous peoples' land in Mondulkiri province.[30] The couple are involved in Shukaku Inc., which in February 2007 was granted a 99-year concession to develop 133 ha of land around Boeung Kak lake in Phnom Penh city.[31] The project is being developed in a joint-venture with a Chinese investor and has resulted in the displacement of more than 4,000 families and is the dispute over which Mrs Chea Dara committed suicide in November 2011.[32] Lau Meng Khin and his wife are also both directors of a company which is a subsidiary of China's largest dam building company, Sinohydro Corporation.[33] At a cost of $280 million, Sinohydro Corporation is constructing Cambodia's largest hydropower dam, in Kampot province, with finance from China's Exim Bank (ibid). Additionally, the couple own Cambodia International Investment Development Group.[34] This company is reportedly involved in a number of Chinese joint-ventures including a special economic zone and coal-fired power plant in southern Sihanoukville town and a bauxite exploration and processing project in north-eastern Mondulkiri and Kratie provinces.[35]

This case provides clear examples of the three modalities of land grabbing and 'grand corruption'. First, the power and influence Pheapimex holds in Cambodia has apparently enabled the company to ignore legal safeguards and due process, for example, being able to retain concession rights to more than 30 times the legal limit. Second, the company was reportedly able to work with government enforcement agencies to issue threats, arrest and bring charges against community activists in order to protect the company's commercial assets. This has had the impact of blocking community activists' attempts to get justice. Third, since gaining rights to the Pheapimex concession, Lau Meng Khin and his wife have reinvested their assets and furthered their economic position, which has in turn strengthened their relationship with the country's elite. This is evident in the couple's involvement in a number of other economically significant projects, particularly those involving Chinese investments.

Case Study 2. Kong Yu and Kong Thom: Undermining accountability mechanisms

In August 2004, Mrs Keat Kolney, the sister of Deputy Prime Minister and Former Senior Minister for Economy and Finance H.E. Keat Chhuon, and the wife of Secretary of State for Ministry of Land Management H.E. Chhan Saphann, announced she had purchased 450 ha of land from the villages of Kong Yu and Kong Thom, Ratanakiri province (EWMI, 2009, p. 13; Interviews with lawyers working on the case, November, 2012). This land, she claimed, was bought on a private basis, through more than 100 land transfer documents (EWMI, 2009, p. 16; CLEC, 2008). The indigenous Jarai minority communities of Kong Yu and Kong Thom dispute this claim saying they have been living and working this land for generations and despite the lack of title, according to the Land Law, it belongs to them collectively (EWMI, 2009, pp. 12–13; Amnesty International, 2008, pp. 8–9).[36] Sixty-five households in these two villages have lost ancestral agricultural land, burial grounds, spirit forests and natural resources on which their livelihoods depend (Walker, 2009; CLEC, 2008).

According to the villagers, between March and August 2004, they agreed under duress to give 50 ha of their land to local authorities, who told them the area was being taken to re-distribute it to disabled soldiers. This process involved villagers signing (by thumbprint) numerous documents on 20 August of that year approving the land transfer of 50 ha (some of the documents were in Khmer language which many do not read, and others were blank). They were not given copies of these documents (EWMI, 2009, pp. 12–13; Amnesty International, 2008, pp. 8–9). Approximately one week later, villagers explained, Keat Kolney arrived, accompanied by District and Commune government authorities and military officials, to distribute gifts and envelopes of money to the community (EWMI, 2009, p. 13; CLEC, 2010, p. 1). At this 'ceremony', villagers were asked to sign receipts for the gifts, again in a language they could not read, which in fact turned out to be contracts for the sale of the land; a fact the villagers were not informed about until the following day (CLEC, 2010, p. 2; EWMI, 2009, p. 13; Amnesty International, 2008, p. 9). Advocacy groups report that upwards of $20,000 was paid to local officials to complete this transaction (Asia Human Rights

Commission, 2007). Lawyers acting on behalf of the villagers also allege fraud, such as backdating land receipts and half of the land transfer receipts being signed by individuals who have never lived in either village and thus have no right to transfer village land, including local authorities (CLEC, 2008, p. 1; CLEC, 2010, p. 1–2).

Within a month villagers were prevented from accessing their fields and forest as the land was cleared to plant rubber by Keat Kolney. Between 2004 and 2007 communities tried to get their land back by filing complaints to government officials, holding public protests, filing petitions and contacting the media. However, these strategies failed, so on 23 January 2007 villagers filed civil and criminal complaints against Keat Kolney in the provincial court (Asia Human Rights Commission, 2007; EWMI, 2009, p. 13; Amnesty International, 2008, p. 9–10). A lawyer working on the case described it as a ' . . . no clearer example in Cambodia today of the rich and powerful exploiting the poor and marginalized. And no better opportunity for the judicial system to finally play its role in upholding the law and protecting the rights of ordinary citizens against the abuse of power'.[37]

Unfortunately, such optimism has been dashed. After more than 6 years since the lawsuit was filed, the provincial court has dropped criminal charges against Keat Kolney and is yet to decide if the civil case will move to trial (Kuch, 2012a, 2012b; Interview with lawyers working on the case, November 2012). Since 2007 five different provincial court judges have been assigned to the case but none have taken action to investigate the original civil complaints filed by the communities who lost their land (Kuch, 2012c; Interview with lawyers working on the case, November 2012). Local media reports this as being due to political interference from supporters of Keat Kolney, describing how the provincial president of the court stated that judges were too scared to get involved in the case (Kuch, 2012b; Neou, 2010). Meanwhile criminal charges of collusion, defamation and fraud were acted on by the provincial prosecutor against six of the most prominent community activists in 2007 and 2010, at the request of Keat Kolney (Amnesty International, 2008, p. 8; Kuch, 2012a, 2012b; Interview with lawyers working on the case, November 2012). Consequently, lawyers defending the case allege that judges have prioritized civil and criminal charges against the communities, instead of the communities' lawsuit relating to the land grab (CLEC, 2010, p. 3–4; Interview with lawyers working on the case, November 2012; Kuch, 2012a).

Community members and their lawyers have faced continued threats, harassment and intimidation, and had their most basic human rights violated (e.g. freedoms of assembly, association and speech). On numerous occasions lawyers have been prevented from entering the village, money has repeatedly been offered to individuals to drop the case, misinformation has been spread to confuse the community (such as their case having been lost or their lawyers having been imprisoned) (CLEC, 2010, p. 2; Amnesty International, 2008, p. 8; Interview with lawyers working on the case, November 2012).

In 2007, Keat Kolney is reported to have written to the Cambodian Bar Association accusing lawyers working on the case of incitement. Lawyers allege this resulted in an investigation into their work. The President of the Bar Association has publicly denied initiating such steps but has admitted to calling the lawyers to a meeting (CLEC, 2010, p. 3; EWMI, 2009, p. 14; Amnesty International, 2008, p. 15; Lawyers Rights Watch Canada, 2009, p. 6).[38] Keat Kolney also met directly with several of the lawyers during this time, making thinly veiled threats for their security if they continued their work on the case.[39] The clearing of land taken from the villagers and planting of rubber has continued throughout these legal proceedings despite an order from the provincial court judge in October 2008 to cease company operations (CLEC, 2010, p. 3; EWMI, 2009, p. 16).

By the date of publication, the dispute was ongoing. The case remains without a judge at the provincial courts and subsequently lawyers working with the affected communities are attempting to bring it to national level courts. Meanwhile the communities themselves continue to fight for justice.[40]

Like Pheapimex, the Keat Kolney case provides examples of the breadth and depth of ways in which 'grand corruption' inter-relates with land grabbing in Cambodia. Her connections appear to have enabled her to illegally acquire 450 ha of indigenous peoples' land through threats, deception and fraud. The systemic failures within the judicial system to respond to the civil and criminal charges filed by affected communities against Keat Kolney, in comparison to the swift action by the courts when she then filed complaints against those same community members are also reportedly due to her connections.

Reversing an unvirtuous circle: Analysis and conclusions

These two case studies from Cambodia highlight a number of forms and modalities of the nexus of grand corruption and land grabbing. They provide examples of how powerful and influential companies and private individuals can grab land, through the manipulation of state power and authority. They then exemplify how such powerful actors employ strategies of structural violence to retain control of the land, in some instances despite the best efforts of reforming elements of the state. As a result, victims are powerless to fight against licensed exclusions which are violently transformative; in other words 'violent exclusions'.

What is most evident from these cases is that in countries such as Cambodia, corruption and elite capture create a durable inequality (following Mosse, 2007, p. 21) wherein efforts by these communities to seek justice which rely on state functions are likely to fail; in these cases for 14 and 10 years, respectively. Given the prevalence of corruption in many of the countries seeing increased commercial interest in land investments and lack of understanding of the modalities of this dynamic, this conclusion should serve as a critical warning.

If what could be termed an 'unvirtuous circle' of corruption and land grabbing in countries such as Cambodia is to be reversed, then reform-orientated actors (those within and beyond government agencies) need to recognize the structural and institutionalized violence within the state and its rulers, and their subsequent vulnerability to corruption. These implications could not be better described than by Cockcroft:

> Thus the common characteristics of corruption in today's world includes the close relationship between personal enrichment and political survival, the willingness of international partners to participate in corrupt stratagems, and the extent to which dual systems facilitate this and make it very difficult for formal institutions to control the corruption at the heart of the process.
> (Cockcroft, 2012, p. 42)

Mosse went so far as to conclude that development policies and programming attempting to end inequality within such a context would inevitably be co-opted (2007, p. 22). I tend towards a more (cautiously) optimistic view. Policy makers, scholars and the media need to invest adequate resources in better understanding land grabbing and its relationship with corruption, and look for solutions beyond the state. A more nuanced and situated understanding of corruption needs to inform policy responses for land, building on the work of Nuijten and Anders (2009). Other natural resource sectors such as oil, gas and mining and timber, where the dynamics of the relationship between corruption and resource governance is addressed through the 'resource curse' lens, may also offer appropriate starting points.

Current reform agendas, especially those promoted and supported by international development agencies, have a tendency to prioritize overly technocratic, 'silver-bullet' solutions. This is not surprising given that the programming and monitoring of overseas development aid is increasingly jointly negotiated between development agencies and the country in question.[41] Cambodia is an example of how development frameworks and benchmarks for the land sector have evolved from those which measured progress towards governance objectives, to targets and indicators which are simply legalistic and technocratic. This has occurred while land rights in the country have become increasingly sensitive and central to political discussions, suggesting evidence of the co-option Mosse (2007) described.[42] The country is also a clear example of how strong legal frameworks on paper can be easily ignored and manipulated, especially if the international development community turns a blind eye. Therefore, it must be recognized that reform and accountability mechanisms addressing land grabbing and corruption in countries such as Cambodia tackle an inherently political and politicized issue and therefore must be designed to be robust enough to counter potential 'interference'. If the degree of robustness cannot be assured through programme design, then development agencies should consider scaling up their work in these areas directly with non-state actors, such as civil society groups and international investors.

Finally, to present the communities involved in both case studies, as simply victims to social, economic and environmental transformations outside their control, does not pay their activism due justice. Both cases have evolved in parallel to national level political transitions which have the potential to be transformative for Cambodia's future. This transition, which culminated in the 2013 general elections and subsequent political protests, is addressed comprehensively in other chapters. While the 'land issue', particularly ELCs, have been at the heart of the 2013 election, it is unclear what implications this political transition will have for land and resource governance in the longer-term. Nevertheless, it is critical that anti-corruption and land reform efforts explicitly recognize and respond to these social, economic, environmental and political transformations.

Notes

1 The total land mass of Cambodia is 176,515 km^2, of this 20.44 per cent is arable (equivalent to 36,079 km^2) according to the CIA, which defines arable land as 'land cultivated for crops like wheat, maize, and rice that are replanted after each harvest', in comparison to permanent crops and other forms of land use, (CIA Factbook, https://www.cia.gov/library/publications/the-world-factbook/geos/cb.html, accessed 16 April 2013, and for CIA's definition of arable land, see https://www.cia.gov/library/publications/the-world-factbook/fields/2097.html, accessed 17 March 2014). Based on this 20.44 per cent figure, the 2,657,470 ha of land allocated to concessions is equivalent to 73 per cent of Cambodia's arable land and 15 per cent of the country's total land mass. Rice paddy cultivable areas in 2011 totalled 2.76 million ha (Prime Minister Hun Sen, Speech at the 'Closing of the 2011–2012 Stocktaking and 2012–2013 Directions Setting Conference of Ministry for Agriculture, Forestry and Fisheries (MAFF)', Royal University of Agriculture, 11 April 2012).
2 Based on analysis of available data by Global Witness in March 2013 from the Cambodian Ministry of Commerce business registration database and the MAFF database. See also Vrieze and Kuch (2012, p. 9) and Global Witness (2013).
3 According to Article 59 of the 2001 Land Law, http://www.opendevelopmentcambodia.net/law/en/Law-on-Land-2001-E.pdf, accessed 22 April 2014.
4 According to Transparency International's annual global corruption perception assessment and ranking, for further details see http://www.transparency.org/country#KHM, accessed 17 February 2014.
5 For the full text of the Tirana Declaration and its background, see http://www.landcoalition.org/about-us/aom2011/tirana-declaration, accessed 03 October 2012.
6 The Voluntary Guidelines on the Responsible Governance of Tenure of Land, Fisheries and Forests in the Context of National Food Security are available at http://www.fao.org/fileadmin/user_upload/newsroom/docs/VGsennglish.pdf, accessed 3 October 2012.
7 According to figures from the Land Matrix database at the time of writing, http://www.landmatrix.org/en/, accessed 24 April 2014.
8 See aforementioned *Journal of Peasant Studies* special issues for examples of such analyses.

Land is life 113

9 For further information see http://www.transparency.org/cpi2011/in_detail, accessed 3 October 2012.
10 The Convention and further information is available at http://www.unodc.org/unodc/en/treaties/CAC/, accessed 1 February 2013.
11 For further details of shadow states and their operations, see Reno (1999) and Funke and Solomon (2002).
12 For definitions and explanation of the 'resource curse' phenomena, see Ross (1999), Ascher (1999) and Le Billon (2012).
13 See Global Witness reports for further details: for Cambodia – Cambodia's Family Trees (2007) and Country for Sale (2009); for Liberia – The Usual Suspects (2003) and Curse or Cure (2011) and for Angola – Time for Transparency (2004). All are available at www.globalwitness.org.
14 For more information on increasing inequality in Cambodia, see http://www.unescap.org/stat/data/syb2011/I-People/Income-poverty-and-inequality.asp, accessed 8 October 2012; and for Angola, see: http://www.irinnews.org/Report/61395/ANGOLA-Poor-marks-for-progress-on-MDG, accessed 8 October 2012.
15 Letters sent by Global Witness to Senator Lau Meng Khin and his wife Choeung Sopheap, to Mrs Keat Kolney and Mr Ky Tech (President of the Cambodian Bar Association at that time), on 29 February 2014.
16 The ELC owned by Pheapimex totalling 335,142 ha of land is 12.89 per cent of the total area of land currently allocated by the Cambodian government (2.6 million ha). For references for the total holdings belonging to Pheapimex see Vrieze and Kuch (2012) and documentation relating to the company available on Open Development Cambodia, http://www.opendevelopmentcambodia.net/, accessed 17 February 2014.
17 Field observations by Global Witness 2003, 2004 and 2005; Interviews with loggers and local residents, 2003 and 2004.
18 Ministry of Agriculture, Forestry and Fisheries ELC profile and lease documents for Pheapimex, at http://www.opendevelopmentcambodia.net/references/Phea_Phimex_21.06.2011.pdf, accessed 17 February 2014.
19 See also the article 'Chinese firm to plant eucalyptus for paper manufacture in Cambodia', *People's Daily*, 25 December 2000, http://english.people.com.cn/english/200012/25/eng20001225_58790.html, accessed 17 February 2014.
20 Interviews with households impacted by Pheapimex's concession from Pursat and Kamping Chhnang, November 2013; NGO Forum on Cambodia (2006, Slide 3); Lang (2002).
21 Interviews with villagers affected from Pursat and Kampong Chhnang provinces, November 2013; Protection of forests in law, as outlined by Royal Government of Cambodia (2002), Articles 29 and 40 and the ELC Sub-decree, Royal Government of Cambodia (2005) Article 5; Ministry of Agriculture, Forestry and Fisheries (2000, p. 49); Royal Government of Cambodia (2006, Article 3).
22 Interviews with villagers affected from Pursat and Kampong Chhnang provinces, November 2013.
23 Interviews with villagers affected from Pursat and Kampong Chhnang provinces, November 2013; Licadho (2004); UN (2004).
24 Interviews with villagers affected from Pursat and Kampong Chhnang provinces, November 2013.
25 The Government of Cambodia awards rights to community groups to manage their forest under Sub-decree number 79 on Community Forestry Management, http://www.forestry.gov.kh/Documents/CF-Sub%20Decree-Eng.pdf, accessed 17 February 2014.
26 Interviews with villagers affected from Pursat and Kampong Chhnang provinces, November 2013.

27 Interviews with villagers affected from Pursat and Kampong Chhnang provinces, November 2013. For further analysis of the land titling and dispute resolution process, see Milne (2013) and Focus on the Global South and Heinrich Boell Foundation (2013).
28 Minutes from a Ministry of Agriculture meeting at the General Headquarters of the Royal Cambodian Armed Forces, 3 February 1997.
29 Images from Cambodian television news footage, 2004, obtained by Global Witness; China-ASEAN business and investment summit, list of participants, http://www.cabiforum.org/foreign.html, accessed November 2004.
30 Lau Meng Khin was previously a Director of the Wuzhishan L.S. Group, as can be seen from the company's registration profile on the Cambodian Ministry of Commerce online database, http://www.moc.gov.kh/Company/Detail.aspx?MenuID=18&NoticeID=2&ID=94, accessed 1 February 2014; Wuzhishan L.S. Group is registered at the same address as Pheapimex in Phnom Penh, on both the Ministry of Commerce database and on the online registration database for their ELC in Mondulkiri province, http://www.opendevelopmentcambodia.net/pdf-viewer/?pdf=references/Wuzhishan_LS_Group__21.06.2011.pdf, accessed 1 February 2014.
31 Lau Meng Khin was previously both the Chairman and a Director of Shukaku Inc., according to the company's registration profile on the Cambodian Ministry of Commerce online database, http://www.moc.gov.kh/Company/Detail.aspx?MenuID=18&NoticeID=2&ID=4997; according to this database on 2 May 2012, both positions were transferred to his wife: http://www.moc.gov.kh/Company/Detail.aspx?MenuID=18&NoticeID=2&ID=2264; See also UN-OHCHR (2007, p. 11). Shukaku's involvement in the Boeung Kak Lake case was also reviewed by the World Banks' Inspection Panel in 2010, during their investigation into a complaint to the World Bank from the communities threatened with eviction by this project.
32 Details of the Chinese investment involvement in Shukaku's operations in Boeng Kak Lake are available here: http://www.inclusivedevelopment.net/bkl/, accessed 20 May 2014; and the company's business relations were also covered by various Cambodian and Chinese media outlets, for example, Strangio and Titthara (2010).
33 According to company registration information for Sinohydro (Cambodia) United Co Ltd issued by the Cambodian Ministry of Commerce on 7 April 2006; See also Grimsditch (2012).
34 According to the company registration information for Cambodia International Investment Development Group available from the Cambodian Ministry of Commerce online database, Mr Lau Meng Khin was a Director of the company between 2006 and 2010, while his wife currently holds the positions of Board Director and Chairman of the company, and the company is registered at the same address as Pheapimex in Phnom Penh, http://www.moc.gov.kh/Company/Detail.aspx?MenuID=18&NoticeID=2&ID=6370 and http://www.moc.gov.kh/Company/Detail.aspx?MenuID=18&NoticeID=2&ID=408, both accessed 20 May 2014.
35 As described by the introduction on the website of Sihanoukville's Special Econmic Zone: http://www.ssez.com/en/company.asp?Ione=3; http://www.cambodiainvestment.gov.kh/list-of-sez.html, accessed 23 February 2014. See also Lan Lan (2010); 'Miner encroaches on ancestral lands', Radio Free Asia, 22 June 2011, http://www.rfa.org/english/news/cambodia/bauxite-06222011171620.html, accessed 20 May 2014; 'Erdos Hongjun Investment Plans to Build a Refinery in Cambodia', The CM Group, 1 December 2011, http://cmgroup.net/en/blogs/industry/articles/erdos_hongjun_investment_plans_to_build_aa_refinery_in_cambodia, accessed 20 May 2014; Weinland and Kunmakara (2011); Weinland (2011).

36 According to Chapter 3 of Cambodia's 2001 Land Law, indigenous ethnic minorities (such as the Jarai of Kong Yu and Kong Thom) are eligible to register traditionally owned land under collective title. However, due to delays in the passing of government regulations, indigenous communities were not able to begin registering their collective land until 2009, 5 years after this sale is alleged to have been agreed.
37 Mrs Peung Yok Hiep, Director of Legal Aid of Cambodia, quoted in a joint press statement regarding the lawsuit filed by the communities of Kong Yu and Kong Thom villages against Keat Kolney, 23 January 2007, http://www.licadho-cambodia.org/press/files/139JointPRKong%20YuRattanakiri07.pdf, accessed 18 February 2014.
38 Under the name of Global Witness I wrote to the President of the Cambodian Bar Association during this period, on 29 February 2014, asking for his comment on his involvement in this case. By the time of publication, no reply had been received.
39 Personal communication with a lawyer previously working on the case, February 2014.
40 Interview with lawyers working on the case, November 2012 and January 2013.
41 For further information on the principles of 'aid effectiveness', see http://www.oecd.org/dac/effectiveness/, accessed 3 February 2014.
42 For further analysis of this transition and the Cambodian Government's repeated failure to meet land sector development targets, see Global Witness (2009) Country for Sale, http://www.globalwitness.org/library/country-sale, accessed 20 May 2014.

References

ADHOC. (2013) 'A turning point? Land, housing and natural resources rights in Cambodia in 2012', http://adhoc-cambodia.org/wp-content/uploads/2013/02/ADHOC-A-Turning-Point-Land-Housing-and-Natural-Resources-Rights-in-2012.pdf, accessed 16 April 2013.

Amnesty International. (2008) 'Cambodia: A risky business – Defending the right to housing', September 2008, ASA 23/014/2008, http://www.amnesty.org/en/library/info/ASA23/014/2008, accessed 20 May 2014.

Anseeuw, W., Alden Wily, L., Cotula, L. and Taylor, M. (2012) 'Land rights and the rush to land: Findings of the global commercial pressures on land research project', International Land Coalition, Rome, http://www.landcoalition.org/sites/default/files/publication/1205/ILC%20GSR%20report_ENG.pdf, accessed 8 October 2012.

Ascher, W. (1999) *Why Governments Waste Natural Resources: Policy Failures in Developing Countries*, John Hopkins University Press, Baltimore.

Asia Human Rights Commission. (2007) 'Urgent action appeal: Jarai indigenous communities face displacement after land stolen by politically-elite businesswoman', http://cambodia.ahrchk.net/docs/landcase_clec_jan2007.pdf, accessed 18 February 2014.

Borras Jr., Saturnino M. and Franco, J. (2010) *Towards a Broader View of the Politics of Global Land Grab: Rethinking Land Issues, Reframing Resistance*, ICAS Working Paper Series No. 001, Initiatives in Critical Agrarian Studies, Land Deal Politics Initiative and Transnational Institute, Amsterdam, The Netherlands.

Borras Jr., Saturnino M., Hall, R., Scoones I., White, B. and Wolford, W. (2011) 'Towards a better understanding of global land grabbing: An editorial introduction', *Journal of Peasant Studies* 38(2), pp. 209–216.

Brady, B. (2010) 'The Cambodian Army: Open for corporate sponsors', *Time Magazine*, 9 June 2014, http://content.time.com/time/world/article/0,8599,1995298,00.html, accessed 17 February 2014.

Brown, K. (2008) 'Book review of *Escaping the Resource Curse*, M. Humphreys, J. D. Sachs, and J. E. Stiglitz (eds)', in *ECSP Report*, Issue 13, 2008–2009, http://www.wilsoncenter.org/sites/default/files/ECSPReport13_Brown.pdf, accessed 8 October 2012.

Cambodian Human Rights Committee. (2009) 'Losing ground: Forced evictions and intimidation in Cambodia', CHRAC, Phnom Penh, http://www.chrac.org/eng/CHRAC%20Statement%20in%202009/Losing%20Ground%20FINAL.compressed.pdf, accessed 17 February 2014.

CLEC. (2008) *Update in Kong Yu and Kong Thom Land Dispute*, Cambodian Legal Education Centre and Legal Aid of Cambodia, Phnom Penh.

CLEC. (2010) *Kong Yu Case: Illegal Acquisition of Indigenous Peoples' Land*, Report prepared for UN-OHCHR, Cambodian Legal Education Centre.

Cockcroft, L. (2012) *Global Corruption: Money, Power and Ethics in the Modern World*, I.B. Tauris and Co, London and New York.

Deininger, K. and Byerlee, D. (2011) 'Rising global interest in Farmland: Can it yield sustainable results', World Bank, Washington DC, http://siteresources.worldbank.org/INTARD/Resources/ESW_Sept7_final_final.pdf, accessed 8 October 2012.

Dwyer, M. B (2012) *The Formalization Fix? Land Titling, State Land Concessions and Geographical Transparency in Contemporary Cambodia*, Paper presented at the International Conference on Global Land Grabbing II, October 17–19, Land Deals Politics Initiative and the Department of Development Sociology at Cornell University, Ithaca, New York, http://www.cornell-landproject.org/download/landgrab2012papers/dwyer.pdf, accessed 20 May 2014.

EWMI (East-West Management Institute). (2009) *Cambodia Programme on Rights and Justice*, Final Report, Cooperative Agreement No.442-A-00-03-00193-00, October 2003 through December 2008, pp. 12–13.

Focus on the Global South and Heinrich Boell Foundation. (2013) 'Moving forward: Study on the impacts of the implementation of Order 01BB in selected communities in rural Cambodia', http://focusweb.org/sites/www.focusweb.org/files/Student%20Volunteers%20Report_%20ENG.pdf, accessed 17 February 2014.

Funke N. and Solomon, H. (2002) *The Shadow State in Africa: A Discussion*, Development Management Policy Forum Occasional Paper No. 5, Addis Ababa.

Galtung, J. (1969) 'Violence, peace and peace research', *Journal of Peace Research* 6(167), pp. 175–177.

Global Witness (2009) 'Country for sale: How Cambodia's elite has captured the country's extractive industries', http://www.globalwitness.org/library/country-sale, accessed 22 August 2014.

Global Witness. (2010) 'Global witness urges Cambodia's donors to condemn sponsorship of military units by private businesses', 5 March, http://www.globalwitness.org/library/global-witness-urges-cambodia%E2%80%99s-donors-condemn-sponsorship-military-units-private-businesses, accessed 17 February 2014.

Global Witness. (2012) 'Hidden crisis: Increase in killings as tensions rise over land and forests', http://www.globalwitness.org/sites/default/files/images/A_hidden_crisis-FINAL%20190612%20v2.pdf, accessed 11 May 2014.

Global Witness. (2013) 'Rubber Barons, How Vietnamese companies and international financiers are driving a land grabbing crisis in Cambodia and Laos', http://www.globalwitness.org/rubberbarons/, accessed 22 April 2014.

Global Witness. (2014) 'Deadly environment, the dramatic rise in killings of environmental and land defenders', http://www.globalwitness.org/deadlyenvironment/, accessed 11 May 2014.

Global Witness, International Land Coalition and Oakland Institute. (2012) 'Dealing with disclosure: Improving transparency in decision-making over large-scale land acquisitions and investments', http://www.globalwitness.org/library/dealing-disclosure, accessed 8 October 2012.

Grimsditch, M. (2012) 'China's Investments in hydropower in the Mekong region: The Kamchay Hydropower Dam, Kampot, Cambodia', http://www.bicusa.org/wp-content/uploads/2013/02/Case+Study+-+China+Investments+in+Cambodia+FINAL+2.pdf, accessed 17 February 2014.

Gupta A. (1995) 'Blurred boundaries: The discourse of corruption, the culture of politics, and the imagined state', *American Ethnologist* 22(2), pp. 375–402.

Hall, D. (2011) 'Land grabs, land control and Southeast Asian crop booms', *The Journal of Peasant Studies* 38(4), pp. 837–857.

Hall D., Hirsch, P. and Tania, M. L. (2011) *Powers of Exclusion: Land dilemmas in Southeast Asia*, NUS Press, Singapore.

Kuch, N. (2012a) 'Summonses Issued in Keat Kolney Case', *Cambodia Daily*, 31 January 2012, http://sahrika.com/2012/01/31/summonses-issued-in-keat-kolney-case/, accessed 20 May 2014.

Kuch, N. (2012b) 'Mired in land disputes, villagers find no remedy in courts', *Cambodia Daily*, 1–2 September 2012, http://sahrika.com/2012/09/01/mired-in-land-disputes-villagers-find-no-remedy-in-courts/, accessed 20 May 2014.

Kuch, N. (2012c) 'New Judge appointed to Keat Kolney land dispute case', *Cambodia Daily*, 5 October 2012, http://sahrika.com/2012/10/05/new-judge-appointed-to-keat-kolney-land-dispute-case/, accessed 20 May 2014.

Lan Lan. (2010) 'Cambodia wants more investments from Chinese firms', *China Daily*, 19 September 2010, http://www.chinadaily.com.cn/business/2010-09/19/content_11323467.htm, accessed 12 May 2014.

Lang, C. (2002) 'The pulp invasion – Cambodia: Land grabs, logging and plantations', http://chrislang.org/2002/12/01/the-pulp-invasion-cambodia/, accessed 17 February 2014.

Lawyers Rights Watch Canada. (2009) *Concerns about the Independence of Lawyers and Judges in Cambodia*, Written statement submitted by MRWC, a non-government organization in special consultative status 28 August, prepared for the UN Human Rights Council 12th Session.

Le Billon, P. (2012) *Wars of Plunder*, Hurst and Co., London.

Levi, M. (1988) *Of Rule and Revenue*, University of California Press, Berkeley and Los Angeles.

Licadho. (2004) 'Threats to human rights defenders in Cambodia', http://www.licadhocambodia.org/reports/files/71HRDPaper2004.pdf, accessed 17 February 2014.

Licadho. (2011) 'Pushed to the edge: The death of the Boeng Kak Lake activist, Video', http://licadho-cambodia.org/video.php?perm=27, accessed 17 February 2014.

Licadho. (2013) '2012 in review: Land grabbing, the roots of strife', http://www.licadho-cambodia.org/articles/20130212/133/index.html, accessed 24 March 2013.

McMichael, P. D. (2012). 'The land grab and corporate food regime restructuring', *The Journal of Peasant Studies* 39, pp. 681–701.

Milne, S. (2013) 'Under the leopard's skin: Land commodification and the dilemmas of indigenous communal titling in upland Cambodia', *Asia Pacific Viewpoint* 54(3), pp. 323–339.

Ministry of Agriculture, Forestry and Fisheries. (2000) 'Cambodia tree seed project/Danida', *Proceedings from National Priority Tree Species Workshop,* Phnom Penh 15–16 August, Annex IV Endangered or Rare Species, http://www.treeseedfa.org/uploaddocuments/Proceedingworkshop.pdf, accessed 3 April 2013.

Mosse, D. (2007) *Power and the Durability of Poverty: A Critical Exploration of the Links between Culture, Marginality and Chronic Poverty,* Chronic Poverty Research Centre, Working Paper 107, Anthropology Department, School of Oriental and African Studies, University of London.

Neef, A. and Touch, S. (2012) *Land Grabbing in Cambodia: Narratives, Mechanisms, Resistance,* Paper presented at the International Conference on Global Land Grabbing II, October 17–19, Land Deals Politics Initiative and the Department of Development Sociology at Cornell University, Ithaca, New York.

Neou, V. (2010) 'Chief Judge says Judge scared in Kolney case', *Cambodia Daily,* 4 August 2010, http://chiatkh.blogspot.co.uk/2010/08/chief-judge-says-jjudge-scared-in.html, accessed 20 May 2014.

NGO Forum on Cambodia. (2006) *Fast-wood Plantations, Economic Concessions and Local Livelihoods in Cambodia: Field Investigations in Koh Kong, Kampong Speu, Pursat, Kampong Chhnang, Mondulkiri, Prey Veng and Svay Rieng Provinces,* Phnom Penh, Cambodia.

Nuijten, M. and Anders, G. (eds) (2009) *Corruption and the Secret of Law: A Legal Anthropological Perspective,* Ashgate, Burlington, Vermont.

Peluso, N. L. and Lund C. (2011) 'New frontiers of land control: Introduction', *Journal of Peasant Studies* 38(4), pp. 667–681.

Phalla, L. and O'Toole, J. (2010) 'Document shows ties among RCAF, government and private sector', *Phnom Penh Post,* 4 March, http://www.phnompenhpost.com/national/document-shows-ties-among-rcaf-government-and-private-sector, accessed 17 February 2014.

Pollack, E., Cotula, L., Blackmore E. and Guttal S. (2014) 'Agricultural investments in Southeast Asia: Legal tools for public accountability, International Institute for Environment and Development', http://pubs.iied.org/12573IIED.html?k=cotula, accessed 17 February 2014.

Reno, W. (1999) *Warlord Politics and African States,* Lynne Rienner Publishers, Colorado, London.

Reno, W. (2000) 'Clandestine economies, violence and states in Africa', *Journal of International Affairs* 53(2), pp. 435–437.

Ross, M. (1999) 'The political economy of the resource curse', *World Politics* 51, pp. 297–322, http://academics.eckerd.edu/moodle_support/ecUser/EPFiles.php/moodle_20101/653/Ross__The_Political_Economy_of_the_Resource_Curse.pdf, accessed 8 October 2012.

Royal Government of Cambodia. (2001) 'Land law', http://www.opendevelopmentcambodia.net/law/en/Law-on-Land-2001-E.pdf, accessed 22 April 2014.

Royal Government of Cambodia. (2002) 'Forest law', http://www.forestry.gov.kh/Documents/Forestry%20Law_Eng.pdf, accessed 20 May 2014.

Royal Government of Cambodia. (2005) 'Sub-decree on economic land concessions', http://www.cambodiainvestment.gov.kh/sub-decree-146-on-economic-land-concessions_051227.html, accessed 17 February 2014.

Royal Government of Cambodia. (2006) 'Sub-decree on forest and non-timber forest products allow for export and import', http://www.forestry.gov.kh/Documents/Sub-Decree-forest-Pro-Imp-Exp-Eng.pdf, accessed 20 May 2014.

Royal Government of Cambodia. (2008) *Technical Working Group on Forests and the Environment,* Joint Monitoring Indicator Reporting 2007–2008: Summary Analysis Based on Detailed Report, Phnom Penh.

Springer, S. (2013) 'Illegal evictions? Overwriting possession and morality with law's violence in Cambodia', *The Journal of Agrarian Change* 13(4), pp. 520–546.

Strangio, S. and Titthara, M. (2010) 'Chinese linked to filling of lake Boeung Kak Project', *Phnom Penh Post,* http://cambodiatonight.blogspot.com/2010/01/chinese-linked-to-filling-of-lake.html, accessed 12 May 2014.

Transparency International. (2011) 'Corruption in the land sector', http://www.fao.org/docrep/014/am943e/am943e00.pdf, accessed 8 October 2012.

Un, K., and So, S. (2011) 'Land rights in Cambodia: How neopatrimonial politics restricts land policy reform', *Pacific Affairs* 84(2), pp. 289–308(20).

UN. (2004) 'UN rights expert calls for independent probe into mob killings in Cambodia', 15 November 2004, UN News Centre, http://www.un.org/apps/news/story.asp?newsid=12525&cr=&cr1=#.U3tGVii9bGs, accessed 20 May 2014.

UN-OHCHR (Office for the High Commissioner for Human Rights, Cambodia). (2007) 'Economic land concessions: A human rights perspective', http://cambodia.ohchr.org/WebDOCs/DocReports/2-Thematic-Reports/Thematic_CMB12062007E.pdf, accessed 17 February 2014.

Vrieze, P. and Kuch, N. (2012) 'Carving up Cambodia one concession at a time', *Cambodia Daily,* 10–11 March 2012, p. 9.

Walker, R. (2009) 'Cambodia: A land up for sale?' *BBC World Service,* 12 August 2009, http://farmlandgrab.org/6789, accessed 18 February 2014.

Weinland, D. (2011) 'Erdos Group plans laid bare', *Phnom Penh Post,* 3 August 2011, http://www.phnompenhpost.com/national/erdos-group-plans-laid-bare, accessed 20 May 2014.

Weinland, D. and Kunmakara, M. (2011) 'China firm plans bauxite processing plant in Kratie', *Phnom Penh Post,* 30 December 2011, http://www.phnompenhpost.com/business/china-firm-plans-bauxite-processing-plant-kratie, accessed 20 May 2014.

World Bank. (2010) 'Investigation report: Cambodia: Land management and administration project (Credit No. 3650 – KH)', http://siteresources.worldbank.org/EXTINSPECTIONPANEL/Resources/Cambodia_LMAP_for_WEBSITE.pdf, accessed 23 February 2014.

6 Contested development and environment

Chinese-backed hydropower and infrastructure projects in Cambodia

Michael Sullivan

Introduction

Contests between notions of 'development' and 'environment' have constantly been fought in the international arena since at least 1992 when the United Nations Conference on Environment and Development (UNCED) held in Rio de Janiero, Brazil, attempted to reconcile the two concepts. The outcome of the conference – neatly and presciently summed up by Wolfgang Sachs (Sachs, 1995, p. 4) – was the recognition by governments of the 'declining state of the environment, but the insistence of the re-launching of development'. Eight years later, the World Commission on Dams (WCD), backed by a host of international agencies including the United Nations and the World Bank, stated in its final report, 'Dams and Development', that there is no 'justifiable doubt that [large] dams have made an important contribution to human development' creating considerable benefits', but in 'too many cases an unacceptable and often unnecessary' social and environmental price has been paid to secure those benefits. Furthermore, it added the lack of equity in the distribution of benefits has called into question the value of many dams in meeting water and energy development needs when compared with the alternatives (World Commission on Dams, 2000, p. xxvii). Since the publication of the report, large hydropower dam projects have developed into a multi-billion dollar market (Hill, 2013).

The primacy of the developmentalist compulsion confirmed at UNCED in 1992, and reaffirmed at subsequent global meetings, has in large part driven the development of the large hydropower project market irrespective of the WCD findings. Nowhere has this been more evident than in China. Rapid industrialization and exponential economic growth in recent decades has led China into a preeminent position as the world's leading investor in hydropower dam projects. Viewed as a clean alternative to coal-based fossil fuel energy, China has more large dams than any other country including the world's largest, the Three Gorges Dam. The environmental and social devastation caused by this and many other of China's 28,000 dams are according to activist groups like International Rivers profound, and are likely to get worse.[1]

For strategic geo-political as well as economic reasons Chinese state-owned enterprises (SOE) and financiers are also involved in hundreds of large hydropower projects in 74 countries around the globe, including those that make up the Greater Mekong Sub-Region (GMS) of which the Chinese province of Yunnan and the Guangzi Zhuang autonomous region are a part.[2] Countries in the sub-region like Cambodia are of significant strategic importance to China. Likewise, Cambodia derives enormous benefits in terms of trade, aid, investment and infrastructural development from its relationship with China. Chinese SOE's and banks are involved in several large infrastructural projects involving large hydropower dam projects in Cambodia.

Academic research alongside the work of NGOs is gradually coming to terms with the political and socio-economic implications of Chinese hydropower projects in Cambodia and the GMS more generally. In the 1990s researchers like Phil Hirsch (1996) and Karen Bakker (1999) were beginning to engage in analysis of the politics and potential impacts of hydropower in the Mekong region. More recent work by François Molle *et al.* (2009) provided excellent coverage of contestation surrounding livelihoods and governance of hydropower in the region. However, with the exception of recent studies by Urban *et al.* (2013) and the work of Carl Middleton and Sam Chanty (2008) and Mark Grimsditch (2012), extensive research has yet to be done on the impact of Chinese funded and built hydropower projects in the GMS and more specifically in Cambodia. This chapter sets out to examine the nature of the relationship between China and Cambodia in the context of these projects and begins to address some of the questions surrounding the short-term benefits and long-term environmental and social costs already found in the existing literature.

In the last decade, China's involvement in infrastructure development in Cambodia has grown considerably. Driven by its own regional strategic interests and Cambodia's need for physical infrastructure for socio-economic development, China has been investing heavily in major Cambodian projects such as those involving hydro-electric dams, roads and bridges. China's rise to prominence in Cambodia's infrastructural development has generated broader debates about the nature of what appears to be a mutually beneficial relationship between the two states. Typically these debates revolve around the discussion of short- and long-term impacts and benefits of Sino-Cambodian partnerships. In particular, some environmentalists and development practitioners along with ordinary Cambodian citizens are concerned about the trade-offs between short-term socio-economic gains and the longer-term impact on the provision of public goods and environmental services. For the most part, these concerns arise from the manner in which the Cambodian government engages with Chinese SOEs and the seeming lack of a serious commitment to environmental and social safeguards. The politics and economics of China's role in the transformation of Cambodia's natural environment and society are deeply contested, and conflicts over the trajectory of the country's development are likely to continue for some time to come. This chapter looks at these broader issues and debates and considers the scale, impact and implications of the relationship between China and the Cambodian government's development of large infrastructure projects, such as hydropower dams.

Cambodia's relationship with China

In December 2011, the Cambodian Prime Minister Hun Sen presided over the official opening of the country's first large hydropower dam on the Kamchay River in the south west province of Kampot. It was planned and built by Sinohydro Corporation, a Chinese state-owned hydropower engineering and construction company and financed by one of China's three large import-export banks, China Exim. The Kamchay dam is the first in a number of large hydropower projects intended to provide Cambodia's need for a relatively cheap and reliable source of electricity. Burdened with excessive charges and unreliable delivery, Cambodia's electricity supply system is seen by policy makers and international advisors as constraining economic and social development and acting as a disincentive for foreign and domestic investment. Government ministers and foreign experts frequently espouse the benefits of stable electricity for economic competitiveness and the attraction of investment for manufacturing and agricultural industries (Xinhua, 2013a). Furthermore, in terms of household consumption only about one-quarter of the Cambodian population are currently on the national grid.

As the Prime Minister pointed out energy and other physical infrastructure problems in Cambodia have persisted for years. China's involvement in helping to address these, however, is relatively recent. Destruction caused by continuous civil war and conflict throughout the 1970s and 1980s, followed by an extended period of political instability in the early 1990s up to the beginning of the 2000s, prevented any serious and sustained development of physical infrastructure. War and the virtual loss of an entire generation are devastating enough, but the greatest recent impediment to rebuilding and reconstruction of physical infrastructure has been political in nature. The struggle for control of the Cambodian state in the 1980s and 1990s created a political-economic system that de-prioritized sustainable development in favour of preservation and the entrenchment of the state itself. As well as political survival, the control of state power meant access to and control over international aid and investment flows since 1991. In a reciprocal exchange of political loyalty and access to resources state powerholders and subordinates have for the most part ensured immediate personal interests have been met largely at the expense of the national interest. Control is mediated through extant patronage networks melded to the bureaucratic power of the state in a neo-patrimonial nexus that intentionally blurs any distinction between public and private interests (Bratton and van de Valle, 1994).

Under these circumstances, particularly in the early to late 1990s, essential infrastructure such as major road links were re-built and repaired, but the work and materials were of such poor quality that they would be washed away in the rainy season. The same process was often repeated the following dry season with the same results. At the end of the 1990s, the situation had to improve if Cambodia was to take full advantage of integration into the regional ASEAN group and wider international capitalist markets. Before that could happen, the struggle over state control was fought out. Using authoritarian controls, Hun Sen and the Cambodian People's Party (CPP) ensured they emerged as winners in what was a fundamentally flawed election in 1998 (International Crisis Group, 1988). A period of relative political stability accompanied by high macro-economic growth followed.

It is within this evolving political-economic milieu that relations between China and Cambodia grew in the mid-1990s. They developed at a time when Cambodia's political elites were spiralling towards crisis. Relations between Cambodia's Co-Prime Ministers Prince Ranariddh leader of the royalist Funcinpec Party and Hun Sen began to deteriorate in 1996 ending in the violent removal of Ranariddh by armed forces loyal to Hun Sen in July 1997.[3] At the same time, Chinese and Cambodian officials began to open up diplomatic and political channels exchanging visiting delegations. Interestingly, these visits were conducted almost exclusively by members of the CPP, some of whom were Sino-Khmers who maintained links with China, and Hun Sen himself.

Cambodia–China, partnership for the 21st century

Relations with China have gone from strength to strength in the 21st century. In June 2013, Chinese and Cambodian dignitaries gathered in Phnom Penh to celebrate 55 years of diplomatic relations in what was designated as the 'Cambodia–China Year of Friendship'. Two years previously relations were strengthened with the creation of the 'comprehensive strategic partnership of cooperation'. For Cambodia this strategic partnership has meant billions of dollars of direct development assistance and investments. Numerous technical and economic cooperation projects have been done and signed, in all areas of trade and investment, infrastructure, telecommunications, energy, manufacturing industries, extractive and agro-industries, security, defence, and cultural and educational exchange. Some estimates suggest that from 1994 to 2012 China invested approximately $9.17 billion and Chinese companies consistently top Cambodia's foreign direct investor tables. China is also one of Cambodia's major providers of direct development assistance through soft loans and grants, and the total volume of bilateral trade is expected to reach $5 billion by 2017 (Xinhua, 2013b).

In return for lavish investments and aid, China receives significant political and economic benefits from a grateful Cambodia. Politically, Hun Sen and the Royal Cambodian Government (RGC) have consistently supported China's 'one-country' policy recognizing its territorial claims over Taiwan. Economically, Cambodia continues to play an important strategic role in China's regional 'go southwest' strategy (Chen and Stone, 2013). China's south western province Yunnan and the autonomous economic zone Guangxi Zhuang Autonomous Region which form part of the GMS are seen by Beijing as key gateways to China's economically and politically important Southeast Asian neighbours. Cambodia is an integral part of China's strategic plans for access via rail networks from Kunming in Yunnan province to Singapore and the opening up of the Cambodian port of Sihanoukville. Cambodia's natural resources, land, timber, minerals, petroleum, hydropower, cheap labour and historical cultural links are particularly attractive to Chinese business. Mainland Chinese manufacturing firms supported by international quotas have played a central role in the development of the textiles and garment industry, the powerhouse of Cambodia's recent economic boom (Bargawi, 2005).

Chinese relations for better or worse?

For a country the size of Cambodia the scale of Chinese involvement in virtually all sectors of the economy is huge. Close ties between China and Cambodia's political and economic elites seemingly reinforced by a shared sense of historical ties and cultural links appear to make doing business of all kinds more amenable and beneficial. However, on the margins of these close political-economic ties questions have been raised about what exactly the benefits of this special relationship with China are for the majority of ordinary Cambodians.[4] The textiles and garments industry is often held up by proponents of the view that relations with China are enormously beneficial. To be sure there is empirical evidence to show that there are positive correlations between improvements in livelihoods poverty reduction and the garment industry. At the same time, the industry has been mired in controversy surrounding employee–management relations. Since the mid-1990s, there have been numerous disputes, strikes and demonstrations by workers protesting against pay and conditions and generally poor treatment by factory owners and management. It is precisely these and other apparent downsides in others spheres that have given rise to the debate about the political and economic costs-benefits of the special relationship (Chandary et al., 2011).

Nowhere are the boundaries of the cost-benefit debate more clearly delineated than in the area of physical infrastructure especially hydropower projects. In modern materialistically impoverished contexts like the Cambodian countryside, there is a standard list of assumed benefits that comes with improved road and transportation networks including reduced travelling times from place to place, access to greater employment opportunities, access to health and education facilities, increase in land values and prices of agricultural produce, that is, market access and commodification. Of course, the assumptions are that employment opportunities and good quality health and education already exist in provincial capitals, which is not necessarily always the case before good quality serviceable roads are in place. On the negative side, as values and market access increase so does dispossession of land through 'grabs' by predatory political and economic elites, sometimes in partnership with foreign interests. This state-backed predation of land and resources is now a major source of rural discontent and conflict; the political ramifications of which have been simmering beneath the surface for some time, but are now actively manifest within the body politic.

Chinese companies with their partners in government have been busy in the last 5 years rehabilitating and reconstructing roads and building large bridges in Cambodia, especially in the Northeast of the country and across the Mekong and Tonle Sap rivers close to the capital Phnom Penh. Because of the immediate obvious benefits related to journey times and access to resources transportation and road projects are not subject to the same scrutiny as other large infrastructure projects like hydropower. The scale, impact and implications of Chinese-backed dam building in Cambodia are highly controversial on many different levels drawing together political, socio-economic and environmental concerns. In the same way as Cambodia needs good transport infrastructure, cheap reliable sources of energy are needed for the country's development (Cambodian Development Research Institute, 2013). Supplying those needs through the construction of hydrodams with Chinese planning and financing seems to be the RGC's preferred method for achieving development goals.

The idea of using hydropower to help solve problems of energy supply in Cambodia is not new. In 1968 a 12 Mega Watt (MW) hydropower plant, the Kirirom 1, in Kampong Speu province was built with help from Yugoslavia, but it was partially destroyed and fell into disuse after 1975. The project was re-built by a Chinese state-owned enterprise (SOE) China Electric Power Technology Import and Export Corporation and re-commissioned in 2002 under a 30 year Build Operate Transfer contract. A 120 km 115 Kv (high voltage) transmission line provides electricity to Kompong Speu and Phnom Penh (Middleton and Chanty, 2008, p. 32). Plans to build a dam in Kamchay in the 1960s were abandoned as Cambodia was drawn into the Second Indo-Chinese war. The resurgence of interest in building new hydropower projects began in the 1990s but was, because of social and environmental concerns, controversial from the beginning (Grimsditch, 2012). By 1996 the debate about the overall viability of hydro power in Cambodia was well underway. Government proponents and international partners like Chinese SOE typically viewed the projects as offering a rational, relatively clean and reasonably affordable solution to the country's energy problems.

As well as providing for its own electricity needs Cambodia could, according to the advocates of hydropower, become a net exporter of electricity earning much needed foreign exchange. It was further argued that cheap reliable sources of power would attract foreign investment and kick start industry. In addition, flooding – a serious problem in Cambodia – could be better controlled and used to help irrigate farmland thus boosting the agricultural sector.

Critics by contrast gave a much more pessimistic prognosis, warning of economic, environmental and social disaster. Given that most of the proposed projects were to be built in remote conservation areas, the negative social and ecological impacts threatened to outweigh any potential benefits. Contrary to the view that it was an affordable source of energy, critics also pointed out that the construction and maintenance involved may be more prohibitive than proponents had calculated, likely requiring private investment subjecting the projects to vested interests at the expense of the consumer, and increasing the nations' debt burden. Other environmental and ecological costs included the potential of loss of biodiversity, a negative impact on vitally important fisheries and the related problem of the loss of livelihoods and displacement of traditional communities (Post Staff, 1996).

Moreover, on closer inspection the motives of the proponents of hydropower projects, in particular Chinese SOEs, cast doubts about who in the long run would benefit. Large state corporations like Sinohydro are closely tied to China's geo-political and foreign policy objectives and are overseen by the State Council.[5] A central component of China's 'going out' strategy is the acquisition of natural resources beyond its borders to fuel and maintain high levels of economic growth and development. The potential for acquiring cheap low-carbon sources of electricity from hydropower in the riparian states of the GMS like Cambodia, Laos, Vietnam and Myanmar to power China's own thriving economic areas' are enormous. Scholars like Urban *et al.* (2013, p. 132) argue that there is 'a direct link between creating hydropower' in these countries and importing it back to China to support 'over-stretched' domestic energy markets. Furthermore, the expansion of overseas markets for Chinese firms is another significant aspect of China's going out strategy. The 'bundling' of Chinese aid, trade, investment and concessional loans for hydro-electric dams in places like Cambodia are often linked with the export of electricity and the importation of Chinese goods (ibid). Aside from the environmental issues, questions could be asked about whether or not the benefits of hydropower will actually reach the poor and vulnerable groups that government proponents and their international partners claim they will.

Enabling political environment for China

As the debate heated up it soon became apparent to the Cambodian government that there was a reluctance on behalf of multilateral agencies like the Asia Development (ADB) and World Bank as well as some western bilateral donors to support these projects directly because of this negative social and environmental risk. Part of the problem, in addition to the overall financing of the projects, was the thorny issue of commitment to international standards related to assessments of environmental and social impacts. China and Chinese SOEs involved in the hydropower sector appeared to be less concerned with environmental and social safeguards than counterparts elsewhere. Nothing illustrated this better than the construction, beginning in 1994, of the world's largest hydropower project the 'Three Gorges Dam' on China's Yangtze river. Problems associated with this project are multiple and entangled taking environmental, ecological, geological and human welfare concerns to new heights (Bosshard, 2011).

What concerns critics of the Cambodian government's prioritization of hydropower power projects is China's apparent willingness to forego these concerns in favour of immediate and short-term socio-economic and political returns for the Cambodian government and Chinese corporations. Particularly worrying is that China's poor record in this regard is matched by the current Cambodian government's own disregard for any opposition to policies or behaviour that challenges the dominant political economic structures of power. For a number of years, irrespective of repeated concerns about the disproportionate negative social and environmental costs expressed by local and international NGOs and village representative groups the Cambodian government along with Chinese partners have pushed through hydropower projects without proper oversight (Chakrya and Strangio, 2009). More recent examples include staunch opposition to the hugely controversial Stung Cheay Areng dam in Koh Kong province and the Lower Sesan II dam in Stung Treng province. These projects threaten to destroy what conservationists describe as vitally important ecological areas displacing thousands of people and affecting the livelihoods of tens of thousands of families who rely on them (Worrell and Seangly, 2013; See also, Worrall, 2013; Hul, 2014).

The presence of foreign NGOs working alongside national organizations and advocacy groups ready to challenge government policies such as hydropower has been problematic for Hun Sen, especially on the basis of their human rights implications. Consequently, over the last two decades Hun Sen's relations with Cambodia's largest multilateral and bilateral donors, the World Bank, IMF, ADB, UN, EU, Japan, various western powers and the capitalist countries of ASEAN have been mixed. While Cambodia gratefully accepted aid and investment, the regime has been less than sanguine about apparent donor concerns with democratic reform, good governance and commitment to the covenants and conventions of the 'Universal Declaration on Human Rights'.

While these items do regularly feature in the pronouncements of some donors, they have historically stopped short of imposing any conditions that would effectively alter the underlying structures of power. As a consequence, key democratic reforms in areas of the judiciary, civil service and elections have not been enacted and serious civil, political and other rights are routinely violated.[6] Paradoxically, the reforms advocated by some western donors could potentially undermine the political stability that they have worked hard to promote and sustain. Similarly, because many of the rights abuses are perpetrated by members of the regime and/or individuals connected to it, a climate of impunity for the wealthy and powerful persists.

The unwillingness of western donors to push the RGC too hard for reforms and compliance with international covenants and conventions doesn't stop Hun Sen from chiding them for making what are seen as unreasonable demands to act in these areas (Gillison and Kimsan, 2007). By contrast, in recent literature on the subject and in the media, Hun Sen is often quoted commending China for its no questions asked, no strings attached approach to its dealings with the RGC (Ciorciari, 2013). In reality, there isn't a great deal of difference between the Chinese way of doing things in Cambodia and the approach taken by major western donors. Both are interested in securing political stability and security to facilitate their own geo-strategic interests via trade aid and investment. That said, one key difference is that some international NGOs, many from the western liberal democracies working in Cambodia do demand accountability and transparency from their own home governments and regularly expose the RGC's failings and shortcomings.

Although there are indications that the situation may be changing, Chinese political leaders engaged with Cambodia do not demand the same levels of scrutiny, accountability and transparency expected by non-state actors in the west. Moreover, the same could be said for Chinese companies and state-owned enterprises involved in hydropower projects in Cambodia. In the final analysis, historically Cambodia's geo-political position has meant Cambodian leaders of all political-economic orientations have had to balance carefully relations with powerful neighbours to the north (China), east (Vietnam) and west (Thailand). Having western powers as friends outside of the region to counterbalance these powerful Asian neighbours is still important for Cambodia. However, in the absence of an apparent willingness on the part of Cambodia's western donors to become involved in hydropower in Cambodia or oppose it on environmental and social grounds, China's willingness to do so seems to make good economic and political sense for Cambodia's leaders.

In this favourable political environment Chinese sate-owned companies and corporations are currently involved in a total of nine hydropower projects in Cambodia, including the controversial Cheay Areng and Lower Sesan II projects.[7] The impact and implications of Chinese built and financed dams in Cambodia – especially if the proposed projects go-ahead – are profound and complex. While government officials and other vested interests continue to extol the developmental virtues of hydropower, others scrutinize and question the overall long-term benefits for the majority of

Cambodians. The point of departure for a critical analysis often begins with an examination of the manner in which China and Chinese companies and the Cambodian government actually do business. Obtaining accurate and clear information and data like EIAs from Cambodian government sources has not always been straightforward. As well as general administrative and procedural shortcomings government ministries are notoriously opaque and often unforthcoming in matters of a politically sensitive nature.

The development of hydropower falls under the auspices of three ministries each led by senior members of the CPP's Central Committee, the Ministry of Industry Mines and Energy, the Ministry of Water Resources and Meteorology and the Ministry of Environment (MoE). As reserved domains of power and influence, the CPP party leadership tightly controls these and other key ministries. Dealing with the higher echelons of the administration can be easy or difficult depending upon the extent to which your interests are in harmony with those of the party leadership. For China and Chinese companies the process of securing approvals, contracts and licences for hydropower projects has been fairly straightforward. Hun Sen and his ministers are fully behind Chinese involvement in Cambodian hydropower development (Coghlan, 2008). All large multi-million dollar investments or projects have to pass through the Council for the Development of Cambodia and be ultimately approved by the Council of Ministers. The Prime Minister Hun Sen sits at the head of both bodies.

Problems arise when the political-economic edifice around which the CPP's power and control is built is challenged from the outside by those with an interest in holding the government to account for failures to uphold the rule of law, international covenants, commitments to human rights or other recognized standards of behaviour. As things currently stand, Chinese companies and state-owned corporations involved in hydropower projects outside of China are expected to follow the laws of the host country.[8] Over the last two decades the Cambodian government's record in upholding the rule of law and implementing and enforcing regulatory frameworks in cases that threaten vested interests connected to the ruling elite is and continues to be dismal.

Chinese hydropower and environmental and social impacts

By contrast other international organizations and local advocacy groups directly involved in hydropower issues in Cambodia, like International Rivers, Mekong Watch and the 'Three Rivers Protection Network' do not partner directly with government ministries. Organizations like these are very active in publicizing and organizing campaigns to raise awareness of the environmental and social impact of hydropower projects, and regularly challenge the government's position. International Rivers in particular pays close attention to Chinese backed projects. One of the central concerns of all these organizations is the manner in which the Environmental Impact

Assessments (EIA) and Social Impact Assessments (SIA) for these projects are handled by the Cambodian government and their Chinese partners. These are intended to provide assessments of environmental, social and other impacts of proposed development projects to inform decision-makers and the public before final decisions and commitments are made. A full EIA for Cambodia's first major dam project on the Kamchay river was completed only months before the project itself came online. The EIA process for the Kamchay project was problematic from the outset thus justifying the concerns of NGOs and advocacy groups pushing for greater transparency and public consultation.

The Kamchay experience raised many questions and fears about environmental and social safeguards for other projects already underway. The chief concern is not necessarily whether EIAs and SIAs are conducted, although that is still a significant worry, but whether there is the political will to ensure any potential problems and issues identified by the assessments are accurately reported and adequately dealt with by the authorities. Laws and regulations to govern and protect the environment and natural resources and ensure safeguards do exist (Grimsditch, 2012, pp. 33–36). These also include provisions for public consultation and participation in decisions that will impact upon local community access to natural resources and livelihoods. However, a recent report on the Kamchay conducted by an international consultant found that there are 'considerable gaps in the application and implementation of the safeguards that should apply to such projects' (ibid., p. 32).

In spite of the legislative framework, public consultation and participation in the EIA process for the Kamchay project was virtually non-existent (ibid., p. 37). Indeed, the project was conceived, planned and decided upon behind closed doors between the government and the Chinese companies and representatives without much regard for coherent plans to mitigate and deal with any adverse environmental and social effects. The dam was built in Bokor National Park a supposedly protected area of 140,000 ha of land. The park provides a habitat for a diverse number of species including large mammals such as elephants, tigers and sun-bears. In total, according to the EIA within the project area there are 37 species of mammals, 68 bird species, 23 reptile and 32 fish species. Overall the project takes up almost 2,300 ha or 20 km^2 of land including the dams' two reservoirs. Disruption to wildlife in the project area is expected, but any negative impact is considered by proponents of the project to be outweighed by the benefits (Grimsditch, 2012, p. 19). To make way for the project's facilities, large areas have been deforested, according to some reports from local people who rely on the forest for part of livelihoods and former park rangers. In addition, illegal logging has taken place in areas outside of the project area. It is estimated that approximately 3,000 ha of ever-green forest including bamboo was lost (ibid., p. 20).

For people and communities living in the area, the project has impacted upon their lives in several different ways. The first major impact people reported was a marked deterioration in the quality of water. The provincial town of Kampot and the surrounding areas receive their drinking water from the Kamchay river. While short-term negative effects on water quality during the construction phase are expected, the longer-term impact on hydrology in general is uncertain. Changes to the river's flows causing a build-up of sediment and the intrusion of salt from the nearby gulf of Thailand may have a negative on agricultural land. Some farmers lost productive land including commercial fruit trees to make way for project infrastructure. They did receive some compensation, but are still left with reduced incomes, with few alternatives to recoup losses. Local communities who rely on non-timber forest products for their livelihoods were affected most by the project as access to the most productive areas has been restricted by the project. Incomes from a local beauty spot on the river near the dam have also been significantly affected as the numbers of tourists visiting the site have dropped since construction of the dam began (ibid., p. 25).

The pushing through of the Kamchay project behind closed doors without public consultation and without a full EIA clearly demonstrated the government's and its Chinese backer's disregard for environmental and social safeguards. As a test-case for Cambodia's commitment to securing environmental and social safeguards in future hydropower plans the forecast is not favourable. Other proposed Chinese financed and built projects like the Cheay Areng in the Cardamoms, the large Sambor project in Kratie and a number of other projects on the Sesan and Srepok rivers in the country's northeast will have enormous environmental and social costs.[9] The impacts of projects currently under construction in the Cardamom Mountains have also given national and international organizations and advocacy groups further cause for concern.

As part of their campaign to raise awareness of the environmental and social costs of projects like the proposed Cheay Areng dam, International Rivers have been going directly to the Chinese companies involved with their concerns. In a letter sent in June 2013 to the CEO and President of China Guodian Corporation, the project's investor, International Rivers pointed out the project's 'reputational and operational' costs due to the expected environmental and social impacts. The projects reservoir will flood 2,000 ha of land belonging to the indigenous people sometimes referred to as *Khmer Daum*, requiring the relocation of perhaps as many as 400 families (Tittihara *et al.*, 2013). If the project goes ahead it will block the flows of the river 'destroying downstream habitats for wild fish' which are vital to the local economy, and also altering the natural seasonal flow of the water which will affect agriculture over a large area. The dam would also flood the habitat of 31 endangered fauna species including the Siamese crocodile, and other threatened animals like tigers, Asian elephant, pileated gibbons and rare fish. The letter politely but firmly explained that the company could expect conflict and public protests if the project went ahead (International Rivers, 2013).

What is interesting about the Cheay Areng case, as the letter pointed out, was that another prominent Chinese hydropower Company 'China Southern Power Grid' (CSPG) had previously backed out of the project, apparently due to the enormous risks involved and possible public protests. According to International Rivers, an inter-ministerial meeting with CSPG and NGOs to discuss the project prompted the Ministry of Interior to 'request that the company work with conservation organizations to mitigate the dam's impacts' (ibid.). The fact that NGOs were invited to the meeting and had their concerns heard was perhaps a positive sign that public consultation was beginning to be taken seriously by government ministries. However, the letter also noted at the time that Guodian had not followed up on the MoE request to work with the conservation NGOs. Moreover, the findings of the EIA for the project which was approved by the government have to date not been made public.

Any positive signs there may have been regarding public engagement with the Cheay Areng project has been overshadowed by the involvement of CPP senator and tycoon Lao Meng Khin and his wife both of whom are board members of Sinohydro. Sinohydro replaced Guodian after it withdrew its interest citing financial unfeasibility of the project – suggesting motivations maybe more to do with short-term personal gain rather than the long-term sustainability of the project (Pye, 2014a). International Rivers again drew attention to a number of issues related to the large Stung Tatay project situated in the southern Cardamom range. The project is being built by China National Heavy Machinery Corporation operating in Cambodia under the project name Cambodia Tatay Hydropower Company Limited and has been under construction since 2010. Problems and inconsistencies in the design and implementation of the project pointed out by International Rivers included insufficient public engagement and consultation, omission from the Project Design Document of the serious impact the project will have on bio-diversity in the Cardamom Mountains, and the possible violation of Cambodian laws including the 1996 Environment and Protection and Natural Resource Management Law and the 2008 Protected Area Law.

International conservation and Chinese dams

As has already been mentioned, donors have not pushed too hard for reform because to do so could threaten the stability of the system within which they operate. For international NGOs and advocacy groups critical of government officials' complicity in business activities causing environmental and social damage, this situation can make dealing with the authorities at all levels particularly troublesome. For the staff of local Cambodian NGOs and individuals working in advocacy groups, it can be extremely dangerous, even fatal. The termination of the UK-based campaign organization Global Witness as Cambodia's Official Independent Forest Monitor in 2003 for its work in exposing government links to illegal logging is illustrative of the difficulties faced by organizations concerned with effective governance of natural resources. The organization was later barred from Cambodia and its staff threatened with violence by the Prime Minister's brother if they dared to return after releasing a damning report linking members of the Prime Minister's family to rampant illegal logging (Global Witness, 2007).

A decade or so later, the Global Witness experience and its treatment at the hands of the government still resonates with those who recall some of the worst of the illegal logging excesses post-UNTAC. However, more recent cases concerning large well-endowed international conservation organizations suggest that the functioning of the Cambodian elite political-economic system may have circumscribed their engagement and compromised principles and actions upon which their organizations are founded. In the last 10 years or more, organizations like Conservation International (CI), Flora and Fauna International (FFI) and Wildlife Alliance (WA) have built close working relationships with the Cambodian government. Both CI and WA are working in areas close to large Chinese-backed hydropower projects in the Cardamom Mountains in South West Cambodia. The Cardamoms form part of the second largest contiguous evergreen forest area left in mainland Southeast Asia in what has been dubbed a global 'bio-diversity hotspot'. The area was designated the Central Cardamoms Protected Forest (CCPF) within which there are four protected areas, in 2002 by the Cambodian government.[10]

The murder in April 2012 of Cambodia's well-known and inspirational environmental and social activist Chut Wutty, once again placed illegal logging and international conservation organizations working in the Cardamoms into the spotlight. Wutty, the founder and director of Natural Resource Protection Group (NRPG), was shot and killed by a 'security guard' while investigating large-scale illegal logging in an area not far from hydropower projects. Two large Chinese dam projects the Stung Atay and the lower Roussey Chhrum have been completed, and the third, Stung Tatay is close to completion in the Cardamoms. A highly controversial fourth is in the early stage of construction in the densely populated and bio-diverse area of Cheay Areng in Thmar Bang district in Koh Kong province. It was subsequently discovered that the security guard that shot and killed Wutty was a military policeman apparently in service to a Cambodian logging company, Timbergreen, which is licensed to clear areas for the Tatay dam project reservoir. It is common knowledge among national and international activists, villagers and researchers alike that illegal logging with links to the Cambodian government is taking place outside of the designated reservoir areas (Cambodia Watch-Australia, 2012).

The killing of Chut Wutty drew worldwide media attention. International organizations like CI became embroiled in an ensuing controversy when they denied any knowledge of large-scale illegal logging going on in the area. CI funds and coordinates protection programmes in the CCPF are working closely with Forestry Administration officials and the military to prevent illegal logging and to protect the forest. In an attempt to defend itself against accusations made in the English language *Phnom Penh Post* of complicity and 'turning a blind eye' to the problem, CI pointed out that it only provides logistical support via grants to the Cambodian Forestry Administration to support monitoring and patrolling of the CCPF and is not involved on the ground in enforcing regulations and law (Lang, 2012). Critics argue that these type of responses from large well-funded International Conservation organizations like CI amounts to a 'green washing' of the problems (Milne, 2012). That is to say, either the denial of the existence of the problem or an unwillingness to engage with partners in government to tackle the problems seriously compromises conservation efforts, and efforts to deal with the impact of the dams. That said, recent statements by FFI and CI concerning the scrapping of the Cheay Areng dam suggests they may be becoming less skittish in their approach to government approved projects (Pye, 2014b).

The conscious or unconscious co-option of seemingly well-intentioned international organizations and donors attempting to work within the Cambodian political-economic system is nothing new. Beginning with UNTAC and the massive influx of international aid for reconstruction and development, elements within government have been particularly adroit in maintaining a facade of cooperation while protecting vital interests that can undermine or compromise international partnerships. The annual pledging and disbursement of aid by intentional donors despite the government's abysmal record in following through on stated commitments to reform provide some of the best illustrations. Overtime, various questionable cultural relativistic and historical arguments have been deployed to explain the nature of these relationships. Implicit in these arguments is the condescending idea that somehow Cambodia and Cambodians, because of recent history, are not ready for democracy, while attempts by individuals and groups on the outside of the system pushing for democratic change are ignored or downplayed.

Conclusion

Fears and worries highlighted by some national and international NGOs and advocacy groups about environmental and social safeguards surrounding these controversial hydropower projects are well-founded. The threats posed to people's livelihoods, the loss of bio-diversity over large swathes of some of Cambodia's and the region's pristine forested areas are grave, and if not checked could cause further irreversible damage. Supposedly cheap and reliable supplies of electricity provided by hydropower to meet the country's obvious energy needs shortfall seems, at first glance at least, to be a rational and logical proposition.

However, profound environmental and social changes wrought by these projects are inherently geo-political in nature and intimately linked to the motives and interests of foreign actors like the Chinese government and Chinese corporations and business. Furthermore, the projects are often linked and overlapped by other 'development' projects like mining, and agri-business, and associated problems like illegal logging and land grabs suggesting a link between these and hydropower development. The transformation, privatization and commodification of land use and livelihoods of traditional and rural communities alongside bio-diversity loss and declining fish stocks are thus key sites of contestation generating political conflicts at the local, national and international levels. What this amounts to is the clash of political-economic interests and agendas of a wide variety of local, national and international state and non-state actors each with their own competing and contested ideas about what it means to develop and how to do it.

In these circumstances, challenges to the government's dealings with Chinese companies involved in hydropower projects can be perfunctorily dismissed or subjected to obfuscatory administrative and bureaucratic engagement resulting in indeterminate government responses. As a result international standards and best practices as they relate to hydropower projects and environmental and social safeguards in Cambodia are routinely downplayed or ignored. National laws and regulations governing the project design and environmental and social assessments of the impacts are regularly flouted by government officials and their Chinese partners. For international conservation organizations working in the areas where these projects are being built or proposed these circumstances present a dilemma. For some caught between their government partnerships and commitments to conservation they find their positions compromised, resulting in them remaining silent on the huge impacts on indigenous people's livelihoods, and the suspected illegal logging activities of Cambodian companies engaged in the hydropower projects in collusion with local authorities.

In the absence of a public commitment by the Cambodian government and its Chinese partners to seriously address environmental and social safeguards, the situation is unlikely to change in the foreseeable future. In the meantime the debate about the costs and benefits of hydropower in Cambodia will continue until the importance of the debate for Cambodia's future needs and long-term sustainable development is recognized by political forces with the foresight and power to allow alternative voices to be heard.

Notes

1 See China's Global Role in Dam Building, http://www.internationalrivers.org/campaigns/china-s-global-role-in-dam-building, accessed 6 November 2013. See also The Three Gorges Dam http://www.internationalrivers.org/campaigns/three-gorges-dam, accessed 6 November 2013.
2 The GMS also includes, Laos, Myanmar, Thailand and Vietnam. For background information see http://www.adb.org/countries/gms/main, accessed 5 October 2013.

3 Funcinpec is the French acronym *Front Uni National Pour un Cambdodge Indépendent, Neutre, Pacifique et Coopératif*, which translates to National United Front for an Independent, Neutral, Peaceful and Cooperative Cambodia.
4 Personal interview with Sam Rainsy Party Parliamentarian, March 2011, Phnom Penh. See also Makara (2012).
5 Sinohydro Corporation, www.chincold.org.cn/chincold/zt/first/others/webinfo/2009/08/1281417028948733.htm, accessed 21 November 2013.
6 Report of the Special Rapporteur on the situation of Human Rights in Cambodia (formerly the Special Representative of the Secretary General for Human Rights in Cambodia), http://cambodia.ohchr.org/EN/PagesFiles/Reports/SR-SRSG-Reports.htm, accessed 5 August 2013.
7 See International Rivers, 'Overseas Dams List', http://www.internationalrivers.org/es/node/3611, accessed 11 November 2013.
8 More recently in 2013, the Chinese Ministry of Commerce and the Ministry of Environmental Protection released new 'Guidelines for Environmental Protection in Foreign Investment and Cooperation'. Although they are non-binding, they are as International Rivers points out Chinese government policy and provide a useful tool for NGOs and civil groups when 'holding Chinese companies responsible for environmental and social impact overseas', http://www.internationalrivers.org/resources/chinese-government-guidelines-for-overseas-investment-7934, accessed 24 November 2013.
9 See, for example, http://www.internationalrivers.org/campaigns/cambodia, accessed 6 December 2013.
10 These are the Cardamoms Protected Forest, the Phnom Samkos wildlife sanctuary, Phnom Aural and the Southern Cardamoms Protected Forest.

References

Bakker, K. (1999) 'The politics of hydropower: developing the Mekong', *Political Geography* 18, pp. 209–232.
Bargawi, O. (2005) *Cambodia's Garment Industry-Origins and Future Prospects,* Economic and Statistics Analysis Unit ESAU Working Paper 13, Overseas Development Institute, London.
Bosshard, P. (2011) 'Chinese government acknowledges problems of the Three Gorges Dam', 15 May, www.internationalrivers.org/blogs/227/chinese-government-acknowledges-problems-of-three-gorges-dam, accessed 15 October 2013.
Bratton, M. and van de Valle, N. (1994) 'Neo-patrimonial regimes and political transitions in Africa', in Pak (2007a) *Accountability and Neo-Patrimonialism in Cambodia: A Critical Literature Review,* The Cambodian Development Research Institute (CDRI) Working Paper 34, Phnom Penh, Chapter 4.
Cambodian Development Research Institute. (2013) *Cambodia's Development Dynamic: Past Performance and Emerging Priorities,* September, Phnom Penh.
Cambodia Watch-Australia. (2012) 'Timber Green Company Ltd at Vey Bey point, Koh Pao village, Bakkhlong sub-district, Mondol Seima District, Koh Kong province where Vuthy was murdered', 30 April 2012, http://camwatchblogs.blogspot.com/2012/04/timber-green-company-ltd-at-vey-bey.html, accessed 17 October 2013.
Chakrya, K. S. and Strangio, S. (2009) 'Villagers gather to express dam concerns' *The Phnom Penh Post*, 25 September 2009.
Chandary, O., Chanhang, S. and Dalis, P. (2011) *Assessing China's Impact on Poverty Reduction in the Greater Mekong Sub-Region: The Case of Cambodia,* CDRI Working Paper 32, Cambodian Development Resource Institute, Phnom Penh.

Chen, X. and Stone, C. (2013) 'China and Southeast Asia: Unbalanced development in the Greater Mekong Sub-Region', *The European Financial Review*, August 20.
Ciorciari, J. D. (2013) *China and Cambodia: Patron and Client?* International Policy Center Working Paper No 121, University of Michigan, Gerald R. Ford School of Public Policy.
Coghlan, M. (2008) *China's Poverty Footprint in Cambodia*, Oxfam, Hong Kong.
Gillison, D. and Kimsan, K (2007) 'Donor discontent may not lessen donor largesse', *The Cambodia Daily*, March 3.
Global Witness. (2007) 'Family trees', 31 May 2007, http://www.globalwitness.org/library/cambodias-family-trees, accessed 18 October 2013.
Grimsditch, M. (2012) *China's Investment in Hydropower in the Mekong Region: The Kamchay Hydropower Dam Kampot, Cambodia*, World Resources Institute, Washington, DC.
Hill, J. (2013) 'Global hydropower set to exceed $75 billion through to 2020. The energy collective', October 20, http://theenergycollective.com/joshshill/290736/global-hydropower-set-exceed-75-billion-through-2020, accessed 20 October 2013.
Hirsch, P. (1996) 'Large dams, restructuring and regional integration in Southeast Asia', *Asia Pacific Viewpoint* 27(1), pp. 1–20.
Hul, R. (2014) 'Chinese push Sesan Dam talks with Hun Sen', *The Cambodia Daily*, January 23.
International Crisis Group (ICG). (1998) 'Cambodia's flawed elections: Why Cambodia will not be ready for free and fair elections on 26 July 1998', *Asia Report*, No 2, 16 June.
International Rivers. (2013) 'Letter from International Rivers to Guodian Corporation', 24 June 2013, http://www.internationalrivers.org/files/attached-files/20130624-letter_to_guodian_re_cheay_areng_dam_english.pdf, accessed 20 October 2013.
Lang, C. (2012) 'Conservation International turns a blind eye to illegal logging in the Cardamom Mountains Cambodia', red-monitor.org, 19 January 2012, http://www.redd-monitor.org/2012/01/19/conservation-international-turns-a-blind-eye-to-illegal-logging-in-the-cardamom-mountains-cambodia/, accessed 20 October 2013.
Makara, K. (2012) 'Opposition urges China checks', *The Phnom Penh Post*, 17 August 2012, http://www.phnompenhpost.com/business/opposition-urges-china-checks, accessed 20 October 2013.
Middleton, C. and Chanty, S. (2008) *Cambodia's Hydropower Development and Cambodia's Involvement*, International Rivers and the Rivers Coalition in Cambodia, Phnom Penh.
Milne, S. (2012) 'Chut Wutty: Tragic Casualty of Cambodia's dirty war to save forests', New Mandala, 30 April 2012, http://asiapacific.anu.edu.au/newmandala/2012/04/30/chut-wutty-tragic-casualty-of-cambodia%E2%80%99s-dirty-war-to-save-forests/, accessed 5 November 2013.
Molle, F., Foran, T. and Käkönen, M. (eds) (2009) *Contested Waterscapes in the Mekong Region, Hydropower, Livelihoods and Governance*, Earthscan, London.
Post Staff. (1996) 'Rivers of power: The dam debate hearts up', *The Phnom Penh Post*, September.
Pye, D. (2014a) 'Power couple linked to Sinohydro project', *The Phnom Penh Post*, 13 March.
Pye, D. (2014b) 'ECO groups slam Areng dam', *The Phnom Penh Post*, 3 April 2014.
Sachs, W., 'Global ecology and the shadow of "development"', in Wolfgang Sachs (ed.) (1995) *Global Ecology: A New Arena of Political Conflict*. Zed Books. London and New Jersey, p. 4.

Tittihara, M., Boyle, D. and Cheony, D. (2013) 'Last days of a valley damned', *The Phnom Penh Post*, 8 February.

Urban, F., Nordensvard, N., Khatri., D., Wang, Y. (2013) 'An analysis of China's investment in the hydropower sector in the Greater Mekong Sub-Region', *Environment, Development and Sustainability* 15(2), pp. 301–324.

World Commission on Dams. (2000) *Dams and Development: A New Framework for Decision-Making*, Earthscan, London and Sterling, VA.

Worrell, S. (2013) 'NGOs ask PM to axe Koh Kong dam plans', *The Phnom Penh Post*, 20 December.

Worrell, S. and Seangly, P. (2013) 'An unsettling prospect', *The Phnom Penh Post*, 17 December.

Xinhua. (2013a) 'China-invested hydropower dam operational', February 23, http://www.china.org.cn/business/2013-02/23/content_28041286.htm, accessed 20 October 2013.

Xinhua. (2013b) 'Cambodia China celebrate 55th anniversary of diplomatic ties' 20 June 2013, http://english.peopledaily.com.cn/90883/8291601.html, accessed 5 November 2013.

Part 2
Interventions in natural resource management

7 Managing protected areas in Cambodia

The challenge for conservation bureaucracies in a hostile governance environment

Richard Paley

Figure 7.1 Rangers demarcating the Community Zone inside a protected area.
Source: Photo by R. Paley.

Introduction: Management responses to a protected area system under threat

Protected areas (PAs) have a long history as the preferred response to human impact on natural ecosystems (Margules and Pressey, 2000) and recent decades have witnessed an unprecedented expansion of the global protected area network (Jenkins and Joppa, 2009). During this period there has been considerable debate over the merits of community-based approaches to PA management versus the more exclusive 'fortress conservation' mode (Kramer et al., 1997; Brockington, 2002), but PAs remain the defining strategy for conservation (Adams, 2004). The modern Cambodian PA system was established by Royal Decree in 1993. Twenty three PAs were created, encompassing a quarter of the country's land surface including some of its most diverse and species-rich landscapes. The Royal Decree also invested the Ministry of Environment (MoE) with responsibility for the management of the PA system, and though other areas have subsequently been gazetted under different jurisdictions, the MoE remains Cambodia's primary authority for PAs.[1]

From their inception Cambodia's PAs have been under increasing threat from unsustainable resource exploitation and unregulated infrastructure development (Lacerda et al., 2004). The instigators of these threats include a wide array of social and state actors ranging from the rural poor, for whom the country's forest areas are a critical livelihoods resource, to police or military personnel and members of the civil administration. In recent years, the acceleration in uncontrolled forest conversion fuelled by expansion of agriculture and land speculation has superseded both illegal hunting of wildlife and logging of luxury timber as the most pervasive and damaging threat. Indeed, so serious was the rate of land conversion in Roniem Daum Som Wildlife Sanctuary during the early 2000s that by 2004 the MoE had reluctantly de-gazetted 78 per cent of its original area. This acceleration in natural resource depletion has been given additional impetus by the stability and economic growth enjoyed by Cambodia over the past decade which has been accompanied by rapid expansion of agro-industry, tourism, extractive industries and infrastructure (Hughes and Un, 2011; EU, 2012).

Formal designation of conservation areas has provided few safeguards against the environmental and socio-economic impact of these developments. New road networks transect conservation areas, opening them up to settlement and resource extraction. In 2012, four large-scale hydropower projects were under construction in southwest Cambodia alone; and at least 13 other projects were subject to feasibility studies across the country, many of which overlapped with PAs (Grimsditch, 2012). Numerous economic land concessions for the production of commodities such as rubber and sugar have been granted in PAs and are major drivers of land conversion as well as magnets for further settlement. Mining exploration licences have been granted inside more than half Cambodia's PAs (NGO Forum, 2008). Commercial tourism concessions have also been approved within a number of PAs, most notably in Ream National Park where approximately 25 per cent of its land area has been allocated for development of a single tourism resort (Pye and May, 2014). Indeed the Cambodian human rights organization, Licadho, claims that PAs have been specifically targeted in the granting of land concessions, and that 10 per cent of the PA system had already been allocated by 2012 (Vrieze and Naren, 2012).

The response of MoE and its international partners to these threats has tended to follow a classic and formulaic approach. This focuses predominantly on the proximate causes of biodiversity loss and natural resource degradation and gives insufficient emphasis to larger scale pressures and the complex set of drivers which underlie them. When explaining their lack of conservation success, PA managers usually emphasize practical challenges ranging from impassable roads and endemic malaria to the difficulty in detecting illegal activity at night and over vast forest areas. Suggestions for improving PA performance emphasize the need for what Gibson (1999) referred to as 'bureaucratic' solutions, which focus on addressing inadequacies in staff capacity and resource availability while ignoring broader institutional, social and political factors. The inevitable deduction from this is that what is required to make PAs more effective is further investment in training, infrastructure and equipment. The majority of Cambodian PAs are certainly underfunded and current government budgets only cover modest staff salaries, uniform issue, basic park infrastructure and irregular payments for sundry costs. Managers must operate under a range of constraints including inadequate staffing, equipment, transport and office facilities.[2] So lacking in resources and levels of activity are many of Cambodia's PA's, that they can justifiably be classified as 'paper parks' (ICEM, 2003; MoE, 2006).

The situation is different in the select group of PAs which receive financial and technical support from international donors or conservation NGOs.[3] In these, budgets are sufficient to cover most operational costs and thereby sustain much more active management, and PA staff generally possess the skills and materials necessary to carry out a more comprehensive and sophisticated range of management interventions. These interventions are broadly consistent with international concepts of best practice, and go beyond an exclusive reliance on protection and law enforcement. Instead they employ a range of strategies that focus on engaging local resource users to achieve conservation objectives such as participatory planning, environmental education and community natural resource management (Clements *et al.*, 2008; Long, 2008), which are also increasingly articulated in Cambodian environmental legislation and policy (Kim and Sy, 2005).

Nevertheless, in spite of receiving greater technical and resource inputs, none of the donor or NGO-supported PAs shows significantly greater resilience to external threats and pressures than their unsupported neighbours. So while 'bureaucratic' factors or technical 'best practice' may contribute to success they are not sufficient to determine management outcomes; meaning that other variables must be at play. As Cumming (2004) pointed out, once certain minimum levels of funding and staffing are achieved, other factors emerge as important drivers of management effectiveness.

This chapter seeks to identify those drivers of PA performance by examining both the MoE and the political and social context in which it operates. Its principal focus is at the PA level but reference is also made to the MoE at national level, since the latter's engagement with PA issues has a direct bearing on their performance. The chapter begins by focusing on the organizational characteristics of PA management authorities and the extent to which they conform to the model of a rational bureaucracy. This leads on to an exploration of the factors which constrain the MoE from conducting effective park management. The conclusion of this analysis is that these 'constraining factors' are both integral to the organization and are products of a hostile political, social and economic operating environment, characterized by poor governance and a pervasive culture of corruption and patronage throughout the state apparatus.

The views expressed in this chapter are based on the author's own observations, as well as formal interviews and *adhoc* interaction with conservation practitioners, community representatives, government officials and international donors during a decade of work and research in Cambodia from 2000 to 2010. From 2008 to 2009 the author undertook field research focusing on the MoE and its capacity to address the challenges facing PAs. As part of that research semi-structured interviews were conducted with all PA directors (or their deputies), and detailed case studies of management effectiveness were carried out in two PAs using techniques adapted from organizational ethnography, including extended periods of time observing PA staff at their duties. Where the study of organizations is concerned there is a tendency to adopt a language and perspective, which is peculiarly Western in outlook. This is no doubt true of the discussion and analysis in this chapter. Nevertheless, I hope conservation practitioners in Cambodia and beyond will still find them relevant and useful.

Internal organizational characteristics influencing PA management performance

Formal and informal structures and processes

The MoE's inability to successfully address the threats facing its PAs is partially attributable to weaknesses that are evident at all levels of the organization from the individual PA management units to the headquarters in Phnom Penh. The essence of the problem, and one that is not unique to Cambodia, is that like many government agencies particularly in developing countries, the MoE is a parody of the Weberian ideal of a rational bureaucratic organization (see Weber, 1973; Scott, 1998). The formal characteristics which should define such organizations, integrity, strict adherence to organizational goals, advancement on merit, transparent rewards and sanctions, and committed leadership, are either absent or present in a weakened form. In their place a culture of institutionalized corruption and patronage, discussed later in this chapter, dominates.

Outwardly the MoE conforms to the pattern of a rational bureaucratic organization structured and managed for the efficient achievement of its objectives. Goals are defined with varying degrees of clarity, and are reproduced in formal structures which group staff according to the various tasks assigned to the organization. Though the official hierarchy is fairly flat, with few intervening grades between senior and junior staff, there is a rigid distinction between these levels, and management operates in an ostensibly 'top-down' fashion, the emphasis being on command and control rather than initiative and self-motivation. Subordinates customarily show deference to their seniors and eschew displays of overt disobedience. However, as in all organizations, formal structures and processes are subject to interpretation and modification by the members. So while PA management organizations appear to function according to officially proscribed patterns, closer examination reveals a range of unorthodox arrangements and practices.

Maintaining day-to-day control over activities within PAs is problematic for their directors, who are often far-removed physically from their staff and unable to communicate with them easily. The result is that those working in remote field stations become used to acting semi-autonomously, referring to higher levels of authority only when it suits them. This infrequency of direct supervision promotes a 'centrifugal effect' in opposition to the centralizing tendency of formal management structures (Kaufman, 1993), which mirrors the centre-periphery tensions and limitations on state capabilities which are characteristic of many developing countries (Migdal, 1988). Under these conditions, I observed that coordination between functional components (whether protection, community extension or ecological research) becomes more difficult as each pursues its own narrowly defined goals, and the discretionary powers of subordinates flourish alongside formal control systems. In this way the directors' orders become '. . . like authorless texts; once the words are set in motion, the manager ceases to control their meaning' (Gergen, 1992, p. 220).

Authority in PAs is officially associated with rank and status, reinforced to some degree by cultural and normative expectations that emphasize obedience and hierarchical conformity (Bit, 1991; Pearson, 2005). But owing to the weakness of the supporting regulative framework, I found this authority to be implied rather than absolute. In fact it is unclear what formal controls and sanctions PA managers have at their disposal to ensure compliance with organizational goals, rules and procedures. Government instructions for civil servants (RGC, 2000) state clearly the standards of conduct and discipline expected of officials in the execution of their duties, but make no mention of the penalties for breaching these standards or mechanisms for applying them. Formal evaluation of individual staff is non-existent, and few MoE staff have a clear terms of reference against which their performance can be assessed. Occasionally rangers will have their short-term contracts revoked by the PA director for poor performance or misconduct but for staff employed as part of the permanent civil service this would require the sanction of the Minister for Environment and is almost unheard of.[4] In 2005 I observed an investigation in which five PA staff confessed to bribery and misappropriation of confiscated timber. The four rangers involved were sacked, but the permanent MoE officer was merely reassigned within the provincial Department of Environment (DoE). In this context of weak and ill-defined authority multiple chains of command often develop, through which PA managers reinforce their control by circumventing uncooperative colleagues and routing instructions through more malleable subordinates. Conversely disgruntled subordinates exploit their connections to higher levels of government to by-pass the official chain of command. This leads to a web of rival authorities and loyalties all competing for legitimacy, often as a means to gain access to or control over resources and always leading to confusion over responsibilities and resentment between colleagues. In this chaotic managerial arena what authority PA directors do exert is largely derived from the benefits they can bestow on their subordinates. These institutional links between patron and subordinate which facilitate the unofficial flow of resources up and down the levels of hierarchy are referred to in Cambodia as *khsae* meaning 'string' or 'connection' (Hughes, 2006; Jacobsen and Stuart-Fox, 2013).

Constraints on protected area staff performance

Many of those I interviewed working in Cambodia's PAs admit that poor staff performance is a major inhibitor of successful management outcomes. This is often ascribed to low technical capacity and inadequate financial compensation for demanding work in remote and challenging environments, but this explanation is incomplete.

Staff capacity is certainly an issue in most PAs, including those supported by international organizations. Rangers are almost invariably drawn from local communities, so educational levels are low and illiteracy is common. The quality of rangers would be improved if selection procedures were more rigorous. In many PAs there is no procedure, while in others applicants are selected on the basis of a simple résumé and an interview with the director; use of aptitude tests is very limited. This leaves the process open to abuse and the possibility that selection will owe more to personal connections and the ability to pay than suitability for the job. This in turn makes rangers more biddable and susceptible to incorporation in patron-client relationships. Nevertheless, regardless of the method of recruitment, most rangers join having acquired field skills from previous experience as soldiers, policemen or from time spent harvesting forest resources, and are therefore qualified to carry out their tasks to a basic level at least. Moreover, being drawn from communities in or adjacent to the PAs where they work, they possess an innate understanding of the immediate context in which they operate enabling them to make rapid assessments of any enforcement situation. In August 2008, I witnessed rangers conducting a quick analysis of recent land clearing. Based on factors such as distance from the nearest village and proximity to the road, they rightly concluded the clearing had been instigated by a land speculator from outside the PA rather than local farmers wishing to extend their land.

Capacity is more of a problem among PA technical staff conducting ecological surveys or community extension work. In provincial DoEs it is difficult to find candidates with the required knowledge, potential or interest to learn a more sophisticated set of skills. Yet with mentoring from international organizations and secondment of staff from the MoE in Phnom Penh, some PAs are developing a cadre of proficient staff capable of implementing conservation interventions of greater breadth and complexity than just law enforcement. The most serious capacity issues I identified were at the PA management level. Many directors have occupied their positions for a considerable time. The average duration in 2008 was over 4 years, which enabled them to develop an acute grasp of the social and political complexities of their work. However, they still lacked sufficient conservation knowledge and management skills to devise PA strategies, co-ordinate technical activities or oversee administrative and financial systems without the support of external advisers. Nevertheless, these issues of technical capacity are gradually being addressed; meaning they alone cannot explain the poor performance of Cambodia's PA staff.

As in any organization, levels of motivation and morale are equally important in determining staff performance (Scott, 1998; Evans and Rauch, 1999). A variety of factors serve to sap morale and weaken commitment to MoE goals, but PA staff and their managers tend to highlight the role of inadequate financial remuneration particularly for enforcement rangers. The government salary for a basic ranger is approximately $35 per month, and the flat staff hierarchy provides few opportunities for increasing salary through promotion. Delayed payment of up to 3 months and misappropriation of salaries by some supervisors serve to further diminish the incentivizing effect of a ranger's official wage. Even salary supplements of up to 500 per cent offered to some rangers by international NGOs are considered insufficient recompense given the arduous nature of the job. Patrolling over long distances, while negotiating physical obstacles in seasonally inclement weather, is physically very demanding. Add to this the stress of confronting seemingly intractable problems, in a risky and unpredictable operating environment with minimal support from other government agencies or the higher echelons of their own ministry, and it is easy to appreciate how morale and motivation could suffer. Especially frustrating for the rangers is the frequency with which their superiors or the courts order the release of influential suspects or their employees without prosecuting cases fully. A ranger patrol leader related to me how he returned to his station from escorting an offender to the provincial courts, only to learn that the accused had already returned to his village having paid a bribe. Unsurprisingly therefore, when questioned by me about law enforcement, rangers peppered their responses with references to 'wasted effort', and the 'pointlessness' of their work.

In Cambodia the norms and values prevalent among rangers' families, communities and colleagues which might compensate for the absence of other incentives are not conducive to reinforcing PA goals. Rangers have learnt to repeat stock phrases about the necessity of 'preserving the forest', but there is no recognized moral imperative to conserve nature either in the abstract or the sense of protecting valuable natural resources from rapacious outsiders. The hierarchy of obligations after self is to family, friends and then colleagues, and where this conflicts with conservation objectives the former normally prevails.[5] This clash of values has repercussions for their relations with the communities among which they live and work and to whose members they are often related. Rangers described how behaviour perceived as over-zealous is widely resented by local residents. In most cases the reaction is confined to verbal abuse or minor acts of spite or harassment, but it occasionally extends to threats of physical harm. However, fear of personal injury is not the key factor here. More potent is the sense of communal and familial attachment which overrides the rangers' identification with the MoE and its objectives. Locally recruited rangers are understandably sympathetic to fellow villagers who are often poor and/or marginalized, and it is partly guilt combined with fear of ostracism that induces them to pursue their enforcement activities with less than full vigour. PA technical staff generally seem more motivated, perhaps, because many of the negative aspects of ranger life – the risk, the antagonism and the constant physical strain – are not as prevalent in their work. They also receive higher salaries and are aware that the knowledge and experience they acquire as part of their work are likely to open up better employment opportunities for them in the future.

Few PA directors exhibited significant leadership qualities.[6] Remote, seemingly uninterested, and adopting an authoritarian style more likely to induce fear than encouragement, they expressed little enthusiasm for their responsibilities or commitment to conservation. Many were candid about their sense of political vulnerability and their reluctance to face up to competing and powerful interests, adopting a 'live and let live' attitude instead. Their staff often complained that when they encounter difficult or complex management situations, particularly those involving influential elites, managers seem more concerned with avoiding repercussions than ensuring PA regulations are upheld. Thus, they frequently postpone decisive intervention until it is too late to influence the outcome.

Corruption among PA staff

> All rangers want to be rich and follow the example of the leadership, all therefore do corruption in a big or small way.
>
> (Former Phnom Samkos protection team leader, August 2008)

Many PA staff are involved in corruption linked to the patronage systems characteristic of the Cambodian bureaucracy (Calavan *et al.*, 2004). The primary reason advanced to explain why PA staff engaged in corruption was a desire for self-enrichment, in some cases spurred on by the example of those further up in the hierarchy. External pressure or intimidation from within and outside the MoE can also play a part. Poor employment conditions tend to make staff more susceptible to inducements and less concerned at the prospect of losing their jobs if they are caught.

PA managers enmeshed in a system of *khsae* are expected to make regular payments to their superiors and to political party funds. They recoup these costs through minor acts of embezzlement and the receipt of regular contributions in cash or valuable natural resources from the rangers working for them. Specific examples related to me include making unofficial deductions from ranger salaries and supplements and exacting a commission on the sale of ranger positions from one individual to another. The rangers in turn make up their losses and supplement their salaries though a range of illicit practices. Some clear land inside the conservation zone for their own use, others sell illegally cut timber which they have confiscated – sometimes to the very individuals from whom it was seized. Most exploit their official positions managing state resources by 'taxing' the law. This can be through extorting money from those habitually involved in illegal activity, such as chainsaw operators or transporters of illegal timber; or alternatively by misappropriating all or part of the fines that they levy in the course of their duties. In some PAs a particular team is earmarked by superiors to carry out most of the corrupt activities, causing resentment among other teams which are thereby excluded from such opportunities.

Corruption is facilitated by the fact that managers often concentrate their rangers in a few main locations with limited rotation of staff between them, thus enabling them to form the bonds with each other and those engaged in illegal activity that support corrupt practices. But it has thrived in large part because there are no effective institutional sanctions to suppress it. Even though the Protected Areas law (Article 64) states unequivocally that PA staff that are negligent or participate in illegal activity will be subject to prosecution, they know that in practice this rarely happens; not least because those responsible for maintaining discipline and correct conduct are frequently beneficiaries of corruption and patronage themselves. It is not entirely unknown for senior MoE staff to face disciplinary action, as the removal of the director of Virachey National Park for collusion with illegal loggers demonstrated (Ironside and Yik, 2007); though in that case there was widespread feeling among conversation practitioners that government action was prompted by pressure from donors and the director's failure to fulfil his obligations to those he was linked to by *khsae*, rather than a desire to uphold Cambodia's laws.

Aside from acting as a disincentive to proper performance of duties, corruption has other insidious effects. It reduces efficiency by creating leakage from limited budgets. It can lower self-esteem, and therefore morale, by making rangers look incompetent when bribes secure immunity for flagrant offenders, and it can weaken organizational cohesion by generating resentment against superiors who embezzle salaries or towards colleagues who receive a greater share of the proceeds. Furthermore, corruption generates negative perceptions of PA staff among communities, especially when it involves inconsistent and partial implementation of the law, making it more difficult to secure local co-operation in pursuing PA objectives. The observed contradiction that PA staff whose performance is routinely poor, do sometimes pursue PA objectives with determination and courage was explained to me as reflecting their need to perform effectively enough to justify continued employment, particularly in PAs supported by international donors or NGOs. In the case of more senior staff, the occasional rigorous application of PA regulations can also serve as a demonstration of power which in turn facilitates subsequent efforts to extort or secure bribes.

Support for PAs from the Ministry of Environment

> GDANCP doesn't know how to solve the problems [confronting PAs], or if it knows it doesn't have the capacity, or if it has the capacity it doesn't have the credibility.
>
> (Senior technical officer, MoE, 2009)

As the parent organization for 23 PA authorities, the MoE and its constituent General Department for the Administration of Nature Conservation and Protection (GDANCP), which is responsible for overseeing the protected area network, should be (1) a source of competent technical advice and sound management guidance and (2) a mediator between the ministry and its external environment. But the ministry is not competent to provide the former and has insufficient influence and status within government to provide the latter. As a result, it often fails to provide adequate support to PA staff in addressing issues that require greater capacity and authority than is available at site level; namely those involving the Royal Cambodian Armed Forces (RCAF) or police or commercial enterprises linked to senior political figures. This promotes a sense of abandonment among PA directors and the suspicion that GDANCP and the Ministry at large are indifferent to the challenges they face.

Weak in terms of power compared with the Ministry of National Defence and insignificant in terms of revenue generating potential compared with the Ministries of Industry, Mines and Energy or Agriculture, Forestry and Fisheries, the MoE's conservation goals have been definitively relegated to a subordinate position in a national policy agenda that privileges rapid economic development over sustainable growth. From such a position of weakness, it is unable to intervene to ensure that local decisions and actions affecting PAs are guided by long-term perspectives rather than political and economic opportunism and elite interests.

The MoE also exhibits many of the same internal defects as individual PA authorities, namely low technical and managerial capacity, indifferent leadership and the distortion of staff behaviour by patronage and corruption. Evidence for direct involvement in corruption, at least among junior and middle management staff, is less apparent than at PA level, but significant incentives to diverge from official goals exist. Consequently decision-making is more often determined by considerations of personal benefit and aversion to risk than by a balanced and informed judgement of what will achieve optimal outcomes. Appointments made on the basis of political and familial connections rather than aptitude reduce further the competency and credibility of a workforce already characterized by low skill levels.

In one respect, however, the MoE differs from the PA management authorities. Most of the latter are formally structured in ways that reflect the actual tasks they perform. However, in the process of elevating the department responsible for PAs to a 'General Department', the MoE has created an inflated and confused structure comprised of a plethora of offices with ambiguous responsibilities and insufficient skilled staff to fill newly established positions. This has exacerbated an already serious problem of overlap and competition between different offices in the MoE and GDANCP in particular, leading to a further reduction in efficiency and effective support to PAs.[7] In practice the ministry has never functioned entirely in accordance with its formal structure. Staff regularly find themselves undertaking activities outside their official remit, partly owing to the absence of clear job descriptions for many positions, but also because certain departments and individuals are considered insufficiently competent to do demanding tasks even when these accord with their specified roles. For example, compilation of the Programme of Work for PAs (2008) and the conduct of a Management Effectiveness Tracking Tool (METT) survey of the entire PA system (2008–2009) were assigned to teams from the Departments of Planning and Legal Affairs and Environmental Impact Assessment, respectively, rather than the GDANCP which has formal responsibility for PAs. Intense rivalry between the different elements of the MoE manifests itself in efforts to by-pass other groups or individuals, or to refrain from co-operating with them. All of which undermines the ministry's ability to function as a cohesive entity.

Filling the vacuum: NGO support to PAs

Lacking support from their parent ministry, PA authorities rely heavily on their long-standing partnerships with international NGOs to address their organizational deficiencies. The presence of well-motivated and capable international advisers has clearly done much to generate better management performance. However, I believe these improvements constitute a largely cosmetic and temporary antidote to what are persistent underlying organizational problems. Advisers working closely with PA staff can facilitate short-term improvements in performance through providing clarity of direction, impartial monitoring of staff conduct and a modicum of protection from pressure to engage in corruption. Yet my research indicated that these effects are at best modest, and last only as long as the close working relationship is maintained.

Improvements in performance achieved through NGO partnerships do not represent an enduring change in the values, perspectives or assumptions of PA staff. Moreover, programmatically, the focus of NGOs still seems to be on addressing 'technocratic' issues, such as staff capacity, resource availability and technical approaches. I suspect this is not simply because their status as partners of the MoE, and the dependency which that implies, acts as a deterrent to tackling these more contentious issues, but because, like their national counterparts, they simply have no clear idea how to set about solving what seem to be intractable problems.

The political and social context and its impact on PA management

Of course not all park staff lack competence or motivation. There are remarkable individuals who struggle to perform their duties properly even within an organization that seems neither to appreciate nor support their efforts. These individuals find themselves constrained by the nature of their organization and facing opposition from a range of inimical external interests. Organizations like the MoE are not hermetically sealed from the political, social and economic environment in which they are embedded. Context is as significant in determining PA management outcomes as are the MoE's objectives, structure and internal processes. Details may differ between areas, but the agents and processes that shape local contexts are broadly similar and only their relative significance changes. Common to all are the conflicting institutional arrangements and contradictory policy agendas that produce an environment in which many of the key actors are antagonistic to the PA by default. A distorted system of governance reduces PAs to a form of patrimonial domain, where the need to secure votes and/or wealth for themselves and their patrons, encourages local elites to facilitate, engage in or ignore unsustainable behaviour (Le Billon, 2002; Global Witness, 2007).

Proximate stakeholders and their relationship to PAs

It is unsurprising that conflict should arise between PA authorities and local residents heavily dependent on the resources within conservation areas. Well planned and executed programmes may help to reduce friction and foster cooperation, but they do not bring about an end to illegal resource use or land conversion. Even when local communities realize current levels of use are unsustainable, present subsistence needs and market-driven demands take precedence. But in Cambodia the main challenge to achieving conservation objectives comes not from local communities but from other elements of the state. To some extent this is due to structural problems in that, notwithstanding the clear legal basis for the MoE's authority over the PAs, the post-conflict re-constitution of the state left other national and local government agencies with overlapping, competing but frequently legitimate mandates and jurisdictional claims over significant parts of every PA.

So numerous and widely distributed are the police and military in Cambodia that all PAs have multiple detachments in close proximity to them. Poorly paid, inadequately resourced and under-employed, they resort to illegal harvesting of natural resources and land clearing to sustain themselves, and engage in commercial-scale resource extraction to generate large incomes for their commanders.[8] Managing the activities of the police and RCAF is highly problematic because they are two of the most powerful and ruthless entities in Cambodia. PA staff claim that direct opposition is usually dangerous and ineffectual, and therefore they have adopted a range of non-confrontational strategies including direct appeals to commanders to control their subordinates, or attempts to harness the authority of the police to regulate the military and vice versa, but with only limited success.

Law, governance and the culture of impunity

Until recently, PA management in Cambodia was guided by a diffuse, ambiguous and in some cases inconsistent set of laws, decrees, circulars and other regulations, which could be used to support contradictory positions on the same issue (Obendorf, 2006). Enactment of the Protected Area Law in early 2008 went a considerable way towards addressing these shortcomings and providing a coherent and comprehensive legal framework for PA management. The PA law is much better integrated with related Cambodian legislation than its predecessors (Dunai, 2008). More importantly it does much to clarify PA system objectives, institutional jurisdiction, and what can and cannot be done inside PAs. Nevertheless, though much of the necessary regulatory and institutional framework is in place to support effective management, the governance environment within which management takes place is in many respects unfavourable.

> We have the law, but everyone knows the law is not respected. So how can we enforce it effectively?
> (Ranger station commander, Lomphat Wildlife Sanctuary, March 2008)

Under current governance arrangements in Cambodia, PA legislation and the authority it confers are consistently undermined by actions of politicians, bureaucrats, businessmen, police and the RCAF. None of these interlinked groups or individuals is motivated by public service or the 'national interest'; instead they chiefly work for narrower personal, family or political interests. Or rather they use the culturally acceptable concept of furthering family interests to justify their participation in a system by which the ruling party has effectively merged the private interests of these elites with its own. Furthermore, the state organizations and agencies to which these elites belong fund their existence and derive much of their power, either from the illegal exploitation of PA resources or extracting unofficial revenue from rent seeking and other forms of corruption linked to such resources (Gottesman, 2003; Un and So, 2011). This results in a situation in which the very entities that PA authorities most need to co-opt to their cause are the most implacably opposed to it. Notwithstanding the occasional and superficial displays of collaboration which their mandates require, these entities focus on subverting or circumventing PA authorities through a variety of strategies which range from contrived incompetence to open obstruction and direct involvement in illegal activity.

The subordinate position of PA managers within the government hierarchy makes it very difficult for them to compel these powerful interests to comply with conservation regulations without support from other institutions of the state. Yet PA managers claim their appeals to the obvious sources of that support, the higher levels of government and the judiciary, seldom yield positive results. Some provincial courts appear to be scrupulous and timely in their application of the law, even awarding custodial sentences where appropriate, but most tend towards inconsistency and procrastination. This is often ascribed by the courts themselves to excessive workloads, but it is also attributable to corruption. PA staff note that powerful or wealthy individuals and organizations are able to ignore or violate the law with impunity. Although poor villagers are sometimes punished by the courts relatively severely, the rich and powerful are invariably able to secure release or at least a reduced punishment for themselves or their employees, occasionally with the added bonus of having their confiscated contraband and equipment returned to them. Indeed disillusionment with the judicial process has led some PA managers to adopt a policy of not submitting cases to court but imposing fines instead, thereby at least ensuring that offenders incur some direct cost for their actions while simultaneously generating funds for both the MoE and in some cases the rangers involved, who receive a proportion of the fine taken. However, this can also create incentives for MoE rangers to engage in rent seeking and extortion. In addition to the failings of the court system, this impunity rests on a capacity to intimidate those enforcing the law. PA staff of any rank who are scrupulous in carrying out their protection duties put themselves at risk, particularly if they go so far as to submit cases to court. For the most part the intimidation is restricted to threats directed at individuals or their families, but can be more extreme. I interviewed a director of Kirirom

National Park who claimed that a hand grenade had been thrown near his house to persuade him to cease opposition to land encroachment.

In this bleak implementing environment populated by frequently hostile actors, many PA staff and MoE officials expressed to me the belief that a new approach based on flexibility and compromise will in the long-term achieve the conditions necessary for key stakeholders to be co-opted into supporting PAs and contributing to achieving their objectives. In most conservation scenarios compromise and trade-offs are essential if accommodation between conflicting yet equally legitimate agendas is to be realized. But under the conditions that this chapter has outlined, it is very difficult to conceive how such an accommodation could be brought about on any terms that would be favourable to conservation. The local authorities, RCAF and police conduct themselves in the manner that they do because it is the course that will secure them maximum wealth and power. Placating these proclivities as a matter of organizational policy will at best lead to inconsistency and confusion and at worst reinforce institutionalized toleration of malfeasance.

Conclusion

The Cambodian PA system is beset with threats, both in terms of excessive local resource exploitation, and broader pressures engendered by national socio-economic policies and political imperatives. In response, PA management authorities have deployed a range of strategies of growing technical sophistication, but with little discernible success. This demonstrates the gulf between idealized models of international best practice in PA management and the realities encountered by those implementing them, and is further confirmation that the relative merits of technical approaches to conservation do not sufficiently explain management outcomes.

This chapter has examined other more fundamental drivers of protected area management success. It finds that a complex array of factors relating to institutional structures and processes shape the actions of PA management organizations and the behaviour of their members. The MoE may be modelled on Weber's bureaucratic ideal, but this is largely a façade which barely conceals a very different type of organization. Weberian principles, espousing an impersonal hierarchy delineated along clear functional lines with staff selected and promoted on the basis of merit and demonstrable competence, have been substituted by a range of informal processes and behaviours, which are inimical to achieving formal goals. Internal rivalries and the pursuit of personal agendas driven by a range of perverse incentives and disincentives have combined to undermine levels of staff motivation and effectiveness. These are largely the product of an external social, political and economic environment, characterized by corruption and patronage.

The literature on bureaucratic reform advances a range of institutional mechanisms for improving performance through enhanced transparency and accountability (Hirschmann, 1999; Rauch and Evans, 2000; FAO, 2001; Davis, 2004). Such changes would be welcomed by many in the MoE, who are frustrated by institutionalized incompetence and mismanagement within the ministry and the lack of opportunities for advancement without strong links to networks of patronage. But it would take time for this new culture to take root given that the prevailing organizational norms are so entrenched. Moreover, the changes would be unlikely to succeed if they were unilaterally applied to MoE. As I have argued in this chapter, the ministry at both national and protected area level is extremely vulnerable to interference and pressure from other elements of the state apparatus, so in order to achieve a sustained impact on performance, reform of the MoE would need to be carried out as part of a wider initiative incorporating all elements of the national administration and armed forces. Alternatively, non-bureaucratic mechanisms for addressing systemic issues in PA management could be adopted, such as working through semi-autonomous public enterprises, parastatal agencies or private parks (James, 1999; Child, 2004), but again in the Cambodian context there is no reason to assume that they would be any more immune from external pressures than the MoE.

Thus, many of the Cambodians I interviewed were convinced that bureaucratic reform is an essential prerequisite to improving the management of PAs, but that this would not occur without corresponding changes in the governance of the country, and more specifically a move away from rule by powerful elites to fully functioning democracy. However, it is questionable whether sufficient 'political will' yet exists within the ruling party to undertake such reforms. Furthermore, improved governance may not necessarily lead to reduced pressure on PAs. A better governed Cambodia will still be populated by poor rural and urban communities needing more agricultural land and growing quantities of energy. However, perhaps at least the decisions relating to land use and resource exploitation will be made through more transparent and equitable processes.

Notes

1 Since 2002 a further eight PAs of various categories have been established under the authority of the Forest Administration.
2 Staff densities in Cambodian PAs average one ranger for every 34 km^2 (author's data) compared with one per 9 km^2 in Indonesia (McQuistan et al., 2006).
3 These include multi-lateral donors such as the European Union, the Global Environment Facility, UN Foundation and World Bank as well as international NGOs such as Conservation International, Fauna & Flora International, Wildlife Alliance, the Wildlife Conservation Society and the World Wide Fund for Nature.
4 'Rangers' here refers to PA staff primarily assigned to law enforcement duties, who are more often than not engaged on annual contracts. In some PAs there are additional staff carrying out more technical duties who are usually permanent MoE employees.
5 A slight caveat; some Cambodians, particularly those from indigenous minorities, hold animist beliefs which promote greater respect for the natural world.

6 It is illuminating that only one director I interviewed explicitly referred to leadership as an important element in effective management.
7 The new structure even includes an 'Office of Office Supplies'.
8 Timber extraction played a critical role in sustaining military forces on all sides during the decade of conflict preceding the integration of the Khmer Rouge and in underpinning the formation of the current Cambodian state (see Le Billon, 2002).

References

Adams, W. M. (2004) *Against Extinction: The Story of Conservation*, Earthscan, London.
Bit, S. (1991) *The Warrior Heritage: A Psychological Perspective of Cambodian Trauma*, Seanglim Bit, El Cerrito, California.
Brockington, D. (2002) *Fortress Conservation: The Preservation of the Mkomazi Game Reserve, Tanzania*, James Currey, Oxford.
Calavan, M. M., Briquets, S. D. and O'Brien, J. (2004) *Cambodian Corruption Assessment*, USAID, Washington.
Child, B. (2004) 'Park agencies, performance and society in Southern Africa', in B. Child (ed.) *Parks in Transition: Biodiversity, Rural Development and the Bottom Line*, Earthscan, London, pp. 125–163.
Clements, T., John, A., Nielsen, K., Chea, V., Ear, S. and Meas, P. (2008) *Translinks Case Study: Tmatboey Community-based Ecotourism Project, Cambodia*, Ministry of Environment and Wildlife Conservation Society, Phnom Penh, Cambodia.
Cumming, D. (2004) 'Performance of parks in a century of change', in B. Child (ed.) *Parks in Transition*, Earthscan, London, pp. 105–124.
Davis, J. (2004) 'Corruption in public service delivery: Experience from South Asia's water and sanitation sector', *World Development* 32(1), pp. 53–71.
Dunai, A. (2008) 'The protected area law of Cambodia: A legal evaluation', *Cambodian Journal of Natural History* 2008(1), pp. 29–40.
EU. (2012) *Country Environment Profile*, European Union Delegation, Phnom Penh, Cambodia.
Evans, P. and Rauch, J. E. (1999) 'Bureaucracy and growth: A cross-national analysis of the effects of "Weberian" state structures on economic growth', *American Sociological Review* 64(5), pp. 748–765.
FAO. (2001) *State of the World's Forests 2001: Part II, Key Issues in the Forest Sector Today*, Food and Agriculture Organisation, Rome.
Gergen, K. J. (1992) 'Organization theory in the postmodern era', in M. Reed and M. Hughes (eds) *Rethinking Organization: New Directions in Organization Theory and Analysis*, Sage, London, pp. 207–226.
Gibson, C. C. (1999) *Politicians and Poachers: The Political Economy of Wildlife Policy in Africa*, Cambridge University Press, Cambridge, UK.
Global Witness. (2007) *Cambodia's Family Trees: Illegal Logging and the Stripping of Public Assets by Cambodia's Elite*, Global Witness Publishing, Washington, DC.
Gottesman, E. (2003) *Cambodia after the Khmer Rouge*, Silkworm Books, Chang Mai, Thailand.
Grimsditch, M. (2012) *China's Investments in Hydropower in the Mekong Region: The Kamchay Hydropower Dam, Kampot, Cambodia*, World Resources Institute, Washington, DC.
Hirschmann, D. (1999) 'Development management versus Third World bureaucracies: A brief history of conflicting interests', *Development and Change* 30(2), pp. 287–305.

Hughes, C. (2006). 'The politics of gifts: Tradition and regimentation in contemporary Cambodia', *Journal of Southeast Asian Studies* 37(3), pp. 469–489.

Hughes, C. and Un, K. (2011) *Cambodia's Economic Transformation*, NIAS Press, Copenhagen.

ICEM. (2003) *Lessons Learned in Cambodia, Lao PDR, Thailand and Vietnam*, Review of Protected Areas and Development in the Lower Mekong River Region, International Centre for Environmental Management, Indooroopilly, Australia.

Ironside, J. and Yik, B. (2007) *Participation of Indigenous Brao and Kavet People in the Management of Virachey National Park, North-eastern Cambodia*, Paper presented at Community Participation in Virachey National Park: A Workshop on Collaborative Management, August 2004, Phnom Penh, Cambodia.

Jacobsen, T. and Stuart-Fox, M. (2013) *Power and Political Culture in Cambodia*, Asia Research Institute Working Paper Series 200, National University of Singapore, Singapore.

James, A. N. (1999) 'Institutional constraints to protected area funding', *Parks: The International Journal for Protected Area Managers* 9(2), pp. 15–26.

Jenkins, C. N. and Joppa, L. (2009) 'Expansion of the global terrestrial protected area system', *Biological Conservation* 142(10), pp. 2166–2174.

Kaufman, H. (1993) *The Forest Ranger: A Study in Administrative Behavior*, The Johns Hopkins University Press for Resources for the Future, Inc., Washington, DC.

Kim, S. and Sy, R. (2005) *Collective Experiences of Action Research and Facilitation on Community Forestry and Community Protected Area*, Ministry of Environment, Royal University of Agriculture, and Forestry Administration, Phnom Penh, Cambodia.

Kramer, R., van Schaik, C. and Johnson, J. (1997) *Last Stand: Protected Areas and the Defense of Tropical Biodiversity*, Oxford University Press, Oxford.

Lacerda, L., Schmitt, K., Cutter, P. and Meas, S. (2004) *Management Effectiveness Assessment of the System of Protected Areas in Cambodia Using WWF's RAPPAM Methodology*, Ministry of Environment, Phnom Penh, Cambodia.

Le Billon, P. (2002) 'Logging in muddy waters: The politics of forest exploitation in Cambodia', *Critical Asian Studies* 34(4), pp. 563–586.

Long, K. (2008) 'Prey Koh Biodiversity Conservation area Management in Kampong Chhang Province', *Tonlé Sap Biosphere Reserve Bulletin* 5, pp. 14–18.

Margules, C. R. and Pressey, R. L. (2000) 'Systematic conservation planning', *Nature* 405(6783), pp. 243–253.

McQuistan, C. I., Fahmi, Z., Leisher, C., Halim, A. and Adi, S. W. (2006) *Protected Area Funding in Indonesia: A Study Implemented under the Programmes of Work on Protected Areas of the Seventh Meeting of the Conference of Parties on the Convention on Biological Diversity*, Ministry of Environment of Republic of Indonesia, Jakarta.

Migdal J. S. (1988) *Strong Societies and Weak States: State-Society Relations and State Capabilities in the Third World*, Princeton University Press, Princeton, New Jersey.

MoE. (2006) *Third National Report to the Convention on Biological Diversity*, Ministry of Environment and National Biodiversity Steering Committee, Phnom Penh, Cambodia.

NGO Forum. (2008) *Monitoring the Implementation of the 2007 CDFC Joint Monitoring Indicators and the National Strategic Development Plan 2006–10*, NGO Position Papers on Cambodia's Development in 2007–2008, The NGO Forum on Cambodia, Phnom Penh, Cambodia.

Obendorf, R. J. D. (2006) *Legal Analysis of Forest and Land Law in Cambodia*, Community Forestry International, Phnom Penh, Cambodia.

Pearson, J. (2005) *The Multi-Cultural Iceberg: Exploring International Relationships in Cambodian Development Organisations,* International NGO Training and Research Centre: Praxis Note No. 8, VBNK, Phnom Penh, Cambodia.

Pye, D. and May, T. (2014) 'Friends in high places', *The Phnom Penh Post,* 24 March 2014, http://www.phnompenhpost.com/national/friends-high-places accessed 3 May 2014.

Rauch, J. E. and Evans, P. B. (2000) 'Bureaucratic structure and bureaucratic performance in less developed countries', *Journal of Public Economics* 75(1), pp. 49–71.

RGC. (2000) *The Duties of Civil Governmental Officials,* Royal Government of Cambodia, Phnom Penh, Cambodia.

Scott, W. R. (1998) *Organizations: Rational, Natural, and Open Systems,* Prentice Hall, New Jersey.

Un, K. and So, S. (2011) 'Land rights in Cambodia: How neopatrimonial politics restricts land policy reform' *Pacific Affairs* 84(2), pp. 289–308.

Vrieze, P. and Naren K. (2012) 'In the race to exploit Cambodia's land and forests, new maps reveal the rapid spread of plantations and mining across the nation', *The Cambodia Daily,* 10–11 March, p. 4.

Weber, M. (1973) 'Bureaucracy', in J. M. Shafritz and J. S. Ott (eds) *Classics of Organization Theory,* Wadsworth, Belmont, pp. 80–85.

8 In whose name and in whose interests?

An actor-oriented analysis of community forestry in Bey, a Khmer village in Northeast Cambodia

Robin Biddulph

> Increasing understanding and awareness among poor communities of their environment will encourage them to conserve forest areas and develop them in a more sustainable manner. This initiative will make a difference to the lives of thousands of poor forestry-dependent people.
> (Winston McColgan, Chargé d'Affaires of the EU delegation in Phnom Penh, quoted in a press release on the 2005 launch of the EU/Oxfam GB community forestry programme in Cambodia)

Introduction

Community forestry is not only a technical response to a resource management problem, but also a political contest, with NGOs lobbying to wrest control of resources from central state authorities, and governments seeking to accede to local demands without giving up key resources and prerogatives. This chapter investigates what happened in a village in northeast Cambodia when international and national NGOs secured the cooperation of the Cambodian government to implement a programme of community forestry.

Community forestry belongs to the community-based natural resource management (CBNRM) family of approaches derived from theories of common pool resources and common property regimes. The theoretical contention is that, under certain conditions, community ownership and management may be preferable to either state management or individualized ownership. Broadly, those conditions include a common pool resource which cannot readily be sub-divided, a community which can effectively exclude outsiders, a resource which offers significant and sustained benefits to the community and a level of internal organization and communication (institutions) to enable the community to manage the resource (Ostrom, 1999). In so far as CBNRM involves citizens being accorded certain rights within a formally constituted association recognized and regulated by the state, it may be characterized as a civil society approach to conservation.

Researchers who have examined CBNRM cases have emphasized the importance of not only discussing people's motivations in terms of self-interest, institutional development and a single resource. They argue that research must acknowledge that people are situated in complex landscapes and are embedded in broader cultural, economic and political contexts (Cleaver, 2000; Peters, 1987; Mosse, 1997). An actor-oriented approach responds to this critique by viewing community forestry through the lens of people's wider interests and connections rather than simply in terms of the achievement of policy-makers' objectives (Long, 1992).

Community forestry has been advocated in Southeast Asia as a win-win policy which can deliver both livelihood improvement and forest conservation. While this advocacy has secured a place for community forestry in the policy mainstream, its simplification and optimism has been critiqued by a number of researchers in the region. In Indonesia and the Philippines, it has been suggested that the forest-dependent conservation-oriented communities routinely depicted by CBNRM advocates are rarely found on the ground (Li, 2002). In Thailand the agricultural priorities and claims of forest communities have been found to have been systematically overlooked by community forestry actors (Walker, 2004). Meanwhile, in Cambodia it is suggested that community forestry lacks significant promise as a tool for poverty reduction because only degraded forest with minimal economic potential has been approved for community forestry (Sunderlin, 2006; McKenney *et al.*, 2004). Nevertheless, the finding that community forests seem to be better protected than state-managed forests has encouraged conservation-oriented researchers to continue to lobby for more widespread promotion of community forestry (Lambrick *et al.*, 2014; Fichtenau *et al.*, 2002), and the donor-supported National Forestry Programme 2010–2029 includes a target of 2 million ha of Cambodian forest being under the management of approximately 1,000 fully recognized community forestry groups (Royal Government of Cambodia, 2010). As we will see, state recognition of community forestry may be a double-edged sword; on the one hand, it gives communities a degree of legitimate discretion; on the other hand, by making community management temporary and conditional, it may effectively extend the reach of the state giving it greater control over forest territory and paradoxically making it easier to exclude local people from forests.

By examining one village's experience of community forestry this chapter subjects the policy claims of community forestry advocates to critical scrutiny. It asks whether NGO interventions have enabled local communities to organize and pursue their own interests. The research from 2006 to 2009, followed a period during which initial enthusiasm in the village was gradually eroded and gave way to despair as the community forestry leader gave up and the commune chief was reported to be selling the community forest land illegally for migrants to farm (see Table 8.1). As such, the chapter also asks what went wrong, and whether alternative approaches might have yielded different results.

This chapter proceeds by presenting the case actor-by-actor, including the researcher as one of the actors. The term actor here is used very broadly

162 *Robin Biddulph*

Table 8.1 Time-line of community forestry in Bey 2002–2009.

2002	Small regional NGO rejects Bey as a potential community forestry site
2003	EU issues a call for proposals for its forestry in developing countries programme
2005	EU/Oxfam adopt Bey as a community forestry site
2006	March: Committee elected in Bey, CF area marked, progress pending Casotim approval
2006	July: Research begins
2007	Sporadic patrolling by Bey CF leader both inside and outside the marked area
2008	CF leader sees CF in Bey as failed; NGO sees it as postponed
2009	March: Research completed

with groups, organizations and government offices to be treated as 'actors' and not always being broken down to the level of individual agency that a purer interpretation of actor-orientation would imply. This case is then discussed with respect to broader lessons that might be learned, including with respect to alternative ways of simultaneously pursuing livelihood and natural resource management goals.

Community forestry actors in Bey[1]

The researcher

In this depiction of a case of community forestry in rural Cambodia during a 3-year period, I am not only an observer and analyst, but also an actor. I had my own agenda and the way in which I pursued that agenda has shaped the account which I develop in this chapter.

An earlier generation of rural development studies had suggested that development policymakers and practitioners tended to systematically misrepresent rural lives and livelihoods (Ferguson, 1994; Porter *et al.*, 1991; Mitchell, 1995). Assumptions were made that enabled development industry actors to imagine legitimate and effective interventions. However, these assumptions also ensured that outcomes could never be as intended in project designs. I wanted to discover whether these earlier lessons had been learned or whether the development industry was still simplifying and fictionalizing reality in ways that made interventions appear promising while guaranteeing their irrelevance.

By spending time in Bey over an extended period, I sought to identify an issue that was important in the everyday lives of villagers, and see how that issue was addressed in development policy and practice. Over a 3-year period between 2006 and 2009 I spent a week in Bey every wet season and a week in every dry season, so a total of 6 weeks in addition to other short visits to the village in between these times. I worked in a research team comprising two young students (one male, one female) with rural backgrounds, an older woman from a rural village in north-west Cambodia and myself. We gathered information through a village census taken in 2006 and repeated in 2008, through two livelihood surveys in the wet and dry seasons in 2008, but most of all through repeated unstructured interviews and observations, including developing life histories of eight case study households with whom we developed particularly close relationships.

On the first morning of our stay in the village on 27 July 2006, members of the Forestry Administration (FA) summoned about a third of the villagers to a meeting in order to inform them about an edict from the Prime Minister that had resulted in the drawing of a map of the village area that identified significant areas which were currently inhabited, but which were state forest and must therefore be vacated. The FA representative repeatedly assured the villagers that 'the state cares about you' but that the forest was needed for national development and that villagers did not have the right to live in it. Explaining the meanings behind the various positions articulated in that meeting requires a longer story than can be recounted here (see Biddulph, 2010). Suffice it to say that while community forestry policy narratives suggest supportive and harmonious state-society relationships, the reality on the ground was complex and involved conflicting interests and agendas.

The community: Segmentation and personalities

Imagining a village as a 'community' is always to some degree a simplification (Li, 2002; Mosse, 1997). People living in the same village do at least have that in common, however, they will also differ in many ways. Villagers living alongside each other may have radically different life stories, livelihood portfolios, political allegiances and degrees of wealth and connectedness. There may be common interests and there may be harmonious relations within a village, but this should not be assumed.

In the case of Bey, a major source of difference and dynamism were the varied origins of the villagers. At the beginning of our research three broad groups were apparent: native villagers born and brought up in Bey comprised 48 per cent of adults; in-migrants from within Chhlong district who were familiar with the landscape but who were born and brought up in the trading villages along the Mekong comprised 26 per cent, and in-migrants from neighbouring Kampong Cham province comprised 26 per cent. However, these proportions were changing rapidly as even during the research the population grew from 83 households in October 2006 to 135 households in October 2008.

The livelihood orientations and capacities of different households reflected the origins of household members. Those born in the village had grown up without a school. Their parents' livelihoods had been forest-dependent in the sense that they found food locally, grew some crops and rice on temporary plots in the forest and traded forest products (especially resin from hardwood trees) for rice and other goods.

Adults born elsewhere in Kratie who moved to Bey were mainly people who had moved to the village from timber trading villages on the Mekong. This migration was a slow trickle, as one or two households moved into the village each year from the 1980s up to the early 2000s. They had grown up in villages with schools and in an environment where many people ran businesses, with profits reinvested and capital accumulated. This orientation was reflected in the fact that all seven small stores in the village were owned by people who had come to the village from the Mekong. The economic rise of this group paralleled the developments in logging in the village. Peace came to the village with the defection of local Khmer Rouge units in 1994, and this was when deforestation began on a significant scale. Initially, this was conducted by a joint-venture logging company, Casotim (Cambodia Soviet Timber) which used its own trucks and heavy machinery with little benefit to villagers. However, a logging ban signalled a change in the style of logging. The company subcontracted to local merchants who placed sawmills in the forest. Logging-related activities became the major source of livelihoods in Bey. Migrants from the Mekong operated as small entrepreneurs while native villagers were mainly employed as labourers in the cutting and transporting. The imbalance in economic relations was illustrated when one of us overheard one of the educated migrants negotiating a deal with a native villager and cheating on the price.

A new and much more rapid wave of immigration from neighbouring Kampong Cham province gathered pace from 2005. These in-migrants came to Bey in the hope of acquiring land for agriculture. Some were wealthier, often middle-aged couples who had left adult children on their land in Kampong Cham. Others were poorer, often newly married couples who had never owned land in Kampong Cham. They had all grown up in a landscape where upland crops were grown, and they intended to introduce such crops to the village including cassava, runner beans and groundnuts in the short term, and in the longer term, tree crops such as rubber, cashew and mangoes. The poorer migrants were initially dependent on working as agricultural labourers outside the village while they saved money to acquire land. However, the better off households started farming directly and enjoyed early success. In 2008 the coincidence of good market prices and a good harvest enabled some to earn $1,000 per ha from their cassava.

The success of the new arrivals, allied to the fact that opportunities from logging were becoming fewer and required more travel, transformed the aspirations of people throughout the community. Although logging had dominated livelihoods for some years, nobody believed that this could continue much longer. The hopes of most villagers, whether they were born in Bey or had come from the Mekong or from Kampong Cham, now revolved around securing enough agricultural land to base a livelihood on. This was easier said than done. Households had typically acquired 4–5 ha of land. Long-term residents had simply claimed land from the forest. Newcomers had (notwithstanding the illegality of such transactions) purchased land as they arrived. However, only a small minority reported clearing more than half a hectare of the land that they had claimed. And for those who did, in 2009 cassava prices were lower, and profits were hit by rain during the harvest period. Nor were the challenges facing villagers limited to those related to farming and agricultural markets. As we will see, the villagers were not the only actors looking to lay claim to the available land.

While the diverse origins of villagers gave individuals different comparative advantages, this did not result in factionalization. This was partly because 30 per cent or more of the households contained both natives and in-migrants, but largely because the newcomers were seen as an asset to the village. Nonetheless, there were some serious conflicts in the village which would make any attempt at collective action challenging. These revolved principally around three men: the deputy village chief, the head of the community forestry and the village school principal. Personal enmities were such that anything supported by one of these men would be likely to be opposed or undermined by the other two.

The head of the community forestry group was a former Khmer Rouge commander who settled in the village after defecting. At the meeting with the FA he was the one person who asked questions. Why did the FA target people in the villages and not the big people operating sawmills in the forest? What was the role of the company Casotim in the management of forests in the district? The forestry official eventually suggested that other villagers should ask questions, but they responded firmly that they liked his questions. Forceful and energetic, he had been elected as chair of the community forestry committee when it was formed in early 2006. During 2006 and 2007, he was often away on training courses and at meetings related to community forestry, which he said provided his main income at that time. He had struggled, however, to secure practical support for community forestry. He explained that the site chosen was 6 km southwest of the village because he had followed advice to locate the community forest away from the village so that it did not overlap with land illegally claimed by villagers for agriculture. With hindsight, given the distance and also the remoteness from the routine journeys of villagers, he felt that this had been a mistake. On the other hand, it is difficult to see how the community forestry initiative could have survived if it had attempted to dispossess villagers of their agricultural lands. The community forest leader had also organized villagers to confront people violating forest laws outside the designated community forestry area, confiscating chainsaws and handing them over to the FA. However, he reported that the chainsaw owners simply paid the FA and got them back again. On top of these difficulties, he finally reported in late 2008 that the new commune chief had started selling plots of land in the community forest to new migrants. He said he loved the forest, but that he had failed with community forestry and instead was now working for another NGO setting up self-help savings and credit groups.

The Bey village chief was a mild character, native to the village and not particularly articulate or literate. If villagers needed something done, they turned to the deputy village chief. He and his wife had come to the village from the Mekong together in 1994 and ran a shop in their house. On the evening after the FA had threatened villagers with eviction, he distributed blank sheets of paper and instructed villagers how to write protest letters. He was also, it was suggested (but always quietly and usually obliquely) a major trader in land and timber. On the subject of community forestry he was ambivalent. He questioned the legitimacy of the whole process, saying that the election of the committee had happened when he was not in the village and that it had not been a proper election. The 'wrong' person was in charge.

The village teacher, also from the Mekong, had initially been popular in the village, especially among the young men with whom he socialized in the evenings. However, due to his engagements in the land and timber business and his absences from the classroom his popularity had waned rapidly. He claimed to be well-connected and to have had business dealings with the Prime Minister's brother. He had secured land to the east of the village claiming to be in cooperation with the Prime Minister's daughter (though nobody could verify the identity of the young ladies in silk outfits and air-conditioned vehicles who came to visit the site one time when we were not present). Villagers in a neighbouring village with claims to that land protested, soliciting help from the community forest chief in Bey. Meanwhile, the teacher was also in a bitter land dispute with the deputy village chief over land behind the school.

As we can see, interests in timber and land have shaped the politics of the village. While most of these interests are informal or illegal, they are nevertheless considered legitimate locally and are to some degree unofficially tolerated or even sanctioned by local authorities and the Casotim company. Inevitably, the prospects of the community forestry initiative were shaped by these informal interests and the local politics that they generated.

The regional community development NGO

The Southeast Asia Development Programme (SADP) was not active in the village during our research period. However, its director, an American who spoke and wrote fluent Khmer, recalled having been in the area a few years before our research began. SADP had become involved in community forestry as a result of learning about the role of resin in the incomes of people in forest areas (e.g. Cock, 2004). SADP therefore sought to help villagers to organize against logging companies who ignored regulations protecting resin trees.

The SADP director recalled having travelled to Bey in about 2002 and inquired into the livelihoods situation there. He had quickly concluded that this was primarily a logging village with no resin-based livelihoods to defend. He had therefore continued his journey south and east to other communes in the district where the situation was different.

His general experience was also relevant. When community forestry began to be advocated in Cambodia, he had become interested because he saw it as a tool with which to continue to protect resin-based livelihoods. However, he soon found that official sanctioning of community forestry obstructed rather than facilitated such protection. FA officials would now work with communities to identify sites, and he found that the sites chosen were inevitably severely degraded with no high-value resin trees. In this way he observed community forestry functioning as a spatial container for activism. The FA allowed villagers to invest energy on low value patches of degraded forest, but (much as the community forestry leader in Bey had experienced) they were strongly discouraged from seeking to participate in forest management anywhere else. Community forestry, he found, was used by the FA to limit people's assertion of their rights under the Forestry Law rather than to extend them. These experiences in the early 2000s were precursors to similar experiences that have been documented elsewhere (Milne and Adams, 2012), and which generated the evasion hypothesis which suggests that externally sponsored intervention tends to get diverted away from the problems it claims to address (Biddulph, 2010, 2011).

The EU project

SADP saw no rationale for pursuing community forestry in Bey, but others did. In 2003 the European Union called for proposals for a programme entitled 'Program on Tropical Forests and other Forests in Developing Countries'. The international NGO Oxfam GB responded and secured 1.6 million Euros of funding for a 5-year (2005–2010) project implemented in eight provinces (Oxfam GB, 2005).

The objective of the European Union programme was 'the conservation and sustainable management of forests in developing countries'. The European Union had a delegation in Cambodia but no technical staff. Monitoring was conducted through missions from various consultancy companies based in Europe. Such visits lasted only a few days and were mainly focused on administrative issues relating to compliance with the programme document.

Staff at the delegation in Phnom Penh were friendly and receptive. They facilitated a meeting with one of the monitors and an open discussion of findings. However, they did not have practical authority over the project. The authority was the project agreement itself and (as was made clear in large bold, capitalized text on the first page of the application form) this was not something that was subject to amendment.

Oxfam GB – Contractor to the European Union

Oxfam GB had had long experience in Cambodia. During the isolation of the 1980s it had provided direct technical assistance to the government, helping for example with the rehabilitation of the Phnom Penh water infrastructure. An Oxfam country director wrote 'Punishing the Poor' in protest at Cambodia's treatment by the international community (Mysliwiec, 1988). During the 1990s as multi-lateral and bilateral donors came to Cambodia, Oxfam shifted into community development work and implemented its own projects. By the 2000s, as a result of both changes in the organization and judgements about the capacity of Cambodian organizations to implement projects directly, it operated as an advocacy NGO working through local partners.

On the strength of the EU funding, Oxfam GB was able to open three provincial offices to support the community forestry programme which operated in six provinces with an NGO partner in each province. A manager and three young field officers were installed in the Kratie provincial office during our research. I asked them about the tension between the agricultural aspirations of the villagers and the community forestry orientation of the programme and how they thought such tensions could be resolved. The young field officers were new in their roles; their first priority related to the NGO's use of funds and donor compliance (the main issue raised by the EU monitors). On consideration, and in separate interviews, they answered that 'it was not Oxfam's responsibility' but the local NGO's to deal with community issues. However, they felt that the correct course of action for the local NGO would be to educate the villagers. The NGO workers, one of them said, must 'explain the importance of forests to the villagers so that they would learn to value their environment, and then they would understand that they should support the community forestry'.

The NGO in the provincial town – Sub-contracted by Oxfam GB

The local NGO sub-contracted by Oxfam to manage the community forestry programme in Kratie had previously worked in Chhlong district but not with community forestry. They defined themselves as a community development organization. One morning when we arrived from the village, the director was at the office training young community development workers. He explained that the essence of being a community development worker was being with the people, listening to them and showing solidarity with them. He invited them to reflect on what sort of clothing would be appropriate when they were working, and they decided that they should not wear their expensive jewellery or fancy watches and clothes in the villages.

The good intentions articulated at the training meeting regarding spending time in communities were, however, difficult to realize in the context of the resources allocated in the EU/Oxfam GB budget. The NGO had two staff members working on community forestry; an older man and a younger women who both travelled together to do their work. There were 28 community forests in the programme. In other words, even if they had spent all of their time working in the villages, they could not have spent more than one day in each village per month. In practice, they spent most of their time in meetings and doing administration, so they had considerably less than one day per month per village available to support community forestry.

On our first trip to the NGO office after our first week in Bey, we presented our initial findings in the hope of getting some validation and some pointers towards issues we might have missed. However (and unsurprisingly given what we then learned about the levels of staffing), the NGO's response was to accept everything that we said, and to explain that we had spent far more time in the village than they had and therefore we knew best. In relation to the difficulties that the community forestry leader was having in mobilizing the community, the NGO staff responded that there was indeed an issue there and that they would seek to organize a second election in order that a more 'active' committee could be assembled. This was done and, predictably, did nothing to make villagers more enthused to take long walks to a small patch of degraded forest of no particular livelihood or symbolic value to them.

In collaboration with FA officials, the NGO had helped the community to map the community forest site. They had also set in motion the process of getting full recognition for the proposed site. This, they said, required approval from the company Casotim. They reported that the Casotim boss was enthusiastic, and that the paperwork just needed to be signed. The FA and the provincial office of the regional NGO the Regional Community Forestry Training Centre (RECOFTC) were said to be following up on this matter.

The district forestry administration office

The closest FA office to the village was in the district town of Chhlong. After our first encounter with the officials in the village, I returned to the FA office after each village stay. Frequent staff turnover made the cultivating of relationships difficult. The official who presented the eviction order to the villagers in July 2006 had only served 2 months in the province. Within 2 years he had been moved to another province. I was usually met with courtesy and often with friendliness. Staff shared coffee breaks and lunches and talked of their patrols and showed me wood taken from smugglers and vehicles that they had impounded. However, I rarely met the same person more than once. My understanding of the way that the office worked, the personalities and attitudes of the staff and the interests they were pursuing therefore remained superficial in comparison with what we learned about villagers' interests and motivations.

One objective of going to the FA offices was to ask about the concession company. In particular, I was seeking to get an introduction to the local company boss. The FA officials invariably reported that he was away in Phnom Penh. It was difficult not to draw the conclusion that their de facto role within the shadow state system was as a gatekeeper restricting access to Casotim rather than, as the NGOs suggested, facilitating such access.

The company

Casotim stands for Cambodia Soviet Timber. The company began as a joint-venture (51 per cent Cambodian, 49 per cent Russian) and in 1996, was granted a 142,000 ha concession covering most of Chhlong and much of Snoul district in Kratie province. Their head office address in Phnom Penh during the research was on Norodom Boulevard, in the apparently deserted former Czech embassy.

Following investigations into forest management initiated by complaints about the World Bank's support to the Cambodian government's timber concessions programme, all concessionaires had been required to submit new forest management plans. Casotim, as far as could be ascertained, had never done this and researchers in Phnom Penh were surprised to learn that the company was still operating at all.

In Chhlong, however, the compound at the district town remained, and the local boss had his house opposite that compound. He had the title *Okhnya* which is awarded by the Cambodian state to business people who have made a contribution to national development. This is usually in the form of an infrastructure donation worth at least $100,000.

Having failed to gain access to the *Okhnya* via the FA, I decided to approach him directly. The first motorcycle taxi I approached refused to take me to that address citing fear of the security guards. However, I eventually found a willing taxi and by chance, I arrived just as the *Okhnya* was crossing the road from his house to his compound.

I introduced myself and he invited me to the terrace by his house overlooking the Mekong. We sat in the company of his wife and relatives, and discussed the village and the concession. His answers were clear and decisive. No, there was no prospect of the company allowing Bey's community forestry project to proceed. Yes, he had heard that the commune chief had been selling land there and he was in the process of taking him to court for that. Yes, the company would be prepared to allow villagers to have up to 5 ha per household of private agricultural land near their village. However, he doubted whether the villagers had the labour and the equipment to farm such large plots.

When asked about development plans, he explained that Casotim had secured permission from the government for a 15,000 ha plantation which would be cleared and planted 1,500 ha at a time over the coming 10 years. In the seventh year the proposed plantation site would cover most of the agricultural land currently claimed by villagers from Bey. Friendly and happy to share information he fetched a copy of the Master Plan with ministry signatures and stamps and a detailed map attached and gave it to me. Along with this cooperativeness was a healthy suspicion. While I took notes he discreetly recorded our interview on his mobile phone and took my photograph. Relatively wealthy, powerful figures such as the *Okhnya* do not appear in community forestry policy narratives, which feature only a homogenized community and a remote but supportive state. However, his attitudes and decisions were clearly of key significance for the livelihoods of the people of Bey.

Towards a political ecology of community forestry

One purpose of political ecology is to repoliticize depoliticized environmental narratives (Greenburg and Park, 1994). This is achieved in two ways. First, it looks at issues of power and marginalization. If a population is dependent on a fragile, marginal landscape, political ecologists will tend not to simply look for technical solutions that might make either the landscape more productive or the population's use of it more sustainable. Rather it will ask why this particular group of people have been marginalized from wealth and power to the extent that they are dependent on meagre natural resources. Second, it looks at issues of representation. Why has the problem been represented in this way, and who are the winners and losers from such a representation?

During the period of this study, Bey was a complex, dynamic village. A native population who had previously depended on forests for their livelihoods lost that livelihood base as a result of deforestation, which itself was a result of a brand of elite politics that favoured off-budget plundering of natural resources in order to maintain political stability (Le Billon, 2000). The short-term resource boom resulting from illegal logging and illegal trading of land and the longer term prospects for illegally converting forest to long-term agricultural use attracted new migrants into the village; some wealthier and some poorer. Their future aspirations revolve in the short term around securing land for agriculture and in the longer term around enabling their children to secure salaried employment. Villagers are not, however, able to secure agricultural land because elite figures in the shadow state prefer to allow Casotim to function as the de facto resource manager and prefer not to allow the population to develop rights that would infringe on Casotim's ability to make decisions. An elite collaboration between the state and large concession companies functions contrary to the interests of the local population. The FA meanwhile, following longer traditions in the political ecology of forest management in Southeast Asia, claims legitimacy in terms of being the steward of a national resource for the national good, but in fact flouts the law and simply takes the side of the rich against the poor (Bryant, 1997; Peluso and Vandergeest, 2001).

If the politics of power and marginalization are rather clear, with obvious winners and losers, the politics of representation are slightly more complex.

Who gains from representing the situation above as a case of a forest dependent community wishing to regain stewardship of the resource upon which it depends? The villagers do not appear to benefit; as we have seen, they are not forest dependent and their priorities lie elsewhere. Neither does Casotim seem to benefit. If the company was concerned to use community forestry as a façade behind which to conceal its plans, the *Okhnya* could easily have continued with the fiction of the company being in the process of approving the proposed site. Two sets of actors significantly gained from the representation of Bey as a place where community forestry made sense. First, the FA, which could strengthen its own authority by legitimating community forestry (see Sikor and Lund, 2009) while also acquiring a façade of developmental respectability for its gatekeeping for Casotim. Second the European Union, Oxfam GB and the local NGO, all of whom were able to secure funding and organizational reproduction by claiming to be serving the interests of the people and of forest conservation.

Conclusion

What insights can be drawn from the case of Bey that might have wider application in similar contexts? I will briefly present three perspectives that may be of value, namely common property theory, community development practice and political society versus civil society.

Bey viewed through the lens of common pool resource theory

Elinor Ostrom's whole career might be characterized as an investigation of the conditions required for a population to develop the institutions for community-based management. However, before such internal processes of communication and rule-making are considered there are some very basic pre-requisites that are needed to make pursuit of community based management worthwhile.

> For users to see major benefits, resource conditions must not have deteriorated to such an extent that the resource is useless, nor can the resource be so little used that few advantages result from organizing.
> (Ostrom, 1999)

The first is that the resource to be managed is sufficiently valuable to justify community investment. Eleven hundred hectares of degraded forest located away from villagers' agricultural land and travel routes simply was not a resource that justified villagers' engagement (Biddulph, 2010). The question about the value of the resource was asked by SADP, and the answer led them to not pursue community forestry in Bey. The question had clearly not been asked by the European Union, Oxfam or their local partner. It is perhaps the first question that should be asked when community forestry is proposed or when proposals are analysed. Researchers in Cambodia have long advocated that community forestry should be implemented in higher value forests (McKenney *et al.*, 2004). Organizations supporting community forestry should perhaps stop judging themselves in terms of the number of community forests approved, and instead judge themselves in terms of the value and potential sustainable yields of forests allocated to community management.

Conservation and development practice

The essence of community development practice is that local knowledge should be valued and that development workers play the role of facilitators, enabling people to find common goals and to achieve them together. However, planned intervention always comes with its own agenda and interests (Mosse, 2001; Long and Ploeg, 1989). There is therefore always the risk that educated development workers working with poor people will see themselves not as facilitators, but as educators, telling the poor people what they should think, what they should value and why; this risk is familiar to those researching Cambodian development assistance (O'Leary, 2006). In this case, the project design did not allow any flexibility or learning. When villagers' interests did not match the community forestry policy narrative the response of NGO staff could not be to listen to the villagers or to amend the approach, it could only be to tell villagers that they should value community forestry. The prescribed, top-down structure of the EU/Oxfam programme made proper community work impossible even if it had been properly resourced.

The European Union and Oxfam GB developed a project design that involved community development workers spending less than a day a month in villages. This was within the framework of an engagement of just 5 years. As was apparent in Bey, it is fanciful to imagine that significant change might be achieved so quickly and with such flimsy resourcing (c.f. Korten, 1980). This under-resourcing was aggravated by the hierarchical bureaucratic structures of the European Union and Oxfam GB, which have the highest paid, highest status positions occupied by people in Brussels, Oxford and Phnom Penh, while the lowest paid, least experienced people are tasked with supporting the work on the ground – and given only the remit to fulfil the pre-determined objectives in the plans.

Political society versus civil society

One striking finding from this research was that the organizations which represented themselves as intermediaries between the community and Casotim (the local NGO, RECOFTC, the FA and to an extent Oxfam) actually served more as a barrier interposed between the community and the company. Meanwhile, when I actually secured an audience with the *Okhnya* at Casotim (by avoiding these supposed intermediaries and seeking him out directly) his responses were much more in tune with the priorities expressed by villagers; he was not interested in community forestry, but stated that the company was prepared to allow villagers up to 5 ha per household of agricultural land. It appeared possible that villagers would have been better served by negotiating directly with the company rather than allowing their interests to be represented by intermediaries.

Such a possibility is somewhat heretical particularly given other incidents in which Casotim has been implicated. After our research was completed, Casotim was accused of being responsible when a 14-year-old girl was shot dead during a protest by villagers in a neighbouring commune (Titthara, 2012). The *Okhyna*'s answers to me cannot be assumed to represent what Casotim would actually be prepared to do in the way of accommodating local people's interests. However, the heresy is more fundamental than this concern with the quality of Casotim's motives. Neither what villagers wanted (to claim forest land and convert it to agriculture), nor the role that Casotim played (de facto resource manager and local authority) are legally mandated. A negotiation between villagers and Casotim would not be grounded in the legal rights of either party. Partha Chatterjee's (2004) work on political society and civil society provides an illuminating perspective here. He suggests that civil society is essentially based on legal entitlements to citizenship, and as such is the preserve of a very narrow section of society in most of the world. By contrast, he suggests that most poor people, in most of the world, tend to be dependent on field level government agencies, who in turn have an incentive to respond to demands from the poor in order to maintain legitimacy (see also Walker, 2012). Political society generates temporary agreements which informally allow people to live in places where they have no legal right to live, and to conduct business for which they do not have the correct official licences.

In 1973 both the *Okhnya* and the deputy chief of Bey were young men living near the Mekong in Chhlong. The *Okhnya* came back from studying in Phnom Penh with long hair. The deputy village chief warned him that the Khmer Rouge were in charge, that they disapproved of long hair and that he should get it cut as soon as possible.

There are no guarantees that old, decades-long relations could provide the basis for productive negotiations for the villagers of Bey. However, conceptualizing this as a political society problem rather than a civil society problem, and searching for potential common ground and negotiating possibilities seems a more promising approach than facilitating villagers to follow the bureaucratic steps outlined in the Community Forestry sub-decree and the Community Forestry *prakas*, which lead only to a weak and contingent right to a severely degraded natural resource.

If solutions to the problems faced by people in villages such as Bey are to be grounded in the situations of the villagers, then this implies recognition of the competing interests and conflicts within the village, and the informal and illegal nature of the livelihoods of the villagers. An actor-oriented approach valuably sheds light on the politics, and indeed the political ecology, of village life, and enables potential allegiances and negotiations to be imagined. However, it also provides a fundamental challenge to established actors in the development industry, whose interventions must be planned and justified in advance both to head office bureaucracies in donor capitals and to national ministries. How can development organizations, which are civil society to the bone, possibly engage meaningfully with political society solutions?

Note

1 Bey is a pseudonym for a village in Chhlong district of Kratie province.

References

Biddulph, R. (2010) 'Geographies of evasion. The development industry and property rghts interventions in early 21st century Cambodia', PhD thesis, University of Gothenburg, Sweden.

Biddulph, R. (2011) 'Tenure security interventions in Cambodia: Testing Bebbington's approach to development geography', *Geografiska Annaler: Series B, Human Geography* 93(3), pp. 223–236.

Bryant, R. L. (1997) *The Political Ecology of Forest in Burma 1824–1994*, University of Hawai'i Press, Honolulu.

Chatterjee, P. (2004) *The Politics of the Governed: Studies in Postcolonial Democracy*, Columbia University Press, New York.

Cleaver, F. (2000) 'Moral ecological rationality, institutions and the management of common property resources', *Development and Change* 31(2), pp. 361–383.

Cock, A. (2004) 'Forest destruction for poverty reduction: The Tum Ring rubber plantation', *Watershed* 9(3), pp. 30–39.

Ferguson, J. (1994) *The Anti-Politics Machine: "Development", De-politicisation, and Bureaucratic Power in Lesotho*, University of Minnesota Press, Minneapolis.

Fichtenau, J., Beang, L. C., Sothea, N. and Sophy, D. (2002) *An Assessment of Ongoing Community Forestry Initiatives in Cambodia – Implications for the Development of a Forestry Extension Strategy*, GTZ/Department of Forestry and Wildlife, Phnom Penh, Cambodia.

Greenburg, J. and Park, T. K. (1994) 'Political ecology', *Journal of Political Ecology* 1(1), pp. 1–12.

Korten, D. (1980) 'Community organisation and rural development: A learning process approach', *Public Administration Review* 40(5), pp. 480–511.

Lambrick, F. H., Brown, N. D., Lawrence, A. and Bebber, D. P. (2014) 'Effectiveness of community forestry in Prey Long forest', *Cambodia. Conservation Biology* 28(2), pp. 372–381.

Le Billon, P. (2000) 'The political ecology of transition in Cambodia 1989–1999: War, peace and forest exploitation', *Development and Change* 31(4), pp. 785–805.

Li, T. M. (2002) 'Engaging simplifications: Community-based resource management, market processes and state agendas in upland Southeast Asia', *World Development* 30(2), pp. 265–283.

Long, N. (1992) 'From paradigm lost to paradigm regained? The case for an actor-oriented sociology of development', in N. Long and A. Long (eds) *Battlefields of*

Knowledge: The Interlocking of Theory and Practice in Social Research and Development, Routledge, London and New York, pp. 16–43.

Long, N. and Ploeg, J. D. V. D. (1989) 'Demythologising planned intervention: An actor perspective', *Sociologia Ruralis* 29(3–4), pp. 226–249.

McKenney, B., Chea, Y., Tola, P. and Evans, T. (2004) *Focusing on Cambodia's High Value Forests: Livelihood and Management*, Cambodia Development Resource Institute/Wildlife Conservation Society, Phnom Penh, Cambodia.

Milne, S. and Adams, W. (2012) 'Market masquerades: Uncovering the politics of community-level payments for environmental services in Cambodia', *Development and Change* 43(1), pp. 133–158.

Mitchell, T. (1995) 'The object of development: America's Egypt', in J. Crush (ed.) *Power of Development*, Routledge, London and New York, pp. 129–157.

Mosse, D. (1997) 'The symbolic making of a common property resource: History, ecology and locality in a tank-irrigated landscape in South India', *Development and Change* 28(3), pp. 467–504.

Mosse, D. (2001) '"People's knowledge", participation and patronage: Operations and representations in rural development', in B. Cooke and U. Kothari (eds) *Participation: The New Tyranny?* Zed Books, London, pp. 16–35.

Mysliwiec, E. (1988) *Punishing the Poor: The International Isolation of Kampuchea*, Oxfam, Oxford.

O'Leary, M. P. (2006) 'The influence of values on development practice: A study of Cambodian development practitioners in non-government organisations in Cambodia', PhD thesis, La Trobe University, Melbourne, Australia.

Ostrom, E. (1999) 'Revisiting the commons: Local lessons, global challenges', *Science* 284(5412), pp. 278–282.

Oxfam GB. (2005) *Grant Application Form: Promoting Community Forestry in Cambodia*, Oxfam GB/European Commission, Phnom Penh/Oxford.

Peluso, N. L. and Vandergeest, P. (2001) 'Genealogies of the political forest and customary rights in Indonesia, Malaysia, and Thailand', *The Journal of Asian Studies* 60(3), pp. 761–812.

Peters, P. E. (1987) 'Embedded systems and rooted models', in B. McCay and J. A. Acheson (eds) *The Question of the Commons*, University of Arizona Press, Tucson, pp. 171–194.

Porter, D., Allen, B. and Thompson, G. (1991). *Development in Practice: Paved with Good Intentions*, Routledge, London.

Royal Government of Cambodia. (2010) *National Forest Programme 2010–2029 (Unofficial Translation)*, Forestry Administration, Phnom Penh, Cambodia.

Sikor, T. and Lund, C. (2009) 'Access and property: A question of power and authority', *Development and Change* 40(1), pp. 1–22.

Sunderlin, W. D. (2006) 'Poverty alleviation through community forestry in Cambodia, Laos, and Vietnam: An assessment of the potential', *Forest Policy and Economics* 8(4), pp. 386–396.

Titthara, M. (2012) 'Security forces strip, handcuff women in Kratie amid eviction', *Phnom Penh Post*, http://www.phnompenhpost.com/national/security-forces-strip-handcuff-women-kratie-amid-eviction, accessed 22 May 2012.

Walker, A. (2004) 'Seeing farmers for the trees: Community forestry and the arborealisation of agriculture in northern Thailand', *Asia Pacific Viewpoint* 45(3), pp. 311–324.

Walker, A. (2012) *Thailand's Political Peasants: Power in the Modern Rural Economy*, University of Wisconsin Press, Madison.

9 The forest carbon commodity chain in Cambodia's voluntary carbon market

Sango Mahanty, Amanda Bradley and Sarah Milne

Cambodia's most recent wave of conservation interventions promote market-based schemes that aim to secure forests by selling the ecosystem services they provide. Most prominent among them are performance-based payments to conserve the carbon stored in trees and forests, known as REDD, or 'reducing emissions from deforestation and forest degradation'.[1] Driven by international efforts to mitigate climate change, these measures create a market for the carbon that is held in forests and soil, or 'forest carbon'. A relative newcomer to forest carbon trade, Cambodia currently has six REDD projects under development, with two now close to monetising the resulting carbon credits.

Like other global commodities, the production and trade of forest carbon rests upon transactions that involve a range of actors[2] and institutions[3] (Appadurai, 1986), extending from a specific locality to international buyers that are trying to offset their carbon emissions. The creation of verified carbon credits, which are the 'commodity' form of forest carbon, begins in a place: a forested, yet often inhabited landscape. This process of carbon credit 'production' requires specialized institutions and knowledge, usually facilitated by international NGOs, donors and the private sector, with the blessing, if not active involvement, of state actors. To ensure that payments are only for 'additional' carbon stored, producers must demonstrate new actions or changes in behaviour from 'business as usual' scenarios around the use of forested land. Under the now widely recognized market standards, tradeable units of forest carbon only exist after a project is validated and verified according to the standards[4]. A third party must then periodically verify the quantity of credits produced by the scheme and their continued legitimacy (Bumpus, 2011, more fully outlines the workings of the carbon market).

This production process can be thought of as a commodity chain, involving complex social relations among diverse actors, within prevailing political and economic relations and institutions (Ribot, 1998). 'Commodity chain analysis' therefore examines the actors, relationships, transactions, contexts and resource/benefit flows associated with a commodity's production right through to its end-use (Gereffi and Korzeniewicz, 1994). Applying this approach to the nascent commodity chain for forest carbon, we examine emerging power and knowledge dynamics in this next wave of Cambodia's conservation and development interventions, and consider their future viability and equity.

In examining the forest carbon commodity chain, we focus on two projects in Cambodia, both aimed at the voluntary carbon market. International non-governmental organizations and the Cambodian government facilitate these projects. The first, in Oddar Meanchey Province, is a collaboration between the NGO, Pact and the Forestry Administration, which evolved from a grassroots community forestry (CF) initiative. The second, in Seima Protection Forest (SPF), Mondulkiri Province, evolved from an ongoing conservation project facilitated by the Wildlife Conservation Society (WCS) and the Forestry Administration (FA).

Our research builds upon several threads in the commodity chain analysis literature. Initially, we consider whether forest carbon is subject to the same political-economic disparities afflicting other global commodities, in which consumers at the 'centre' dictate the terms to producers who are at the 'periphery' (Gereffi and Korzeniewicz, 1994). We then explore how the costs and requirements of international institutions to standardize forest carbon trade, notably the Verified Carbon Standard (VCS) and the Climate Community and Biodiversity Standard (CCB), figure in potential disparities. Information limitations and uncertainties associated with the nascent forest carbon market make it difficult to undertake detailed quantitative analysis of inputs, outputs, prices and value addition, which often feature in commodity chain or 'filière' studies (Raikes and Jensen, 2000). However, we do examine the positioning and roles of key agents that mediate forest carbon production and exchange, and how they generate and capture value. Finally, we examine factors influencing various actors' access to the potential benefits of forest carbon trade and the forests and land that underpin it (c.f. Ribot and Peluso, 2003; Mahanty et al., 2013).

Our analysis uses project documents that are in the public domain. We also draw on discussions with project staff and data accumulated through our past and ongoing engagements with the two REDD projects. Bradley was a project coordinator with the Oddar Meanchey project between 2008 and 2012. Mahanty and Milne are undertaking ongoing research on REDD in Cambodia, which involves field research at the SPF. Milne also worked as a technical advisor to WCS between 2011 and 2012. For both sites, draft versions of this chapter were provided to current project staff, inviting corrections and comments.

The voluntary carbon market in Cambodia

The global voluntary carbon market responds to private sector demand for mechanisms to offset or reduce greenhouse gas emissions for ethical and/ or reputational reasons. This differs from the 'compliance' market, which is driven by mandated caps on greenhouse gas emissions. The UN's Clean Development Mechanism for Kyoto Protocol signatory countries and the

EU Emissions Trading Scheme are examples of the latter (Peters-Stanley and Yin, 2013).

Globally, the voluntary market is smaller than the compliance market, but it is still sizeable, trading $516 million in 2012 (Peters-Stanley and Yin, 2013). Within the voluntary market, forest carbon schemes provide some 32 per cent of carbon credits in 2012, competing with credits from renewable energy and efficient cook stoves, among others (ibid). Carbon credit prices may vary by project type (e.g. energy versus forest carbon), start date, region and overall demand and supply (ibid). Recent commentary flags a possible imbalance between the growing global supply of forest carbon credits and current demand in the voluntary market, which is currently the only means for selling carbon credits from conservation or land use interventions (Conservation International, 2013). In Cambodia, the voluntary market has so far been the most influential avenue for carbon credit transactions, mainly due to substantial donor investment in REDD.

Voluntary carbon markets represent the newest wave in the valuation and management of forested land in Cambodia (Milne, 2013), making them particularly significant to this volume. As a country with high forest cover and a high deforestation rate due to factors such as weak law enforcement, illegal logging and rapid conversion of forested lands for agriculture (see Chapters 1 and 2, this volume), Cambodia is an attractive location for REDD because of the potential for significant emissions to be avoided if forest loss is reduced.

The Royal Government of Cambodia (RGC) is a primary player in REDD, given the numerous laws and regulations that reinforce state ownership and control over the country's natural forests. These include the Forestry Law (2002), the Protected Areas Law (2008), the Land Law (2001) and various sub-decrees such as the Community Forestry Sub-Decree (2003) and Sub-decree 143 (2009) specifically for the SPF (WCS and FA, 2013). This regulatory mosaic divides forest jurisdictions between the Ministry of Agriculture Forestry and Fisheries, which managed the forest estate, and the Ministry of Environment, which manages the country's system of 23 protected areas. Apart from this legal framework, REDD is also ensconced in policy documents such as the National Forest Programme,[5] which outlines the RGC's intent to pursue 'sustainable forest financing' through market mechanisms.

The Oddar Meanchey and Seima projects were the first REDD projects to gain official government recognition, and are the most advanced towards trading forest carbon.[6] Now officially labelled 'REDD demonstration projects' both are expected to inform policy and ultimately become integrated within Cambodia's national REDD system, although the specific arrangements for this are still to be determined (Bradley and Shoch, 2013).

Oddar Meanchey and Seima REDD Projects: Actors, institutions and value creation

In the analysis below we consider the key actors involved in forest carbon production and trade in Oddar Meanchey and Seima, and their roles and relationships. We then examine how formal and informal institutions shape forest carbon production and trade from the local to the international level. Finally, we examine how these interactions contribute to the creation and maintenance of value along the forest carbon commodity chain, and how this might shape the distribution of REDD's risks and benefits.

Oddar Meanchey

The Oddar Meanchey Community Forestry REDD project was initiated in late 2007 by the American NGO Community Forestry International (CFI), who was succeeded by Pact in 2009 when CFI met funding difficulties. Terra Global Capital (TGC), a California-based company joined early as a partner, providing technical support to the project in return for an equity share of future credits. Remaining credits would then flow to the RGC, for management and distribution among partner institutions and communities. The FA was a key partner in the project's development, given its jurisdiction over the forest estate and its role as the RGC's designated seller of forest carbon credits. The Council of Ministers issued an official project endorsement (Government Decision No. 699) and the Danish aid agency (Danida) provided the first year of funding. This high-level commitment prompted central and provincial government officials to back the project and to step up forest law enforcement.

Local community forestry (CF) groups in Oddar Meanchey, who play the greatest role in forest patrolling, are among the most critical project actors. The REDD project area of 64,000 ha is spread across 13 non-contiguous CF areas ranging from 383 ha to 18,261 ha. Efforts to achieve legal recognition of these areas were already underway in 2007, through CFI and its local NGO partner, Children's Development Association (CDA); but the process was moving slowly and donor funding was inconsistent. The REDD initiative was therefore seen as an avenue to finance CF activities sustainably and to gain stronger government recognition. With CFI and CDA's assistance, the CF groups formed a CF Network (CFN) to enable structured and province-wide representation of the 13 community groups involved, comprising about 7,000 households. With technical support from TGC, CFI (and later Pact) then coordinated data collection and project design to satisfy the voluntary market standards, including consultation with local stakeholders and negotiation of forest tenure and benefit-sharing arrangements.

As the project moved towards external validation and verification, additional actors got involved. These included the Validation and Verification Bodies (VVBs), which are approved third-party auditors contracted by the project developer. In this case, donor funds supported validation by a German firm named Tuv Sud and verification by the American firm Scientific Certification Systems. In addition, international and Cambodian legal firms and carbon market intermediaries were engaged to support the upcoming sale. A Chicago-based firm, Dentons, provided pro bono legal advice[7] and training on carbon transactions. Meanwhile, a Phnom Penh-based Cambodian-American lawyer was hired to review the requisite legal documents in the Cambodian legal context, to explain the key terms to the FA, and to assure the RGC of the legitimacy of the transaction. In September 2013, the first issued credits were deposited in the 'Markit credit registry', which is an online platform to facilitate carbon credit transactions between buyers and sellers. Both the registry and the market regulators (i.e. the arbitrators of the international standards, VCS and CCB) charge a per credit fee when credits are issued. A market intermediary or broker facilitates transactions, which initially was Carbon Neutral in this case.

The first sale of a portion of the Oddar Meanchey REDD credits was announced on Microsoft's public blog in April 2013. This was 5 years after the project's inception, yet still in advance of the formal issuing of credits. While the volume and price of credits were not disclosed, this transaction was seen as a relatively small-scale advance purchase, limited to TGC's share of credits under the first issuance. Although there were several additional offers to buy credits from the RGC at that time, the government was apparently not prepared to process the necessary purchase agreements in a timely manner. Thus, the slow Cambodian political process did not conform to market expectations for an efficient exchange.

Our account of the Oddar Meanchey REDD project highlights the wide range of actors involved, all either contributing to, or hindering, the production of carbon credits (see Table 9.1). These actors are from civil society organizations (CSOs), government and the private sector. Some have had enduring involvement, such as local communities and the FA, while others, such as donors, VVBs, legal counsel and market intermediaries, were only involved at specific junctures, according to their own interests and specialized skills. For instance, market intermediaries only engaged when credit issuance was imminent. Similarly, given the RGC's limited capacity to understand or facilitate the potential inputs of REDD service providers, the project's primary implementing partner (initially CFI, then Pact) took on a critical role in coordinating the forest carbon production process.

Furthermore, the actors had differing incentives for their involvement in the commodity chain (see Figure 9.1). Financial rewards, both immediate and expected, were a factor for many actors. But non-financial benefits also came into play such as CF tenure rights for communities; reputational gains for groups such as TGC, Denton's and Pact; opportunities for conservation and development NGOs to promote their organizational goals; and, for some donors, the potential to gain political influence. These intangible benefits may cloud a financial analysis of the forest carbon commodity chain, but they appear critical to project proponents' engagement in REDD.

Final decisions on revenue distribution are yet to be confirmed, but the RGC has agreed that participating communities will get at least 50 per cent of net income, once project expenses have been covered. But these expenses remain ambiguous. For example, budgets show that project costs are significantly higher in the first 5 years of implementation, when systems and capacities are being built, and when forest enhancement may be conducted to boost future emissions reductions. The average annual budget during these early years, for Oddar Meanchey, is expected to be $1.2million. However, expenses should roughly halve after the first 5 years, leaving more net income for communities, assuming credit sales of a reasonable volume and price (at least $5 per tonne). Despite these spending fluctuations and market uncertainties, the project at least hopes for a positive cash flow in time.

Somewhat more problematically, the speculative nature of the carbon market creates significant uncertainty for some actors as to whether or not they will be compensated for their investments. For example, TGC and Pact both invested their own resources to move the project forward; and community members have also invested their time and resources, largely on a voluntary basis, in the perilous work of forest patrolling. In contrast, actors like CFI, Cambodian legal counsel and the VVBs have already been compensated for their work. This occurred before credit sale, using donor funding. Such arrangements absorb all risks for these actors, yet they also highlight the key issue that REDD market financing alone may not be sufficient for forest conservation.

Mondulkiri (Seima Protection Forest)

The REDD project at SPF has evolved from a joint conservation program initiated in 2002 by the WCS and the FA to strengthen management of this former logging concession. Their ongoing collaboration, with involvement from various NGOs over time, has aimed to conserve and restore biodiversity values and encourage compatible local livelihoods through improved law enforcement and strengthened local resource management. An important motivation for development of the REDD project was the opportunity to raise conservation financing at an expanded and sustainable scale, to counter threats to the forest reserve from mining, agro-industrial plantations, illegal timber trade and population growth (WCS and FA, 2013).

The 189,513 ha core area covered by the proposed REDD project contains a significant population of ethnic Bunong People (12,879 in 2010), for whom the forest is considered spiritually and economically important (WCS and FA, 2013, p. 1). While Bunong are the dominant ethnic group, a small Xtieng community also resides there, and there has been a rapid influx of Khmer lowland migrants to the area looking for land and labour opportunities. Major indigenous livelihood activities include rain-fed rice farming, cash crop farming (previously cashew, increasingly cassava) and resin-tapping in forested areas. Economic land concessions (ELCs) have recently eaten into the protected forest's buffer zone, creating a locus for

Table 9.1 Key actors in the Oddar Meanchey (OM) and Seima carbon schemes.

Category	Roles	OM (specific actors)	Seima (specific actors)
Royal Government of Cambodia	Project partner; approve credit sale; receive/distribute revenues	Forestry Administration (FA); Council of Ministers	FA
International NGO (primary)	Lead implementing partners; project development; securing funding; field coordination; implementation oversight	Community Forestry International and Pact	Wildlife Conservation Society (WCS)
Int. NGO (service provider)	Technical advice	Birdlife International; Women Organizing for Change in Agriculture and Natural Resource Management	Winrock International
Cambodian NGOs and local civil society organizations	Service provision e.g. livelihood activities, local capacity building, communication, facilitate representation	Community Forestry Network; Children's Development Association; Monks' Community Forestry	Community Legal Education Centre; Cambodia Rural Development Team; Development Partners in Action; My Village International
Village level entities	Community representation; Free Prior and Informed Consent (FPIC) participation; implementation of actions to reduce forest carbon emissions	13 Community Forestry Groups	Community Forest Management Committees (3 villages); Residents[8] of 20 villages (17 key villages; 3 'other user' villages); 10 Indigenous Community Commissions

(continued)

Table 9.1 (continued)

Category	Roles	OM (specific actors)	Seima (specific actors)
Private Sector (technical service providers)	Technical advice on carbon accounting; legal advice on agreements and contracts; validation and verification body (VVB)	Terra Global Capital LLC; Dentons (Int. legal counsel); Sok Siphana and Associates (Cambodian legal counsel); Tuv Sud; Scientific Certification Systems (VVB)	Forest Carbon; Sok Siphana and Associates (Cambodian legal counsel); Scientific Certification Systems (VVB)
Private sector (marketing and purchase)	Sales support and broker/intermediary function; risk insurance; credit purchase	Carbon Neutral; Code REDD; Markit Registry; Overseas Private Investment Corporation Microsoft (buyer)	None yet
Donors	Funding for project development: Project Design process, FPIC, validation, legal advice	Danida; Clinton Climate Initiative; United Nations Development Programme; Japan International Cooperation Agency; UN Food and Agriculture Organization	Asian Development Bank-Biodiversity Conservation Corridor Initiative; Institute for Global Environmental Strategies; Japan International Cooperation Agency; Singapore International Foundation; Translinks; UN-REDD; Winrock, MacArthur

The forest carbon commodity chain in Cambodia's voluntary carbon market 185

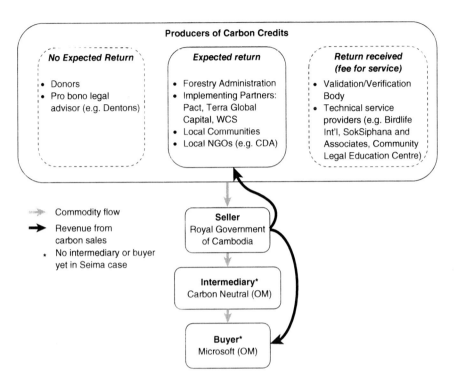

Figure 9.1 The forest carbon commodity chain for Oddar Meanchey and Seima Protection Forest.

Source: This figure was developed by the authors from data available on the two projects.

illegal logging. Furthermore, a dormant mining exploration concession covers much of the protected forest. In this very dynamic context, the project aims to secure 'additional' carbon through better planning and law enforcement; the encouragement of sustainable community land use, particularly through limits to agricultural expansion in the core area; and the provision of support for indigenous communal land titling as a basis for community resource management and exclusion of new migrants. The project also promotes 'alternative livelihoods that reduce deforestation', such as community-based ecotourism, agricultural extension, and non-timber forest product enterprises (WCS and FA, 2013).

In August 2013, in line with VCS and CCB requirements, a project design document (PD) was released for public comment (WCS and FA, 2013). This document was several years in the making, with dedicated financing from 2008 onwards for various aspects of project development (ibid, p. 205). Organizations and groups with a significant and visible role in developing the forest carbon scheme, as mentioned in the PD, are shown in Table 9.1. Importantly, before release of the PD and to comply with CCB standards, WCS conducted a process of securing 'free prior and informed consent' (FPIC) from participating villages, a process that involved multiple public consultations and negotiations over 2011–2013.

Project document submission is a critical moment in the commodification of carbon credits, signalling readiness for them to be validated and registered for trading (see Figure 9.1). This is the culmination of years of negotiation and decision-making about the nature of the REDD intervention, the areas and people involved and the likely distribution of associated benefits. However, the negotiations have not ended with PD submission.

The benefit distribution arrangements are yet to be finalized for Seima, and are the subject of discussion between the FA-housed REDD taskforce, WCS and UN-REDD. A policy document on the subject was prepared and circulated by WCS, but is yet to gain RGC approval. Like in Oddar Meanchey, the FA is the RGC's designated project proponent for carbon credit transactions, but revenue flows are likely to be handled by the Ministry of Economics and Finance.

Until now WCS has been the lead technical organization facilitating the 'production' of verified forest carbon credits in Seima, and its efforts have been financed by a substantial funding allocation[9] of $645,251 (WCS and FA, 2013, p. 205) for work on carbon accounting and other technical aspects of REDD, through Winrock and MacArthur Foundation, and the gaining of community consent through FPIC, financed by *Japan International Cooperation Agency* (JICA) and others. The UN-REDD program in Cambodia also provided small grant funding to WCS for the development of policy briefs. Together, these donors or project financiers have effectively subsidized the production of verified carbon credits from Seima, but they will not receive direct financial returns from resulting credit sales. There is an expectation, however, that a share of carbon revenues will finance many of the running costs of the SPF, which should reduce the fundraising burden on WCS and FA. As with Oddar Meanchey, there may be perceived non-financial rewards from participation in REDD for some actors, for example, achievement of forest management and community livelihood objectives for WCS and others; demonstration of forest carbon markets for climate change mitigation for donors; and the enhanced reputations that follow.

Residents of the 20 villages in and around the carbon production area are another key interest group and are potential beneficiaries of carbon sales. Among them, WCS has identified a particular role for the indigenous Bunong in REDD implementation, as future recipients of indigenous communal land title, seen as an important 'co-benefit' of carbon trading. Through the linking of REDD and indigenous land tenure, it is hoped that Bunong people will have an incentive to contribute to carbon 'production' by limiting their agricultural expansion in the core area of the SPF, and resisting forest incursions by in-migrants looking for land and timber. More broadly, both Bunong and Khmer residents in the target villages will be expected to adhere to land use agreements, supplemented by user permits for forest resources and livelihoods support. So far, REDD-related agreements have been limited only to household and village-level consent forms for FPIC, with other arrangements pending.

In Seima, as with Oddar Meanchey, several indirect players exert important influences over the implementation of the carbon schemes and their ultimate outcomes. Some of these, such as provincial and local authorities, have a recognized role in the forest carbon commodity chain. Others, such as tycoons (*Okhnya*) with land and timber interests, concessionaires and the military, are not directly engaged in the REDD scheme but will strongly influence project outcomes through their role in the wider political economy within which carbon production and trade occurs. Ultimately, the generation of credits may rely upon behaviour change among these powerful actors that are 'external' to the forest carbon commodity chain (see Cambodia Daily, 29 May 2014).

Experiences in Seima also highlight the importance of FPIC and state approvals to establish the legitimacy of the forest carbon production arrangements and the perceived 'permanence' of the carbon credits produced. Seima has gained particular recognition for its attention to FPIC in the 20 targeted villages, since it provides the first instance of FPIC implementation in Cambodia that adheres to international guidelines (e.g. Anderson, 2011; UNREDD, 2013). This involved a series of community consultations over a 2-year period for the purposes of local awareness-raising, provision of independent legal advice, negotiation of village-level agreements with the FA and ultimately the gaining of 'approval to proceed with REDD' at a household-level through thumb-printed consent forms in late 2012.[10] The village-level agreements were then signed by village, commune and community committee chiefs, with the FA, at a formal FPIC signing ceremony in January 2013 (Figure 9.2). Authorization of the PD by the FA then took several months, as in Oddar Meanchey, with project documents released for public review in August 2013.

A 'validation audit' of the REDD project then took place in November 2013 to register the scheme under VCS and CCB standards. This audit process highlighted that validators with the technical skills to audit carbon accounting systems may be less skilled in assessing the 'social licence' aspects of a scheme, which in this case were assigned to a second member of the validation team. Furthermore, the experience revealed inconsistencies between the VCS and CCB standards. The former requires communities to commit to REDD for the full duration of the project, while the CCB's adoption of FPIC provisions require ongoing community engagement in project decisions. The Seima validators also raised questions about how projected carbon credits could be guaranteed in light of the project's plan to set up indigenous communal titles within the project area, especially with the rapid and confusing issuance of individual titles by government officials in many of the same areas, leading up to the 2012 election (Milne, 2013). These tenurial issues are yet to be resolved.

Figure 9.2 Village representatives and the Mondulkiri provincial governor sign the REDD+ Free Prior and Informed consent agreement at a public ceremony, January 2013.

Source: Photo by S. Mahanty.

Key steps in the creation of value for forest carbon

Both projects are governed by rules and procedures for the voluntary carbon market, which are designed by the international bodies VCS and CCB. These in turn intersect existing national and subnational laws and local norms where projects are implemented. Together, these formal and informal rules structure the forest carbon commodity chain, underpinning the production of verified credits and the addition or generation of market value. Table 9.2 compares the key steps in the commodity chain for the two projects.

As the official owner of Cambodia's forests, government approval is the first milestone in the production of forest carbon credits. Accordingly, the RGC is the recognized seller of carbon credits in both the Oddar Meanchey and Seima project agreements. In both cases, these approvals took time and relationship building as, without a specific law or policy on REDD, Cambodian government officials were initially wary of carbon 'cowboys' who might profit from unscrupulous private deals. The assertion of government ownership over carbon benefits was an important precondition for future trade in Cambodia.

Tenure clarity is an important enabling condition for accessing the carbon market, and it also influences the value of carbon credits. The CCB standards emphasize the importance of clear tenure arrangements and a review of these is standard procedure. Under VCS, land tenure disputes result in an increased project 'risk rating' and fewer credits to the project proponent. Therefore, even though both projects fall under the jurisdiction of the FA, resolving local tenure claims has been a key requirement for both projects. In Oddar Meanchey, CF groups gained renewable 15-year management agreements for the 13 forest parcels making up the project area.

Table 9.2 Key steps in forest carbon production and exchange.

Stage	Specific steps	Oddar Meanchey	Seima Protection Forest
Production of validated and verified forest carbon credits	Government endorsement of project	Government Decision No. 699 (May 2008)	MOU with RGC
	Clarify tenure arrangements	CF Agreements with 13 communities	Forest user rights and communal land title already formalized for some communities, with further clarification foreshadowed in REDD benefit-sharing arrangements
	Community consultation/ consent (FPIC)	Training and awareness raising followed by a consultation workshop with representatives from each CF	FPIC process run by WCS-FA team, with third party community legal advisors and indigenous language translators
	Submission of project documents and deeds	Submit PD; follow rules of VCS and CCB; collect extensive data	Submit PD; follow rules of VCS and CCB; collect extensive data
	Complete validation	August 2012 Follow rules of VCS and CCB	November 2013 Follow rules of VCS and CCB
	Increase forest protection activities to deliver carbon credits	Additional support for patrols and forest protection	Stepped up forest law enforcement
	Complete verification	September 2013 Follow rules of VCS and CCB	Verification process still to be concluded. Follow rules of VCS and CCB
Purchase of credits via intermediary	Sell credits	First sale to a buyer (Microsoft) in mid-2013; Carbon Neutral served as an intermediary with the buyer	No buyer identified yet (April 2014)

In Seima, WCS aimed to promote tenure clarity by supporting indigenous communal title applications by Bunong villagers in the project area. These efforts to accommodate local resource rights are supported by Cambodian laws, but their implementation can be complicated by REDD. For instance, in Oddar Meanchey, the standard CF Agreement template was modified to prohibit commercial timber harvesting and to recognize communities' rights to receive carbon benefits, with the RGC serving as an aggregator. Meanwhile in Seima, validators have questioned whether indigenous communal title can even meet VCS requirements for forest management, and further clarification is required.

Securing local consent to participate in REDD is critical for market access. The need for FPIC is driven by international principles (e.g. the UN Declaration on the Rights of Indigenous Peoples) and REDD-related guidelines, to ensure the 'legitimacy' of the carbon credits being produced and to reduce risk. For both projects, efforts were made to facilitate FPIC, often with significant investment. But ambiguity still exists in defining acceptable FPIC processes, for example, in determining whether local participants understand the information they receive and whether they are represented with transparency and accountability (Mahanty and McDermott, 2013).

Benefit-sharing arrangements to distribute carbon revenues have also been a key negotiating point between government and other claimants. In both projects, validation has proceeded without benefit-sharing arrangements being finally agreed, due mainly to government reluctance and market uncertainty. One critical question is the level of return to participating communities. In Oddar Meanchey, the FA has agreed in writing to 'maximize' benefits to communities to at least 50 per cent of net income, but it is unclear if this extends to Seima. A second concern is the level of return to project partners. In both cases, there has been no approval of long-term budgets or arrangements for dividing responsibilities and revenues. For instance, Pact has proposed a management fee of 5 per cent to compensate and incentivize the active participation of FA officials; however, it is unclear if this will be approved by the FA, or indeed whether it even has the authority to do so, given that the Ministry of Economy and Finance presides over government revenues.

Existing relationships between key actors have been a critical factor in benefit-sharing negotiations to date. For example, the FA Director General and other officials apparently expressed concerns about the costs of involving an international NGO like Pact, which could reduce revenues for Cambodian partners. From their perspective, there was a risk that revenues could leave the country to support Pact's headquarters. The FA was also uncomfortable when Pact, as a not-for-profit organization, described its involvement in and contribution of its reserve funds to the Oddar Meanchey project as an 'investment'. Yet without Pact's value-adding efforts and potential, the project would be impossible. Such dynamics have delayed progress for Oddar Meanchey. On the other hand, the FA and WCS have a 'tighter' relationship, built on over a decade's cooperation in Seima and elsewhere. Interpersonal relationships between key decision-makers in the FA and long-term WCS advisors also appear to have been central to the FA's responsiveness to WCS's suggestions and meeting requests about REDD. Furthermore, WCS's historical involvement in designing Cambodia's REDD Roadmap would also have played a role, as the key UN-REDD technical consultant was seconded from WCS at the time. This made the 'implementation conditions' for WCS somewhat more favourable, although both international NGOs must work hard to maintain good working relations with the rather unpredictable and politically embedded FA.

In order to produce carbon credits, both projects have had to outline 'additional' actions to step up forest protection and reduce deforestation and forest degradation. Carbon methodologies (and associated knowledge) define how these ground-level actions translate into 'emissions avoided' or carbon credits. At the two sites, project investments focus on enhancing forest patrols, fire control, reducing firewood or timber extraction, and reducing agricultural expansion. Such activities must be carefully monitored and reported on a regular basis to maintain certification of credits, and hence, market access. In Oddar Meanchey, since start-up funds were short, many communities voluntarily organized forest patrols, expecting that the sale of carbon revenues would eventually provide some financial compensation for their efforts. In Seima, enforcement responsibility rests primarily with the FA; but REDD revenues are expected to strengthen enforcement, as well as support community land use agreements and indigenous land titling.

The last three major steps in forest carbon production, namely the submission of project documents, validation and verification bring together local, national and international institutions, with associated power asymmetries. Several international standards exist, although the VCS and CCB are most commonly used and recognized, and generally secure the highest market value. In both projects, the use of these standardized scientific methodologies required significant investment and international technical expertise. In Oddar Meanchey, technical inputs were compensated with an equity stake in future credits; while in Seima, consultants were paid a fee-for-service, or WCS used in-house expertise or that of its academic collaborators.

Finally, the purchase of carbon credits by an international buyer from the Cambodian government signifies the point of forest carbon exchange. The Oddar Meanchey project has already received purchase offers, while Seima aims to sell credits in 2014–2015. However, buyers' demands for clarity and efficiency may contrast sharply with the Cambodian government's opaque internal decision-making processes. In contrast with revenue from competing resource uses such as illicit timber extraction, individual officials may not directly benefit from REDD revenues and could be less supportive in facilitating sales. Even the Director General of the FA admitted his uncertainty about whether he had the authority (not to mention will) to contract a sale of carbon credits. Those outside the government, including implementing partners, struggle to navigate these relationships and identify (honest) strategies to speed up lengthy deliberations. Local communities are also excluded from this process. That said, it is possible that the Oddar Meanchey project will pave the way for future REDD projects, including Seima, and the sales process will become more efficient over time. A recent Government Decision (*Sor Chhor Nor* 1552) is an important development: it was issued to guide the sale of carbon credits, establish a floor price and designate who the official signatories should be on purchase agreements. In the meantime, a lack of responsiveness by the RGC could negatively affect market demand for Cambodian REDD credits.

Discussion

The Oddar Meanchey and Seima cases highlight that the forest carbon commodity chain is grounded within and shaped by the political economy of resource exploitation in Cambodia. National and international institutions together shape the roles and power of different actors, which are both internal and external to the commodity chain. Ultimately, these complex and delicate negotiations that make up the commodity chain shape access to the benefits of carbon trade.

Actors and relationships

In both projects, the historical political economy of Cambodia's forests positions the RGC and the FA as central players in REDD. They influence how quickly the process moves, with evidence that capacity and political will may be lacking at times. The question of how forest carbon schemes compare with alternative resource deals such as ELCs and timber extraction is also significant. For both projects, international NGOs have played a critical role as mediators. These NGOs have had to work closely with the government rather than, for instance, operating as a watchdog or neutral facilitator. Although the government is the 'seller' of the carbon credits, it only takes up this role through coaxing by NGO actors. Correspondingly, after investing significant resources in REDD development, NGOs are equally if not more vested than the government in the forest carbon commodity chain. This nexus between project facilitators and government actors highlights the forest carbon commodity chain's reliance upon 'webs of interdependence', particularly at the production stage. In Cambodia, these vital and often personal connections can be opaque and also fragile in the face of changes to staffing within government and NGOs, and political shifts; introducing an element of risk to forest carbon production.

Furthermore, accounting for verified carbon credits is highly technical. No Cambodians are (yet) sufficiently skilled to undertake deforestation modelling or PD preparations, creating dependence upon outsiders as well as higher costs. Knowledge brokers such as the validators and technical service providers are therefore assured of a return for their contribution to the 'production' of carbon credits, regardless of the sale price or whether a sale is ultimately realized. In the Cambodian context, these 'transaction costs' – such as payments to knowledge brokers – have so far been borne by donors and facilitating organizations rather than from carbon revenues. But if these costs remain high, then this will discount the potential returns that local actors may receive from forest carbon. Given limited global financing, both for project development and purchase of the credits, this problem will likely persist.

Quite apart from international dynamics, both schemes are strongly influenced by Cambodia-based actors external to REDD. Concessionaires, tycoons and the military are not directly engaged in the forest carbon production and exchange, but are highly influential and visible within the broader political economy, due to their lucrative interests in ELCs and timber extraction (see Chapter 5). These interests in timber, land and agricultural products feed into commodity chains that directly compete with REDD. Indeed, some actors within local government, communities and the FA may simultaneously engage in and benefit from competing commodity chains, by wearing 'multiple hats'. In time, this could represent a significant challenge for REDD implementation, as actors in forest and land-based commodity chains weigh up whether the benefits they accrue from REDD compete favourably with these alternatives. If not, it is possible that external actors and competing interests will gradually encroach upon the forests that are designated for carbon production and, in so doing, reduce or undermine the production of carbon credits. The operation of these indirect or external actors is relatively new to commodity chain studies, but has clear significance for the long-term viability of carbon markets.

Institutional influences on carbon trade and the interplay of new and existing institutions

The political economy of natural resource use in Cambodia frames different actors' roles in the carbon market and their capacity to benefit. This setting is highly contested and power laden, with ongoing contests over land and forest resources. While both REDD projects are attempting to 'settle' tenure contests through mechanisms like CF agreements and indigenous land title, these arrangements may be dynamic and not always respected in practice. For example, in Oddar Meanchey, the military has established camps and cleared forest in at least three of the officially recognized CF areas (Kuch and Blomberg, 2013); and in Seima, powerful external actors may disregard indigenous communal title (Milne, 2013). Thus, although recognition of title may be seen as a more secure basis for communities to claim rights to carbon revenues, the reality is often more contested (Mahanty *et al.*, 2013). New forest carbon-specific institutions (VCS, CCB that are developed without reference to these underlying and often conflicted institutional contexts, may fail to identify potential pitfalls and risks.

Our analysis also highlights the market role played by FPIC. Often framed as a 'safeguard', FPIC here becomes a stage in the forest carbon production process, in vouching for the legitimacy of carbon credits and reductions in market risk. Yet the reality on the ground may be that local people's 'consent' is based on cultural protocols or trust in a long-time NGO partner, rather than understanding of the intervention or engagement from a position of empowerment. Indeed, the power asymmetries between local villagers and project actors may be hard to overcome, as seen in mining and forest certification projects (Mahanty and McDermott, 2013). This, combined with the overall complexity of explaining the timeframes and transactions of REDD, can influence FPIC outcomes, even where project facilitators intend to meaningfully engage communities.

The influence of international carbon standards on local institutions, particularly the social safeguards they demand, is also striking. For instance, the desire to obtain CCB approval convinced government and other stakeholders of the need to guarantee significant benefits to communities, and to put in place formal grievance mechanisms as well as worker safety protocols around REDD. All of these would be unusual in a typical development project or concession agreement.

Value addition along the commodity chain

Unlike typical physical commodities, where value is added through processing, aggregation and transportation, much of the value addition for forest carbon occurs through the complicated negotiations and knowledge transactions that are required to produce trusted and saleable carbon credits.

In this sense, the process of value addition resembles a complex commodity like a car, where numerous transactions and labour inputs are required before a car is driven out of the factory. For forest carbon, value is added through the application of processes set out in the VCS and CCB standards, which together 'embed' market legitimacy and trust in the final product. Processes such as FPIC, social and environmental co-benefits, and government sign-off, collectively signify moments of value addition, culminating in the production of a verified carbon credit. Accounting and validation/verification standards are thus critical to the legitimacy and perceived quality of forest carbon units. Yet their methodologies inevitably simplify the social dynamics that drive deforestation, making modelling difficult. These methodologies are continually being evaluated and revised to improve their accuracy and credibility; indicating how value is generated through scientific credibility and 'faith' in the model.

Critical analyses of carbon markets highlight the risk that markets for forest carbon privilege carbon values over other forest values (e.g. Boyd *et al.*, 2011). Yet our analysis highlights that value creation for forest carbon may be rather fragile and contingent, subject to the vagaries of delicately negotiated relationships upon which forest carbon's production depend and the maintenance of trust at every point along its fragile commodity chain.

The flow of benefits and risks

Uncertainty and volatility are inherent to the global forest carbon market, creating risks and opportunities. Most fundamentally, project developers require estimates of expected credits and revenues in order to motivate the actors involved. However, continuing uncertainty around carbon price makes such estimates difficult, and overestimation can create disappointment that ultimately undermines a carbon project. In this uncertain context, the RGC has been very cautious with REDD, as reflected in a former FA Director General's remark: 'Don't talk about cooking the fish until you've caught it'. Compared with other forms of conservation, forest carbon trade may also lead to new kinds of competitiveness and less transparency among project facilitators, since REDD design elements and market knowledge can provide a 'market edge'. Commodity chain analysis has made some of the actors and resource flows more transparent than they otherwise are.

The dependencies created through forest carbon's highly technical underpinnings, position intermediaries and knowledge brokers to benefit from carbon trade, regardless of whether sale ultimately occurs or the desired price achieved. This is consistent with early predictions that knowledge brokers would be well positioned to gain a significant share of revenue from forest carbon markets (Munden Project, 2011). However, if financial transfers mainly benefit intermediaries, will there be enough resources to shift land use decisions and implement ground-level actions to reduce deforestation? A slump in the market would further jeopardize these fundamental environmental goals, by reducing the number of projects being developed. Intermediaries will not be immune from the resulting reduction in returns.

Finally, in both cases, it is noteworthy that benefit-sharing arrangements were not agreed ahead of marketing the carbon credits. This situation adds a further layer of uncertainty, on top of that created by a volatile carbon price. This creates a risk for local communities engaged in carbon production, whose bargaining power is arguably the weakest; but it also creates a risk for REDD, since lack of community support could ultimately undermine conservation objectives and project sustainability.

Conclusions

Forest carbon is an atypical and abstract commodity, with a material basis in forests and land, and the institutions, actors and power dynamics that this entails, but also founded in complex knowledge transactions. Analysing its commodity chain is a complex undertaking but provides important insights.

First, our analysis shows that forest carbon 'production' is the most complex phase of the carbon commodity chain, with its multiple actors and multi-directional resource flows. Some actors benefit before the forest carbon even enters the market, while others continue to sponsor its production with seemingly no financial returns (yet), but perhaps driven by conservation, climate change or reputational objectives. Worldwide, very few projects have reached the stage of investing carbon revenues back into on-the-ground activities to reduce deforestation and degradation, and for the most part have relied heavily on external funding. Further research is necessary to determine if the market can be truly self-sustaining.

Second, commodity chain analysis has allowed us to consider how the institutional context influences the production and exchange of forest carbon, particularly the interplay of formal and informal, and/or international and local institutions governing forests and land. Importantly, the role of hidden actors and ongoing contests over forested land show that it is not just the institutional arrangements on paper that matter, but how they are realized in practice. In the Cambodian context, competing interests in land and forests could ultimately undermine REDD, especially if actors in the forest carbon commodity chain must wear 'multiple hats'. The schemes are also vulnerable to the delicate and contingent negotiations across scales upon which forest carbon production and exchange depend.

Similarly, our analysis of the potential benefits and risks from REDD indicates potential asymmetries. The intermediaries and knowledge brokers involved in producing verified carbon credits are, at least in the short term, well positioned to benefit from carbon trade. Without these intermediaries, the momentum for forest carbon markets may disappear. Yet, without sufficient revenues reaching the actors who determine land use or implement actions to reduce deforestation, REDD's contribution to climate change mitigation may be heavily compromised. Thus, REDD in Cambodia (and elsewhere) faces a significant challenge to achieving equitable benefit and risk sharing, given the plethora of players and their asymmetrical and power-laden relationships around knowledge and resource access.

Finally, compared with traditional conservation, the use of market-based tools like REDD appears to create new sensitivities and practices around information-sharing and perceived 'risk'. In a market context, processes like FPIC become a means to demonstrate market legitimacy and reduce market risk; the danger being that the original community empowerment agenda is lost to a 'check-box' approach.

An important question then emerges about whether the marketization of forest carbon reduces openings for learning and collaboration, which were once encouraged in conventional conservation and development projects. Such openness, in sharing both positive and negative experiences, is essential as actors in Cambodia move forward with plans for national-level REDD; navigate the challenges of achieving meaningful FPIC; and strive for transparency around methodologies for calculating baselines and accounting for carbon, while coping with the complexities of carbon trading agreements and benefit sharing. Only through open collaboration can a national approach to REDD fully incorporate and learn from voluntary schemes such as those at Oddar Meanchey and Seima, and thus address the challenges ahead.

Notes

1 The acronym REDD is typically used in the voluntary carbon market. UN-hosted negotiations over compliance markets for carbon emissions use the acronym REDD+, where *plus* adds *sustainable forest use practices*.
2 Social actors are individuals and groups that are capable of decision-making and agency (Hindess, 1988, p. 45; Long, 1992, p. 22), including individuals, capitalist enterprises, state agencies, NGOs and so on.
3 Institutions refer here to formal and informal rules and norms (Ostrom, 2005), rather than organizations.
4 Validation is an evaluation of the consistency between REDD project design and the carbon accounting methodology, which occurs once the project preparation phase is completed. Thereafter, verifications occur periodically to review and quantify emissions reductions generated by the project.
5 Royal Government of Cambodia, 2010. NFP, http://www.twgfe.org/nfp/Living_NFP_doc.php, accessed January 2014.
6 Other schemes under development include Prey Lang REDD project (Conservation International), Kulen Promtep REDD project (WCS), Southern Cardamom REDD project (Wildlife Alliance), Siem Pang REDD initiative (Birdlife International), Siem Reap CF REDD project (Fauna and Flora International) and a new project in Battambang Province (Maddox Jolie Pitt Foundation). These projects are divided between the Ministry of Environment (MoE) and the FA, with NGO partners.
7 SNR Denton valued this at over $93,837.
8 Residents were variously engaged in REDD. For example the FPIC process, at the request of the FA, required that households be considered as the fundamental 'consent giving' body; but formal village-level representative bodies (e.g. the Indigenous Community Commissions or *sahakoum* formed for indigenous land title) were also engaged in FPIC, along with local government bodies like the commune councils.
9 Note that this figure excludes operational costs like staff time and other technical inputs from WCS.
10 This household level agreement is not a requirement of international FPIC guidelines, but was requested by the FA.

Acknowledgements

The authors acknowledge the helpful comments from the following individuals: Scott Settelmyer, TerraCarbon LLC; Sarah Sitts and Julien Brewster, Pact; Wolfram Dressler, University of Melbourne. They thank Pact and WCS staff for sharing information on the Oddar Meanchey and Seima projects. Aspects of this paper were supported by an Australian Research Council Discovery grant (DP120100270 The Political Ecology of Forest Carbon: Mainland Southeast Asia's New Commodity Frontier?). The views expressed here are those of the authors and do not necessarily represent those of funders or other informants.

References

Anderson, P. (2011) *Free, Prior, and Informed Consent in REDD+: Principles and Approaches for Policy and Project Development*, RECOFTC, Bangkok.

Appadurai, A. (1986) *The Social Life of Things: Commodities in Cultural Perspective*, Cambridge University Press, Cambridge.

Bradley, A. and Shoch, D. (2013) *Survey and Analysis of REDD+ Project Activities in Cambodia*, TerraCarbon LLC.

Boyd, E., Boykoff, M. and Newell, P. (2011) 'The "new" carbon economy: What's new?' *Antipode* 43, pp. 601–611.

Bumpus, A. G. (2011) 'The matter of carbon: Understanding the materiality of tCO$_2$e in carbon offsets', *Antipode* 43, pp. 612–638.

Conservation International. (2013) *REDD+ Market: Sending out an SOS*, Conservation International, Arlington, Virginia.

Gereffi, G., and Korzeniewicz, M. (1994) *Commodity Chains and Global Capitalism*, Praeger, Westport, CT.

Hindess, B. (1988) *Choice, Rationality, and Social Theory*, Vol. 22, Unwin Hyman, Boston, London.

Kuch, N. and Zsombor, P. (2014) 'As forests fall, carbon credit plan faces collapse', http://www.cambodiadaily.com/news/as-forests-fall-carbon-credit-plan-faces-collapse-59938/, accessed 29 May 2014.

Kuch, N. and Blomberg, M. (2013) 'Cambodia's carbon credit scheme still not making gains', http://www.cambodiadaily.com/archives/cambodias-carbon-credit-scheme-still-not-making-gains-43865/, accessed 29 April 2014.

Long, N. (1992) 'From paradigm lost to paradigm regained? The case for an actor-oriented sociology of development', in N. Long and A. Long (eds) *Battlefields of Knowledge: The Interlocking Of Theory and Practice in Social Research and Development*, Routledge, London, pp. 16–43.

Mahanty, S. and McDermott, C. L. (2013) 'How does "Free, Prior and Informed Consent" (FPIC) impact social equity? Lessons from mining and forestry and their implications for REDD', *Land Use Policy* 35, pp. 406–416.

Mahanty, S., Dressler, W., Milne, S., and Filer, C. (2013) 'Unravelling property relations around forest carbon', *Singapore Journal of Tropical Geography* 34(2), pp. 188–205.

Milne, S. (2013) 'Under the leopard's skin: Land commodification and the dilemmas of Indigenous communal title in upland Cambodia', *Asia Pacific Viewpoint* 54(3), pp. 323–339.

Munden Project. (2011) 'REDD and forest carbon: Market-based critique and recommendations', http://www.mundenproject.com/forestcarbonreport2.pdf, accessed 23 August 2011.

Ostrom, E. (2005) *Understanding Institutional Diversity*, Princeton University Press, Princeton, NJ.

Peters-Stanley, M. and Yin, D. (2013) *Maneuvering the Mosaic: State of the Voluntary Carbon Markets 2013*, Forest Trends' Ecosystem Marketplace and Bloomberg New Energy Finance.

Raikes, P. and Jensen, M. F. (2000) 'Global commodity chain analysis and the French filière approach: Comparison and critique', *Economy and Society* 29(3), pp. 390–417.

Ribot, J. C. (1998) 'Theorizing access: Forest profits along Senegal's charcoal commodity chain', *Development and Change* 29(2), pp. 307–341.
Ribot, J. C., and Peluso, N. L. (2003) 'A theory of access', *Rural Sociology* 68(2), pp. 153–181.
Royal Government of Cambodia. (2010) *National Forest Programme 2010–2029*, Phnom Penh, Cambodia.
UNREDD. (2013) *Guidelines on Free, Prior and Informed Consent*, UNREDD Programme Switzerland, Geneva.
Wildlife Conservation Society and the Forestry Administration (WCS and FA). (2013) *Reduced Emissions from Deforestation and Degradation in Seima Protection Forest*, Wildlife Conservation Society Cambodia, Phnom Penh.

Part 3
Social movements and radical responses to transformation

10 What about the 'unprotected' areas?

Building on traditional forms of ownership and land use for dealing with new contexts

Jeremy Ironside

Introduction

Conservation discourse typically divides territory into protected and 'unprotected' areas. This is unsatisfactory in Cambodia as protected areas or national parks can hardly be considered 'protected' with large areas allocated for plantation agriculture and mining, opening the door for widespread illegal logging in the process. Forested areas outside these parks are also undergoing widespread transformation driven by the substantial potential revenues from logging, plantations and land grabbing (see Chapters 2 and 5, this volume). This raises the question of what exactly is the meaning of biodiversity conservation and a protected area system in the Cambodian context, and also what other ways might there be to maintain biodiversity and support sustainable development in the country's forested areas.

Throughout Southeast Asia the very idea of a protected area free from human use and impact, following the 'Yellowstone model' (Stevens, 1997), is largely a foreign concept. It is more accurate to talk about 'humanized ecosystems' (Galhano-Alves, 2008) in this region. This highlights the problem of artificially separating people from nature, and also the false dichotomy that is created in separating agricultural and forest areas (Adams and Hutton, 2007). Using Ratanakiri Province in the far northeast of Cambodia as an example, I wish to question these forest-agriculture dichotomies by exploring models and examples of traditional forms of land ownership and use. Ratanakiri Province is of interest in this regard because it has maintained over 80 per cent forest cover (primary and secondary) up until the very recent past (Fox, 2002), despite the presence over centuries of indigenous groups and their rotational swidden agriculture practices. This raises the possibility of other approaches for managing biodiverse areas. Instead of conservation efforts treating forests in isolation, they should instead be located in a larger ecological, socio-cultural and economic setting (Puppala, 2013). I argue in this chapter, therefore, that such alternative approaches, exemplified in the mixed use landscapes that resulted from traditional systems of communal management, can provide us with another paradigm or model for maintaining ecosystems and balancing conservation with use in natural areas. The case of upland forested areas in Ratanakiri, Cambodia, therefore allows us to explore the integration, as opposed to the separation, of people and nature.

From this discussion, I wish also to explore alternatives to state management of protected areas, given the onslaught which these areas have been under in Cambodia over the past decade or more. Developing locally driven alternative management scenarios, which emphasize the connection between people and land, inherently requires understanding the cultural links between the use of natural resources and their protection. Studies of local communal management of natural resources have shown that where local groups have management authority over their resources, use has been able to be combined with maintaining overall biodiversity (Basurto and Ostrom, 2009; Fairhead and Leach, 1996; Ostrom, 1990). Understanding the way that traditional forms of land and forest management have shaped the forested landscape in Ratanakiri can therefore help in developing communal models of forest conservation and agricultural land use in and around these areas.

I begin this chapter with a brief discussion of conventional land use paradigms and some new ideas that are challenging these. Following this, I discuss the importance of the study site and the methods I used to understand land uses and how these are changing. I then examine Ratanakiri Province as a place where contrasting land uses and ownership systems exist side by side. I explore the land use systems that have been traditionally practiced by the area's indigenous populations and some examples of how these are operating in the contemporary context. In addition to this, I present a case of community conservation that is building on cultural norms to adapt to present day pressures. I conclude this chapter with a call for greater consideration of communal land management options as a way to reconcile biodiversity conservation objectives with the livelihood needs of local communities.

Rethinking conventional conservation and land use paradigms

Ideas of separating humans and nature are deeply rooted in Western culture, and in conventional conservation thinking (Colchester, 1994). Seventeenth century enlightenment thinkers such as John Locke, Thomas Hobbes and René Descartes, for example, were influential in providing a philosophical basis for transforming natural areas in the name of progress and civilization (Freyfogle, 2010; Pattberg, 2007). Locke's ideas about clearing and claiming land in a wild state to create value provided sanction for the exploitation and control of nature (ibid). This urge to transform nature provided a strong justification for colonization, as the conversion of commonly held 'waste' into privately owned agricultural land became regarded as a natural progression (Locke, 1960, in Manzo, 1995, p. 235). Ideas of social evolution at the time also meant that non-Western cultural beliefs were devalued, and Western attitudes to nature came to predominate (Rist, 2002).

As a result of this thinking, in contemporary times, common pool resources such as forests, pasture and drylands, which are important both for livelihoods and biodiversity conservation, often continue to be seen as 'wastelands', and continue to be privatized, enclosed and taken over for industrial agriculture and other purposes (Puppala, 2013). Industrial forms of agricultural production, in turn, tend to adopt a monocultural vision of land-use, focused on planting large areas to a single species. This kind of management attempts to create ecological equilibrium through technically oriented management aimed at 'controlling the resource to increase the predictability of yields' (Berkes *et al.*, 2000, p. 1259). These systems are inherently unstable and lack the ability to absorb disturbance and change. This lack of resilience in the face of changing conditions is masked by technologies dependent on fossil fuels to maintain yields (ibid).

Challenging these monoculture approaches, new perspectives from non-equilibrium ecology and post-structural thought are now leading to a reappraisal of the role of humans in managing and creating ecosystems, and to a rethinking of forest-agriculture dichotomies (Tonneijk *et al.*, 2006; Steinmetz, 1996). A greater recognition of the unpredictability of nature and of the existence of multiple perspectives on nature in society has brought about a new appreciation of the way local ecosystems are managed and maintained by small-scale human disturbances. There is also increasing recognition of the way this kind of management is able to accommodate 'extreme spatial and temporal variability' (Neumann, 2005, p. 77). From this thinking, local management practices are now more recognized as having contributed to or maintained the appearance of wilderness in several areas; and many so called 'pristine forests' can be seen, in fact, as highly modified, complex and dynamic mosaic landscapes (Pimbert and Pretty, 1995).

Viewed from this perspective, disturbance processes and change can be seen as crucial for creating and maintaining natural diversity. This, in turn, is a major factor in maintaining the stability and functioning of ecosystems (Steinmetz, 1996; Pimbert and Pretty, 1995). Protecting areas against periodic disturbance and adaptation, therefore, can actually reduce their diversity and the ability of ecosystems to maintain their functions (Sandberg, 2007). Instead of attempting to 'preserve the wilderness', conservation thinking needs to consider managing ecosystems to allow for and accommodate change. The role of disturbance, however, continues to be underappreciated in conservation practice (Hagerman *et al.*, 2009).

This highlights the importance of understanding management practices based on deep, local ecological knowledge, that work with 'ecocycles and recurrent small disturbances' (Sandberg, 2007, p. 616). There is a need to better understand the way indigenous farmers recognize and work with these dynamic natural processes, and the way disturbance impacts on forest and biodiversity conservation (Tonneijk *et al.*, 2006; Neumann, 2005). We need to also call into question the standard dichotomy of traditional and modern land use; and the pervasive stigmatization of 'traditional' land use as unproductive and backward, as seen, for example, in government plans for the economic development of Cambodia's northeast (e.g. Master Plan for CLV-DTA, 2004).

Given the looming problems of climate change and ecosystem instability, production systems that are diverse and resilient, and able to rebound after severe disturbance, are increasingly being seen as preferable to large monocultures (Meinzen-Dick and Mwangi, 2008). As a result, there is now greater thought going into maintaining the extensive nature of ecosystems, and into maintaining 'complex mosaics' and 'patchy landscapes' (Sandberg, 2007, pp. 614, 618). In some cases, conservation practice is also now moving towards thinking beyond spatial models focused on barriers and zones of 'protection', to broader concepts of sustaining functional landscapes (Hagerman et al., 2009). This, in turn, requires looking beyond present models of formal, centralized state governance of land and nature, which often view traditionally managed areas as available for transformation.

From this, I argue, we need a fresh understanding of property arrangements that can accommodate more diverse land uses. Such arrangements can offer interesting possibilities for integrating productive land uses into forested landscapes, including agroforest systems or mixed landscapes that incorporate the production of, for example, rubber, fruit and nut trees, honey, spices, herbal medicines, resins, coffee, tea, mushrooms, tubers, rattan, bamboo, timber trees, animal forage, animals and fish, among other things (Cairns, forthcoming; Penot, 2007). Some of this is underway with, for example, rotational swidden farmers, largely on communal land, intensifying their systems through combining the management of productive species in fallow areas with soil fertility regeneration (Cairns, 2007). Building on this, I explore the potential role of land contiguity, cooperation and complexity in developing productive land use systems that can better withstand external shocks. Rather than viewing traditional land use practices as inferior, as mainstream conservation discourses often do, I argue that these practices provide a basis for building alternatives to the destructiveness of present land use models.

Methods

Given its remoteness, Ratanakiri Province provides an interesting case study of forest-based communally managed agricultural production systems. These systems continue to persist, even if over the past decade or more, the province has seen drastic clearing of forest areas, local communities' fallow land and agricultural fields for rubber plantations. Local and national elites and plantation companies have been involved in what essentially has been a large scale land grab (Global Witness, 2013; COHCHR, 2012; CHRAC, 2010). Over this period there has also been a much more modest process of communal land titling. The existence of these different land uses, literally side by side, provides an opportunity to examine the land use dynamics on a fault line between different models of land ownership and use.

Research for this chapter consists of investigations into land use and social change, and into community beliefs around the protection and use of forest areas in four villages, conducted during 2010 and 2011, and updated during visits in 2013 and 2014. These four villages were chosen because they represent varying impacts of land use, land ownership and livelihood changes underway in Ratanakiri Province. One village (Pierr-Tampuan ethnic group) was one of the first of three villages in the country to receive its communal land title in 2012, covering 920 ha for 94 families, or 456 people. Another two villages (Beine-Tampuan with 387 people and Jet-Kreung ethnic group with 689 people) demonstrate models of traditional communal land use that also incorporate newer cash crops. Beine Village also demonstrates the pressure these systems are under due to the demand for land to plant rubber. The fourth village (Moine-Tampuan with 203 people) has lost 60 per cent of its original lands to outside buyers[1]. It is, however, involved with neighbouring villages, in an effort to maintain a pristine volcanic lake in community hands and to develop alternative livelihoods from eco-tourism. Research consisted of focus group discussions and semi-structured interviews with key informants, including community leaders, government authorities, NGO staff and agricultural merchants and with randomly selected villagers. Community mapping, trend analyses and village walks were also carried out. In addition, time was spent observing a process of cultural reinvigoration by Moine and neighbouring villages as part of their attempts to maintain control over their sacred lake.

Introduction to Ratanakiri Province: Land use change on the forest frontier

Situated in the northeastern corner of Cambodia, bordering Laos to the north and Vietnam to the east, Ratanakiri Province has been rapidly opened up to the outside world over the past decade or more. This is partly because of the existence of a 2,000 km^2 (200,000 ha) upland plateau of fertile red basalt soils in the centre of the Province. This plateau has traditionally drawn swidden cultivators, due to its productivity and its capacity for rapid fallow regrowth. However, these soils are now also in demand by outsider cash cropping farmers and concession companies for rubber, soybeans, corn, cassava and cashew nuts.

The eight indigenous groups found in Ratanakiri made up 58.9 per cent of the province's 150,466 population in the 2008 census (MOP, 2009). These groups range in size from a few hundred people to the largest group, the Tampuan, with a population of 30,888 (ibid). Despite their different languages, they share common cultural practices and livelihood systems, including swidden cultivation and hunting and gathering from the forested environment which, until recently, surrounded them. The system of swidden cultivation practiced in the Province consists of alternating periods of cultivation of small (1–2 ha) pieces of land with longer periods of rest to allow forest regrowth and soil fertility replenishment.

Trend analyses conducted in the four villages showed a generally adequate level of food self-sufficiency from this form of land use in the past. Before the fighting (in the 1960s), villagers commented that people usually had sufficient rice and other food to eat, and there were plenty of animals and other resources in the forest when they were short. People said they were often able to grow enough upland rice to sell a surplus. This is not to say, however, that life is/was easy. Ratanakiri and neighbouring Mondulkiri Province, also with a high percentage of indigenous peoples, have the highest poverty rates in the country (UNDP, 2010).

Plans for the development of this region go back to the French, and were continued by the post-independence Cambodian government under Prince Sihanouk (Meyer, 1979).[2] Following the failure of policies to encourage Khmer migration to this area, in the early 1960s, the Sihanouk government chose the classic formula of Western colonialism, namely the granting of large agro-industrial concessions for rubber, as its development model for Ratanakiri (ibid). By 1968 this rubber planting had to be halted due to escalating conflict in the province, partly created by the dispossession caused by this plantation development. Local populations resisted, revolted and became willing recruits and supporters of the then fledgling Khmer Rouge army. Only 2,000 ha of a planned 8,000 ha were able to be planted.

Now again, plans are in place for the northeastern Cambodian provinces of Ratanakiri, Mondulkiri, Stung Treng and Kratie to become the 'fourth development pole of Cambodia' by 2015, based on mining, agro-industry, forestry and eco-tourism (COHCHR, 2007, p. 16).[3] These four provinces form part of the so-called Cambodia, Laos and Vietnam Development Triangle (CLV-DTA). Couched in neoliberal terminology, the Master Plan for this Development Triangle outlines a programme to make use of 'under-utilized economic potential' in these 'least developed territories' (Master Plan for CLV-DTA, 2004, p. 10).[4] The aim is to create a 'market-oriented commodity producing economy' (ibid, p. 92), with good potential seen for high-value cash crops such as coffee, rubber, cashew and pepper and animal-raising.

Implicit in this development vision is a radical plan of transforming groups of self-employed subsistence farmers into producers for the market economy and workers for large-scale commodity production. Continuing a process, going back to French colonial times, of bringing order and control to 'unruly' and 'wild' forested areas and people, the Master Plan envisions permanent settlement to stabilize the indigenous minorities, in order it is claimed, to mitigate deforestation and protect the environment (ibid).[5] Ethnic minority groups are portrayed as having difficult lives, whose 'production, customs and practices remain backward' (ibid, p. 129).

The land rights of the indigenous groups are not mentioned in this Master Plan. However, in between the lines is the denial of existing settlement and use patterns, and a justification for displacement and dispossession. The allocation of land concessions is resulting in loss of land and forest areas important for livelihood security, and in particular the widespread appropriation of fallow areas, necessary for fertility regeneration. Several reports document the abuse of local communities' land rights by concession companies (Global Witness, 2013; COHCHR, 2012, 2007; CHRAC, 2010; Ironside and Nuy, 2010). Large areas of land transferred from community to company control have resulted in social upheaval and ecological degradation.

Perhaps the greatest tragedy is that, since the 1960s, there has been no attempt to learn from and incorporate the local populations' knowledge of land use and the natural milieu to aid the development of appropriate land uses in this area (Meyer, 1979). Governments in Phnom Penh have seen no reason to listen to the local peoples' advice or to incorporate them into development projects and agricultural change.

This lack of recognition of local peoples' knowledge is partly a result of concepts of civilization, which throughout Southeast Asia have come to be defined in terms of sedentary populations cultivating lowland rice with land use rights over defined parcels. This allowed for the easy collection of taxes to support hierarchical kingdoms and empires (Scott, 2009; Dove, 1985). Upland groups who rotated their agriculture fields in forests, remained outside a kingdom's sphere of control and revenue collection, and came to be labelled as 'nomadic', anarchic, wild, savage and uncivilized (ibid). Their deep knowledge of the natural milieu, therefore, is considered of little relevance by the lowland decision-makers and planners.

In this sense, development plans in these upland areas are less about making them productive and local populations prosperous, than they are about ensuring 'their economic activity [is] legible, taxable, assessable and confiscatable or, failing that, to replace it with forms of production that [are]' (Scott, 2009, p. 5). Hidden within arguments about making land more productive, and ideas about transforming Ratanakiri into an 'economic engine', therefore, is a colonialist discourse of bringing order and control to unruly areas through monoculture and enclosure. This has also led to the conventional views that privately owned monoculture plantations equal development, and that plantations can be defined as 'forests' (Dove, 1993, 1985; Blaikie and Brookfield, 1987). Cambodian government officials justify the widespread replacement of natural forests with plantations on these grounds (Vannarin and Lewis, 2013).

Learning from traditional land use in Ratanakiri

Understanding the way culture is shaped by the surrounding environment and the way nature is also socialized helps in understanding the way particular land use practices are adapted to their milieu. Latour (1993) uses the term 'nature-culture hybrids' to explain these interrelated feedback loops.

210 *Jeremy Ironside*

In this section I explore the nature-culture relationships found among indigenous groups in Ratanakiri, in order to understand their potential contribution to developing more socially and environmentally appropriate forms of land use.

While there has been much discussion about the negative impact of swidden agricultural systems with increasing population and land pressure (Cramb *et al.*, 2009; Padoch *et al.*, 2007), of interest for this discussion, as mentioned, is the way these systems have, up to the very recent past, integrated forests and agriculture, and the communal systems of land management that allowed for this. This is shown, for example, in a longitudinal land-use change study in Ratanakiri between 1953 and 1996, which found that over this 43-year period overall forest cover (primary and secondary) remained between 77 per cent to 96 per cent of the landscape, depending on the area (Fox, 2002). This occurred in spite of the fact that between 50 per cent and 81 per cent of the landscape was used for swidden farming over this period. While 77 per cent to 96 per cent of the landscape remained under forest or secondary growth, land cover on any particular plot may have changed several times (ibid).

This indicates the way local people managed land for both agricultural production and forest regeneration, and this in turn sustained and promoted significant biological and agrobiological diversity. Mosaics of in-use and regenerating fields allowed for a range of products for subsistence and commerce. Figure 10.1 shows an aerial photo of this kind of land use taken in 1953. Communal rights to use the village land were combined with private use rights of particular areas, for example, when a given field was in use. Once the field was no longer productive, private use rights were relinquished in favour of another area and the land was allowed to regenerate. These areas of regenerating young and old fallows provided significant 'semi-wild' production.[6] Land use arrangements aimed at promoting forest regrowth also resulted in a dispersed population distribution over the landscape (Fox, 2002; Bourdier, 1995). That is, autonomous villages communally managed swidden agriculture areas of sufficient size to allow for rotation of agricultural fields and for fertility building fallow areas. These culturally distinct land-use practices contrast dramatically with the sedentary practices of the lowland rice-growing cultures and with contemporary agro-industrial visions now being implemented in upland areas, as outlined in the Development Triangle Master Plan. These sedentarist visions of land use tragically overlook two key points: that the art of tropical land use depends on spatial management and mobility is a key aspect of this (Neugebauer *et al.*, 1995).

This spatial management and the mobility this entailed can be seen in Figure 10.2, which shows the way traditional land distribution resulted in a decentralized, dispersed arrangement of villages over the landscape. This served to spread impact widely and allowed sufficient time for recovery rather than concentrating land use and preventing regeneration. This even distribution of populations over the landscape can

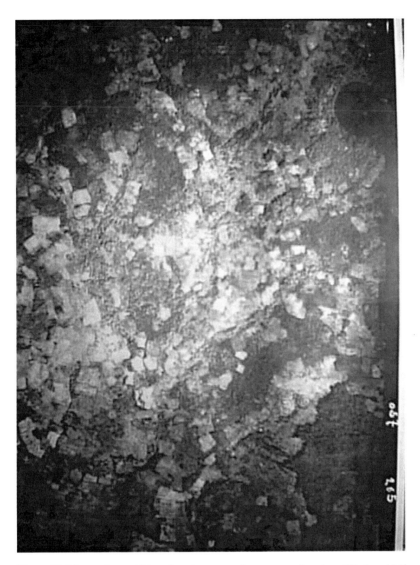

Figure 10.1 Intensive swidden farming near the present-day site of Ratanakiri's provincial capital, Ban Lung (which was established only in the 1980s), revealed by a 1953 aerial photograph. The 800 meter-wide Yeak Laom volcanic crater lake can be seen in the top-right of the photo. The area in the southern part of this photo was planted in rubber in the 1960s.

Source: J. Fox, East West Centre.

be seen in a forested district in Ratanakiri, where villages were found to have maintained a fairly constant population density of around 30 people per km² within their village boundaries (Fox, 1997). This points to a balanced demographic impact on the forested environment, reinforced by traditional regulations preventing the encroachment of one village onto the territory of another. While these systems are now less able to function, for reasons discussed above, in some areas this even dispersal of villages over the landscape still persists. The common cultural and practical need

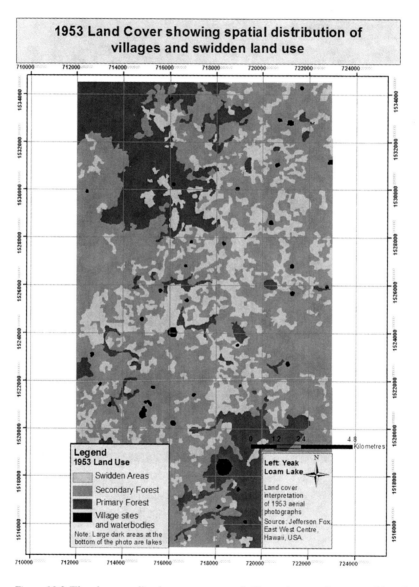

Figure 10.2 The decentralized arrangement of village sites on the central basalt plateau in the centre of Ratanakiri Province in 1953.

Source: J. Fox, East West Centre.

to allow for forest regeneration therefore, until quite recently, resulted in landscape-wide ecological diversity.

Contemporary forest/agriculture systems in Ratanakiri

In contrast to the single species monocultural vision of agricultural production, as discussed, communal systems offer possibilities for integrating food and non-food crops, commercial and subsistence production and cultivation with the collection of 'wild' resources. The possibilities for diverse livelihood strategies from these systems demonstrate the potential of communal land management options and provide a foundation for adaptations and new strategies. This section provides some examples of this land use diversity that is common in these systems. This includes a case of the protection of a local sacred site by the surrounding communities, now being used for eco-tourism.

Beine Village: The overturning of a forest/agriculture system

One example of an integrated forest/agriculture system was found in Biene Village in 2010–2011. Land use mapping carried out as part of this research revealed 228 ha of forested areas in the village preserved for the collection of forest products and for cultural reasons (see Figure 10.3). Figure 10.3 also shows how villagers organized their land use into different categories, enabling mobility over the areas designated for upland swidden farming. Out of the 720 ha designated for swidden agriculture, only 10 per cent (70 ha) was actively being used as swidden fields along with around 45 ha planted permanently in cashew nuts. This means 228 ha of forest land and 605 ha of regrowing fallow in various stages of regeneration was available to villagers for grazing, collection of wild foods and other resources. This mix of active upland swidden fields, fallow, cashew trees and forest areas provided a diversity of both commercial and subsistence production. As well as income from selling tobacco, pigs, sesame, cashew nuts and soybeans, surpluses from subsistence production and products from the forest were also sold or used for community and religious obligations. Social events where produce is shared, in turn, form the basis of the community cohesion needed for communal land management. Tragically, however, since 2011 villagers were forced to clear large areas of their fallow land and use them for planting cassava, rice and soybeans to prevent a rubber company from claiming 'unused' land. In the process villagers lost the vital regeneration function their fallow areas played.

Pierr and Jet Villages: Incorporating the old with the new

Pierr Village provides another example of a communal system, now with a communal land title, which demonstrates a diverse land use incorporating

214 *Jeremy Ironside*

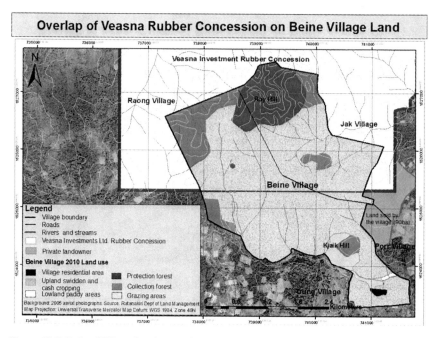

Figure 10.3 Beine Village land use, also showing the overlapping claim by a rubber company.
Source: Ironside, 2012.

commercial production. The village has established a sound economic base, largely through planting 190 ha of cashew trees on the 835 ha allocated for agriculture in their land use plan. While this is a considerable area of agricultural land being devoted to a single crop, family cashew orchards, generally between one to two hectares, are interspersed with upland rice fields and fallow regrowth and some forest areas across the village landscape. This dispersal of different land uses provides some diversity, and also works to maintain some ecosystem function in the form of minimizing erosion, protecting watersheds and providing habitat for smaller wildlife. During the 2011 and 2012 harvest seasons, annual income for an average family with one to two hectares of cashew trees was between $369 and $738. With an overall income for the village as a whole for the 2011 and 2012 harvest seasons of $90,000 and $50,000, respectively, this village is contributing to the government's economic and poverty alleviation goals by producing an export crop. Most families also sell a wide range of agricultural products from their upland swidden fields in the Ban Lung market, the provincial capital, 10 km distant. Villagers' net income from cashew nuts, bananas, papayas, vegetables (eggplants, gourds, chillies, sweet potato, corn, wild vegetables, bamboo shoots), herbs, ginger, chickens and some fish from a nearby hydroelectric reservoir, compares favourably with the average Cambodian GDP per capita for 2010 of $830.[7] Importantly, village leaders explained that no families are landless in the village and no one goes hungry. With some support, production systems like this could be further refined, diversified and strengthened for better land use and livelihood outcomes, and to provide a model for other villages.[8]

Jet Village in O Chum District is a further example of a village balancing ecosystem management at the landscape level with the productive use of village land. An important means for achieving this has been controlling land alienation, through strong traditional governance and community cohesion. This has allowed for the maintenance of traditional forms of land use, and therefore overall ecosystem function. Strong community management, for example, has allowed for the regulation of new land uses, such as cashew production, preventing any one family from planting more than 5 ha. This maintenance of ecosystem function can be seen from a land use change study carried in Jet and two other villages, which found that deforestation rates in Jet Village from 1989 to 2006 were at a moderate rate of 0.86 per cent per year (Fox *et al.*, 2008). In another village where governance was weak and solidarity was fragmented as a result of disputes over land sales, forest loss over this same 17-year period was found to be up to 5 per cent per year (ibid).

Traditional and evolving culture-nature relationships in Ratanakiri, therefore, exhibit expert understandings of natural regeneration processes and cycles, and the value of diversity. These relationships, and the property arrangements they are based on, can enable both productive systems and the maintenance of natural processes.

Moine Village: Building on cultural foundations

Another aspect of culture-nature relationships in Ratanakiri is the protection of certain areas in the landscape which villagers believe are inhabited by powerful spirits. In local peoples' cosmology protection of these areas and paying respect to the spirits that inhabit them link directly with ensuring good harvests and village well-being. In this way, the integration and connection between forests and agriculture is culturally reinforced. As Fox (2002, p. 116) points out 'in a swidden agriculture system the perceived dichotomy between agriculture and forest is for the most part artificial. Swidden fields, secondary forests, and mature forests are all part of the same agroecosystem'.

This certainly is the case with the pristine, 800 m diameter Yeak Laom (Yak Rlom, Tampuan) crater lake and its surrounding protected forest of over 200 ha (see Figures 10.1 and 10.2). As the home of the Yeak Loam communities' most powerful spirit, this lake is the centre of their spiritual beliefs. Villagers have never cut the forest in the crater area, and a community leader reported that most still do not swim in the lake, out of fear and respect for the spirit.[9]

In 1998 the five villages of Yeak Loam Commune managed to secure a 25 year agreement with the Ratanakiri provincial government to allow them to manage the lake and surrounding forest. The community's management philosophy, based on their beliefs, is to keep the area in its natural state and to maintain access for all for a minimal entrance fee. Community members have consistently said they are not interested in modernizing and developing the lake, they just want to protect it. These communities see this lake as important for their future livelihoods from eco-tourism but, as discussed in a 2010 community meeting, the area is also highly valued for forest resources which supplement their agricultural activities including bamboo, bamboo shoots, vines, rattan, fish, small animals, forest fruit and poles. The importance of this lake and the surrounding forest resources has also increased over recent years as the Yeak Loam communities have gradually lost large areas of their land and almost all their former forest areas to land grabbing and alienation.

Seeing the income potential of this pristine lake, however, government officials and business interests have become impatient with the community's management philosophy. These outside people see the current income from entrance fees as miniscule compared with what could be made through infrastructure development, the building of upmarket accommodation and the installation of cable cars, among other things. 'This is the era of development not protection', and 'the community lacks business acumen, and there is no progress', provincial officials are reported to have said to lake committee members (Lake committee member, pers. comm., 2010).

With the awarding of a tourism concession over a nearby hill (on the border of Yeak Loam Commune), there are rumours that the tourism company also wants control over Yeak Loam Lake. This fight over the lake is, therefore, a fight over Yeak Loam villagers' cultural, and perhaps economic, survival and is truly a clash of development and political forces in the province. To deal with this challenge, the five communities decided they needed to build a meeting house to protect their culture, and where people can come together to discuss issues impacting them. They see this as a foundation for all their future joint efforts: a place to reinvigorate their culture and beliefs, strengthen solidarity, resolve problems, develop strategies, gain new skills, facilitate community-to-community exchanges and attract tourists. The meeting house is also intended to serve as a physical structure symbolizing their claim to the lake.

This clash of development visions highlights the way in which villagers are applying the tools of communal management in defence of their lake. They are seeking to stand together against powerful outsiders on their own cultural foundations. This community-driven process ultimately means rejecting much of what is considered to be 'conventional development', and rejecting forms of progress that devalue cultural traditions. This is therefore a celebration of difference rather than conformity; a form of development based on cultural diversity rather than on standardization and uniformity. As is shown by the symbolism of building the meeting house, the message is that culture must be the foundation of all change and progress[10]. As a local leader pointed out, 'culture and ceremonies are closely connected to managing land, forest, mountains and the lake'.

This case provides a vital contrast to the common solution of privatization generally offered to protect and manage natural resources (Demsetz, 1967; Hardin, 1968). Despite the economic forces now impacting on this area, Ratanakiri's indigenous cultures continue to see land as more than just a commodity, encompassing spirituality, concepts of territory and ownership, and the means of livelihood security. Bearing in mind the parable of the Little Man with the Big Stone, which is actually a jewel (Dove, 1993), the powerful deem it not correct for small villagers to be in possession of what is literally the jewel in Ratanakiri's tourism crown. If Yeak Loam communities are able to maintain their lake, there is every possibility they will be able to determine their own development and prosperity.

The communal land management option

The above examples indicate some important principles for sustainable land use, especially in forested environments. These include decentralized settlement and property rights which allow for periods of rest and recovery; encouragement of diversity and working with natural processes; management based on knowledge and skills formed from local experience; protection of watershed and other key areas and the maintenance of modest demands on the surrounding environment. These principles contrast sharply with the land degradation and deforestation caused by sedentarized agriculture, monocultures and concentrated populations (Ishii-Eiteman, 2008), and which is now being witnessed in Ratanakiri. From this, I argue that, communal property arrangements which build on and integrate traditional practices and beliefs appear to hold promise for land use that is more in tune with ecosystem needs and processes. In suggesting this, I am not intending to defend swidden agriculture per se, which clearly must also adapt to increasing land pressure and social change, but rather to call for efforts to better understand and build on the positive aspects of these systems.

A key lesson from these swidden systems in Ratanakiri is that the sustainability of traditional farming systems depends on diversity. This means mixing a range of crops and agricultural production strategies, within a diverse and productive natural landscape producing a range of resources. Locally managed communal land, it seems, can accommodate and encourage such diversity and flexibility. Evidence from Pierr, Beine and Jet villages also indicates that the self-sufficiency, diversity and resilience generated by these mixed 'agricultural' landscapes allows for a degree of livelihood security, which in turn can assist community members to resist land selling and alienation.

Working with integrated systems, however, means getting away from focusing on improving the yield of any one part, and focusing more on improving the integration between the parts. This means it is necessary to understand and work with the interconnectivity, complexity and diversity of both social and natural systems. Unfortunately communities do not receive support in intensifying the integration of their systems, partly because technical land use 'experts' are generally not trained to understand or work with these kinds of approaches. There is also little learning and sharing of experiences from these systems for wider application. In contrast to the technical support that simplified large-scale monocultures have benefited from, the attention received by small-scale indigenous forms of forest-based land use is negligible (Fox, 2000; Dove, 1993). The problem is not so much the unviability of traditional practices, but the persistence of a dominant monocultural view of forests and agriculture.

It seems that where communities have been able to choose for themselves, such as those discussed in this chapter, many decide that communal, rather than individual, models best suit their aspirations. Models of economic development, therefore, are needed that build on communal cultures, or at least are not completely hostile to them. However, instead of options that allow communities to cooperate, individualist models, which risk loss of individual families' land and livelihoods, are generally the only option available in standard agricultural development practice. Dependency on individualist monoculture cash cropping and their consequent 'mono-livelihood' strategies, only increases small farmers' vulnerability. In the age of climate change and volatility in yields and markets, fixed boundaries and monocultures are hardly likely to provide the flexibility or the diversity needed by communities and the environment for survival.

In this light, I argue that communal land titling can potentially be a way to safeguard the livelihoods of many vulnerable communities, and allow for the evolution and adaptation of their land use systems. The underlying racism, however, inherent in the discourse of 'civilized outsiders' and 'backward indigenous locals' prevalent in debates over the management of upland forested areas in Southeast Asia (Scott, 2009; Dove, 1985), means that there is little opportunity for objectively analysing and learning from indigenous land use systems. There is certainly a need to try new cropping systems, but most new models fail to build on or integrate local systems. As discussed, in the drive to develop large-scale monocultures, there is little consideration by government planners or agri-business interests of the social and environmental costs of their activities; nor is there any real attempt to incorporate the time tested local culture-nature adaptations that communal forms of land management could offer.

A more mature culture-land relationship is needed, therefore, to replace the fragmentation created by predominant private property arrangements. Property-rights institutions designed for the production of single products from simplified ecologies need to be reworked and adapted (Sandberg, 2007, p. 619). Polyculture production systems that embrace diversity and which work with complex arrangements of plants, animals, forests and farms can offer a bridge between natural and human systems, but the key issue is what kinds of property arrangements will facilitate these approaches. Communal and mixed tenure options appear better suited for accommodating the social and ecological complexity needed for landscape-level management approaches.

Conclusion

In this chapter I have argued that it is difficult to deal credibly with ecological destruction in 'unprotected' areas, when this is in fact the basis of conventional land use. Unfortunately these kinds of management approaches are now impacting on Cambodia's so-called protected areas. I have also argued that unprotected areas need much greater consideration in conservation discourse, because of the generally limited recognition that agriculture is at the centre of human relations with nature (Duncan, 1996, in Friedmann, 2008). Wilderness protection is often given a much higher priority in contemporary conservation than finding ways for humans to integrate into the local ecology. The inherent contradiction between conserving pristine areas and the ecological destruction of the 'unprotected areas' in the name of modernist agriculture is little recognized.

Indigenous land use systems in Ratanakiri, while by no means perfect, can therefore provide a starting point for developing an alternative perspective, and a basis for new land use models. Indications from this study are that communal management can potentially encourage diverse and decentralized land use configurations that are important for sustainability. Rotational land use and the encouragement of diversity, which communal systems can accommodate, well appear to be important aspects in maintaining the integrity of forests, grazing lands and other natural areas.

In forested upland areas, rather than creating rubber monocultures, I argue that it is more appropriate to develop new/old forms of productive and varied land use. The swidden lands could be a highly productive mix of cropping, agroforestry and fallow. Options for wildlife management in degraded or more open dry forest areas could also be experimented with. With secure communal tenure, several possibilities for maintaining forest systems and generating economic return are possible. Therefore, I suggest that the preservation of forested landscapes needs ultimately to consider the role and function of biodiverse land use. The case studies I have discussed above indicate the value of forest fragments and secondary growth forests, and from this new conservation paradigms that incorporate human-impacted lands can emerge (Fox, 2002).

Given the importance of diversity and mobility in the maintenance of forested landscapes, a rethink of concepts such as productivity and efficiency is also needed, to consider the overall productivity of multiple products from diverse landscapes which are able to adapt and accommodate changing climatic conditions. To work with the chaos of natural systems, a new language of movement, flexibility and resilience is needed to replace the vocabulary of equilibrium, stability, balance and predictability that has dominated agricultural and conservation planning. From this study, flexible communal property rights which allow for periods of use and forest regeneration allow agriculture and forest to be maintained in a dynamic tension. I argue that the conventional models of agriculture also need to embrace an agricultural future based on the diversity of natural systems.

This reorientation of agricultural practice, however, is a challenging process. Dialogue among grassroots people, who understand the local system relationships and dynamics, is essential for reducing the significance of boundaries, and coordinating and dealing with complex natural systems. Dynamic and overlapping property arrangements can ultimately only operate with a thorough knowledge of the local social and ecological context. Property arrangements, therefore, need to be formulated and regulated by empowered local communities. Learning from communal systems in Ratanakiri has shown the key role that community institutions play in managing land and in mediating the various interests in that land.

To summarize, while communal land titling and management are certainly not the whole answer to the problems which indigenous groups face in Ratanakiri and throughout Cambodia, it offers an opportunity to think differently about the way land use is conceptualized and actualized. Skills need to be developed, experiments need to be tried and systems need to be built to demonstrate to other communities, locally and farther afield, what is possible. Instead of separating people from nature, cultures which have developed ways of working with their natural environment need to be seen as places for mutual learning about how to rebuild our culture/land relationships.

Notes

1 Village names are pseudonyms.
2 Cambodia gained its independence in 1953.
3 The other main areas of economic activity in the country are Phnom Penh, Siem Reap and Sihanoukville.
4 The authorship of this report is unknown, but it was prepared in Hanoi and is likely a Vietnamese government document. It continues to guide development decision-making in Ratanakiri as witnessed by the March 2010 Development Triangle meeting held in Ban Lung, Ratanakiri (see Marks, 2010). This report can be found at http://clv-triangle.vn/portal/page/portal/clv_en/819086/1305933?p_page_id=819086&p_cateid=825523&item_id=8597958&article_details=1, accessed 27 January 2014.
5 The Master Plan states that the 'ethnic minority groups' ... practice of forest burning for cultivation land and inconsiderate forest exploitation has rapidly decreased the forest area, consequently having serious negative impacts on the ecological environment' (Master Plan for CLV-DTA, 2004, p. 97).
6 See for example Steinmetz (1996, p. 63) who reports on the Karen ethnic group in Thung Yai Naresuan Wildlife Sanctuary in Western Thailand. They prohibited the raising of domestic livestock for food and instead 'raise animals by caring for

the forest', maintaining rules for forest management which keeps disturbance to a sustainable level.
7 Source National Institute of Statistics http://www.nis.gov.kh/index.php/en/, accessed 28 January 2014.
8 A further example of the potential of communal systems to satisfy economic and biodiversity objectives are the rubber agroforest systems planted by communal swidden farmers in Indonesia. Jungle rubber agroforests cover 2.8 million ha and account for 80 per cent of Indonesia's rubber production (Zomer et al., 2009). Indonesia accounts for 24 per cent of the world's rubber production (ibid). Much of this is produced in gardens of around a hectare along with swidden families agriculture practices (Dove, 1993). These multiple use forest gardens are being cleared for oil palm due to temporarily depressed rubber prices (Potter and Badcock, 2001) further demonstrating the predominant monocultural thinking behind conventional agro-industrial agriculture. Forest dwelling swidden farmers in Malaysia and Indonesia also grow on their communal lands, often in multistrata agroforests; rattan, pepper, coffee, dammar (tree nut), sago, coconuts, durian, benzoin, cinnamon and other spices (Zomer et al., 2009; Dove, 1993). The 12 million ha of natural rubber in extractive reserves in the Brazilian Amazon is a further notable example (World Agroforestry Centre, 2009).
9 This lake is also a Cambodian national icon, cemented into the nation's folklore through songs, stories and so on.
10 The meeting house and the strict protection of spirit areas are powerful elements of indigenous culture in Ratanakiri.

References

Adams, W. M. and Hutton, J. (2007).'People, parks and poverty: Political ecology and biodiversity conservation', *Conservation and Society* 5(2), pp. 147–183.
Basurto, X. and Ostrom, E. (2009) 'Beyond the tragedy of the commons', *Economiadelle Fonti di Energia e dell Ambiente* 52(1), pp. 35–60.
Berkes, F., Colding, J. and Folke, C. (2000) 'Rediscovery of traditional ecological knowledge as adaptive management', *Ecological Applications* 10(5), pp. 1251–1262.
Blaikie, P. and Brookfield, H. (eds) (1987) *Land Degradation and Society*, Methuen Publishers, London.
Bourdier, F. (1995) *Knowledge and Practices of Traditional Management of Nature in a Remote Province*, Report of a Research Mission on the Theme of Environment in Cambodia, under the Sponsorship of AUPEL/UREF (October 1994–July 1995) (Unofficial English translation December 1995 by Dr Carol Mortland), East West Center, Honolulu.
Cairns, M. (ed.) (2007) *Voices from the Forest: Integrating Indigenous Knowledge into Sustainable Upland Farming*, RFF Press, Washington, DC.
Cairns, M. (ed.) (forthcoming) *A Growing Forest of Voices*, Earthscan, UK.
CHRAC. (2010) *Still Losing Ground: Forced Evictions and Intimidation in Cambodia*, The Cambodian Human Rights Action Committee, Phnom Penh, Cambodia.
Colchester, M. (1994) *Salvaging Nature: Indigenous Peoples, Protected Areas and Biodiversity Conservation*, UNRISD Discussion Paper No 55, UNRISD-IIED-WWF, Geneva.
COHCHR. (2007) *Economic Land Concessions in Cambodia: A Human Rights Perspective*, Cambodia Office of the United Nations High Commissioner for Human Rights, Phnom Penh, Cambodia.

COHCHR. (2012) *Addendum to the Report of the Special Rapporteur on the Situation of Human Rights in Cambodia*, Cambodia Office of the United Nations High Commissioner for Human Rights, Phnom Penh, Cambodia.

Cramb, R. A., Pierce Colfer, C. J., Dressler, W., Laungaramsri, P., Trang Le, Q., Mulyoutami, E., Peluso, N. L. and Wadley, R. L. (2009). 'Swidden transformations and rural livelihoods in Southeast Asia', *Human Ecology* 37, pp. 323–346.

Demsetz, H. (1967) 'Toward a theory of property rights', *American Economic Review Papers and Proceedings* 57, pp. 347–359.

Dove, M. (1985) *The Agro-Ecological Mythology of the Javanese and the Political Economy of Indonesia*, Reprint no. 84, East West Center, Honolulu, pp. 1–36.

Dove, M. (1993) 'A revisionist view of tropical deforestation and development', *Environmental Conservation* 20(1), pp. 17–25.

Fairhead, J. and Leach, M. (1996) *Misreading the African Landscape: Society and Ecology in a Forest-Savannah Mosaic*, African Study Series, No. 90, Cambridge University Press, Cambridge.

Fox, J. (1997) *Customary Boundaries in Ratanakiri—A Study of 3 Villages in Poey Commune*, (unpublished), East-West Center, Honolulu.

Fox, J. (2000) 'How blaming "slash and burn" farmers is deforesting mainland Southeast Asia', *Asia Pacific Issues* 47, pp. 1–9.

Fox, J. (2002) 'Understanding a dynamic landscape: Land use, land cover, and resource tenure in Northeastern Cambodia', in S. Walsh and K. Crews-Meyer (eds) *Linking People, Place, and Policy: A GIScience Approach*, Kluwer Academic Publishers, Boston, pp. 113–130.

Fox, J., McMahon, D., Poffenberger, M. and Vogler, J. (2008) *Land for My Grandchildren: Land Use and Tenure Change in Ratanakiri: 1989–2006*, Community Forestry International and the East West Center, California and Honolulu.

Freyfogle, E. (2010) 'Property and liberty', *Harvard Environmental Law Review* 34(1), pp. 75–118.

Friedmann, H. (2008) Book review, 'The global food economy: The battle for the future of farming by Tony Weis', *Journal of Agrarian Change* 8(4), pp. 618–623..

Galhano-Alves, J. P. (2008) *From Land to a Simulacrum World; An Anthropological Essay on the History of an Agricultural Geo-Policy: The Elimination of Communitary Land Use Systems and Its Ecological, Socio-Cultural, Psychological and Political Effects,* Paper presented at Governing Shared Resources: Connecting Local Experience to Global Challenges, 12th Biennial Conference of the International Association for the Study of Commons, Cheltenham, England, July 14–18.

Global Witness. (2013) *Rubber Barons: How Vietnamese Companies and International Financiers Are Driving a Land Grabbing Crisis in Cambodia and Laos*, Global Witness, London.

Hagerman, S., Dowlatabadi, H., Satterfield, T. and McDaniels, T. (2009) 'Expert views on biodiversity conservation in an era of climate change', *Global Environmental Change* 20(2010), pp. 192–207.

Hardin, G. (1968). 'The tragedy of the commons', *Science* 162(3859), pp. 1243–1248.

Ironside, J. (2012) 'Thinking outside the fence: Exploring culture/land relationships, a case study of Ratanakiri province, Cambodia', PhD thesis, University of Otago, Dunedin, New Zealand.

Ironside, J. and Nuy, B. (2010) *Development with Identity: Assessment of the Impact of Tenure Security from Legal Entity Registration in Indigenous Communities in Cambodia (Mondulkiri and Ratanakiri Provinces)*, DANIDA, Phnom Penh, Cambodia.

Ishii-Eiteman, M. (2008) 'New era for agriculture?' *Food First Backgrounder, Institute for Development Policy* 14(2), pp. 1–4.

Latour, B. (1993) *We Have Never Been Modern*, Harvard University Press, Cambridge, MA.

Manzo, K. (1995) 'Black consciousness and the quest for a counter-modernist development', in J. Crush (ed.) *Power of Development*, Routledge, London. pp. 228–252.

Marks, S. (2010) 'Governments, investors to map Ratanakiri investment', *Cambodia Daily*, March 12, Phnom Penh, p. 31.

Master Plan for CLV-DTA. (2004) 'Socio-Economic Development Master Plan for Cambodia-Laos-Vietnam Development Triangle, Hanoi', http://clv-triangle.vn/portal/page/portal/clv_en/819086/1305933?p_page_id=819086&p_cateid=825523&item_id=8597958&article_details=1, accessed 27 January 2014.

Meinzen-Dick, R. and Mwangi, E. (2008) 'Cutting the web of interests: Pitfalls of formalizing property rights', *Land Use Policy* 26(1), pp. 36–43.

Meyer, C. (1979) 'Les nouvelles provinces: Ratanakiri – Mondolkiri', *Revue Monde en Développement* 28, pp. 682–690.

MOP. (2009) *2008 Cambodia Population Census,* CELADE Population Division, ECLAC, National Institute of Statistics, Ministry of Planning, Phnom Penh, Cambodia.

Neugebauer, B., Gast, H., and Richter, J. (1995). *Ecologically Appropriate Agri-culture: A Manual of Ecological Agri-culture Development for Smallholders in Development Areas.* German Foundation for International Development (DSE), Food and Agriculture Development Centre (ZEL), Feldafing.

Neumann, R. (2005) *Making Political Ecology,* Hodder Arnold, London.

Ostrom, E. (1990) *Governing the Commons: The Evolution of Institutions for Collective Action,* Cambridge University Press, Cambridge, New York.

Padoch, C., Coffey, K., Mertz, O., Leisz, S. J., Fox, J. and Wadley, R. L. (2007). 'The demise of swidden in Southeast Asia? Local realities and regional ambiguities', *Danish Journal of Geography* 107(1), pp 29–41.

Pattberg, P. (2007). 'Conquest, domination and control: Europe's mastery of nature in historic perspective', *Journal of Political Ecology* 14, pp. 1–9.

Penot, E. (2007) 'From shifting cultivation to sustainable jungle rubber: A history of innovations in Indonesia', in Cairns M. (ed.) *Voices from the Forest: Integrating Indigenous Knowledge into Sustainable Upland Farming,* RFF Press, Washington, pp. 577–599.

Pimbert, M. and Pretty, J. (1995) *Parks, People and Professionals Putting 'Participation' into Protected Area Management,* UNRISD Discussion Paper No 57, UNRISD-IIED-WWF, Geneva, pp. 1–49.

Potter, L. and Badcock, S. (2001) *The Effects of Indonesia's Decentralisation on Forests and Estate Crops in Riau Province: Case Studies of the Original Districts of Kampar and Indragiri Hulu,* Bogor, Centre for International Forestry Research, Indonesia.

Puppala, J. (2013) 'Land matters for the environment – especially the commons', https://www.devex.com/en/news/land-matters-for-the-environment-especially-the/81798?source=DefaultHomepage_Center_8, accessed 10 October 2013.

Rist, G. (2002) *The History of Development: From Western Origins to Global Faith,* 2nd Edition, Zed Books, London.

Sandberg, A. (2007) 'Property rights and ecosystem properties', *Land Use Policy* 24(4), pp. 613–623.

Scott, J. (2009) *The Art of Not Being Governed: An Anarchist History of Southeast Asia,* Yale University Press, New Haven.
Steinmetz, R. (1996) *Landscape Ecology and Wildlife Habitats: An Indigenous Karen Perspective in Thung Yai Naresuan Wildlife Sanctuary of Western Thailand,* Wildlife Fund Thailand, Bangkok.
Stevens, S. (ed.) (1997) *Conservation through Cultural Survival: Indigenous Peoples and Protected Areas,* Island Press, Washington, DC.
Tonneijk, F., Hengsdijk, H. and Brindaban, P. (2006) *Natural Resource Use by Agricultural Systems: Linking Biodiversity to Poverty,* Plant Research International No. 406, B.V., Wageningen.
UNDP. (2010) *Current Status of Cambodian Millennium Development Goals (CMDG) (Draft),* United Nations Development Programme, Phnom Penh, Cambodia.
Vannarin, N. and Lewis, S. (2013) 'Hun Sen Shares Vision of Rubber Plantation Boom', *Cambodia Daily,* 22 February 2013, http://www.cambodiadaily.com/archive/hun-sen-shares-vision-of-rubber-plantation-boom-11253/, accessed 27 January 2014.
World Agroforestry Centre. (2009) 'Smallholder Rubber Agroforestry System Project',http://www.worldagroforestry.org/newsroom/media_coverage/new-studies-predict-record-land-grab-demand-soars-new-sources-food-energy, accessed 15 October 2013.
Zomer, R. J., Trabucco, A., Coe, R. and Place, F. (2009) *Trees on Farm: Analysis of Global Extent and Geographical Patterns of Agroforestry,* ICRAF Working Paper no. 89, World Agroforestry Centre, Nairobi, Kenya.

11 Cultures and histories of resistance in Cambodia

Margaret Slocomb

Introduction

The cosmic battle between gods and demons depicted on the magnificent *bas relief*, the Churning of the Sea of Milk, at Angkor Wat is a graphic metaphor for the friction that lies at the heart of all social change, and a reminder that resistance to power is as essential to that creative process as the exercise of power itself. While there has been close scrutiny and analysis of the excesses of the state in Cambodia, particularly with regard to the post-colonial and contemporary eras, a comprehensive study of Cambodia's 'cultures of resistance' and the people's engagement with power has yet to be written. This chapter aims only to explore the issue from an historical perspective in the hope that this will shed some light on contemporary state-society relations, a central theme of this book.

While the gods and demons in the creation myth may have met in equal combat, the same is hardly true in traditional societies when a rural peasantry confronts the coercive power of the state in open protest. Even when allied with victorious revolutionary forces, the outcomes for the Cambodian peasants after 1975, and again in the decade following 1979 were mainly negative. As Barrington Moore noted (1966), in a revolution the peasants provide the dynamite to bring down the building, but gain little or nothing from the subsequent reconstruction (p. 480). The same can be said of the widespread millenarian movements that have punctuated Cambodia's history. Like similar 'flashes in the pan' that occurred elsewhere in world history, very little came of them, and even though some persisted for decades, they were eventually crushed.

The failure of a revolution or a rebellion that grew around the myth of a saviour-leader, however, was never the end of the Cambodian peasants' resistance to the constant demands made on them by the state for labour, military conscription and a share of the harvest surplus. These persistent grievances were (and increasingly are) aggravated by the inexorable encroachment by the state and its cronies onto essential natural resources of land, water and fuel that the traditional inhabitants regard as their own by customary right. The everyday forms of resistance in their arsenal are typically, in James C. Scott's (1985) term, the 'weapons of the weak': passive noncompliance including foot-dragging, feigned ignorance, pilfering and so on; exit rather than voice, so long as a land frontier exists and control over manpower rather than land remains the basis of surplus extraction; and avoidance protest rather than defiance and confrontation (pp. 31, 245). In the long run, these weapons have proved more effective in defending the peasants' interests than open protest that is likely to provoke a retaliatory, violent response from the state. The element of fear, he adds, helps to structure their view of the options available to them. Therefore, acts of resistance may be clandestine as, for instance, when lowland rice-farmers deliberately damage the gates in an irrigation channel, or when rubber tappers deeply score the bark of hevea trees or start spot fires on the plantation. When such acts of sabotage are rare and isolated, Scott believes they are of little interest; but when they form a pattern, however uncoordinated and unorganized, this counts as resistance. In sum, he considers resistance as 'actions that involve at least some short-run individual or collective sacrifice in order to bring about a longer-range, beneficial goal', and that it is the fusion of self-interest and resistance that provides the 'vital force' of peasant resistance (pp. 291, 295).

Unfortunately, the everyday acts of peasant resistance are rarely the subject of historical record. Nevertheless, the record is clear that in Cambodia, the subordinate rural class, whether Khmer or of other ethnicity, has consistently resisted state efforts that would deny its own minimal claims to survival with dignity and justice. In the light of contemporary struggles over land and natural resources in Cambodia, the record of the past suggests that the outcome of the epic tug-of-war is still far from certain.

The historical context of resistance, 1863–1979

> We know our people. None is more calm and peaceful than they are. However, facts have often shown that they are subject, under the influence of certain malcontents, to excitation, to brusque anger that can make them instantly lose all judgement and that renders them blind and furious.
>
> King Monivong, to Resident Superior Lavit, 10 April 1929 (*Résidence Supérieure du Cambodge* [RSC]: File 2799)

We can only surmise how and why ordinary people summon the courage to engage in mass protests that bring them into confrontation with the state's vastly superior coercive forces. In Cambodia's case, given the relative frequency of protests and the huge number of participants they attracted in the past and still attract, it would be foolish to dismiss them as anomalies or pathological disturbances of the 'natural' order of things. Peasant farmers and oppressed or simply despised ethnic minorities everywhere have much cause to defend and dispute, particularly during times of profound political change when even the most fundamental certainties can be altered without their knowing. Legal anthropologist, Simon Roberts (1979), suggested that the ostensible issues about which people quarrel must depend largely upon the beliefs that are held, the values subscribed to and the forms of organization prevailing in the society concerned (p. 48). In purely material terms, what there is to quarrel about depends largely on how the people make their living. Therefore, in traditional rice-farming communities the most obvious points of contention are land and other natural resources, debt and taxes. Cambodian history suggests, however, that non-material concerns always mattered just as much as the purely material. Those with power, whether foreign overlords, as in the case of the Vietnamese and the French or local and educated elites, in their relations with indigenous minorities and the rural peasantry, were accustomed to interpreting the behaviour of their subjects in terms of their own political objectives. Such rational interpretations of popular resistance were useful for justifying the harsh restoration of order, but obviously inadequate for winning trust and cooperation. Even in those rare instances where cooperation seemed to be assured, however, the goals of the participants proved to be at variance.

Millenarian and traditionalist rebellions

The people's reverence and respect for their king, the symbol of karmic merit and moral authority, ignored the structural limitations on his temporal power. The Cambodian monarchy is not hereditary and Khmer kings always competed for the throne against rivals, usually full or half-brothers, who built their own power bases and maintained factional loyalties far from the court. The French declared their protectorate over Cambodia in August 1863 at a time when intense rivalry for the throne had already caused serious loss of both territory and population to neighbouring states, and when the power and prestige of the monarchical institution itself was very weak. The diminishing reputation of the king, coinciding with the alarming military presence of the French and their obvious determination to interfere not only in the affairs of state but in Khmer cultural traditions as well, gave rise to fears of an impending catastrophe. Historical circumstances such as these provided an ideal opportunity for a charismatic and righteous warrior-saviour to usurp the throne and restore the moral order.

For 25 years after the death of King Ang Duong in 1860 and the election by the royal court of his successor, Norodom, Cambodia was engulfed in waves of rebellion that were led, for the most part, by his sibling, Sivutha. For some of that time, there were also separate revolts led by two pretenders, Achar Soa and Pu Kombo. The claims to the throne by these two men were entirely spurious. Milton Osborne (1997) noted that Achar Soa was a former slave and that the charismatic Pu Kombo belonged to the small ethnic minority of the Kuy. In the unsettled conditions and for a disoriented and credulous peasantry, Osborne continues, what was important in both instances was not the veracity of their claims, but the fact that they made them, since only a member of the royal family or a claimant could mount an effective rebellion against the king. For 2 years until his capture in December 1867, Pu Kombo rallied as many as 10,000 peasant supporters in the southeastern part of the country near Ba Phnom. They sacked villages that resisted them and led raids on French military outposts. These were typical millenarian revolts led by men who claimed supernatural powers and adorned themselves with occult paraphernalia. Their bands of followers believed that they were responding to a moral crisis and that catastrophe could be averted only by a righteous ruler. The millenarian impulse, Anne Ruth Hansen records, proved compelling in Cambodia right through to the end of the nineteenth century with its most powerful expression at the peripheries: on the frontiers, among cardamom pickers, within the ethnic communities (2007, p. 62). It is noteworthy that Pu Kombo in 1866 and Prince Sivutha in 1877 both declared their legitimacy at the ancient cult site of Ba Phnom, as had other millenarian leaders before them (cf. Chandler, 1996).

Prince Sivutha proved far more elusive and effective than the other rebel leaders. In 1877, he built a stockade and raised a force of dissidents at Ba Phnom but the fledgling army quickly surrendered to French-backed forces, although Sivutha escaped to the northeast along the Mekong where he maintained his own small and impoverished royal court. The capitulation by Norodom to the terms of the 1884 Convention which consolidated French control over the kingdom was the spark for open revolt. In January 1885, a French military post at Sambor in northern Kratie province was attacked by partisans of Sivutha (Osborne, 1997). Within 4 days of this attack, there was general disorder over most of Cambodia. Two years of general unrest, banditry and armed resistance ensued that eventually required a force of 4,000 French troops to quell it. There was strong suspicion among the French that Norodom was in secret contact with Sivutha and that letters bearing the royal seal were circulating through the realm, but nothing could be proved, although insurgents near Kampot told the French they fought because the king had ordered them to do so. There was no doubt whatsoever concerning Sivutha's involvement. He may have claimed that he was fighting to protect Cambodia's ancient traditions, but given his lifetime distrust of Norodom and his indefatigable ambition to be king, Milton Osborne regards his call for unity as opportunistic (p. 221).

The motive for this heroic rebellion against the French was not nationalist or even proto-nationalist. It was, rather, traditionalist: the people rose up in response to the call of their monarch, as they would again following King Sihanouk's call after the *coup d'état* of March 1970. When the king had won sufficient amendments to the 1884 Convention, including the power to pardon or punish those who had taken part in the uprising, he ordered the insurgents to lay down their arms, travelled into the troubled regions and urged the people to submit to his authority and to that of the French. By 1888, even Sivutha had given up his decades-long fight for the throne and retreated to a jungle redoubt far upriver on the border with Laos.

Anti-colonial resistance

The French reconstructed the Khmer monarchy as part of a broader construction effort, Nicola Cooper (2001) suggested, for a coherent, stable and homogenizing image of both Indochina and of its own role in this Southeast Asian empire (p. 91). This image was of course false, but in order to justify the violence done to their colonial subjects, the French needed to believe in the efficacy of their *mission civilisatrice*, and this meant, in part, turning a blind eye and a deaf ear to the stirrings of genuinely nationalist discontent throughout the peninsula that were exacerbated by the misery caused by the global economic depression of the 1930s, and that would crystallize into something like a nationalist movement even in Cambodia in the 1940s. For the most part, however, overt organized resistance to the French by the Khmer majority was rare. The rural Khmers did their best to ignore the French presence, evaded taxes as best they could, and continued to take their grievances to their monarch for resolution.

In 1933, the Protectorate Administration submitted its annual report on the situation in Cambodia with the following assessment of the average farmer's response to the calamity:

> The Cambodian, despite the hardships of these times, has maintained his serenity and good spirits. A carefree thinker, he calmly waits for better days, indifferent to or rather ignorant of the upheavals shaking the world's economic structures. He simply notes that the produce of his *chamcar* or his rice field sells poorly or not at all and that the tax burden weighs more heavily on his shoulders. He thus resigns himself to a harsher life, avoiding the taxman whenever he can but keeping his good state of mind.
>
> (RSC: File 499 Box 38)

Observations like these abound in the official colonial documents. The French had created an image for themselves of Cambodia as 'the last exotic Asian paradise', to borrow Michael Vickery's phrase; they believed that Khmers were asleep, child-like and passive in the face of authority and hardship (Kiernan and Boua, 1982, p. 90). By 1933, it is reasonable to accept that the latest generation of French officials had forgotten the bloody strife that occurred during the early years of the Protectorate, but more recent events should have sounded a warning that these cultural stereotypes were quite useless for interpreting their relationship with the people, let alone for predicting trouble. On most occasions, the French were simply annoyed by peasant recalcitrance and mystified by Cambodian mass protests.

Over a period of 3 months in the dry season of 1915–1916, as many as 100,000 Cambodians took part in a series of political demonstrations, some peaceful and others violent, that were ostensibly against the French tax and *corvée* regime (Osborne, 1978). The *corvée* was in two parts: *prestations* of 10 days per year where farmers could pay three piastres in lieu of labour, plus *réquisitions* that, in practice, were unlimited. *Corvée* labour was paid at the rate of 30 cents (of one piastre) per day, but as this was below the free market rate for paid labour, resentment festered. At first, the protests involved large groups of peasant farmers converging on Phnom Penh to present their grievances to the king for resolution. On 7 January 1916, for example, more than 2,000 peasants descended on the royal palace and then departed peacefully after receiving the monarch's assurance that their complaints would be heeded. It was noted that the majority of the demonstrators were unarmed and peaceable, while their leaders were considered to be men of some education and experience of the world beyond their native village; there were suggestions that Buddhist monks may have played a role in promoting the protests. Perhaps, it was the polite demeanour of the protesters that persuaded the French administration, along with the king, to decree that for the year of 1916, all *prestations* could be paid in cash rather than in labour. Two days later, a crowd of around 5,000 peasants who had been waiting on the river bank opposite the palace assembled before their king and departed as before. This was more or less the end of such demonstrations, but, according to Osborne, 'a worried and largely uncomprehending French administration had seen the passage of at least thirty thousand peasants through the capital' (p. 222).

In the provinces, by contrast, armed protesters threatened violence over the *corvée* issue. On 30 January 1916, King Sisowath placated a crowd of 10,000 that had assembled at Tonle Bet, across the river from Kompong Cham town. After the king departed, however, parts of the crowd began molesting Chinese and Vietnamese traders and fishermen and sacking their property. Even the residence of a Cambodian governor was threatened. The king returned to Kompong Cham and peace was again restored, but similar protests erupted all over the country with the exception of the northwest. In all, more than 20 Cambodians were killed by French forces during the protest movement.

The 1916 affair showed that the people still regarded their king as the ultimate arbiter for their grievances, but what alternatives did they have? Low-level intervention by the village chief, for instance, was unthinkable in such an issue. Archival records show that the French courts were kept very busy, but mainly with the concerns of the *colons*, and Chinese and Vietnamese businessmen. Ordinary Cambodians only appeared in court to face charges or to receive punishment. The tax burden fell disproportionately on them, as the French freely admitted, and very little of it was returned in the form of social benefits.

Perhaps, none of these legitimate complaints were in the minds of those who killed Felix Bardez, the *résident* of Kompong Chhnang, along with two

Cambodian aides in Kraang Laev village during Khmer New Year in 1925 (Chandler, 1996). Bardez had spent over 10 years in Cambodia and was said to be an experienced administrator, so why he chose to appear in a village during a traditional holiday period to collect delinquent taxes is a mystery. Like a man at the end of his tether, he seized and bound three of the assembled villagers as hostages. In the pandemonium that ensued, Bardez and the other two officials were punched to the ground and beaten to death. The villagers then headed for the provincial capital with the idea of attacking the French *résidence*, but they were intercepted by militiamen and forced to return to the village. Punishment was swift and harsh. Over the following weeks, 19 suspects were rounded up and sentenced to death or long imprisonment terms. The name of the village was changed by royal decree to Direchan, or 'bestial' and the villagers were ordered to conduct cleansing ceremonies on the anniversary of the killings for the next 10 years.

Instances of direct action against the French were rare in colonial Cambodia. David Chandler (1996) noted that the Bardez incident revealed 'a reservoir of indigenous violence' that under normal circumstances would have worked itself out on other villagers, or on Cambodian officials. 'But whether it can be treated as a prologue to nationalism', he adds, 'is less clear . . . Evidence at the trial suggests that when their fervour waned and the crowd had been dispersed they returned, ashamed, to the village and before long were turning one another in to the police . . . ' (p. 158).

Indigenous resistance

At the level of direct action, it was people of the tribal minorities who were the most successful in resisting French encroachment on their territory and on their culture. They were organized, persistent and fearless, and their resistance won grudging admiration from the French despite the heavy toll in life on both sides. The attack on the remote French outpost of Le Rolland, as one example of these guerrilla raids, was documented in official reports and dramatically re-told in the colonial press. The following account is derived from RSC Files 14411 and 29360 in the State Archives of Cambodia.

During the night of 4–5 March 1935, Poste Le Rolland, the fortified headquarters of the French military delegation in the Haut Chhlong, the high plateau of what was then northeast Kratie province where the borders of Cambodia, Annam and Cochinchina met, was attacked by a band of Phnong insurgents armed with spears, bows and arrows. Five French were killed and three were grievously wounded in the raid. Three Phnong prisoners accused of murder in an earlier affray disappeared.

On the basis of preliminary investigations and his own visit to the area the following month, the Resident Superior of Cambodia, Richomme, reported that militants from a dozen or so villages had taken part in the attack which he described as 'an operation of great energy whose aim was the destruction of the post, the massacre of the garrison and especially of the Europeans'. He added that most of the villages that had taken part had since been abandoned and destroyed, the jars smashed, animals killed and the rice reserves burnt to demonstrate that it was not possible 'to assassinate Europeans with impunity'. In fact, this was just the most recent in a series of guerrilla-style attacks on the French presence in the region. Between 1910 and 1933, four French commanders, along with their escorts and local officials had been ambushed and killed. Reprisals then had been 'timid' in Richomme's opinion because of difficulties of access in a largely unknown region, but he promised that future action would involve 'measured repression, firm and effective; the reinforcement of all posts; and pacification of the troubled zone'.

Despite the bellicose tone adopted by these high level official reports, the *colons* of Indochina generally regarded the hill tribespeople as noble savages. Their resistance to the imposition of French colonization was understandable, even commendable, it was felt. Rather than crushing their native will and independence, the French saw their purpose as luring these 'men of the forest' into inevitable submission to the *mission civilisatrice*. This attitude was shared by the military officers, including Captain de Crèvecoeur, the commanding officer at Le Rolland, who reported unequivocally that the 1935 attack, like the earlier ones, was a further episode in the struggle by the Phnong to defend their independence against the threat of rapid French penetration of their territory. He estimated that 45 villages were part of this movement and that the leader of the revolt was Beu Degn/Pu Tran Lung whose prestige and occult influence made him the very soul of the revolt.

Beu Degn was a Phnong chief who had submitted to French authority about 18 months before the raid on Le Rolland. He had drunk from the jar with the head of the delegation and was appointed *balat*, deputy district chief, by the Administration. He had acknowledged Cambodian Protectorate authority over numerous Phnong villages where he had considerable influence. For reasons unknown to the French, however, Beu Degn simply disappeared one day and entered into dissidence. Matters came to a head when French authorities entered a village and arrested three known associates: the brother of Beu Degn, one of his acolytes, and a sorcerer. These were the prisoners who disappeared on the night of the attack.

During the weeks and months that followed the raid, bridges were burnt and destroyed and the houses of informants razed. The attacks were so well co-ordinated that the Direction de la Sûreté Générale suspected the involvement of external forces, particularly the Communist Party of Indochina whose propaganda was thought to be stirring up 'the primitive spirits of members of certain tribes'. Richomme, however, mocked the suggestion, pointing out that it was hardly likely that the illiterate inhabitants of Haut Chhlong could be influenced by handwritten or printed publications with revolutionary tendencies. Instead of sending security service agents into the area – who would be immediately killed, he delighted in pointing out – Richomme arranged for 20 dogs to be sent to the highlands instead.

Towards the end of May 1935, Beu Degn was captured in the forest. The telegram reporting this victory read: 'Pu Tran Lung prisoner; his wife killed, brother probably wounded in flight, three children aged one to six years. Found one old musket and twenty cartridges'. Another telegram received in Phnom Penh 2 days later announced his death, from wounds received in the course of capture, at Choeng Plah. This post was bombed and completely destroyed in November, exactly 6 months after the Le Rolland raid, a none too subtle reminder that while Beu Degn may have been the soul of the revolt, his death alone was insufficient to end it.

It is interesting to note throughout Cambodian history how often Khmer rebel leaders cooperated with the hill tribespeople. Milton Osborne (1997) believed that Prince Sivutha's strength was probably connected with links he had already established with the hill people living on the edge of lowland Khmer society (p. 214). He adds that the Kuy minority, inhabitants of Prey Lang, the vast lowland rainforest stretching northward from Kompong Thom province, had given their support to a major revolt led by another dynastic rebel prince as early as the 15th century. It has already been mentioned that the pretender, Pu Kombo, may have been of Kuy origin; tribal Stiengs of the Mimot plateau region were said to have joined his forces (Kiernan and Boua, 1982 p. 2). When the Communist Party of Kampuchea (CPK) moved its headquarters to Ratanakiri in 1966, it derived both inspiration and support from the tribal minorities, especially the Jarai, Tapuon and the Brao, hundreds of whom were recruited into CPK units and who acted as cadres, messengers for party leaders and as bodyguards after 1975 (p. 175).

Rebellions within the revolution

Between 1947 and 1954, Cambodians joined the Indochina-wide struggle for independence from French rule. Generally speaking, however, the nationalist movement in Cambodia was neither widespread nor mass-based, and it was the king, Sihanouk, who claimed the credit when independence was won in November 1953. It is not the purpose of this chapter to discuss the post-independence political struggles that eventually brought the communists to power in 1975, or to examine the nature of their regime. This history has already been thoroughly documented and analysed. There are two rebellions in this period, however, that demand attention. The first is the Samlaut rebellion of 1967–1968, which may or may not have been as Ben Kiernan termed it 'the baptism of fire for the small but steadily growing Kampuchean revolutionary movement' (Kiernan and Boua, 1982, p. 166). Even though communist cadres had been at work in the area, the rebellion was more in the nature of a spontaneous outburst against abuses by the military, and certainly Pol Pot, in his version of the Party's history, regarded the Samlaut rebellion as premature. It was, nevertheless, the first reported instance of a popular uprising where land-grabbing was one of the ostensible causes. The historical significance of this event has been noted by at least one leading Cambodian academic and political analyst, Lao Mong Hay, who has drawn direct parallels between it and a current, protracted land dispute in Kratie province (Titthara and Boyle, 2012). The second is the Chikreng rebellion of 1977, which, to the best of my knowledge, is the only recorded popular revolt that occurred within the revolution. Because the protesters were mostly 'base' people, villagers who had remained in the revolutionary zone throughout the civil war and were therefore, by association, supporters of the revolution, their grievances should be viewed separately from those in published survivor reports by 'new' people who escaped from the regime.

Until very recently, Cambodia has never had a serious problem of landlessness. For the most part, the clearing of new land always kept pace with demand. After independence, however, there was a noticeable trend in Battambang province towards land accumulation by wealthy city people, officials and army officers who could manipulate the legal regulations with impunity and assign themselves titles to land, which had already been cleared and occupied by local farmers and convert it into plantations for the fruit, jute and cotton industries (Thion, 1993, p. 42). After 1965, the impact of this trend was compounded by the influx of settlers from Kampuchea Krom who were fleeing the escalating war in South Vietnam. Pailin's population, for instance, doubled between 1964 and 1967 (Kiernan and Boua, 1982, p. 177). The spark for the uprising in Samlaut, about 25 km south of Battambang town and only 15 km from the Thai border, was the forced sale of rice to the government at prices below what the farmers were receiving from black market sales to middlemen or insurgents in Vietnam. The anti-government rebellion that ran its course in Samlaut between March and May in 1967 had developed into a civil war in many parts of the country by the end of the year, specifically in the hill tribe areas of the northeast and other western provinces. The Samlaut rebellion was brutally put down at Sihanouk's orders. According to David Chandler (1991), Sihanouk saw the Samlaut uprising primarily as a personal insult (p. 35). Taking the lead from the French response to the Bardez incident, he ordered the villages razed and renamed. Perhaps hundreds of people died, and there were reports of bounties paid for rebels' heads. Thousands of people went into dissidence and swelled the revolution's forces.

The regime of Democratic Kampuchea was torn apart by factionalism. During its brief term in power, between April 1975 and December 1978, there were at least nine attempted *coups d'état* following which most of the revolution's highly trained and experienced leaders and cadres were executed along with all those on their personal *khsae royeak*, the strings or lines of patronage (Kiernan, 1980). In Chikreng district, located on the periphery of two major provinces and where rice-fields blend into dense lowland rainforest on its eastern edge, the villagers were used as pawns to flush out 'enemies of the state' following the failed attempt by the commanders of their Northern Zone to wrest power from the Pol Pot faction (Slocomb, 2006). In April 1977, former district leaders had been replaced and guards were suddenly without arms when a fear-mongering campaign spread throughout several villages, reminding the people of their hunger and creating a general sense of grievance. Agitators told them that there had to be a new regime and promised that troops would come to support them if they rebelled. The demonstration (*patekam*) lasted 3 days. Angry villagers armed with machetes, sticks, axes and knives marched in a procession and then set upon the guards. The prepared festival at the *sala wat* to celebrate their victory, however, turned into a bloodbath. Instead of the much-anticipated new leaders, the trucks that arrived were full of armed soldiers who immediately turned their guns on the assembled crowd. Many villagers were shot dead, while others were grabbed and executed beside the wat pond. A former village chief who later gathered up the dead estimated that those at the wat numbered between 100 and 150, while a further 30 bodies had been thrown under a bridge at the turn-off to the wat road. The terror continued the following day when all the former local officials were summoned to a meeting in the *vihear*, the temple at the wat. Most of them were then bound, led to the pond and executed. For the next 2 weeks, armed soldiers searched the villages for conspirators whom they killed outright or loaded onto trucks and took away.

The villagers who were asked about the causes of the Chikreng rebellion realized that they had been deceived and they knew why and how they had been deceived. Although it was impossible for them at the time to have known about the machinations at the highest level of the regime, they had a clear understanding of how power functions. They expressed fear and regret but little lasting bitterness about the terrible injustice they had suffered. While the regime held power, the villagers obeyed; then the regime cynically tricked them and killed them for their false loyalty.

Given half a chance, and a small window of opportunity like the few days that the guards in Chikreng were without weapons, there would undoubtedly have been many similar uprisings – what James C. Scott (1979) terms 'revolution within the revolution' – against the autocratic rule of Pol Pot. Radical elites, he notes, denounce this behaviour as adventurism, deviation or anarchy, forgetting, of course, that it is frequently the case that this same radical intelligentsia has usurped a revolution begun by the peasants and put it to ends which its peasant supporters do not recognize. If Samlaut and Chikreng are seen as bookend rebellions, staged a decade apart within the same revolution, then Scott's arguments are indeed valid. The revolutionary project might have had nothing to do with why the peasantry joined it. 'One cannot necessarily assume a consensus of beliefs merely from the joint participation of elites and non-elites in the same movement . . . not without a certain condescension,' he argues (p. 99). Scott might well have been discussing Cambodia's more recent history when he sounded this warning to those seeking common cause with the ordinary villager in political action:

> [A]ny radical elite hoping to mobilize the peasantry confronts not a *tabula rasa* but a rich tradition of prior identifications, a history of organized struggle, and a set of politico-religious ideas all of which will affect whatever synthesis emerges (p. 101).

Conclusion

The end of the Cold War and the consensus among Southeast Asian nations to convert their region into a competitive free marketplace forced a resolution of the conflict on the Cambodian warring parties in 1991. Protracted civil war and revolution meant that Cambodia had arrived late and unprepared at the transformative stage of the world economy to economic (neo) liberalism, but adaptation was made at breakneck speed. Karl Polanyi (1944) described this modern churning phase in state-society relations as the 'double movement', with the forces establishing a self-regulating market acting against those that aimed at the conservation of man and nature (p. 132). These, he argued, were the actions of two organizing principles in society, each setting its own aims and methods, and each having the support of definite social forces.

By the turn of the 21st century, the stage was set for radical change in Cambodia. Predatory state actors quickly allied themselves with the forces of big business corporations such as international logging companies and property developers. The forces representing 'conservation of man and nature' were a little slower to respond. Citizenship duties and obligations had held sway over the notions of human rights and democracy for decades, while conservation of natural resources meant little to people who could quote old school textbooks that described their country as 'a land covered in forests, where lakes and rivers teemed with fish'. As pressure on land and other resources increased, however, and the evidence of illegal logging, land-grabbing, official corruption, and the violence that all this generated became indisputable, popular resistance to the excesses of state power began to grow.

As in the past, resistance will continue to take different forms. The 'weapons of the weak' will be fully utilized, as will challenges to authority, and sometimes even open protest. In the everlasting struggle, the Cambodian peasantry will undoubtedly exhibit all the persistence and courage that they have displayed so many times before. Survival and self-interest, Scott's 'vital force' of peasant resistance, demands nothing less.

References

Chandler, D. (1991) *The Tragedy of Cambodian History: Politics, War and Revolution since 1945*, Yale University Press, New Haven.

Chandler, D. (1996) *Facing the Cambodian Past*, Silkworm Books, Chiangmai.

Cooper, N. (2001) *France in Indochina: Colonial Encounters*, Berg, Oxford.

Hansen, A. R. (2007) *How to Behave: Buddhism and Modernity in Colonial Cambodia, 1860–1930*, University of Hawai'i Press, Honolulu.

Kiernan, B. (1980) 'Conflict in the Kampuchean Communist Movement', *Journal of Contemporary Asia* 10(1–2), pp. 7–74.

Kiernan, B. and Boua, C. (eds) (1982) *Peasants and Politics in Kampuchea 1942–1981*, Zed Press, London.

Moore, B. Jr. (1966) *Social Origins of Dictatorship and Democracy*, Penguin, Harmondsworth.

Osborne, M. (1978) 'Peasant politics in Cambodia: The 1916 affair', *Modern Asian Studies* 12(2), pp. 217–243.

Osborne, M. E. (1997) (1969) *The French Presence in Cochinchina and Cambodia*, White Lotus, Bangkok.

Polanyi, K. (1944) *The Great Transformation*, Beacon Press, Boston.

Résidence Supérieure du Cambodge (RSC), File 2799, Rapport sur la situation du Cambodge 1927–28; File 499, Box 38, Rapport annuel sur la colonisation pour l'année 1932–33; File 14411, Rapports et Correspondances . . . sur la repression des rebellions des Phnongs; and File 29360, Rapport Politique de mois de Jan., 1938., State Archives of Cambodia, Phnom Penh, Cambodia.

Roberts, S. (1979) *Order and Dispute: An Introduction to Legal Anthropology*, Penguin, Harmondsworth.

Scott, J. C. (1979) 'Revolution in the revolution: Peasants and commissars', *Theory and Society* 7, pp. 97–130.

Scott, J. C. (1985) *Weapons of the Weak: Everyday Forms of Peasant Resistance*, Yale University Press, New Haven.

Slocomb, M. (2006) 'Chikreng Rebellion: Coup and its aftermath in Democratic Kampuchea', *Journal of the Royal Asiatic Society* Series 3(16:1), pp. 1–14.

Thion, S. (1993) *Watching Cambodia*, White Lotus, Bangkok.

Titthara, M. and Boyle, D. (2012) 'Mourning villagers flee Kratie after bloody eviction', *Phnom Penh Post*, http://www.phnompenhpost.com/national/mourning-villagers-flee-kratie-after-bloody-eviction, accessed October 2013.

12 A 'people's' irrigation reservoir on the Tonle Sap floodplain

John Marston and Chhuon Hoeur

Figure 12.1 Cambodian and CPP flags erected around the People's Reservoir, as the community appeals for it not to be destroyed.

Source: Photo by J. Marston.

This chapter is about community mobilization and conflict around the issue of irrigation reservoirs in the Tonle Sap Lake floodplain in one subdistrict of Kampong Thom province, Cambodia.[1] As the chapters in this volume

A 'people's' irrigation reservoir on the Tonle Sap floodplain   239

amply illustrate, many of the 'land dilemmas of Southeast Asia' written about by Hall *et al.* in their book *The Powers of Exclusion* (2011) are evident in contemporary Cambodia – the ins and outs of land titling programs, the practical realities of defining protected areas and market penetration by local and non-local actors. While we might quibble on some points and re-combine some of their categories, the area of the Tonle Sap floodplain we are concerned with here is the site of some of these same dilemmas. Such developments on the floodplain – the seemingly unstoppable march towards more intrusive ways of defining control and 'exclusion' from natural resources, is a major historical drama. For the purpose of this chapter, we focus on a fairly peripheral phenomenon as it occurs in relation to these other processes, which is nevertheless of interest as representing grassroots agency: the creation of what was called a 'people's' reservoir. This also links to Hall *et al.*'s discussion of 'collective mobilizations for land and territory' (Hall *et al.*, Chapter 7).

The 'people's' reservoir represented a relatively rare instance when villagers came together to create for themselves the same kind of irrigation reservoir that entrepreneurs were creating elsewhere. Our study relates to Marston's (2011) earlier analysis of academic debates about the nature of Cambodian rural community – or its seeming absence; he has increasingly come to see this issue in terms of community mobilization. Underlying this study is the question: under what circumstances do Cambodian populations mobilize and what are the socio-cultural/political pitfalls of mobilization at the present historical moment.

The question of how social organization relates to water resources has figured in the literature on Khmer social cohesion – in particular in Richard O'Connor's (1995) discussion of 'agro-cultural' complexes in the context of historical succession in pre-modern Southeast Asia. He suggests that Khmer society, oriented to the local use of ponds and reservoirs, has had a different fabric to that found in Thai or Vietnamese society, which were historically more grounded in cooperation needed for the irrigation of rivers and streams. O'Connor's underlying assumptions may also have informed Margaret Slocomb when she wrote about historical cultural resistance to large-scale irrigation projects in Cambodia (Slocomb, 2010, p. 100).

We ask ourselves, does the 'people's' reservoir – and its practical difficulties in implementation – exemplify these tendencies or point to the evolution of new models? The cooperative organization we will describe here might fit into Elinor Ostrom's models of Common Pool Resources (Ostrom, 1990) and we ask the reader to keep in mind this positive model of grassroots empowerment around resources. Unlike the case studies Ostrom uses, the people's reservoir emerged at a moment of historical change and instability, very much subject to historical contingencies, and its final outcome is far from certain. It cannot be understood without taking into consideration the degree to which it represents resistance to other social processes. For this chapter we are less interested in exploring the implications of Ostrom's model than of unravelling and documenting messy, morally complex processes of negotiation around land tenure and environmental, economic, social and political considerations – processes which it seems to us reveal a great deal about changes that have taken place in Cambodia since the early 1990s.

Ecology of the Tonle Sap floodplain

Samprouch subdistrict is one of several subdistricts in Stoung District, Kampong Thom province, which extend from the national road in the direction of the Tonle Sap Lake. The ecology of the Tonle Sap river and lake, described in more detail in Chapter 3, affects much of what we recount here. The flood pattern in and of itself makes questions of land tenure complicated. Who has the right of access to the land when it is not flooded and the right to use receding water for irrigation purposes?

Historically, the Tonle Sap floodplain is associated with the use of 'floating rice' – varieties of long-stemmed rice which grow with the rising floodwater. Zhou Daguon, a 13th century Chinese visitor to the court of Angkor, describes this technique, which was still widely practiced in the period prior to the Pol Pot regime (Zhou, 2007). Fox and Ledgerwood (1999) have also shown that there was the historically significant use of the technique of flood recession rice agriculture – that is to say, in contrast to floating rice (which grows with the rising water), water is captured for irrigation purposes as it *recedes* from the floodplain *following* the season of flooding.

In the 1980s, following the Pol Pot regime, the People's Republic of Kampuchea (PRK) government tried to encourage the re-introduction of floating rice, and specific villages and 'solidarity groups' were assigned locations on the floodplain to pursue this; later, as the 'solidarity group' system broke down, locations were assigned to specific families (CAS, 2006). However, the use of the floodplain for floating rice never again became widespread. A variety of reasons are given for this: crops of floating rice were unsuccessful; perhaps, as some farmers say, it was because some varieties were lost under the Khmer Rouge when starving peasants ate seed rice; others have said that ecological changes in the lake has meant greater variation in water levels, making floating rice unreliable. In the 1980s, villagers were also reluctant to farm in areas distant from the National Road for reasons of security – problems of banditry as well as the movement of guerrilla troops.[2] These attempts to re-initiate floating rice agriculture were then largely abandoned (although they provide some claim for land rights at the present time).

Irrigation in Cambodia

Since the late 1980s, a number of large irrigation projects in the Mekong River basin of Cambodia – including the Tonle Sap watershed – have been funded internationally – many of them expansions or renovations of irrigation systems originally built prior to the war or during the Pol Pot period; partly because of their international funding, these have been extensively written about in reports (CDRI, 2010; Öjendal, 2000; Chou, 2010; Khiev, 2010; Ros, 2010; CDRI, 2008). Most of these schemes have involved stream-diversion irrigation – that is to say, the use of flowing water from rivers and streams for irrigation purposes. The Ministry of Water Resources, with the support of international funders, has encouraged the formation of 'Farmer-Water User Groups'.

There has been limited research on gravity-fed systems in which annual floodwaters are captured in enclosed areas to be used gradually for irrigation in the season after which the waters have normally receded – that is to say, varieties of the flood-recession techniques Fox and Ledgerwood (1999) were concerned with. On a small scale, such systems also historically involved community coordination, in what Middleton and Prom (2008) have even described as localized traditions of Community-Based Natural Resource Management. Some large-scale irrigation projects constructed during the Pol Pot period used this technique, including two projects in Batheay District, Kampong Cham which have been successfully renovated since the 1990s.

Reservoirs in Kampong Thom province and Samprouch subdistrict

Stoung district, along the national road, is the last district in Kampong Thom Province as you head northeast towards Siem Reap province. Samprouch is one of the subdistricts lying totally on the Tonle Sap flood plain.[3] While there is some informal marketing, it is close enough to the district town that most market activity occurs there, and the subdistrict has a clearly agricultural focus – with rice farming, cattle grazing, legal and illegal fishing and some other small-scale agricultural production, such as that of watermelon or lotus seed. Housing consists of modest structures on stilts of wood or thatch. There are clearly different levels of economic security, but villagers by and large live close to the subsistence level, and some at levels of poverty difficult for an outsider to understand. Fishing, once a key to survival, has decreased in importance because of (villagers say) decreasing quantities of fish and legal restrictions on access to fish in the Tonle Sap lake on the ponds and lakes of the floodplain. Increased dependence on dry-season rice production, as described in this chapter, has been for some a strategy which makes up for the decreasing fishing activities. Many young men and women, even from families who are relatively secure economically, will now spend periods working as labourers in Phnom Penh, on plantations near the Thai border or elsewhere in Cambodia, or in Thailand itself. Villagers along the national road, and to an even greater degree the families living in Stoung district town, appear more economically secure and more linked to the market economy as it functions in the region and the country as a whole. The reservoirs we describe here in some ways bring the market economy of the district town, the province and the country as a whole to bear on the subsistence economy of the villages.

The phenomenon which provided the setting for what we describe here has been the fairly sudden spurt in the building of this kind of reservoir on the Tonle Sap floodplain during the last decade, mostly by entrepreneurs – but a few administered by the village or subdistrict government or, cooperatively, by groups of peasants. They feed dry-season rice crops using new varieties of fast-growing rice. The growth of this kind of reservoir, which as we shall see has proved very controversial, has been predominantly in the provinces of Bantheay Mean Chey, Battambang, Siem Reap, and, more than anywhere else, Kampong Thom, where it was actively promoted by the provincial governor. Stream-diversion irrigation schemes have been more favoured in the provinces to the southwest of the lake, Kampong Chhnang and Pursat – the projects more widely written about in the literature (Chou, 2010; Ros et al., 2011; Chem et al., 2011). While the entrepreneurial irrigation reservoirs have been less researched than the internationally funded irrigation schemes, there have been notable studies by agronomist Jean-Christophe Diepart (2007a, 2007b, 2010) and development specialists Ngo and Chan (2010). The larger question underlying our research is the relation of these mostly entrepreneurial irrigation schemes to the rural agricultural populations and the trajectory of their social and ecological costs in the first decade of the 21st century – although for the purposes of this paper we will eventually focus more narrowly on one single cooperative reservoir which developed in response to the entrepreneurial reservoirs.

The efflorescence of irrigation reservoirs has environmental, social and political dimensions. Here I will initially speak broadly of Kampong Thom, the province where the construction of reservoirs has been most intensive and most controversial; in the course of this paper we will concentrate on occurrences in Samprouch subdistrict, our fieldwork site.

Supporters of the reservoirs typically tell of visiting the floodplain during the dry-season, looking out at the vast extensions of land, and thinking how greatly it would benefit Cambodia if this land – much of it far from mangrove forests – could be used productively. Accounts of how the reservoirs began in the area vary, but they were apparently the results of experiments by farmers and businessmen formerly involved in floating rice agriculture in Kampong Thom and adjoining areas of Siem Reap province, who were looking for practical alternatives. This captured the interest of the Kampong Thom provincial governor, Nam Tum, who sponsored the construction of model reservoirs, to refine the techniques, and then encouraged more and more construction of reservoirs on the floodplain. One document we have seen dates some reservoirs to 2001 and 2002, and this may be about the time that entrepreneurs began requesting land. They began building in earnest in 2003 and a momentum was created in 2004–2005. In Samprouch subdistrict, the initial wave in which several entrepreneurs acquired land for this purpose was in 2004. The numbers given for the reservoirs vary, partly because not all lists include the smallest reservoirs. In 2012 there were about 18 in Samprouch sub-district and over 100 in Kampong Thom province alone. While the social and environmental impact was initially minimal this began to change as the grid of reservoirs became denser. Adjacent peasant populations were initially skeptical about whether the reservoirs would even function; their attitude changed when land irrigated by reservoirs turned out to be extremely productive. Moreover, the large extensions of land lent themselves well to more mechanized agricultural techniques.

Floodplain land is considered state land and will probably continue to be for the foreseeable future – although part of the context of the events we describe is the fact that the country is in the process of introducing systematic land registration across all provinces. This means, among other things, that populations are particularly sensitive to land tenure and eager to secure land in the hopes that it may represent permanent access.[4]

The 2001 Land Law introduced the possibility of Economic Land Concessions, as is discussed by MacInnes (Chapter 5). While major land concessions are authorized at the national level, the law originally included the provision for smaller land concessions of up to 1,000 ha authorized at the provincial level. The law was changed to eliminate provincially authorized land concessions in 2008. The majority of the Kampong Thom entrepreneurial irrigation reservoirs were authorized provincially under the terms of this provision – although some have been built since 2008 on land with claims to having been purchased. Most are between 100 and 400 ha in size and feed rice growing areas only slightly larger than the reservoir's size.

There are in fact varying degrees of legality regarding the reservoirs: those on land authorized at the subdistrict, district and provincial levels; those authorized only at the subdistrict or district level without ever getting formal permission at the provincial level; those constructed without any permission at all; those constructed after having been 'bought' from peasants, who themselves may have had unclear claims to the land. There is also the question of reservoirs (or the farmland they feed) and environmental law (such as laws governing the Tonle Sap floodplain or the zones which have been restricted for the protection of the Bengal Florican), and the director of the provincial office of the Ministry of Agriculture, Forestry and Fisheries (MAFF) told us that reservoirs violating environmental zones are illegal, even if approved by the provincial government. There are, moreover, questions about whether lands granted by the province as land concessions were ever registered as 'state private land', as required before being granted as land concessions. Finally, in Kampong Thom, contracts for land concessions stipulated that at least 40 per cent of the land would be developed cooperatively with the local community if they so requested, (but despite protests, such cooperative arrangements rarely if ever happened.).[5] If even under the best of circumstances legality has, in practice, an element of negotiation, this has been particularly the case here, where laws themselves are new and ambiguous, governed by authorities with overlapping jurisdictions, and, perhaps, framed from the perspective of legal and cultural traditions alien to Cambodia. The ad hoc ways they are put into practice may also relate to the fact that the socio-economic conditions to which they make reference are also in flux.

Peasants typically refer to the large entrepreneurial irrigation systems as those of *krumhun*, or 'companies', which underlines the degree to which they are recognized as representing agricultural systems qualitatively different from those of the peasants themselves. We however, prefer to see the owners of these reservoirs as in a different category from the companies that acquire large land concessions. The owners of the reservoirs have, in fact, up until now typically been fairly small-scale entrepreneurs, with backgrounds either in floating rice or fishing lots, or business. Some are persons in Siem Reap with longstanding family or business connections in the district; others own businesses in the district town. One in Samprouch was a long-term resident of the subdistrict whose modest house is near the national road. Another, entering the reservoir business later in the process, is a local military officer. They are in many cases less characterized by wealth than the kind of connections which would make them aware of trends in provincial government, and people in a position to take out newly available bank loans. From most peasants' perspective, the capital mobilized to create reservoirs represents wealth beyond their dreams; there are times when, seen as such, an observer would be tempted to paint the entrepreneurs as the drama's villains. However, one should keep in mind that by Phnom Penh standards their wealth is quite modest – and the investment needed to build a reservoir is closer to what someone in Phnom Penh would pay to buy a modest Chinese-style shop-house than the investment one would need to build a shopping centre. For these entrepreneurs, state moves to tear down reservoirs are a disaster. (Their defenders say that the real reason reservoirs are targeted by the state is not for environmental protection, but rather to clear the land for larger-scale investors who are more truly *krumhun*.)[6] The cost of building a reservoir is not out of reach of local capital. (Nevertheless, some seemed well linked to powerful figures at the provincial and national level, and there is speculation by villagers that the capital of powerful figures is behind the reservoirs.)

There is, we believe, so far no documentation of the process whereby the environmental problems posed by the reservoirs came to public attention and Prime Minister Hun Sen came to call for their demolition. As the number of reservoirs multiplied on the floodplain there was more and more attention given to them by environmental NGOs, including FACT (Fisheries Action Coalition Team) and the Wildlife Conservation Society, each of which advocated restrictions on the building of new reservoirs in at least some parts of the floodplain and was in dialogue with government officials about the issue. Probably, however, the opposition which carried the greatest weight came from within different ministries of the government itself. Opposition to the reservoirs was based first and foremost on the fear that the destruction of mangrove forests would mean the disappearance of Tonle Sap fish. Other concerns were that reservoirs were so densely situated that they interrupted normal channels of water flow into the lake. They also sometimes blocked traditional pathways whereby pedestrians, bicyclists and oxcarts gained access to lowlands. Agronomists argued, furthermore, that despite the phenomenal productivity initially shown by the land, this could only be sustained by future extensive use of fertilizers, which could also have negative impacts on the eco-system, and might eventually call into question the systems' profitability. Prime Minister Hun Sen, in one speech broadcast repeatedly on television, even made the broad statement that the reservoirs could result in the lake's disappearance.

All this resulted in the national government's announcement in December 2009 that all the reservoirs would be razed. A scattering of reservoirs were demolished during the first half of 2010, during the period of time when we were jointly looking at this issue; but we were unable to determine any particular pattern as to which reservoirs were destroyed first. There were newspaper reports of further bulldozing of reservoirs since then – a total of 45 in 2010 before rains made it impossible. A March 9, 2011, article in the *Phnom Penh Post* reported that a demarcation process to indicate which reservoirs would be demolished was 25 per cent completed (Khouth, 2011). Nevertheless there has been little if any demolition since then.

Grassroots mobilization

All this provides the setting for what is our principle topic – the mobilization of grassroots rural populations in relation to all this. Any adequate study of the reservoirs must recognize that they have been the locus of significant conflict with local populations. Supporters of the entrepreneurial reservoirs typically say that peasants were indifferent to their construction until it became apparent that they were highly profitable; it was only then they decided they should have a share in the profits. Such statements are hard to evaluate, since we cannot easily construct a chronology of protests. There was indignation quite early about misleading statements attributed to authorities about the nature of the reservoirs – such as that contracts were for 5 years, when in fact they were for 25 years. While not all reservoir projects have generated conflicts, anecdotal evidence points to the fact that there have been *many* protests by villagers in many parts of Kampong Thom province. These have involved issues of compensation, and of their access to land and water in the vicinity of reservoirs. (Tensions of this kind, e.g., were referred to, albeit indirectly, by two of the reservoir owners we were able to interview, as well as NGO specialists on conservation and villagers in Kampong Cham with relatives in Kampong Thom.) While most cases do not have clear documentation, one notable clash in July 2011 in Sangkor subdistrict was covered in the Khmer-language press (Gūlaen, 2011; Kanchestā, 2011) after villagers blocked traffic on the national road for 6 hours. It involved land protests over reservoirs which had resulted in a local activist's imprisonment. The Kampong Thom provincial representative of the human rights NGO, LICADHO, described to us the long history of this conflict.

The most obvious point to be made is that the floodplain was, as Diepart (2007b, 2010) emphasizes, since time immemorial a source of common-pool resources for fishing, grazing of cattle and gathering of non-timber products. The granting of land concessions meant that traditional access to the land was lost – in what could, in classical Marxist terms, be described as primitive accumulation.[7,8] Diepart argues that the value of resources now lost is as great as the value generated by irrigated dry-season rice fields. That is to say, the sum total of the profit generated by the increased production of rice permitted by the reservoirs is not as great as the sum total of what was generated by fishing, grazing of cattle and gathering of non-timber products.

The earliest published account we have found of disputes about the irrigation reservoirs is in a 2006 study by the Center for Advanced Study on land disputes and how they are resolved in Cambodia in the context of new land law and newly decentralized forms of local government. One of three cases the report examines is 2005 land disputes in Stoung district; focusing on a single subdistrict, it examines the history in three villages where disputes arose over the construction of irrigation reservoirs. The building of these reservoirs had been approved by the subdistrict chief. The subdistrict's name is not given but it appears to be one adjoining Samprouch. In two of the three villages there was significant resistance by the local population. In one (Village A), villagers had learned about the project while it was still being negotiated by the subdistrict council:

> Although villagers did not agree to the project, the investor received approval for the project from the provincial authority and started to bring his construction equipment to the location. This movement prompted the villagers to go to the field armed with knives and axes to prevent the occupation of their land and to threaten to burn down the equipment if construction proceeded. The village chief and a commune councilor immediately appeared at the scene and appealed to the angry villagers not to use violence but to solve the dispute peacefully. Both sides agreed to stop the construction work provisionally until the dispute between villagers and the investor could be resolved.
> (Center for Advanced Study, 2006, pp. 52–53)

Through this process opposition party representatives and human rights organizations became involved. Protests and meetings led eventually to the provincial governor deciding 'to stop the implementation of the investment plan and allow the villagers to use the disputed land on condition that they cultivated rice there that year' (Center for Advanced Study, 2006, p. 54). Eventually the investor decided to abandon his plans to build a reservoir. Events in another village (Village B) followed almost the same pattern – a confrontation with armed villagers followed by meetings and a similar decision by the provincial governor – with the only difference being that at the time the report was written the investor had not abandoned his intentions. A third village (Village C) decided that instead of protesting they would push for financial compensation from the investor, and this was negotiated successfully – although some villagers only agreed to this reluctantly, feeling that they had no choice.

It is hard to make generalizations about how the irrigation reservoir projects relate to adjacent rural populations. As we say, it is unquestionable that there has been significant conflict, both between villagers and entrepreneurs and between villagers and authorities who authorized the coming of the entrepreneurs, and in our analysis this relates to something basic to the underlying change in the relationship to resources. But it was also apparent that some reservoirs were the locus of more conflict than others.

A variety of different arrangements between officials, entrepreneurs and villagers have been worked out in different settings. In some early cases, investors built a third reservoir to be used by villagers at the same time they were building two for themselves. This is described by Ngo and Chan as occurring in Chamnar Kraom subdistrict [and investor Lev Vanna told us he had done this in Kampong Ko subdistrict]. The reservoirs of this kind described by Ngo and Chan are administered by subdistrict officials and poorer villagers are given access to the irrigated land from year to year on a rotating basis. Ngo and Chan describe this as the most 'pro-poor' arrangement of the different kinds of reservoirs. It may represent investors' attempts to abide by the contractual agreement to work 40 per cent of the irrigated land cooperatively with villagers. As described by Ngo and Chan, and by the subdistrict officials interviewed, this seems a very positive, non-conflictive arrangement which could have been a model for other places. Unfortunately, this practice has not continued, perhaps because investors came to realize they would not be compelled to keep the 40 per cent requirement. There are no reservoirs with this arrangement in Samprouch.

Some reservoir owners, while maintaining control of the reservoir itself, sell parts of the land it feeds to local farmers; others rent it out and in a few cases there has been sharecropping introduced. Besides the more formal arrangements with land immediately below the reservoir that feeds it, there are increasingly less formal arrangements with peasants using the water as it continues to flow past these fields. Some reservoir owners let farmers use the water for free; others charge nominal fees. (Although commodification is taking place, complex relations of patron-clientism still come to the fore. Villagers in such arrangements sometimes show loyalty to reservoir owners in disputes.)

While villagers in many locations have been opposed to the construction of entrepreneurial irrigation reservoirs, or felt that they were not adequately compensated for loss of access to the land, there are also peasants who, having worked out agreements for agricultural use with one of the entrepreneurial reservoirs, find themselves dependent on this for their livelihood – and are now vulnerable if a policy is implemented whereby reservoirs are destroyed.

The people's reservoir

All this brings us finally to the 'people's reservoir' in Samprouch subdistrict, the topic of this chapter indicated in the title. We should start by pointing out that, despite the way the phrase 'people's reservoir' resonates in English, this is not in the end the story of a particularly leftist or activist project (although it did grow out of earlier protests and can be conceived of as representing a form of resistance to the developments taking place in the province). We would like to describe it as the complex outcome of processes of negotiation, itself marred by accusation of corruption and complicity with authorities and built in environmentally questionable areas – but which nevertheless represents a practical solution of subsistence and the minimization of conflict for at least some villagers.

The pattern of dispute in Samprouch commune is consistent with some of what the CAS study described as taking place in other parts of the province. Although the People's reservoir was already being formed when we did preliminary research in the subdistrict in July 2009, what was most salient in conversations with villagers was a sense of grievance and attempts to organize in the face of that grievance. These grievances took a number of forms (and some may have been more important at different points in time.) There were complaints they were led to believe contracts for reservoirs were for 5 years, when they were for 25 years – or simply that they had been encouraged to put thumbprints on documents without being told their implications. Some villagers were left with the impression that the reservoirs would revert to villagers after a certain number of years, but that was not happening. There were reports that the subdistrict chief encouraged people to 'sell' land to reservoir owners, even though compensation was minimal (and fear that if they did not accept they would receive no compensation at all). There was discussion of different ministries taking different sides in disputes. Villagers had gone to the human rights NGO LICADHO in the provincial town and to other NGOs requesting help. One reservoir owner, C, had police with arms threatening people.

There were also what we now understand to be the complaints of *individual* farmers previously granted access to floodplain land for specific purposes, whose claims were swallowed by the newly built reservoirs, distinct from the general situation of villagers to the degree they had a basis for pursuing their grievances individually with the state. (One man had gone to the provincial capital and had limited success – limited because while his use of the land had been authorized at the subdistrict level prior to the granting of land to the reservoir investor, it had never been authorized at the provincial level. He was pleased with the outcome because others, he said, simply lost all their land because they hadn't dared fight at the provincial capital.)

Community dissatisfaction came to a head in the 2007 subdistrict council elections, when an SRP opposition party candidate was chosen over the incumbent, the candidate of the dominant Cambodian People's Party (CPP).[9] If nothing else, the election of a SRP subdistrict council chief signalled to the provincial governor's office that there were significant problems surrounding the reservoirs that needed to be addressed.

One of the leaders of demonstrations against the reservoirs was a farmer aged around 40 years, who we will call PP. Around this time PP and other protesters came to decide that instead of protesting existing reservoirs they would push to control a reservoir themselves. In our conversation with villagers, PP is commonly identified as the leader of the people's reservoir, although we would later learn it is administered by a committee of three.

They appealed to be given a large plot of land (360 ha) on a tier of reservoirs quite low in the floodplain – one that had already been promised to another investor, C, who had delayed in developing it while he completed another large reservoir. Against C's protests, the land was given to 'the people' of the commune by the provincial governor Nam Tum in March 2006. Nam Tum, as we see it, was trying to solve the longstanding conflict, while cultivating his own relationships of patron-clientism in the area. Representatives of the provincial government attended meetings held with villagers at one of the wats, and from the perspective of those involved, a 'community' was formed with the recognition of the authorities. (They use the term *sahakum* for 'community', a term often used in state projects, suggesting that it was given legal recognition at this time, although, as we see below, it was not.)

Various problems emerged and tensions were still very much in evidence during our field work in the first half of 2010. PP is a relative of the two brothers who were the current and former subdistrict chiefs. There is not too much that distinguishes him from other villagers, but his brother is a village schoolteacher, and he has slightly more education than most of his neighbours.[10] His family was traditionally involved in fish trade. His modest wood house might be slightly bigger than others around it. He became involved in the people's reservoir because of earlier involvement in protest. He was chosen in community meetings as a representative for direct talks with C and another major reservoir owner, K. During this time he was subjected to threats of violence (by, apparently, reservoir owners, themselves well linked to provincial authorities). However, there is no sign he is an activist in the sense of being ideologically motivated. His involvement with the reservoir brought him into increasing contact with Nam Tum, the former governor of the province, still at this time powerful as the president of the provincial council, whose name PP drops in conversation. PP himself has a small 60-ha reservoir which, though built after the people's reservoir, is, he says, on land he acquired prior to the building of the people's reservoir; thus, above and beyond the people's reservoir, he is invested in the economy of the reservoirs.[11]

While Nam Tum and other provincial government officials were present at the meeting creating the reservoir and may have helped to devise the plan, it is by no means clear that there is a legal basis for it. Although in the case of the entrepreneurial reservoirs, contracts were signed, the subdistrict chief told me this wasn't done with the People's reservoir, because 'it wasn't necessary'. The MAFF provincial chief for Kampong Thom told us that the reservoir community had applied for formal recognition as an agricultural cooperative, but he turned it down because farmland fed by the reservoir clearly extended into flooded forest areas, and because he had questions about PP, as a reservoir owner himself, who might be linked to outside interests. The people's reservoir is also not recognized as a Farmer Water User Group by MOWRAM. (There are no formally registered FWUCs in the floodplain area of the Tonle Sap in Kampong Thom.) That is to say, despite villagers' perceptions, it has very little legal foundation.

Upon formation of the reservoir community, rice land fed by the reservoir was assigned to participating families by lottery; 1,009 were each assigned 1 ha. During our research in 2009 and 2010, members were actively clearing areas of flooded forest in this area. This was universally described as extremely hard, backbreaking work. They knew this was illegal and that they could be fined the equivalent of about $200 if they were caught. They knew this was destroying fish spawning grounds, were embarrassed by this fact and laughed sheepishly about it over palm wine – but felt they had no choice if they wanted to survive as farmers. (Villagers until recently supplemented their income significantly by fishing in the floodplain. In a vicious cycle, there is now less fish – perhaps because of the reservoirs – and this forces them to cut down more flooded forests, which will further reduce the fish.)

The chief complaint against the people's reservoir is that, although it pretends to be for all the subdistrict's residents, many have not been able to participate. Of 15 villages in the subdistrict, only 12 participate in the reservoir, and of those 12 villages, some have larger numbers than others. Some of those not participating perhaps simply did not join early enough; some did not feel that they could pay the $200 fee being charged by PP's reservoir association. A fee of this sort of course becomes a means of exclusion (to use the terminology of Hall *et al.*); it discriminates against the poorest of the poor. Anger rose to sufficient pitch that in 2008 a group of subdistrict farmers, of those *not* part of the people's reservoir, went to Phnom Penh to protest at the National Assembly. (Since C is still working to regain the rights to the property, there were accusations that C supported protesters. Some we interviewed said no; there may be some villagers who genuinely feel that cooperative farming agreements with a reservoir owned by C would have been more beneficial.[12]) While Phnom Penh protests did not lead to any national government action, Nam Tum at this time called publicly for the reservoir to be open to *all* villagers in the subdistrict. In response, PP said he would take smaller contributions from other villagers who would then be part of a *second* reservoir when he found the land for one – but couldn't guarantee that he really could do so or promise to return money if he didn't. This led to criticism that he was simply taking money for his own use. There was also criticism by *members* of the reservoir community, who felt that money was required arbitrarily, such as a fee for the right to clear plots of land, and that this money was going into the pockets of administrators and not to the reservoir project as a whole. We cite these stories not to attack PP or the people's reservoir – from what we have heard so far, we think most of PP's actions have been justified – but to convey the sense that the reservoir project is still coloured by doubts and, as it were, undergoing birth pains, with many issues still unresolved. It is to its credit that it brings together participants at marginal levels of subsistence working actively to create the conditions for their continuing livelihood.

During several visits to Samprouch in the first half of 2010, we found that although villagers were aware that some reservoirs were being destroyed, they were fairly nonchalant and optimistic that theirs would be an exception. In July, on our last visit, however, we arrived to find that many villagers affiliated with the reservoir had been at the reservoir site for the last 3 days. This was prompted by the fact that several reservoirs in the neighbouring subdistrict, Msa Krong, had been dismantled in a short period of time by teams arriving by helicopter, and they were afraid that authorities would next move to Samprouch. Members of the people's reservoir camped out for several days, preparing to plead for the reservoir if attempts were made to destroy it. PP later told me that all 1,009 reservoir members were there. (Members were no doubt eager to participate – but we also later heard stories that PP had threated to fine those who did not come.) By the time we arrived, the issue was mostly resolved, but one could see the frames of makeshift shelters where villagers had slept. Around the reservoir they put poles with small Cambodian flags – and under them (conspicuous, since the village had voted for SRP in commune elections) flags with the logo of the dominant CPP (Figure 12.1). Reservoir representatives told us (as did PP when later interviewed) that they were not protesting – they were appealing to the authorities for mercy to spare the reservoir. A helicopter with the Minister of Water Resources and Mineralogy had flown over to inspect the site. Journalists had come from Phnom Penh (but were no longer there when we arrived.) A team of representatives from the different ministries involved visited and finally gave them demarcation markers. They told them to very carefully demarcate the reservoir land boundaries, implying that it would be spared when the demolition of reservoirs finally occurred. This also meant there could be no further clearing of land outside the border markers once they were established. On July 6 they submitted a formal letter petitioning that the reservoir be spared; it was stamped already as having been received by the subdistrict chief, the district chief and the head of the provincial committee; presumably it was to pass on to Hun Sen. That the reservoir would not be demolished was confirmed later to us by a provincial official.

On one visit, PP told Chhuon Hoeur, somewhat arrogantly, that he was the only person qualified to be subdistrict chief. He subsequently stood as CPP candidate for subdistrict chief in the 2012 local elections and won. There has nevertheless continued to be criticism of PP in some sectors of the subdistrict. On a short visit in 2012, soon after he was elected, several villagers told us he had gone too far, and there were stories that he was involved with a group of entrepreneurs illegally clearing areas in the flooded forest inside a now clearly demarcated protected area. (He may have only been involved to the extent that his equipment was used.) We sought him out the day before leaving; he was nowhere to be found, and family members seemed genuinely puzzled that they could not contact him by phone. The following day, on the bus to Phnom Penh, we learned by phone that he had been arrested for his connection with the illegal clearings, together with two other persons – one the Kampong Thom provincial chief for the Ministry of Water Resources. The arrests were reported on national television and in newspapers. (These reports said that further arrests would take place; however, this never happened, suggesting that the three arrested were scapegoats, or that their arrests were intended to frighten others into escaping arrest by bribes.) According to his relatives, he throughout this period had the support of provincial council president Nam Tum, although this was not enough for him to escape a 1-year prison term. During this year, the previous subdistrict chief (representing an opposition party) re-assumed his duties.

Released after 1 year, PP was met at the prison door by a lawyer for Nam Tum who brought him by car to a large Buddhist temple in Phnom Penh where an uncle was head of the wat committee and the abbot is also from Samprouch. There he participated in an elaborate water blessing ceremony intended to liberate him from negative forces accumulated during imprisonment and elevate him to higher spiritual levels of power. Even though, according to Cambodian law, someone with a criminal record may not serve in political office, he was allowed to re-assume his position as subdistrict chief. We made a brief visit to the subdistrict not long after this; the villagers seemed disinclined to talk about his case. In the national elections, held soon after this, in late July, 2013 (not involving any voting for local officials), the subdistrict went for the Cambodian National Rescue Party, a party newly created by the merger of two opposition parties.

While PP's arrest points to the government's determination not to permit reservoirs in newly demarcated protected areas surrounding the Tonle Sap lake, already existing reservoirs, including the people's reservoir, are no longer questioned, and do not seem to be at risk.

Conclusions

What generalizations can we make about changing landscapes, processes of 'exclusion' and community mobilization? We see the events described here as reflecting a major shift in land regime which has to do, not just with new land laws, but changing economic relations and changing relations of the state and other actors to natural resources. Clearly the fact of change draws attention to the fact that relations of 'property' can be ambiguous and subject to negotiation. The situation we examine occurs in an environmentally vulnerable zone at a time of environmental change. The complexities of this setting are then overlaid with the introduction of new irrigation techniques, the exploitation of which is further intensified and complicated by changing property relationships and a general trend towards commodification.

What we describe is a historical adjustment to change, which to some degree could be called 'resistance' – not resistance in the sense of a unified, militant struggle but in a more fluid sense of negotiation, re-adjustment, and, sometimes, compromise. We see degrees of defeat, but we also see rural communities mobilizing in what seems to be new ways – ways which suggest grassroots empowerment but also involve exclusion of other villagers.

From a strictly environmental point of view, the people's reservoir was a negative development, in that it involved further intrusion into the area of flooded forests on the Tonle Sap floodplain. In political terms, it may have in some sense represented defeat, to the degree that the population of a subdistrict which had voted for an opposition party was in the end putting up flags of the dominant party and appealing to it for mercy. One can also say that the people's reservoir was less than successful in the degree to which it was plagued by internal disputes. Nevertheless, we find something positive in the very fact that a group of rice farmers could come together to the extent of creating a working alternative to the privately owned reservoirs that were springing up around them and seemingly squeezing them out of their livelihood.

The people's reservoir did not have the kind of state encouragement that in recent years has been given to community-based natural resource management or Farmer Water User Groups or agricultural cooperatives in other contexts. They did not succeed in getting the kinds of official recognition that these groups did. Nevertheless, we believe that the zeitgeist in which these other kinds of new rural organization flourished may have something to do with the movement created around the people's reservoir. The community came together first out of protest and then out of a common desire to create opportunity for themselves in a difficult situation.

As Marston has written elsewhere (1997, 2005), one must be very careful in applying the term 'patron-clientism' to Cambodia – a term which in its classical formulation referred to stable, longstanding relationships of mutual benefit among actors of markedly different social status – exemplified iconically in the relationship between landlord and tenant-contexts which are not typically found in Cambodia. For want of a better term, we use 'patron-clientism' as it is often used in writing about Cambodia, to refer to any sort of personalized, dyadic relationship with a hierarchical dimension and the suggestion of mutual aid in a chain of such relations. (PP's relationship to provincial council president Nam Tum was, to all appearances, a very recent development, but came to carry enough weight when trouble hit that we can accurately describe it in terms of patronage.) Such relationships are not merely vestiges of 'traditional' life, but deeply entwined with all sorts of 'modern' institutions that are evolving. They can also be very fluid and changing; patron-clientism is not in practice a conservative institution.

The culture of Cambodian rural society puts great emphasis on the sense of justice – an emphasis which may be coloured by the years of socialism, but also no doubt derives from the imperatives of living close to subsistence levels. As in any society, there is indignation over injustice, and it is not surprising that this readily translates into social mobilization.

At the same time, our case study shows how a cultural disposition to patron-clientism (as we have defined it) becomes a factor in the way mobilization plays itself out – in the ways, for example, PP's relationship developed with villagers and provincial-level power brokers – but also in the way some villagers chose to oppose the people's reservoir. It is as though underlying cultural assumptions have their own intuitive logic: for an institution to be durable, it must be enmeshed in patron-client relations.

We do not see political ideology as playing a strong role with the villagers, so much as indignation and practicality. The election of an opposition-party candidate as subdistrict chief in 2007 demonstrates well that in the context of land and water disputes, villagers do take dissatisfaction to the polls. Nevertheless, there was enough commonsense practicality coming into play that, for instance, when there was fear that the reservoir would be razed, members were willing to put up the dominant party's flag and show deference to it while appealing for the reservoir to be saved. PP's subsequent election as subdistrict chief (running for the dominant CPP) may have been further recognition of the practicality of CPP being in power at that particular moment – as well as the simple acknowledgement of his leadership skills. We do not know if the subdistrict's voting for an opposition party in 2013 national elections – part of a surge occurring throughout the country – can be said to be related at all to reservoirs disputes. No doubt the fact that they voted for the opposition previously made it easier for them to do so again. The overall impression is of villagers who will vote in whatever way seems to make practical sense to them, without any great sense that they are beholden to those in power.

Notes

1 The principal fieldwork for this paper was conducted during a 4-month period of research in 2010 with the support of the Center for Khmer Studies with funds from the Committee for American Overseas Research Centers (CAORC).

A 'people's' irrigation reservoir on the Tonle Sap floodplain   255

2 Yet another factor may have been, as one farmer told us, that in the 1980s there were no merchants buying rice in the dry season. The intensification of dry-rice agriculture at the present time comes together with merchants who will buy it – so it makes sense in a way that it didn't in the mid-1980s.
3 Our access to villagers was facilitated by the fact that Chhuon Hoeur is a native of the subdistrict.
4 The controversial Order 01BB initiative, with its plan for an intensive campaign of land titling with the help of teams of youth, began to be implemented in 2012, and as such falls after most of our research, and the narrative of most of the events in this chapter. It nevertheless also points to intensification of the Cambodian government's activity in this direction.
5 Our request to see a copy of the contracts issued by the province and the reservoir owners was denied, and we are uncertain of the exact provisions as well as the underlying logic of this 40 per cent requirement. We speculate that it derives from attempts at safeguards written into the original law – which were, nevertheless, increasingly easy to ignore.
6 Evidence of this possibility is the fact that the Cambodian Development Commission (CDC) has maps which indicate large tracks of the floodplain as possible sites for investors to develop as major, large-scale land concessions. There have already been feasibility studies by Chinese firms into these tracks of land (pers. comm. with anonymous source), which have, however, not resulted in concrete projects. The firm Leopard Capital also attempted to concretize a large project in the floodplain which would have authorization at the national level.

Yet another dimension of the situation is the fact that petroleum has been found in the Tonle Sap Lake and will eventually be exploited. This could be another factor in motivating the state to restrict control of the floodplain areas.
7 It is true that more recent land concession contracts are more likely to stipulate that traditional forms of access to resources – for example, fish ponds – will be maintained.
8 David Harvey (2003), in attempting to develop the concept of primitive accumulation with reference to the present time, uses the term 'accumulation by dispossession'.
9 The SRP candidate was the brother of his opponent, the incumbent subdistrict council chief. The actual political implications of this are unclear, since the power of the new council chief was significantly circumscribed and most decisions continue to be made by CPP. The new subdistrict council chief, however, has been a supporter of the people's reservoir.
10 He also happens to be the cousin of a well-known monk who is now the abbot of a wat in Phnom Penh.
11 One claim used to discredit him is that he used money contributed to the people's reservoir by its members to buy his reservoir.
12 A group of 800 families supported C, who was offering an arrangement whereby farmers could work land fed by his reservoir, paying them between 800 kg to 1,000 kg of rice for each hectare they worked.

References

Cambodian Development Resource Institute (CDRI). (2008) *Framing Research on Water Resources Management and Governance in Cambodia: A Literature Review*, CDRI, Phnom Penh, Cambodia.
Cambodian Development Resource Institute (CDRI). (2010) *Empirical Evidence of Irrigation management in the Tonle Sap Basin: Issues and Challenges*, CDRI Working Paper Series No. 28 (Working Draft), CDRI, Phnom Penh, Cambodia.

Center for Advanced Study (CAS). (2006) *Justice for the Poor? An Exploratory Study of Collective Grievances and Land and Local Governance in Cambodia*, Center for Advanced Study, World Bank, Phnom Penh, Cambodia.

Chem, P., Hirsch, P. and Paradis, S. (2011) *Hydrological Analysis in Support of Irrigation Management: A Case Study of Stung Chrey Bak Catchment, Cambodia*, CDRI Working Paper Series No. 59, Cambodia Development Resource Center, Phnom Penh, Cambodia.

Chou, C. (2010) *The Local Governance of Commonpool Resources: The Case of Irrigation Water in Cambodia*, CDRI, Phnom Penh, Cambodia.

Diepart, J. -C. (2007a) 'Problèmes et enjeux de l'économie rurale au Cambodge: Entre nouvelles gouvernances et réalités paysannes: Le cas de la province de Kampong Thom', PhD thesis, Communauté Praciase de Belgique, Acadamie Universitaire Wallonie-Bruxelles, Faculté Universitaire des Sciences Agronomiques de Gembloux.

Diepart, J. -C. (2007b) 'Recent land dynamics in the Tonle Sap flood plain and its impact on the local communities', *Tonle Sap Biosphere Reserve Bulletin* 3, pp. 20–22, Tonle Sap Biosphere Reserve Secretariat, Phnom Penh, Cambodia.

Diepart, J. -C. (2010) 'Cambodian peasant's contribution to rural development: A perspective from Kampong Thom province', *Biotechnology, Agronomy, Society and Environment* 14(2), pp. 321–340.

Fox, J. and Ledgerwood, J. (1999) 'Dry-season flood-recession rice in the Mekong Delta: Two thousand years of sustainable agriculture?' *Asian Perspectives* 38(1), pp. 37–50.

Gālaen. (2011) 'Krum Tavā Pit Phlūv Jāt Lek 6 Jañ 6 Moṅ Dām Dār Ti niṅ Sumqoy Ṭoḥ Leṅ Birunth Jan Mnâk', *Rāsmī Kambujā*, July 9, pp. 1, 6.

Hall, D., Hirsch, P. and Murray Li, T. (2011) *Powers of Exclusion: Land Dilemmas in Southeast Asia*, University of Hawai'i Press, Honolulu.

Harvey, D. (2003) *The New Imperialism*, Oxford University Press, New York.

Kaṅchestā, V. (2011) 'Pātukamm Pid Kamṇât Phlūv Jāt Lek 6A Sdaḥ Charāchar Râp Moṅ', *Kambujā Thmī*, July 9, pp. 1, 4.

Khiev, D. (2010) 'Challenge of participant irrigation management in Cambodia: The case of Damnak Ampil Irrigation Scheme', MA thesis, University of Sydney, NSW.

Khouth, S. (2011) 'Progress made on illegal reservoirs', *Phnom Penh Post*, March 9 2011, http://www.phnompenhpost.com/national/progress-made-illegal-reservoirs, accessed 9 March 2011.

Marston, J. (1997) 'Cambodia 1991–1994: Hierarchy, neutrality and etiquettes of discourse', PhD thesis, University of Washington, Seattle.

Marston, J. (2005) 'Review Essay: Post-Pol Pot Cambodia', *Critical Asian Studies* 37(3), pp. 501–516.

Marston, J. (2011) 'Introduction', in J. Marston (ed.) *Anthropology and Community in Cambodia: Reflections on the Work of May Ebihara*, Monash University Press, Caufield, pp. 5–20.

Middleton, C. and Prom, T. (2008) 'Community organization for managing water resources around Tonle Sap Lake: A myth or a reality', in M. Kummu, M. Keskinen, O. Varls, (eds) *Modern Myths of the Mekong*, Helsinki University of Technology, Helsinki, pp. 149–159.

Ngo, S. and Chan S. (2010) *Does Large Scale Agricultural Investment Benefit the Poor?* Cambodian Economic Association, Phnom Penh, Cambodia.

O'Connor, R. (1995) 'Agricultural change and ethnic succession in Southeast Asian states: A case for regional anthropology', *Journal of Asian Studies* 54 (4), pp. 968–996.

Öjendal, J. (2000) 'Sharing the good: Modes of managing water resources in the Lower Mekong River Basin', PhD thesis, Göteborg University, Sweden.

Ostrom, E. (1990) *Governing the Commons: The Evolution of Institutions for Collective Action*, Cambridge University Press, Cambridge, New York.

Ros, B. (2010) 'Participatory irrigation management and factors that influence the success of farmer-water user communities: A case study in Cambodia', MA thesis, Massey University, NZ.

Ros, B., Tem, L. and Thompson, A. (2011) *Catchment Governance and Cooperative Dilemmas: A Case Study from Cambodia*, CDRI Working Paper Series No. 61, Cambodia Development Resource Institute, Phnom Penh, Cambodia.

Slocomb, M. (2010) *An Economic History of Cambodia in the Twentieth Century*, NUS Press, Singapore.

Zhou, D. (2007) *A Record of Cambodia: The Land and Its People*, Peter Harris, Silkworm Books, tr. Chiang Mai.

13 Story-telling and social change

A case study of the Prey Lang Community Network

Terry Parnell[1]

Prey Lang[2] is OUR forest. Prey Lang is YOUR forest, too.

Figure 13.1 Kuy woman dressed as an avatar. Pregnant, she completes a long protest walk through the forest. When the child is born, she names it Prey Lang.

Source: Photo by Samrang Priang, Reuters

This is a mantra of Cambodia's Prey Lang Community Network (PLCN), a grassroots group advocating for the Prey Lang forest, made up of people from the Kuy ethnic minority, and other indigenous and non-indigenous forest communities. The PLCN burst into Cambodia's national consciousness in May 2011 after about 200 members and allies painted themselves blue and presented themselves as Cambodia's 'avatars' during a Phnom Penh demonstration.[3] Prey Lang, in north central Cambodia west of the Mekong River, is the last large lowland dry evergreen forest in mainland Southeast Asia, a biodiversity treasure house of internationally recognized significance. It also has high carbon sequestration values and is an important watershed for Cambodia's rice basin. Despite the critical ecological services it provides and its vast size – at least 350,000 ha spanning the intersection of four provinces: Kampong Thom, Preah Vihear, Stung Treng and Kratie – few Cambodians were aware of its existence before the PLCN put it on the map in 2011.

The PLCN has doggedly defended the forest from encroachment while persisting in their demand that Prey Lang not only be conserved but sustainably managed in cooperation with them and forest communities. They have become a national symbol of the land and natural resources rights movement. This is extraordinary in a country where until recently it was widely believed that there was no real social movement, that the majority of poor rural Cambodians lacked the agency and organization to sustain resistance against rampant social injustice characterized by land grabbing and resource capture by Cambodia's elite. The exceptional nature of this achievement is underscored by the fact that just 5 years ago, Prey Lang was remote and barely accessible by roads, making even access between villages difficult. Telephone coverage was limited and unreliable and only minimal government services were available. As a result, poverty rates were high,[4] literacy rates were low and few people living there had ever ventured beyond the forest and nearby villages. The identity of the Kuy, the majority population, an indigenous group who has occupied this area for generations, was fractured, with many Kuy and mixed Kuy disassociated from their ethnic origins.

So what is it that has distinguished the PLCN from the many other Cambodian networks, coalitions and community-based groups that are also advocating their land rights? And how and why did this network emerge in this unlikely situation?

The answers are complex and open to interpretation from a variety of perspectives. This chapter looks at one aspect that this author believes was of fundamental importance to both the network's development and their challenge to forest encroachment; that is, the distinctive role that *narrative*, or stories and story-telling, has played in the evolution of the network, their community organizing, the shaping and delivery of their advocacy to save the forest and the resilience of their stance. The chapter first describes how narrative supported early organizing, delving into the network's background and history and looking at how through story-telling an innovative vision for forest management emerged. It discusses how the PLCN used stories to shape and share their advocacy message to Cambodians and the world, and it considers challenges associated with story-telling in the PLCN's evolution.

Narrative as an organizing tool

The role of narrative has been largely overlooked in the study of social movements despite the central role that story-telling plays (Fine, 1995; Davis, 2002; Fortmann, 1995).

> Neglect from this quarter is especially surprising because social movements are dominated by stories and story-telling, and narrative goes to the heart of the very cultural and ideational processes these scholars have been addressing, including frames, rhetoric, interpretation, public discourse, movement culture, and collective identity.
>
> (Davis, 2002, p. 2)

Marshall Ganz suggests that story is an essential source of social movement power and vital for developing strategy, noting a historical tendency for scholars to focus on discourse analysis. He says that 'story-telling is central to social movements because it constructs agency, shapes identity, and motivates action' (Ganz, 2001, p. 3).

The PLCN's story and their own telling of it illustrates this. However, while much of Ganz's teaching about community organizing, derived from decades of experience in America's civil rights and labour movements, focuses on how to use stories as intentional tools, this chapter examines an organic and intuitive process through which a network of forest community activists and their campaign was born. Arguably, both the network itself and its vision for the forest, emerged – at least in part – from an iterative and natural process of story-telling. This informed the PLCN's development and helped to motivate and galvanize its advocacy and forest protection, while also strengthening their indigenous identity. The chapter also describes how the network began using story-telling, again in a natural and intuitive way, to engage others and build national and international support.

'Stories' are typically characterized as narratives with plots that have a beginning, a middle and an end (Roe, 1991), but the way in which the PLCN uses narrative reflects their own cultural and social representation of story. The development of a story and all its subplots unfold over many iterations, across weeks, months, even years. The framing and details of a story evolve not just to fit an immediate purpose but to accommodate and respond to challenges to the narrative and threats to the forest and its inhabitants. The experience of an evolving narrative reflects the storytellers' and the network's deepening analyses and emerging vision over time. The exact beginning and middle, and supporting details, change many times; the end is often anticipated but not yet known.

As a social process, story-telling need not be empirical. The PLCN's narrative evolution may not represent facts so much as an attempt to create a shared 'truth'. As their narrative evolved, consensus was also built. This is the unifying power of narrative, simplifying complexity, allowing a common vision to emerge (Roe, 1991) and serving as a metaphor for resistance (Fortmann, 1995).

History of Kuy people in north central Cambodia

Prior to 2000, indigenous Kuy[5] and other forest communities lived relatively undisturbed in much the same way their ancestors had for centuries. Even Bayon temple bas reliefs depicting indigenous people, as early as the 12th century, could have been mistaken for those of Kuy and other forest communities in recent times. The Kuy's relation to the Angkorian kingdom appears to have included both market relations (Keating, 2013) and tribute payments.

Broadly grouped with other indigenous people they called Montagnards,[6] the French mostly ignored the Kuy during the colonial period. In the post-colonial era, however, the Sihanouk-led Cambodian government, attempted the assimilation of all indigenous people then termed 'Khmer Loeu' or Khmer highlanders (Bourdier, 2009, cited in Swift, 2013; Baird, 2011). Local administrators were appointed to Kuy areas and Khmer in-migration increased. A new province – Preah Vihear – was split from Kampong Thom, demonstrating new interest in state control over the predominately Kuy area as it was brought under increasing administration.

In the 1960s, assimilation was resisted by indigenous groups in the northeastern province of Ratanakiri, a movement that was eventually co-opted by the Khmer Rouge. There is no record of any similar modern resistance by the Kuy,[7] despite their being one of the country's largest indigenous groups.[8] In the 1970s, assimilation was promoted aggressively by the Khmer Rouge regime who punished the Kuy for speaking their indigenous language (Swift, 2013). Kuy communities were also resettled in lowland areas away from forests, or in newly cleared areas, where they were impressed into rice production. Even after the Khmer Rouge were forced from power in 1979, their domination of some Kuy areas continued well into the 1980s and 1990s,[9] further diminishing Kuy identity. Only some Kuy returned to their former forest communities, while others settled new forest areas or stayed where they were. Following the dissolution of the Khmer Rouge in the late 1990s, Kuy identity was further challenged by renewed and increasing in-migration of Khmer, facilitated by the construction of new roads from 1998 on (Keating, 2013; Baird, 2011). This was exacerbated by the awarding of logging concessions in Kuy areas (Keating, 2013). Not surprisingly, Khmer identity was adopted by large numbers of Cambodia's Kuy people (Swift, 2013). The loss of the Kuy language both reflected and contributed to this trend. Many of Swift's informants expressed the sentiment that to be Kuy one must be able to speak the language and that those who had lost the language are now Khmer (Swift, 2013).

Emerging concerns regarding logging and concessions

In 2002, a grassroots initiative against logging concessions surprised the Cambodian government and the World Bank (WB), which had promoted logging concessions as a way to support sustainable use of Cambodia's forests and to centralize collection of logging royalties. Cambodia's forest communities were alarmed by the pace of deforestation that accompanied logging concessions, threatening their livelihoods and local economies which were largely dependent on non-timber forest products. During an NGO-sponsored meeting in Phnom Penh in 2002, hundreds of forest community representatives from around the country learned that logging concessions, technically subject to the law, were intended to be transparent. That motivated dozens of them to descend on Forest Administration (FA) and WB offices to demand copies of management plans, required of companies by law and intended to be publicly accessible. Neither agency was able to provide the requested documentation. After several days of demonstrations, the Cambodian government quelled the protests by force. In the ensuing melee, a Prey Lang area forest activist, shocked with an electric baton, suffered a heart attack and died (personally conducted interviews with Peter Swift, 19 February 2014 and Sao Sokol 13 and 20 February 2014.) These and other events embarrassed the WB and reflected poorly on Cambodia. Eventually, faced with a formal complaint led by the local NGO Forum, backed up by Global Witness, the WB withdrew from the program, precipitating the Prime Minister's subsequent cancellation of concessions already logged and suspension of those not exhausted. Grassroots activists, who had taken their active non-violent strategy from a similar movement by Cambodia's fishers only 2 years before, hailed this as an important victory, even though their part in precipitating the decree was not widely recognized by the public.

With the forest concessions cancelled or suspended and with the support of a small international NGO whose charismatic expatriate director was trusted around Prey Lang, local activists, along with sympathetic NGO workers and local authorities, began to discuss the idea of commune forestry, a type of cooperative forestry to be undertaken at the commune rather than village level, and thereby offering more protection across a greater landscape. The initiative went so far as drawing up rules for forest use. Among other things, communities committed to maintaining the core zone free of motorcycles, restricting exploitation of certain forest resources and participating in patrols (ibid).

The *national* trend, however, was regulated towards *community* forestry (CF), a form of cooperative forestry at village level, administered by the Forestry Administration. With both donor support and new government regulation focused on this one modality,[10] the idea of commune forestry, another form of cooperative forestry at a broader landscape level, was forgotten. Prey Lang communities received no official support and their initiative languished.

In the meantime, from 2005 to 2010, Prey Lang was among several critical biodiversity areas repeatedly nominated for protection by conservation groups including Conservation International, and some government technocrats. Despite its clear importance, Prey Lang's conservation was rejected again and again, likely because its logging values were so high. Prey Lang remained unprotected.

In 2007, Prey Lang and its broader landscape figured prominently in Global Witness's, *Cambodia's Family Trees,* an investigative report which revealed the extent to which Cambodia's political leaders had profited from both the forest concessions and illegal logging. The government swiftly denounced and banned the report. Prey Lang was further marginalized. For several years after this, when activists questioned officials about Prey Lang or advocated its protection, they were told that Prey Lang did not exist or were asked to locate where the mythical Prey Lang was. Conservation groups by then were also reluctant to become involved in Prey Lang, deeming it too hot an issue or engaging in strictly apolitical, often government-friendly discussion behind the scenes.

Despite the fundamental ecological services it provides to downstream rice and fisheries, Cambodians outside of the immediate forest area, remained mostly ignorant of Prey Lang's existence, having never even heard its name.

PLCN's origins and the role of narrative

The PLCN began to emerge as an informal organization after 2007 when, funded by USAID, international NGO East West Management Institute, working with local NGO partners, began resourcing meetings of activists and forest community members across the forest. Although some illegal logging continued, the forest had remained mostly intact, even though areas to the south were largely compromised first by heavy logging and later by tree plantations. An estimated 80,000–100,000 ha core zone still harboured valuable and rare luxury wood and other endangered species; biologically unique riparian areas thrived. Nevertheless, cognizant of deforestation and land conversion trends around the country, local communities remained concerned. In addition, they had become increasingly discouraged without support to follow through on earlier promising discussions and plans for commune forestry. The injection of funds to support their meetings and communication with one another was welcomed, particularly since news from other parts of Cambodia suggested that the government's adoption of economic land concessions as a vehicle for land conversion represented an even more destructive policy than that of forest concessions. The example of the 6,200 ha Tumring rubber plantation – replacing dense forest – just to their south in Kampong Thom's Santuk District was a clarion call for some activists.[11]

Early meetings, initially organized and facilitated by NGOs, quickly became focused on story-telling and conversations in which participants would recount their historical and cultural links with the forest, describe the forest's value to themselves and others, analyse both internal and external threats and plan forest protection. Stories were an anchoring point for every meeting. While rambling tales were first construed by facilitators and observers as digressions, it soon became clear that these stories were helping the group to internally validate their forest claims and to distinguish themselves as forest protectors, distinct from intruders and other exploiters (whether local or external). Stories relating to their customary livelihoods emphasized their dependence on and knowledge of the forest, and their rightful place within it. Traditional stories, including mythical tales about animals, divine creatures and even Cambodia's royal family, established long cultural ties. While many stories were familiar, speaking them out loud with one another reinforced their traditional identity in the contemporary context.

Many initial narratives focused on threats, describing problems and who was involved with them, but also discussing how offenders were violating indigenous social norms. The threads of these stories often continued over months. An initial story about a problem would devolve into a situational analysis which led to both ideas and consensus-building for interventions. At subsequent meetings, the narrative would continue with accounts detailing actions taken and the responses to them. Archetypes emerged: large companies and veiled intruders were the villains, local interlopers were potential converts and the activists were forest guardians and defenders. This casting of roles differentiated their identity from other forest stakeholders and strengthened their confidence. In the telling of this moral tale, they increasingly represented themselves as vanguards in the fight to save the forest. The government and Cambodia's leaders were initially portrayed as 'parents' who were expected to protect their 'children'. There was considerable debate about how to appeal to the parent for help and compassion.

Meeting participants drew on their historical and cultural links to the forest in narratives that evolved to fit and respond to new threats.[12] For generations, traditional stories had warned against felling giant trees, believed to house powerful spirits, by recounting how past instances had been followed by illnesses or other bad luck. In their new telling, such stories became cautionary tales about the dangers of leaving the forest unguarded. Community members talked about how tree spirits, once considered invincible, were afraid of bulldozers and chainsaws and needed protection, even as they had historically protected forest communities. This was validated by real-life stories of other communities, holding similar beliefs, around the nation. For instance, in meetings with other grassroots activists in Phnom Penh, villagers from a formerly forested area in Kampong Speu told how their community had fallen on bad luck after failing to stop deforestation. One woman said that since her community had not defended the nature spirits, they had lost their protectors and descended into terrible times characterized by water shortages, falling soil fertility, continuing land grabbing and loss of important forest resources. As the implications of deforestation were made clear, inside the network, cautionary tales devolved into apocryphal warnings of what would ensue if the forest was lost. This represents a way in which cultural norms as expressed through stories may serve as informal forest management institutions, thereby supporting conservation (Ostrom, 1990).

Although Khmer was the primary language in meetings, one important Kuy linguistic element was fundamental in shaping the activists' story about the forest. The Khmer name *Prey Lang* is derived from the Kuy, *Koh Lang*, which means *our forest*.[13] The notion that the forest was a shared legacy was a basis for solidarity. It was only natural then that, in the network's incipient stages, activists had already embraced the idea that Prey Lang belongs to everyone, not just its communities. This made the Prey Lang story distinct from that of others around the country who, when responding to land or resource rights conflicts, typically descended into complaints about personal property rights and litanies of personal suffering. While such concerns are both grave and legitimate, and certainly shared by Prey Lang communities, the activists' early identification of the forest as a broadly shared communal resource ultimately gave rise to the idea that PLCN members are not just protecting the forest but are in fact protecting the entire country, even the world, unto future generations.[14]

Instead of focusing solely on individual and community losses of resources, many early network members' stories described ecological services vital to farmers and fishers downstream and warned of potential impacts. This framing of the forest as a communal asset and a heritage for Cambodia's future eventually became a cornerstone in the network's advocacy, one that was picked up on and accentuated in a short video, *Prey Lang: One Forest, One Future*, and it remains fundamental to PLCN's campaign. It was critical in shaping activists' views of themselves as heroes and forest defenders and galvanizing actions that otherwise might have been considered too bold and presumptuous in the Cambodian socio-cultural and political context. This included, over time, a shift away from characterizing themselves as children and the government as parents to a more pro-active projection of themselves as good citizens upholding the law and policing corrupt authorities. While traditional state-society dynamics had constrained resistance, the new paradigm compelled action against poor or unjust governance.

By extension and through the story-telling and discursive process, activists concluded that everyone and anyone can (and should) help to save the forest. This message of responsibility, became another cornerstone in their messaging, and opened the way for a more inclusive campaign than Cambodia had seen to date.

While Khmer and Kuy NGO workers were the main facilitators at this stage, meetings were informal affairs wherein an introductory open-ended question (such as 'what's happening?') would typically progress from story-telling to a conversation between participants that included clarification, analysis, problem-solving and action-planning. Facilitators even prodded participants for and reminded them of their history, including how they had helped end forest concessions and attempted cooperative protection. A repetitive re-telling of this was crucial to participants owning the process, rather than just showing up for an NGO-directed activity; moreover, the collaborative nature of story-telling contributed to consensus-building around both identity and action (personally conducted interview with Pyrou Chung, 22 January 2014). This process gave birth to the network's creation story, detailing their early resistance. It differed from the original tale, pieced together through the recollections of only a few, to describe more organization and a stronger sense of collective agency and intent than had perhaps existed at the time. Nevertheless, it was key to the network claiming the forest protection agenda as their own and not one foisted on them by NGOs.

The best facilitators concentrated on clarifying and deepening questions, identifying inconsistencies or gaps in reasoning, encouraging the contributions of more reticent participants, especially women, keeping the conversation on track when digressions occurred and maintaining continuity from meeting to meeting. This light facilitation role, of a type described by O'Leary and Nee (2001), encouraged discussion *between participants* rather than directing responses to the facilitator. This was central to relationship-building, transferring facilitation skills and roles to the group itself over time and contributing to a stronger sense of shared agency. Participants detailing threats to their communities, and themselves, were challenged to posit responses to the dangers the stories described. Speaking their plans out loud amounted to commitments which then drew in others, increasing the likelihood that plans would be acted on between meetings. Those interventions then became fodder for new stories that focused on their bold actions (personally conducted interview with Pyrou Chung, 22 January 2014). At this stage, those actions mostly targeted local threats such as a community member clearing forest for personal use. The subsequent recounting of an intervention usually told how a group had confronted their fellow, convinced him of the forests' value – usually by using the narratives already developed through the PLCN's internal dialogue – secured a pledge to stop the clearing, and gained a convert. Conversion stories, which also extended to gaining participation of other community members, became more common in the narrative process.

Clearly, story-telling was a critical and culturally appropriate way for participating community members to present and describe issues of concern and build shared agency. Stories which recounted personal and/or community experience, as well as drawing on traditional cultural and spiritual beliefs and mythos, resonated strongly with participants and created opportunities for story-driven analysis that segued seamlessly into problem-solving. The iterative nature of the story-telling, wherein particular narratives would be repeated and embellished with new episodes over successive meetings, resulted in the evolutionary re-framing of stories to accommodate and respond to new problems and shifts in identity and agency. The Kuy-based name, 'Prey Lang', remained an important linguistic device as they elaborated on and extended the story of the forest to include various versions of the future and their role in it. The willingness of NGO facilitators to encourage story-telling followed by conversational analysis and problem-solving was fundamental. It was through this lightly guided iterative process that the shared identity of an actual network emerged.[15]

The case of community forests: Using stories to challenge norms and posit alternatives

Story-telling also shaped the young PLCN's rejection of conventional CF, and led to them challenging status quo development practices which include hierarchical patron-client relationships between government, donors, NGO agents and communities.[16]

Following the cancellation of forest concessions in late 2002, CF quickly gained the support of technocrats, donors and NGO workers as the primary response to grassroots discontent. A sub-decree on community forests was promulgated in 2003. In 2010, the government adopted CF as a key element of the National Forest Programme 2010–2030, mandating one million hectares of community forest to be recognized by 2015. Although the National Forest Programme described six modalities for community-cooperative forest management – including ones that mirrored what Prey Lang communities had discussed in the early 2000s – only the CF model was developed and hence it was the only model implemented.

Whether the motivation was genuinely to protect the rights of forest-dependent communities is a matter of some debate, especially since this era saw the rise of economic land concessions wherein large forest areas were leased to companies to clear and convert them to agricultural production. Hundreds of communities around the country were engaged in preliminary CF planning processes, mostly managed by NGOs who had been solicited for their roles in donor-initiated projects, and premised on four linked assumptions: (1) communities would want to engage in CF, (2) CFs would be adequate to protect both the forest and community forest rights even though other laws were weakly enforced, (3) no other model for recognizing customary (forest) rights or engaging in cooperative forest management and protection was legal or even possible and (4) by virtue of the fact that CF efforts were donor-funded, often NGO-led, and agreed with the government, communities should comply.

In 2009, the idea of CF was introduced to Prey Lang communities in Kampong Thom by various NGOs. Several communities, led by the incipient network, rejected the intervention, and actively discouraged others. Many

NGO workers implementing CF programs were concerned that those NGOs working most closely with the PLCN were responsible for their challenge to the model; that the network was externally influenced against CFs. In fact, it was story-telling between community groups that motivated their response. With many activists now travelling more, participating in workshops with other people from around the country, they were frequently exposed to stories about communities who had accepted CF but had bad experiences. These included reports of communities denied the customary use areas they had requested only to be given rights over inferior forest or even deforested and degraded land instead. Some villages were far from their CFs and some CFs were too small to sustainably and fairly accommodate all the participating households. They also heard about communities pressed to give up any claim to forest beyond their CFs, how economic land concessions with up to 90 year leases, were subsequently surrounding and encroaching CFs which had agreements lasting only 15 years, with their continuation conditional upon the communities sustaining and profitably managing them. They heard how hard it was to defend CFs against encroachment, particularly when military or other powerful interests were involved. Network fears were further borne out by the government's 'leopard skin' policy, an approach through which community land would be conservatively determined and remaining 'state-owned' land provided to concessionaires, making villages and CFs islands in a landscape increasingly dominated by concessions. CFs appeared to be a way to contain communities in small areas, structurally breaking stakeholders into discrete groups, effectively annulling their claims to the greater forest and further dissociating them from each other.[17] Keeping in mind that Prey Lang activists had already been working to defend the forest as a whole, the conventional approach to introducing CFs was met with resistance. Stories from other parts of the country were repeated to Prey Lang communities, and in PLCN meetings they informed analysis of options. In the midst of this, a visiting consultant offered the idea that a forest is a living organism, similar to a person's body. The idea reinforced the network's intuition to advocate for the protection and sustainable management of the forest in its entirety and to resist a CF model isolating pockets of forest (and communities) from one another. The analogy was adopted into the lexicon of the network. Activists routinely explain the forest as an organism to outsiders, noting that if you would not cut a person's body into pieces why would you do the same to a forest.

Such a cross-fertilization of ideas between local communities and various outsiders, including other Cambodian activists, and Khmer and expatriate NGO workers, as well as advocates from other countries, is another distinguishing feature of PLCN's development. PLCN's broad interaction with others, often enabled by NGOs and national and even regional civil society networks, especially the Community Peacebuilding Network (CPN), represents a multi-layered flow of 'social production' wherein new ideas, introduced through narrative and discourse with external participants, are absorbed and reframed for the local context (Appadurai, 1990; Tsing, 2005).

The PLCN's opposition to conventional CFs put the nascent network in direct conflict with both NGOs working on CFs and the FA since they were not just rejecting an accepted intervention but also challenging the social hierarchy of its delivery. Relief only came when donor interest declined and as a result CF organizing efforts in the area waned for a time. In 2013–2014, renewed NGO/government attempts to settle Prey Lang community complaints, at least partly via CFs, met the same arguments as before. However, this time the network had concrete evidence to support themselves: a mapping initiative begun by the PLCN in 2013 found that as many as a third of the CFs in the greater PL area were no longer viable and that another third were under duress. They continued to call for co-management of the entirety of the forest.[18]

While this dynamic was seen by government authorities and some NGOs as mostly contentious (with the PLCN often viewed as obstructionist, obstinate or unrealistic), in fact, it was through story-telling and accompanying analysis that network members challenged a status quo and began to articulate a new vision for the forest and a potential positive end to their evolving story. The unfolding narrative became an opportunity to posit alternative forest management approaches that would not only protect critical ecosystems but also respect indigenous heritage and resource rights, stabilize local economies and leverage the power of communities to guard large areas of forest because it is in their own best interest.

Narrative's role in advocacy

In PLCN's early days, the immediate threats were mostly local and limited, such as poaching, selective logging of luxury wood. Hence advocacy was also mostly local, and directed at village and commune authorities and local interlopers. While the network understood that they could share the fate of other communities which had lost forest and land to concessions, there was not yet a sense of urgency. Like many Cambodians, most were not fully aware of the imminent danger of concessions and assumed a 'wait and see' stance. The first attempt at national advocacy, in 2008, was in regard to mining activities, believed to be connected to an army general. The Preah Vihear community most affected joined other conflict-affected communities from around the country in three rounds of 'coordinated complaints', during which each participating community wrote individual complaints, which were later collated and submitted jointly to ministries, accompanied by press coverage.[19] Other Prey Lang communities joined the third round of complaints; however, this did not yet represent advocacy for the greater Prey Lang.

In late 2009, a company cutting a road through the west side of the forest from Sandan, Kampong Thom to RiepRoy, Preah Vihear, sparked alarm. Some of the government's justification for the road was a logging coupe awarded to a second company, never fully identified.[20] Network members reported that road-building was accompanied by illegal logging and poaching by both the company and outsiders who now had easier access to the forest. However, they were still unready to advocate at the national or international level, for a variety of reasons. Like other grassroots advocates they had difficulty accessing media, they were inconsistent, sometimes even incoherent in articulating their case and unable to provide convincing evidence.[21] Many were afraid of repercussions from their complaints. True to Cambodia's social hierarchy, they sought patrons to be their interlocuters. Statements on Prey Lang were added to an NGO report for Cambodia's Universal Periodic Review (2009), and to similar NGO reports submitted to the United Nations Committee on the International Covenant on Economic, Social and Cultural Rights (2009) and the United Nations Committee on the Elimination of Racial Discrimination (2010). With behind-the-scenes assistance from NGOs in Cambodia, the Asian Indigenous Peoples Pact also submitted a complaint to the Special Rapporteur on Indigenous Rights in 2009. Although the reports and complaint were derived from the nascent PLCN's stories and reports, no network members were directly involved in any report or complaint-writing, or related advocacy.

Nonetheless, PLCN members *were* at the forefront of an impressive CPN demonstration on land and forest issues in 2010. About 200 CPN affiliates, including several PLCN members, had determined to deliver a petition to the Prime Minister's house, affixed with more than 60,000 thumbprints, calling for land and forest law to be upheld. When their legal march was blocked, they undertook a peaceful negotiation that appeared to win over many police. Their demonstration was noted by the Prime Minister in a speech 2 weeks later. While this demonstration was not about Prey Lang, certainly PLCN participants felt their issue was represented by the demonstration and they gained valuable experience in bringing a concern to the national level. Prey Lang participants returned to their communities and network, with new confidence and an inspirational story.

By early 2011, the logging coupe was in full operation and the network was galvanized into action, especially since they had heard that the company that had built the road would also be awarded land for rubber. They then turned consciously to national and international advocacy wherein 'story' continued to play an important role. This manifested in three ways. First, story-telling informed and shaped the network's public messaging, a continuation of the process in which their internal story-telling and related analyses influenced their framing of issues. Hence, we saw the network publicly extending messages such as 'Prey Lang is OUR forest' to a transnational audience.[22] They also projected themselves as good citizens and heroes protecting a shared heritage *for the world*, a role they cast for themselves through their story-telling.

Second, they told their story, based on personal and shared experience, to the public through conventional media. PLCN members first got public attention outside of their locale, particularly that of provincial audiences, via talk radio shows on 'free' radio,[23] in which they would tell the story of the forest, connecting it to the sustainability of fishing and farming communities downstream. Their descriptions of environmental changes accompanying forest loss resonated with other rural communities with similar experience. Thus, the PLCN succeeded in increasing Prey Lang's name recognition as well as a growing sense that the forest was important to other downstream communities. Rural communities dependent on natural resources paid most attention, while urbanites, most importantly in Phnom Penh, took little notice. Overall, they expanded the community of persons who identified with the idea that 'Prey Lang is our forest, too', building a constituency for further advocacy.

Finally, the network adopted and adapted other popular, current stories as vehicles through which to articulate their own story. This was vital to gaining recognition in Phnom Penh, among urban youth, and at the international level, something they had not been able to do via conventional methods. The turning point was in 2011 when a handful of activists saw the release of the popular film 'Avatar' and, even without translation, identified with it. An outsider's suggestion that they paint themselves blue for a national-level demonstration resonated with some PLCN leaders and they determined to present themselves as 'avatars'.

Their demonstration, one of the most creative actions seen up to that time, coupled with positive messaging, attracted the attention of both the international community and urban youth. The story was picked up by international media and was instrumental in gaining the network two international advocacy partners as well as local ones, most importantly an urban youth group. They continued the avatar theme in two later 2011 demonstrations, adding the traditional element of prayer. These included a prayer ceremony in front of the palace at a national shrine and another at the Bayon in the Angkor Complex. The avatar theme was repeated at an Amnesty International press conference in late 2011 on the release of a report which included a profile of Prey Lang activist Pok Hong (Amnesty International, 2011). Hong painted her face blue mid-speech, and was joined by other activists in the audience. She called on everyone to become 'avatars' to protect Prey Lang.

Even when they were not donning the blue face of the film's Na'vi, they were playing out the role through direct action. In a series of ambitious forest wide patrols beginning in late 2011, the network paralleled the Avatar film by challenging forest interlopers, particularly certain rubber concessionaires. In the first attention-grabbing patrol, hundreds of Prey Lang activists spent 2 to 3 weeks walking across the forest, confronting illegal activities along the way and converging at a Kampong Thom rubber plantation where they called for a halt to company logging. Similar patrols followed, each accompanied by new stories: a man was snake-bitten and saved by the quick action of fellow activists; grandparents made the journey despite their age; a woman, six months pregnant, feared her baby had died during a 2-week forest walk but refused to stop, saying that without the forest, her baby had no future. She later named her healthy baby boy Prey Lang (Figure 13.1).

These compelling examples of tenacity and courage attracted more external supporters and allies. Chief among them was prominent environmentalist Chut Wutty,[24] who had long advocated for Prey Lang's protection and who already knew the Prey Lang communities. He joined his efforts with that of the network, becoming a prominent spokesperson, especially to international audiences since he was fluent in English. In doing so, his status became near legendary for how he would challenge forest interlopers and authorities. This time the story was told through video clips posted to YouTube by journalists and friends.[25] When, in 2012, he was killed during a mission with journalists in the Cardamom Mountains, far from Prey Lang, he was lionized as a hero. 'We are all Chut Wutty' became a second mantra of the network and many other land and forest activists. Any tension that they may have felt around Wutty's assertive leadership or some of his advice on strategies and tactics, not completely shared by network leaders, was put

Figure 13.2 Activists from the Prey Lang Community Network and elsewhere attend a solidarity event in memory of Chut Wutty, after his assassination in 2012. The sign says: "We are all Chut Wutty"

Source: East West Management Institute.

aside. By linking their story to Wutty's personal story they not only paid him homage but strengthened their own status in the public eye. Chut Wutty's story was absorbed into the story of Prey Lang and their story was inextricably linked with his.

How social media has contributed to the Prey Lang story

The use of social media to present the Prey Lang story became increasingly important to the network in 2013. It enabled the PLCN's constantly evolving story to be tracked and shared publicly on a more consistent basis, particularly among Cambodian youth and international supporters, creating a sense among at least some followers that the network's struggle is theirs too.

Although a PLCN website, Facebook page and Twitter account were established on the network's behalf by NGOs as early as 2011, they were initially managed by various NGO workers drawing on and reflecting the network's stories but not directly involving them in the social media. In 2012, the Chut Wutty story figured prominently. In 2013, responsibility for the sites began to be transitioned to an allied urban youth group, attracting new followers and extending the reach of the story particularly to Cambodia's urban, educated youth.

While the network was made aware of the website and social media, their understanding of the internet was almost non-existent and they expressed little interest. In 2013, inexpensive internet coverage via smartphones and computers disseminated by NGOs to a few network leaders extended the internet's reach far into the hinterlands.[26] PLCN suddenly became aware of Facebook and its powerful influence as a story-telling venue. Particular PLCN members, serving as 'infomediaries' between the network and online public, began documenting their patrols and advocacy initiatives and became active posters to social media.

An ambitious forest-wide mapping exercise begun in early 2013 also grew their story. Instead of simply documenting their claims and mapping violations, the PLCN mapping team began collecting oral histories about the forest, particularly from elders. At the time of this writing, that project was still underway. NGOs are helping the network translate their immense collection of data into an interactive map offering their own portrait of the forest. This will include recorded oral histories of the forest and its communities, linking the past to the present. Materials will be uploaded onto PLCN's website. The network also plans to create a book.

As of April 2014, the PLCN's Facebook page was 'liked' by more than 8,000 people. Most are Cambodian young people but the page has also attracted followers from around the world. The chief attraction seems to be the constantly unfolding story of the network. Viewers regularly comment on news from patrols and shared photos of illegal activities. When a prominent network elder succumbed to sickness and his death was feared, the story told on Facebook solicited well wishes from around the world.

The limitations of narrative as an organizing and advocacy tool

While story-telling has contributed significantly to the PLCN's continuing network-building and advocacy, it is important to recognize that this has been only one vehicle for its development. The PLCN has also learned and benefited from a parallel indigenous people's movement that has contributed to deepening their identity (Swift, 2013) and a broader grassroots advocacy movement, chiefly through their interactions with and participation in the national CPN, of which they are an affiliate.

Conversely the PLCN's prominence as an advocacy group has almost certainly contributed to both the indigenous people's movement and CPN's development. The network also benefitted from community legal education, undertaken by a number of groups, wherein PLCN members became more cognizant of their rights and how to use the law and evidence to defend themselves.

Story-telling, particularly in the form of gossip and sometimes falsehoods, has on occasion had negative impacts. Stories have been used by some actors, both inside and outside the network, to undercut the reputations of others, manoeuvre for leadership advantages or diminish solidarity. Not surprisingly, the network's best story-tellers have also accrued power to themselves, whether or not they are the best leaders in actuality.[27]

Not all stories about the network are controlled by the network themselves. Outsiders have told contrary stories of the network, representing them as renegades, outlaws, puppets of certain NGOs or political opposition, or naïve, selfish and anti-development. The fact that the network has maintained a fairly consistent message and narrative has helped to mitigate damage in the public eye.

Conclusion

The PLCN's story is one that should interest scholars and practitioners of social change, particularly within the Cambodian context. It demonstrates how traditional stories and narratives of people's everyday lives can be transformed into stories of change. In this regard, story-telling becomes an intrinsic part of a rite of passage from an old paradigm to a new one. It's via stories whereby both the tellers and the audience are challenged to address the 'conflict between the values by which (they) wish the world lived and the values by which it actually does' (Ganz, 2009). From those stories – and the actions they inspire – we see new social production (Appadurai, 1990; Tsing, 2005).

This chapter has described how people around Prey Lang attempted pre-emptive action to fend off logging and land grabs and how those early efforts were not sustained because of the absence of an appropriate platform to support them. Only once concerned individuals, from around the forest, had the opportunity to meet and talk regularly to one another were they able to own their collective responsibility for trying to protect and manage the forest. That said, it is unlikely that meetings alone, particularly ones built on conventional NGO-community relations and prescriptive approaches, would have resulted in the changes demonstrated within the PLCN. The fact that the process was lightly facilitated and resourced, perhaps even under-resourced due to funding and staffing constraints, worked to the advantage of the incipient network. Their natural process of story-telling, one to which they gravitated themselves, thus became a fundamental venue through which they reaffirmed cultural and historical ties to the forest, reclaimed pride in their indigenous identity, and redefined their relationship to one another, to other Cambodians, to the Cambodian government, and even the world.

The stories themselves were – and are – fluid, regularly integrating new ideas. While they have had a beginning, a middle and at least an implied or imagined end, their stories are constantly updated to accommodate new events and analysis. In this way, story-telling has sharpened problem-solving skills, galvanized action and stiffened courage. The PLCN story is one in which Prey Lang community members have re-imagined themselves and their future.

They have also employed narrative in engaging others on the issue of Prey Lang's protection. Their messaging – born out of their stories – is built around several 'unique selling points', including that:

- Prey Lang belongs to everyone, projecting inclusivity;
- PLCN activists are heroes, and responsible citizens, working for the good of the country; suggesting that others should admire them;
- Being indigenous is a source of pride and strength, that their heritage both entitles and prepares them to be forest guardians, a role that benefits everyone;
- Prey Lang, as a whole, can be restored and sustainably managed in cooperation with communities, if only the government and other stakeholders commit to such a model. This is an extraordinary vision in a traditional society dominated by an entitled elite who demand full control.

Narrative has also been fundamental to their resistance against status quo relationships and a prescriptive model of development in which they are the passive recipients of pre-determined solutions. Their challenge to CFs has also challenged the social hierarchy, one that probably would not have happened if their stories had not interrupted CF processes.

Their public identification of themselves with a popular icon – the Na'vi from the Avatar movies – was a device that brought them both national and international attention, especially capturing the imaginations of urban Cambodian youth. Their cultivation of conventional media – particularly radio – and the adoption of social media, first by others on their behalf, and then by infomediaries within the network itself, has helped them to sustain and track their story in public over time. Social media has allowed outsiders to interact with and relate to the PLCN story.

While the PLCN's adoption of a narrative approach may have been more organic than intentional, it nevertheless reflects the power that stories can have to transform both the storyteller and the listener. While other grassroots advocacy groups have employed some approaches similar to PLCN's – public prayer ceremonies, painting faces (even without a story reference) and positing alternative solutions – the PLCN's message of inclusivity, good citizenship, shared responsibilities and benefits has been extraordinary. Overall, the tenor of their message – generally upbeat and courageous – has tended to be received by other Cambodians as constructive, illustrating the potential for new relationships between government and citizens. In this way, the PLCN has been a site of 'cultural production' (Appadurai, 1996) and a source of social change on the cusp of a greater turning. The PLCN's story has also presaged, and perhaps even contributed to a broader paradigm shift demonstrated by Cambodians' response to the 2013 election, in which there was what appeared to be a sudden and broad public demand for change but which is actually reflective of a new story that Cambodians all over the country have begun to tell themselves. It is a story in which they are heroes with the power to rescue themselves. Now the PLCN – and all Cambodians – must decide the ending they will make for this episode in their saga and how they will open their next chapter.

Notes

1 Parnell worked with East West Management Institute's Program on Rights and Justice from 2004 to 2014. As a Grassroots Networking and Advocacy advisor, Parnell oversaw and advised East West Management Institute's (EWMIs) work with the PLCN from 2008 onwards. While she was not involved in field level work, she had the opportunity to observe the network's development over time. This chapter reflects her observations.
2 A transliteration from Khmer, alternatively transliterated as Prey Long.
3 A reference to the Na'vi people in James Cameron's epic film, *Avatar*. The popular local appellation is 'avatar'.
4 Although the area was demonstrably poor, local traditional economies and livelihoods were widely perceived to be adequate by the communities themselves, at least in retrospect. As forest resources declined as a result of encroachment, livelihoods have been reduced, with many network members now looking back on earlier times as ones of plenty.
5 Also transliterated as *Kui, Kuoy, Kuay* or *Kouy*.

6 In English, this roughly translates to 'mountain folk'.
7 See Chapter 11, this volume, for a discussion of the charismatic Kuy leader, Pu Combo, who resisted the French in their early days in Cambodia, around 1860.
8 The Kuy are found in Thailand and Laos as well as Cambodia, with an estimated total population of about 380,000. The number of Kuy in Cambodia was estimated to be more than 23,000 in 2004 (LeFebre, cited by Mann and Markowski, 2005). Most Kuy are found in the provinces of Preah Vihear and northern Kampong Thom, but there are also Kuy in Kratie and Stung Treng, primarily west of the Mekong, within the greater Prey Lang area (Swift, 2013).
9 Cambodia remained in civil conflict until 1999 when the Khmer Rouge, having been gradually brought under government control, was eventually dissolved.
10 See Chapter 8, this volume.
11 Since that time plantations have been significantly expanded in that area. As of early 2014, there were concessions noted on the private non-profit open data website, www.opendevcam.net.
12 This represents a form of cultural production discussed by both Appadurai (1990) and Tsing (2005).
13 The Kuy word for forest, *koh*, has been replaced with the Khmer word for forest, *prey*, joined with *lang*, or 'our' in Kuy.
14 As an example, see the short video *Prey Lang: One Forest, One Future* (USAID/ EWMI, 2008).
15 The group began calling themselves a *bandaing* (network) early on. However, over time their concept of the network has evolved from a network of activists towards a network of communities within a representative collaborative informal association. This parallels the CPN's arc of development. The CPN is a national network of land activists with which the PLCN affiliates.
16 See Henke (2011) for an in depth description of this dynamic between Cambodian NGOs and communities.
17 See Milne (2013) in the context of communal land titling.
18 See Chapter 10, this volume, on the value of landscape-level management.
19 These initiatives were organized by the CPN.
20 Although logging concessions were cancelled or suspended in 2002, Cambodia continued to facilitate logging projects via a system of annual coupes, in which areas would be identified for logging and offered to companies via competitive bids.
21 As grassroots groups emerged in the early 2000s, they were challenged to connect with both journalists and even rights groups. As unknown actors of low-traditional status and thought to have little capacity, they were not trusted and were considered unreliable sources. Hence, more often than not community members' reports of rights violations were given little credence until they could be investigated by national rights monitoring groups. Journalists tended to seek out rights groups as sources and prominent national-level rights personalities for quotes on issues from which they may have been far removed. This improved as grassroots activists, some with NGO assistance, developed both relationships with trusted journalists and improved their capacity for presenting their issues, including offering evidence.
22 Tsing (2005) described this interplay of various stakeholders from local to international levels, describing the involvement of global rights actors as both a risk and an opportunity but one worth taking.

23 Much of Cambodia's media, including radio is strongly ruling party-influenced, if not controlled. Civil society groups tend to use Radio Free Asia, and NGO shows on the Voice of Democracy, which are not government/ruling party controlled, to discuss their issues.
24 Wutty, formerly with Global Witness and later the leader of his own NGO, the Natural Resources Protection Group, was active in early attempts to organize Prey Lang protection, just following the cancellation and suspension of logging concessions. When those failed he continued to monitor Prey Lang and to advise some local initiatives. However, he only became active with the PLCN when they began the forest-wide patrols described above.
25 A simple internet search shows up more than two dozen video tributes posted to YouTube.
26 While smartphones and computers are not common, it only takes one or two users – herein called *infomediaries* – in a community to expose the others.
27 See also Marston, this volume, for more discussion on complexity and potential for contradictions within grassroots action in Cambodia.

References

Amnesty International. (2011) 'Evictions and resistance in Cambodia: Five women tell their story,' http://www.amnesty.org/en/library/info/ASA23/007/2011, accessed 6 May 2014.

Appadurai, A. (1990) 'Disjuncture and difference in the global cultural economy', *Theory, Culture and Society* 7, pp. 294–310.

Appadurai, A. (1996) *Modernity at Large: Cultural Dimensions of Globalization*, University of Minnesota Press, Minneapolis.

Baird, I. G. (2011) 'The construction of "indigenous peoples" in Cambodia', in L. Yew (ed.) *Alternatives in Asia: Reflections on Identity and Regionalism*, Routledge, London, pp. 155–176.

Davis, J. E. (2002) 'Narrative and social movements: The power of stories', in J. E. Davis (ed.) *Stories of Change: Narrative and Social Movements*, State University of New York Press, New York, pp. 3–30.

Fine, G. A. (1995) 'Public narration and group culture: Discerning discourse in social movements', in H. Johnston and B. Klandermans (eds), *Social Movements and Culture*, University of Minnesota Press, Minneapolis, pp. 127–143.

Fortmann, L. (1995) 'Talking claims: discursive strategies in contesting properties', *World Development* 33(6), pp. 1053–1063.

Ganz, M. (2002) *The Power of Story in Social Movements*, Paper presented at the Annual Meeting of the American Sociological Association, Anaheim, California, August 2001.

Ganz, M. (2009) 'Why stories matter', *Sojourner*, http://sojo.net/magazine/2009/03/why-stories-matter, accessed 6 May 2014.

Global Witness. (2007) *Cambodia's Family Trees*, Global Witness Publishing Inc, Washington, DC.

Henke, R. (2011) 'NGOs, people's movements and natural resource management', in C. Hughes and K. Un (eds) *Cambodia's Economic Transformation*, Nias Press, Copenhagen, pp. 288–309.

Keating, N. B. (2013) 'Kuy alterities: The struggle to conceptualise and claim Indigenous land rights in neoliberal Cambodia', *Asia Pacific Viewpoint* 54(3), pp. 309–322.

Mann, N. and Markowski, L. (2005) 'A rapid appraisal survey of Kuy dialects spoken in Cambodia', SIL International, Dallas, Texas.

Milne, S. (2013) 'Under the leopard's skin: Land commodification and the dilemmas of Indigenous communal title in upland Cambodia', *Asia Pacific Viewpoint* 54(3), pp. 323–339.

O'Leary, M. and Nee, M. (2001) *Learning for Transformation: A Study of the Relationship Between Culture, Values, Experiences and Development Practice in Cambodia*, Krom Akphiwat Phum, Battambang, Cambodia.

Ostrom, E. (1990) *Governing the Commons: The Evolution of Institutions for Collective Action*, Cambridge University Press, Cambridge.

Roe, E. M. (1991) 'Development narratives or making the best of blueprint development', *World Development* 19(4), pp. 287–300.

Swift, P. (2013) 'Changing ethnic identities among the Kuy in Cambodia: Assimilation, reassertion and the making of Indigenous identity', *Asia Pacific Viewpoint* 54(3), pp. 296–308.

Tsing, A. L. (2005) *Friction: An Ethnography of Global Connection*, Princeton University Press, Princeton.

USAID/East West Management Institute. (2008) 'Prey Lang: One Forest, One Future, Video', produced by Ben and Jocelyn Pederick, https://www.youtube.com/watch?v=yWMZsBgWXMo, accessed 20 January 2014.

Index

Page numbers in *italic* refer to figures and diagrams.

accountability: hydropower and infrastructure projects 128; land-grabbing 101–2, 103, 108–10; protected areas management 156; REDD projects 190
Achar Soa 227
activism 120, 133, 167; irrigation projects 246, 248, 249; land-grabbing 96, 102, 106, 108, 109, 112; Prey Lang Community Network 260, 262–5, 268, 271–2, *272*, 275. *see also* grassroots movements; resistance
actor-oriented analysis: in community forestry 161–2, 165, 172, 174–5; REDD projects 179–82, *183–4*, 187, 192–3
advocacy 5, 16; hydropower and infrastructure projects 127, 129–32, 134; land-grabbing 95, 97, 99, 103, 108; Prey Lang Community Network 269–73, *272*, 274
agrarian transition 10, 76–80, *79*, 87–9
agri-business 6, 7; state public land 205, 208, 218; Tonle Sap floodplain 53, 65, 66–7. *see also* cash-crops; fertilizers; hybrid rice; pesticides; plantation agriculture
agricultural quality improvement project (AQIP) 82, 83–4
agriculture, traditional. *see* traditional agriculture
agro-cultural complexes 239
aid, international 7, 105–7, 121–5, 131. *see also* hydropower and infrastructure projects

anarchic logging. *see* logging, illegal
Angkor Wat World Heritage Site 14
anthropogenic landscapes 16
anthropological perspectives 9, 14, 60, 98, 144
anti-colonial resistance 229–31, 232
AQIP (agricultural quality improvement project) 82, 83–4
Areng river. *See* Cheay Areng Dam
armed forces. *see* military forces
Asian Indigenous Peoples Pact 270
assassination, of Chut Wutty 133, *272*, 272–3
Australian Aid 81, 82
authoritarianism 11, 15, 17, 18, 29–33, 38; agrarian change 77; hydropower and infrastructure projects 123, 133; land-grabbing 99, 100, 102–3, 106–8, 110; protected areas management 153, 154; resistance 226. *see also* military forces
avatar identity/metaphor *258*, 259, 271, 276

Batheay District, Kampong Cham 241
benefit-sharing, REDD projects 180, *189*, 190, 195, 196
best practice: hydropower dams 135; protected areas management 143, 155
biodiversity 12, 87; hotspots 13, 14, 133; hydropower and infrastructure projects 132, 133, 134; Prey Lang forest 259: protected areas 143, 203
Birdlife International *183*

Index 281

Boeng Trawsaing Lake 64
Boeung Kak Lake 107
Bokor National Park 130
bribery: illegal logging 39; land-grabbing 96, 98, 100–2; protected areas 145, 147, 150. *see also* corruption
bricolage 59. *see also* livelihoods
bunds, rice field 63, 64, 67
Bunong People 182, 186, 190
bureaucratic structures: community forestry 173, 175; protected areas 143, 156. *see also* rational bureaucratic organizations; Weberian state
burning policies, Tonle Sap floodplain 68–9, 70

Cambodia Agricultural Research Development Institute 82
Cambodia-China Year of Friendship 123
Cambodia International Investment Development Group 107
Cambodia-IRRI-Australia Project (CIAP) 81, 82
Cambodia Tatay Hydropower Company Limited 132
Cambodian National Petroleum Authority 58
Cambodian National Rescue Party (CNRP) 28, 252
Cambodian People's Party (CPP) 4, 8, 9, 10–11, 14, 15, 17; hydropower and infrastructure projects 123, 129; irrigation projects 249; land-grabbing 105; post-conflict state 28–9, 32–4, 38, 40–5. *see also* Hun Sen
Cambodian Red Cross 36, 37, 105
Cambodia Universal Periodic Review (2009) 270
capitalism 6–7, 10, 16, 18, 32
carbon credits 177, 179, *185*, 191–3. *see also* forest carbon commodity chain; REDD; voluntary carbon market
Carbon Neutral 181
carbon sequestration 6, 259
carbon trade 12, 14, 15, 177, 193–4, 196. *see also* forest carbon commodity chain; REDD; voluntary carbon market

Cardamom Mountains 11, *21*, *28*, 42, 228, 131–3, 272
cash crops 186; Ratanakiri Province 207–8, 218; rice 76, 81, 82, 86. *see also* plantation agriculture
Casotim (Cambodia Soviet Timber) 164, 165, 166, 170–4
CBNRM. *see* community-based natural resource management
CCB. *see* Climate Community and Biodiversity Standard
CDA (Children's Development Association) 181, *183*
Center for Advanced Study 246, 248
Central Cardamoms Protected Forest (CCPF) 133, 134
CFI. *see* Community Forestry International
Chandler, David 231, 234
change. *see* transformation
charismatic leaders 225, 227
Chea Sim 31
Cheay Areng Dam 128, 131–4
chemicals, agricultural. *see* fertilizers; pesticides
Chhlong forest. *see* Community Forest in Kratie
Chikreng rebellion (1977) 234–5
Children's Development Association (CDA) 181, *183*
China: aid and investment 121–5, 131; Pheapimex concession 105, 106, 107. *see also* hydropower and infrastructure projects
China National Heavy Machinery Corporation 132
China Southern Power Grid (CSPG) 132
Chinese Farm Cooperation Group 105
Churning of the Sea of Milk creation myth 1, 5, 19, 225
Chut Wutty 133, *272*, 272–3
CI (Conservation International) 133, 134, 179, 263
CIAP (Cambodia-IRRI-Australia Project) 81, 82
citizenship, 6–7
class differentiation 77, 80, 84–6, *85*
climate change 5, 14, 54, 206; mitigation strategies 177. *see also* REDD

Climate Community and Biodiversity Standard (CCB) 178, 181, 185–8, *189*, 191, 193, 194
CNRP (Cambodian National Rescue Party) 28, 252
coalition government (1990s) 32–3
cold war 30, 31, 236
colonialism 12–13, 17, 208–9, 229–32, 261
commodification of nature 6, 8, 10, 16
commodity chain analysis. *see* forest carbon commodity chain
commodity frontiers 6–7
common land 39, 65, 68–9
common pool resource theory 205; community forestry 160, 172–3; people's irrigation reservoir 239, 246
communal land management, Ratanakiri Province 217–20
community based natural resource management (CBNRM) 12, 14, 16, 141, 160–1, 241
community fisheries 13, 14
Community Forestry International (CFI) 178, 180, 181, 182, *183*
Community Forestry Network 181, *183*
Community Forestry Sub-Decrees (2003/2009) 179
Community Forest in Kratie (case study) 14–15, *21*, 161–2, 172; common pool resource theory 160, 172–3; community characteristics 163–6; European Union involvement 167–8, 172; Forestry Administration 163, 165, 166, 167, 169–72; NGO involvement 166–7, 168–9, 172; timeline *162*
community forests 2, 13–15, 106, 160–1; forest carbon commodity chain 178, 180–2, *183;* political ecology 171–2; Prey Lang 262, 263, 267–9. *see also* Community Forest in Kratie (case study)
community mobilization. *see* grassroots movements; resistance
Community Peacebuilding Network (CPN) 268, 270, 274
Community Zones, protected areas *141*

compensation: hydropower and infrastructure projects 131; people's irrigation reservoir 245, 247, 248
compliance market, carbon emissions 178–9. *see also* voluntary carbon market
concessions, logging 4, 13, 105, 261–3. *see also* economic land concessions
conflict, social 1, 5, 7–8, 15, 17, 19; hydropower and infrastructure projects 122; protected areas 152. *see also* activism; grassroots movements; resistance
conservation: fortress 141–2; funding 182; hotspots 13, 14, 133; international 132–4; political ecology 11–17; rethinking 204–6
Conservation International (CI) 133, 134, 179, 263
co-option 111, 134
corruption 17, 32; democracy 33; logging 39; people's irrigation reservoir 248; protected areas management 148–51, 154. *see also* bribery; land-grabbing
corvée regime 230
Council for the Development of Cambodia 129
Council of Ministers (CoM) 34, 180, *183*
CPP. *see* Cambodian People's Party
creation stories 1, 5, 19, 225, 263–7. *see also* story-telling
crop booms 97
CSPG (China Southern Power Grid) 132
cultural production 7, 276
culture: of impunity 153–5; of tolerance 31
culture-nature relationships. *see* nature-culture relationships

dams. *see* hydropower and infrastructure projects
Danish aid agency (Danida) 180
decentralization 34–6, 42; indigenous land management practices 210–13, *212*; protected areas management 145

Index

debt, national 126
deforestation *19*, 43, 262; Ratanakiri Province case study 215; REDD 15, 179, 196; *see also* forest(s); logging
democracy 5, 9, 28–38, 43–4; corruption 95, 103, 112; hydropower and infrastructure projects 123, 128, 134
Dentons (American company) 181, *184*
development: and environment 120; interventions 12–13
Development Triangle Master Plan, Ratanakiri Province 208, 210
dispossession of local people 3–6, 8–10, 17, 42, 45; Community Forest in Kratie 165; grand corruption 95–6, 103, 108; hydropower and infrastructure projects 127; Pheapimex concession 106–7; Ratanakiri Province 209; rice production 77, 78; Tonle Sap floodplain 54. *see also* exclusion; land-grabbing
disturbance, role in conservation 205–6
diversified livelihoods. *see* livelihoods
double-movement (Polanyi) 9, 15–16, 17, 19

ecological degradation 4, 5, 18, 38, 43; agrarian change 87; hybrid rice 87; protected areas 143; Ratanakiri Province case study 209, 217. *see also* REDD
ecological impacts. *see* environmental impacts
ecology: non-equilibrium 205; protected areas 147; Tonle Sap floodplain 9, 53–4, 57, 60, 240, 250. *see also* political ecology
economic growth 2, 3, 33, 78, 123, 124
economic land concessions (ELCs) 3–4, 10, *20*, 42–3, 112; Kampong Thom Province 243; land-grabbing 95, 99; logging 262–3; Mondulkiri 182; Pheapimex concession 105–7; protected areas 142
economic liberalization 30–1
economic transformation 2–3
ecosystem management, Ratanakiri Province 215

ecosystem services 6, 12, 15, 177; Prey Lang forest 259, 263, 265. *see also* forest carbon commodity chain
ecotourism 131, 142, 208, 213, 216
education, environmental 143. *see also* schools
EIA (Environmental Impact Assessments) 129–30
ELCs. *see* economic land concessions
electricity supply 122, 125, 126, 134. *see also* hydropower and infrastructure projects
elite accommodation 8, 14, 40. *see also* land-grabbing; patronage networks; tycoons
employment opportunities 54, 95, 102, 103, 106, 125
enclosure 8, 9, 17, 77, 78, 209. *see also* dispossession of local people
entrepreneurial activities 31; agribusiness 79; land-grabbing 100; logging 164; reservoirs 239, 242–5, 247–8, 250, 252
environment, and development 120
environmental impacts: exploitation of protected areas 142; hydropower and infrastructure projects 126, 127, 129–32, 135; reservoirs 243. *see also* ecological degradation
environmental services. *see* ecosystem services
environmental transformation 1, 2–5, 18, 112, 253, 271
ephemeral environments 6, 10, 62–3, 67–8, 70
ethnographic perspectives 9, 14, 60, 98, 144
eucalyptus plantations 105
European Union 167–8, 172, 173
evasion hypothesis 167
exclusion 7, 78, 186; corruption 96–8, 107, 110; people's irrigation reservoir 239, 250, 253. *see also* dispossession of local people; land-grabbing
experts 15, 122, 191, 218. *see also* knowledge
extractive industries. *see* mining; sand dredging

284 *Index*

Facebook 45, 273–4. *see also* social media
facilitation, Prey Lang Community Network 261, 263–7
FACT (Fisheries Action Coalition Team) 244
factory workers 29
Farmer-Water User Groups 241, 250, 253
farming, large-scale. *see* agri-business
fertilizers, chemical 80, 81, 84, 86–8, 106, 245
financing, off-budget 36–8, 43
fisheries 4–5, 9, 53, 55, 57–61, 64–70, 241, 245
floating rice 66, 240, 242, 244
flooding, Tonle Sap river 4, 54–7, 63–8, 70, 240, 242, 244
Flora and Fauna International (FFI) 133
food security 4, 78; due to corruption 97, 102, 103; hybrid rice 76, 77, 82, 86, 87. *see also* integrated forest/agriculture systems
food sovereignty movement *79*, 89
forest(s): frontier 5, 6, 10, 207–9; management plans 170, 262; organizational structures 35; state revenues 38–43, 45. *see also* community forests; deforestation; logging; spirit forests/lakes
forest carbon commodity chain 177, 178, 180–1, *185*, 187–8, 195–6; key actors *183–4*, 192–3; value chain development 194–5. *see also* REDD
Forestry Administration (FA) 134; Community Forestry 163, 165–7, 169–72; Prey Lang Community Network 262, 269; REDD projects 178, 182, *183*, 186, 188, 190–1
Forestry Law (2002) 42, 179
fortress conservation 141–2
free prior and informed consent (FPIC) 186, 187, *189*, 190, 194, 196
French colonialism 12–13, 17, 208, 229–32, 261
frontiers 2, 5–7, 18; of change 1, 5–7, 19; forest 5, 6, 10, 207–9
FUNCINPEC Party 32, 33, 123
funding, international 240–1. *see also* hydropower and infrastructure projects

garment industry 29, 124
General Department for the Administration of Nature Conservation and Protection (GDANCP) 150
geographical study, Tonle Sap floodplain 9, 54, 56, 58, 60
GINI coefficient 78
Global Environment Facility (GEF) 13
Global Financial Crisis 78
global shared heritage 270
Global Witness 97–9, 102, 104–5, 132–3, 262, 263
globalization, farming perspectives *79*. *see also* international perspectives
Gmelina asiatica (Asian bushbeech) shrublands 64–6, 68
gold mining 5
gossip 274. *see also* story-telling
governance. *see* authoritarianism; political ecology; state
gradients, ecological, Tonle Sap floodplain 54, 57
grand corruption. *see* corruption; land-grabbing
grasslands, Tonle Sap floodplain 53, 56, 60, 64–6, 68–70
grassroots movements 8, 9, 16, 18, 39, 44–5; land-grabbing 112; logging concessions 262; people's irrigation reservoir 17, 238, 239, 245–54; Prey Lang Community Network 270. *see also* activism; resistance
grazing, Tonle Sap 68–9, 70
The Great Transformation (Polanyi) 2–3
Greater Mekong Sub-region (GMS) 3, 121
Green Revolution 76, 87
greenwashing 134
gross national income per capita 78
growth, economic 2, 3, 33, 78, 123, 124
Guangxi Zhuang Autonomous Region 124
guerrilla troops 231, 232, 240

hardwoods, tropical 4, *28*, 42, 142, 164. *see also* logging
heavy metal pollution 5
heritage, global 270

Index   285

heroes: Chut Wutty 133, *272*, 272–3; PLCN activists 275
hierarchical structures: challenging 267, 269, 270, 275; European Union 173; protected areas management 145–9, 154, 155; Tonle Sap floodplain governance 57. *see also* power dynamics
Hindu creation myth 1, 5, 19, 225
hope 2, 5, 13, 19
hotspots, conservation 13, 14, 133
human rights 9, 16; hydropower and infrastructure projects 127, 128; land-grabbing 101, 102, 109; protected areas 142; REDD projects 190; reservoirs 246; resistance 236
humanized ecosystems 203
Hun Sen (prime minister) 9, 11, 13, 28, 30–3, 38, 41, 43–4; hydropower and infrastructure projects 122–4, 127–9; Pheapimex concession 105, 107; reservoirs 244–5
hunting, illegal 142
hybrid rice 7–8, 10, 75–7, 89–90; agrarian change 76, 77–80, *79*, 87–9; agricultural quality improvement project 82, 83–4; research findings 84–7, *85*; seed sales and distribution 82–3. *see also* rice farming
hydropower and infrastructure projects 3, 4, 8, 11, 120–4; costs-benefits 124–6; corruption 107; enabling political environment 126–9; environmental and social impacts 126, 127, 129–32, 135; international investment 121–5, 131–5, 240–1; Mekong River 54; protected areas 142

ICDPs (integrated conservation and development project) 12
illegal logging. *see* logging
immigration. *see* migration of human populations
income per capita 78
indigenous land management practices. *see* traditional agriculture
indigenous people 203; forest carbon commodity chain 182, 186, 190; people's irrigation reservoir 248–52; Prey Lang Community Network 261, 265, 267, 270, 274; protected areas management 143; Ratanakiri Province 208–9; resistance 5, 17, 18, 231–3. *see also* dispossession of local people; grassroots movements; livelihoods; migration of human populations
Indo-Chinese war 125
industrial agriculture. *see* agri-business
inequality 38, 44; agrarian change 76, 77; forestry revenues 43; hydropower and infrastructure projects 120; land-grabbing 104, 110, 111; measures 78. *see also* poverty; tycoons
infrastructure projects. *see* hydropower and infrastructure projects
injustice. *see* justice/injustice
integrated conservation and development projects (ICDPs) 12
integrated forest/agriculture systems 210, 213, 214, 217–18
international perspectives: agendas 11, 13, 14; aid 7, 105–7, 121–5, 131; conservation 132–4; dynamics 6–7; investment 121–5, 131–5, 240–1. *see also* hydropower and infrastructure projects; NGOs
International Rivers advocacy group 129, 131–2
international standards. *see* standards
interstitial environments 62, 63–7
investments: international 121–5, 131–5, 240–1; land acquisitions 103–7. *see also* hydropower and infrastructure projects
irrigation projects 240–1. *see also* reservoirs

Japan International Cooperation Agency (JICA) 186
justice/injustice 16, 17, 45; grassroots mobilization 235, 254; land-grabbing 96, 100, 101, 108, 110, 259; logging concessions 265. *see also* human rights

Kamchay River Dam 122, 130–1
Kampong Cham Province *21*, 163–4, 241–5. *see also* people's irrigation reservoir study

Kampong Speu Province 125
Kampot Province 122
Kampuchean revolutionary movement 233
Keat Kolney 108, 109, 110
Khmer Rouge experiment 30, 31, 33, 40, 165, 240
Kirirom 1: hydropower plant 125; National Park 154–5
knowledge: brokers 193, 195, 196; local 209–13, 209; political nature 4. *see also* experts
Koh Kong Province 127, 133
Kompong Chhnang Province 105
Kompong Thom Province 9, 17, 105, 238. *see also* people's irrigation reservoir; Tonle Sap floodplain
Kong Yu and Kong Thom village case studies, land-grabbing *21*, 105, 108–10
Kratie Province 14, 107, 131, 164, 168, 170, 175
Kuy people 261, 265, 267. *see also* Prey Lang Community Network

labour: unrest 3; wage 77. *see also* staff
land acquisitions and transfers, large-scale 103–4
land concessions. *see* economic land concessions
land-grabbing 3, 8–11,31, 39, 95–100, 275; accountability 101–2, 103, 108–10; case studies 105–10, 216-18; definitions 97, 98; political climate 45; protected areas 203; resistance 234; resource curse 103–4, 111; Tonle Sap floodplain 66; unvirtuous circles 102–3, 111–12. *see also* dispossession of local people
Land Law (2001) 108, 179, 243
land management practices, indigenous. *see* traditional agriculture
land tenure, REDD projects 188
land titling 5, 16, 38, 43; forest carbon commodity chain 185; Kampong Thom province 243–4; land-grabbing 97, 104, 234; Ratanakiri Province 218, 220; REDD projects 188, 190; resistance 234; Tonle Sap floodplain 54, 66, 239, 240

land use: conflicts 3; experts 218; Ratanakiri Province case study 207–10; sustainable 185, 203, 206, 210, 217. *see also* agri-business; traditional agriculture
landscapes: patchy 206, 210; pristine 6, 134, 205, 215, 216, 219; Tonle Sap floodplain 62–70
Lau Meng Khin 105, 107, 108, 132
large-scale farming. *see* agri-business
large-scale land acquisitions and transfers 103–4. *see also* land-grabbing
Le Rolland, guerrilla raids 232–3
leadership: charismatic 225, 227; protected areas 148
Least Developed Country status, Cambodia 78
legal frameworks: corruption and land-grabbing 101–2, 108–10, 111; protected areas management 153–5; REDD projects 179, 181
legibility/illegibility, Tonle Sap floodplain study 54, 59–60, 62, 64, 66, 67, 70
leopard skin policy 268. *see also* Order 01
liberalization, state 30–1
life expectancy 3, 78
Little Man with the Big Stone parable 217
livelihoods: agrarian transition 77; community forestry 162–4, 167, 175; hybrid rice 76, 77, 79, 88; Ratanakiri Province 205–6, 210, 213–20; REDD projects 186; resin-based 106, 164, 166, 167, 186, 206; Tonle Sap floodplain 53–5, 57, 59–61, 63, 70, 241
local knowledge 209–13
local people. *see* indigenous people
logging: concessions 4, 13, 105, 261–3; luxury timber 4, *28*, 42, 142, 164; revenues 39–41. *see also* deforestation; forest(s); *and see below*
logging, illegal 4, *21*, 39–41, 43, 45, 203; community forestry 166, 171; hydropower and infrastructure projects 130, 133–5; Mondulkiri project 185; Prey Lang Community Network 263, 270, 275; protected areas 130, 142, 149, 203; REDD projects 179, 186; resistance 236

Index   287

Lower Sesan II Dam 127, 128
luxury timber 4, *28*, 42, 142, 164. *see also* logging

MAFF. *see* Ministry of Agriculture, Forestry and Fisheries
Making Markets Work for the Poor (M4P) approach 78
mapping, Prey Lang Community Network 273
marginalization, social 7, 12, 18, 171. *see also* dispossession of local people; poverty
market economy 2, 3, 14, 16, 31; agrarian change 10, 78, *79*; ecosystem services 12, 15; land-grabbing 104; Ratanakiri Province case study 208; resistance 236
markets, carbon. *see* carbon trade
Markit credit registry 181
mass patronage 8, 34, 36, 43. *see also* patronage networks
media coverage, Prey Lang Community Network 270, 271. *see also* social media
Mekong River 54, 55, 125, 163–4
Mekong Watch advocacy group 129
mercury pollution 5
metaphors: avatar *258*, 259, 271, 276; forest as an organism 268; resistance 261. *see also* story-telling
migration of human populations 7, 87, 88: into Kratie forests 163–5; Khmer people 208, 261
military forces: community forests 268; hydropower and infrastructure projects 133, 134; land-grabbing 105, 106, 107, 108; protected areas management 105, 150, 153, 154, 155. *see also* authoritarianism
mining 5, 135; protected areas 142, 203; Ratanakiri Province case study 208
Ministry of Agriculture, Forestry and Fisheries 58, 179, 243, 250
Ministry of Economy and Finance 34
Ministry of Environment 14, 58, 129, 142–56, 179
Ministry of Foreign Affairs 58
Ministry of Industry Mines and Energy 129

Ministry of Interior 34
Ministry of Water Resources 58, 129, 241
mobility, indigenous land management practices 210, 213, 219, 220
mobilization, community. *see* grassroots movements; resistance
modernization of agriculture. *see* agri-business
Mondulkiri (Seima Protection Forest and REDD) project 178, 179, 182–7, *188*; forest carbon commodity chain *185*; institutional influences 193; key actors *183–4*; key steps in forest carbon production and exchange 187–92, *189*; project design document 185–6
Mondulkiri province 107
monocultures. *see* agri-business; plantation agriculture
mosaics/patchy landscapes 206, 210
myth 1, 5, 19, 225, 264. *see also* story-telling

narrative. *see* story-telling
national debt 126
National Forest Programme 179, 267
national parks 12, 14, 42, 203
Natural Resource Protection Group (NRPG) 133
nature: commodification of 6, 8, 10, 16; spirits 18, 106, 108, 182, 215–17, 264
nature-culture relations 209–13, 215, 218, 220. *see also* story-telling
nature-society relations 1, 2, 3, 5–11, 16, 18, 29
neoliberalism 7, 14, 18, 208
neopatrimonial regime 33–8, 45, 97, 98. *see also* patronage networks
NGOs (non-government organizations): community forestry 160, 166–7, 172; hydropower and infrastructure projects 121, 127, 132, 134; hybrid rice 83; Prey Lang Community Network 262, 266, 267–9, 270, 273; protected area management 150, 151–2; REDD projects 178, 180–2, *183*, 194, 195; reservoirs 244, 246, 248; political

ecology of 2, 9, 11, 13–16; on Tonle Sap 58
non-compliance, passive 225–6. *see also* resistance
non-equilibrium ecology 205
non-human entities 18. *see also* spirit forests/lakes
Norodom Ranariddh 32–3, 123, 227, 228
Norodom Sihanouk 31, 32, 208, 228–9, 233, 234, 261
NRPG (Natural Resource Protection Group) 133

Oddar Meanchey (Community Forestry REDD) project 178–82; forest carbon commodity chain *185*; institutional influences on carbon trade 193; key actors *183–4*; key steps in forest carbon production 187–92, *189*
off-budget financing 36–8, 43
okhnya. see tycoons
opaque transactions. *see* transparency
Order 01 initiative 38, 43. *see also* leopard skin policy
Oryza rufipogon (wild rice) 69
over-fishing 4. *see also* fishing
ownership. *see* land titling
Oxfam 168–9, 172

PAs. *see* protected areas
Pact Cambodia 178, 180, 181, 182, *183*, 195
paper parks 143
parable, *Little Man with the Big Stone* 217
paradox of plenty 103–4
Paris Peace Accords (1991) 30
participatory planning 143
Party Working Group for Helping the Local Level (PWG) 36–8, 44
Party Youth Groups 36, 37
patchy landscapes 206, 210
patronage networks 14, 30–40, 42, 44, 122; hydropower and infrastructure projects 122; protected areas management 149, 151, 156; resistance 234–5
patron-clientism 253–4. *see also* patronage networks

payments for environmental services (PES) 12
people, indigenous. *see* indigenous people
people's irrigation reservoir 248–52. *see also* reservoirs
People's Republic of Kampuchea (PRK) 30–1, 240
PES (payments for environmental services) 12
pesticides 80, 87
Pheapimex concession *21*, 105–8
Phnom Penh 31, 34, 41, 44, 54, 230
Phnom Penh Post 134, 245
photoperiod sensitivity, hybrid rice 80–1
PLCN. *see* Prey Lang Community Network
planning, participatory 143
plantation agriculture 38, 43; hybrid rice 75, 86, 88; land-grabbing 103, 105, 107; market integration 89; protected areas 203; resistance to 234; state public land 205–6, 208, 209, 213, 217–19. *see also* cash crops; rubber plantations
Pol Pot regime 14, 19, 39–41, 107, 125, 168–9, 233, 235, 240–1
Polanyi, Karl 2–3, 8, 15–16, 19
political ecology perspectives 1–2, 4, 8–9, 14–20; community forestry 171–5; environmental transformation 2–5; frontiers of change 5–7; hybrid rice 75, 78; hydropower and infrastructure projects 126–9; land-grabbing 104; post-conflict state 29, 39, 44–5; protected areas 152–5; Tonle Sap floodplain 57–60. *see also* authoritarianism; power dynamics; state
pollution 5, 106
popular resistance. *see* resistance
post-conflict state. *see* state
poverty 12; agrarian change 78, 79; Prey Lang 259; protected areas management 148; Ratanakiri 208; Tonle Sap floodplain 241. *see also* justice/injustice
power dynamics: community forestry 171–2; hydropower and infrastructure projects 127–8;

neopatrimonial regime 34–6; REDD projects 196; scientific studies 64; state 29, 31, 33. *see also* hierarchical structures; state; tycoons; political ecology perspectives
prayer ceremony, Prey Lang Community Network 271
Preah Vihear Province 261
predatory rule 17, 29, 39, 41–3, 45, 100
Prey Lang Community Network (PLCN) 17, *21*, *258*, 258–9, 269, 272, 274–6; advocacy 269–73, *272*, 274; community forests 262, 263, 267–9; Kuy people 261; logging concessions 262–3; social media 272, 273–4, 276; story-telling 259, 260–1, 263–7, 274
Prey Veng Province 10, 75
pristine landscapes 6, 134, 205, 215, 216, 219
privatization 9, 31, 39, 42, 135, 217, 218. *see also* dispossession of local people; land-grabbing; land titling
PRK (People's Republic of Kampuchea) 30–1, 240
productivity, hybrid rice 87–8, 89
Program on Tropical Forests and other Forests in Developing Countries (European Union) 167
project design (PD) document, Seima project 185–6
property rights. *see* land titling
Protected Areas Law (2008) 42, 132, 149, 153–4, 172
protected areas (PAs) 2, 12–14, 20, *141*, 155–6; hydropower and infrastructure projects 130; management challenges 141–4; organizational structure/staffing 144–52; political and social contexts 152–5
Pu Kombo 227–8, 233
Pursat Province 105, 106
PWG (Party Working Group for Helping the Local Level) 36–8, 44

radical responses to change 16–17. *see also* activism; grassroots movements; resistance
Ranariddh, Prince 32–3, 123, 227, 228

rangers, protected areas 144–50
Ratanakiri Province case study *21*, 203–4, 219–20; communal land management 217–19, 220; indigenous practices 16, 205–7, 209–13, *211*, *212*, 218, 219; land use changes on forest frontier 207–9; methodology 206–7; rethinking conservation and land use paradigms 204–6
rational bureaucratic organizations 144, 155
RCAF. *see* Royal Cambodian Armed Forces
Ream National Park 142
rebellions, revolutionary 233–6
Rectangular Strategy for National Development 8
REDD (reducing emissions from deforestation and forest degradation) projects 14, 15, *21*, 177–9, *185*, 195–7; actors and relationships 192–3; benefit-sharing 180, *189*, 190, 195, 196; government role 179, 180, *183*, 188, 192; key steps in forest carbon production and exchange 187–92, *189*; project design document 185–6, 191, 192; voluntary carbon market 178–9. *see also* forest carbon commodity chain; Mondulkiri project; Oddar Meanchey project
regime strengthening, state 41–3
remote sensing 59, 63–4, 65, 69–70
reservoirs 17, *21*, 238–40, *238*, 248–54; ecology of 240, 250; grassroots mobilization 245–8; irrigation projects 240–1; Kampong Thom Province and Samprouch subdistrict 241–5; people's irrigation reservoir 248–52
resin-based livelihoods 106, 164, 166, 167, 186, 206
resistance 5, 7, 9, 15–18, 225–7, 236; anti-colonial 229–31, 232; indigenous 231–3; millenarian revolts 227–9; people's irrigation reservoir 253; reprisals 233, 234–5, 270; Samlaut and Chikreng rebellions 233–6; story-telling 259, 260–1, 263–7, 274. *see also* activism; grassroots movements

resource curse 103–4, 111
resource revenues, state 38–43
resource security, hybrid rice 76, 84–6, 85. *see also* food security
resource conflicts 2, 3, 5, 9, 16, 29; protected areas 142, 143, 152–4; Ratanakiri Province case study 207–9, 210; resistance 225–7, 236; role of experts 218. *see also* dispossession of local people; land-grabbing; logging
revolutions within the revolution 233–6
RGC. *see* Royal Government of Cambodia
rice farming 80–1; floating rice 66, 240, 242, 244; popular resistance 226, 227, 229, 232, 234, 235; Tonle Sap floodplain 53, 59, 64–7, 69. *see also* hybrid rice
rights. *see* human rights
roads. *see* transport infrastructure
Roniem Daum Som Wildlife Sanctuary 142
rosewood (luxury timber) 4, *28*, 42
Roussey Chhrum Dam 133
Royal Cambodian Armed Forces (RCAF), protected areas management 105, 150, 153, 154, 155. *see also* military forces
Royal Government of Cambodia (RGC) 58, 124, 128, *189*
rubber plantations 6, 43, 142, 164, 226; corruption 109, 110; ELCs 206, 207, 208, *211*, 213, *214*, 219; story-telling and social change 263, 270, 271
rural populations: inter-dependence with urban areas 54, 88, 90; transitions 9–10, 77. *see also* livelihoods

SADP. *see* Southeast Asia Development Programme
salaries: income per capita 78; protected areas staff 143, 147, 149
Sam Rainsy Party (SRP) 249
Sambor dam 131
Samlaut rebellion (1967–1968) 233–4
Samprouch subdistrict *21*, 241–5
sand dredging 4
savanna, Tonle Sap floodplain 53, 56, 60, 64–6, 68–70

schools: education statistics 78; off-budget financing 36, 38
Scientific Certification Systems 180, *184*
Scott, James C. 225–6, 235, 236
seed sales and distribution, hybrid rice 82–3
Seima Protection Forest. *see* Mondulkiri project
self-sufficiency, Ratanakiri Province case study 208, 217
Sesan River 131
shadow state 40, 41, 45, 100, 103
shrublands (*Gmelina asiatica*) 64–6, 68
Shukaku Inc. 107
SIAs (Social Impact Assessments) 130
Sihanouk, Prince 31, 32, 208, 228–9, 233, 234, 261
Sihanoukville town 107, 124
Sinohydro Corporation 107, 132
Sisowath, King 230
Sivutha, Prince 228
small-scale farmers. *see* traditional agriculture
SNAs (sub-national administrators) 35
social impacts: change 1–2, 15–17; hydropower and infrastructure projects 126, 127, 129–32, 135; protected areas 142, 152–5; reservoirs 239, 243
social marginalization. *see* marginalization
social media 29, 45, 272, 273–4, 276
social mobilization. *see* grassroots mobilization
socialism, state 30–3
society-nature relations 1, 2, 3, 5–11, 16, 18, 29
socio-ecological systems, Tonle Sap floodplain 7, 53–4, 57, 58, 70
socio-economic class 77, 80, 84–6, *85*
SOE (state-owned enterprise) 121, 125, 126, 127
soil degradation 87
solidarity groups 240
Southeast Asia Development Programme (SADP) 166–7, 172
spirit forests/lakes 18, 106, 108, 182, 215–17, 264
Srepok River 131

SRP (Sam Rainsy Party) 249
staff: income per capita 78; protected areas 144–50
stakeholders, protected areas 152–3, 155
standards: Climate Community and Biodiversity Standard 178, 181, 185–8, *189*, 191, 193, 194; hydropower and infrastructure projects 135. *see also* Verified Carbon Standard
state: changing political climate 44–5; neopatrimonialism 33–8, 45; forestry revenues 38–43, 45; nature-society relations 8–9; off-budget financing 36–8; organizational structure 34–5; political ecology 2, 7, 8, 14, 16, 18, 28–9; predation 17, 29, 39, 41–3, 45, 100; regime strengthening 41–3; role of logging 39–41; socialist-authoritarian origins 30–3. *see also* authoritarianism; land-grabbing
State public land 16, 203–4, 219. *see also* Ratanakiri Province case study
state-owned enterprises (SOE) 121, 125, 126, 127
story-telling, role in resistance 259, 260–1, 263–7, 274
Stoung District 240
stream-diversion irrigation schemes 241, 242
Stung Cheay Areng Dam 127
Stung Tatay Dam 132, 133
Stung Treng Province 127
sub-national administrators (SNAs) 35
subsistence livelihoods, Tonle Sap floodplain 241, 248. *see also* traditional agriculture
sustainable land-use: Mondulkiri project 185; Ratanakiri Province case study 203, 206, 210, 217
swidden agriculture practices. *see* traditional agriculture

Terra Global Capital (TGC) 180, 181, 182, *184*
territorialization 6, 9, 14, 29, 41–3
textiles industry 29, 124
Thmar Bang district 133

Three Gorges Dam, China 120, 127
Three Rivers Protection Network advocacy group 129
timber, luxury 4, *28*, 42, 142, 164. *see also* logging; rosewood
Timbergreen company 133
Tirana Declaration 97
titles, land. *see* land titling
Tonle Sap Basin Authority 58
Tonle Sap Biosphere Reserve 14
Tonle Sap floodplain *21*, 53–4, 70; ecology 54, 57, 240; ephemeral environments 62–3, 67–8; flooding 4, 54–7, 63–8, 70, 240, 242, 244; governance 57–60; interstitial environments 62, 63–7; livelihoods of rural people 59–60; people's irrigation reservoir 248–52; research methods 60–2, *61*; transport infrastructure 125; village case-study *21*, 60–2, *61*, 64, 65, 68, 70
Tonle Sap Lake 4, 5, 9, 35, 55, *55*, *56*
top-down decision-making 35, 70, 145, 173. *see also* authoritarianism
tourism 131, 142, 208, 213, 216
trade-offs: hydropower and infrastructure projects 121; protected areas management 155
traditional agriculture 75–6, 78, *79*; agrarian change *79*, 88–9; Ratanakiri Province 16, 203, 205–15, *211*, *212*, 218, 219; Tonle Sap floodplain 241, 248
transformation 1, 2; agrarian 10, 76, 77–80, *79*, 87–9; continuous vs. discontinuous 8–11, 17, 18, 66; economic 2–3; environmental 1, 2–5, 18, 112, 253, 271; frontiers of 1, 5–7, 19; nature-society relations 5–7; political 44–5; social 15–17, 263, 270, 271
transnational. *see* international perspectives
transparency: hydropower and infrastructure projects 128, 130; land-grabbing 98; organizational structure 37; protected areas management 155–6; REDD projects 190, 191, 195, 196; territorialization 42

Transparency International 96
transport infrastructure 121, 123, 124–5; Preah Vihear province 261; Prey Lang Community Network 269–70; protected areas 142
tropical hardwoods 4, *28*, 42, 142, 164. *see also* logging
Tuv Sud (German company) 180
Twitter 273. *see also* social media
tycoons (*oknha*) 4, 7, 36, 38, 42, 45, 95; Community Forest in Kratie 170–1, 173–4; forestry revenues 43; REDD projects 187, 193. *see also* corruption; land-grabbing

United Nations Committee on the Elimination of Racial Discrimination 270
United Nations Committee on the International Covenant on Economic, Social and Cultural Rights 270
United Nations Conference on Environment and Development (UNCED) 120
United Nations Transitional Authority (UNTAC) 30, 32, 133, 134
Universal Declaration on Human Rights 127. *see also* human rights
Universal Periodic Review (2009) 270
unvirtuous circles, land-grabbing 102–3, 111–12
urban youth, resistance 45, 271, 273, 276

Validation and Verification Bodies (VVBs) 180, 181, 182
value chain development: forest carbon 194–5; hybrid rice 78, *79*
Verified Carbon Standard (VCS) 178, 181, 185, 187–8, *189*, 190–1, 193–4
vicious circles, land-grabbing 102–3, 111–12

Virachey National Park 149
voluntary carbon market 178, 178–9, 182. *see also* forest carbon commodity chain
Voluntary Guidelines on the Responsible Governance of Tenure of Land, Fisheries and Forests in the Context of National Food Security 97

wage labour 77. *see also* salaries
water supply: hybrid rice 84; hydropower and infrastructure projects 131; Tonle Sap floodplain 240–1. *see also* reservoirs
Weberian state 144, 155
Western: colonialism 12–13, 17, 208–9, 229–32, 261; values 11, 144, 204, 209
wildlife 130, 131, 142. *see also* biodiversity; ecotourism
Wildlife Alliance (WA) 133
Wildlife Conservation Society (WCS) 178–9, 182, *183*, *185*, 185–6, 190–1, 244
Women Organizing for Change in Agriculture and Natural Resource Management *183*
workforce. *see* labour; staff
World Bank (WB) 13, 98, 102, 120, 127, 170, 262
World Commission on Dams (WCD) 120
Wuzhishan L.S. Group 107

Xtieng People 182

Yeak Loam Lake 215–17
Yeay Phu (Choeung Sopheap) 105
yields, hybrid rice 80–1
Youth Groups 36, 37
youth, urban 45, 271, 273, 276
YouTube 272. *see also* social media